# America's Struggle with Chemical-Biological Warfare

# America's Struggle with Chemical-Biological Warfare

*Albert J. Mauroni*

Westport, Connecticut
London

**Library of Congress Cataloging-in-Publication Data**

Mauroni, Albert J., 1962–
    America's struggle with chemical-biological warfare / Albert J. Mauroni.
        p. cm.
    Includes bibliographical references and index.
    ISBN 0–275–96756–5 (alk. paper)
    1. Chemical warfare—United States.    2. Chemical warfare—Safety measures.    3.
    Decontamination (from gases, chemicals, etc.)    4. Biological warfare—United States.    I.
    Title.
UG447 .M345    2000
358′.3′0973—dc21            99–041136

British Library Cataloguing in Publication Data is available.

Library of Congress Catalog Card Number: 99–041136
ISBN: 0–275–96756–5

First published in 2000

Praeger Publishers, 88 Post Road West, Westport, CT 06881
An imprint of Greenwood Publishing Group, Inc.
www.praeger.com

Printed in the United States of America

The paper used in this book complies with the
Permanent Paper Standard issued by the National
Information Standards Organization (Z39.48–1984).

10 9 8 7 6 5 4 3 2 1

To the memories of a Chemical Corps leader:

Major General Alan Nord: Deputy Commanding General, U.S. Army Armament Command (1976-1978); Commanding General, White Sands Missile Range (1980-1982); Commanding General, Fort McClellan; and Commandant, U.S. Army Chemical School (1982-1985); died October 24, 1993.

Let me talk to the broader issue—what we are doing in the chemical arena. . . . [It is] an area where we found we were far behind. About six or seven years ago, . . . we reinstituted the Chemical Corps. . . . We are adding . . . chemical units to our divisions and to our separate brigades, so [that] we have the expertise out there to work the chemical area. We have been in the process of bringing in decontamination apparatus, individual protection items, alarms and collective shelters. . . . We are in the process of making up for years of neglect in the defensive area and . . . I think we could show reasonable progress.

—General Edward C. Meyer, March 1982
Hearing before the Senate Appropriations Committee,
Subcommittee on Defense on the FY83 Budget Overview

# Contents

# Tables and Figures

## TABLES

## FIGURES

*Photo essay follows page 134.*

# Preface

This book was originally intended to become the first part of my book, *Chemical-Biological Defense: U.S. Military Policies and Decisions in the Gulf War*. On the good advice of my editor, that book focused on how the Army Chemical Corps contributed to the Gulf War success. While it remains instructive to understand what did and did not occur in the Gulf War (in the realm of chemical defense), to me the more interesting story is how the U.S. military arrived at its state of readiness in the first place. One of the strong conclusions of the last book was that the combat arms community has an inadequate understanding of how chemical-biological (CB) defense equipment and CB munitions are used in a tactical environment. Nothing since the publishing of that book in 1998 has changed that perception.

If anything, examining how CB defense equipment was designed during the 1980s has strengthened my belief. The Army Chemical Corps has the mission to act as the combat arms proponent in identifying nuclear, biological, and chemical (NBC) defense battlefield requirements, in addition to developing doctrine, training chemical defense specialists, and recommending organizational units for the Army force structure. The combat arms community, unfortunately, has also decided that the Chemical Corps requires little additional guidance or oversight, which has resulted in a number of products that were technically world-class but operationally difficult to employ during battlefield conditions. This result is what has been so publicized since the Gulf War as the Army's so-called failure to develop protective clothing that is lightweight, automatic detectors that detect very low levels of chemical warfare agents, and adequate decontaminants to eliminate chemical agent contamination.

The combat arms community's failure to understand the capabilities of CB defense equipment arises from their inability to understand the tactical and operational employment of CB munitions. Since 1968 CB munitions have been routinely included with nuclear weapons in discussions of the U.S. government's arms control agenda, but as political cards rather than as credible weapon systems. The danger is not in this broad inclusion of unconventional weapons (you will pardon me if I do not use the popular phrase "weapons of mass destruction"), but that both the military and the political leadership do not distinguish the widely different potential effects of their employment. While we can argue about the morality of employing unconventional munitions, we cannot argue whether nuclear munitions have far different effects on terrain, equipment, and personnel than do chemical or biological weapons. However, the failure to understand this is exactly what has led to the panic in August 1990 when the U.S. leadership recognized that it would have to deal with Saddam Hussein's CB arsenal.

I divided this book into four parts to identify what I saw as themes in the Chemical Corps's bumpy transition from a technical service branch to a strong operational supporter to the combat arms. In Part I, I have illustrated how the Army turned its back on the Chemical Corps, nearly destroying their own capability to fight in combat operations involving CB warfare. In Part II, I have explained the rationale behind the defensive equipment developed in the 1980s, in addition to the budding binary chemical weapons program. Part III shows where these programs faltered, in part due to technical issues and in part due to the Army's fickle moods. Part IV shows how all the training and equipment development has paid off, in the Gulf War and at home.

The point of this book is twofold: first, to illustrate the history of the Department of Defense's NBC program (both offensive and defensive) that has given us both chemical defense equipment and chemical munitions, and second, to illustrate how the misconception of CB warfare has resulted in a faulty mindset when one discusses the topic of "weapons of mass destruction." It is hoped that the combat arms community will recognize the distinction between classes of unconventional weapons and that they will become more concerned for and involved with the program. Our military leadership must rise above mouthing their concerns about "weapons of mass destruction" and continuing to underfund the development of adequate CB defense programs.

In my previous book I warned against the possibility that the Chemical Corps might be diminished as they move to Fort Leonard-Wood to join the Engineer Corps. The Chemical School officially moved this summer of 1999, and its new commandant, Colonel Pat Nilo, took charge in September. Under the new Maneuver Support Center (MANSCEN), the position of Chemical School commandant, once a two-star general officer, has been downgraded to colonel. The commander of MANSCEN and the Engineer school remains a two-star general officer, and may head the Joint Service Integration Group as the Army's general officer representative. As did happen in 1972, the Chemical School has lost its general officer proponent. As for whether this will diminish the joint service NBC defense program, domestic preparedness program, and CB arms control, only the future will tell; once again, the lessons of history are ignored.

I want to acknowledge the many people that contributed to the success of this book. Most of them were already identified in my previous book, but I will mention again a few key players: Major General (retired) Bob Orton; Major

General (retired) Jan Van Prooyen; Major General (retired) Gerald Watson; Brigadier General (retired) Walt Busbee; Brigadier General (retired) Pete Hidalgo; Colonel (retired) Billy Cook; Colonel (retired) Gary Eifried; Colonel (retired) Chuck Kelly; Colonel (retired) Nate Licata; Lieutenant Colonel (retired) Mike D'Andries; Major Dave Allegre; Mr. Bill Dee; Mr. Don Gober; Mr. Jeff Smart (U.S. Army SBCCOM historian); and Dr. Burton Wright (U.S. Army Chemical School historian). Many others contributed pieces of this history, and I apologize for not naming you all. Very special thanks to a good friend and essential proofreader, Major (retired) Howard Beardsley. As always, thanks to my friends at Praeger Publishers, Heather Staines, Scott Wich and Nicole Cournoyer. Deep thanks to my strongest supporter, my wife Roseann, who continues to be my number one enthusiast and my source of inspiration for my amateur historian aspirations.

# Abbreviations

| | |
|---|---|
| ABC | Atomic, biological, and chemical |
| ABO | Agents of biological origin |
| AEF | Air Expeditionary Force |
| AFB | Air Force Base |
| AMC | Army Materiel Command |
| AMCCOM | Armaments, Munitions and Chemical Command |
| BW | Biological warfare |
| BWC | Biological Weapons Convention |
| CB | Chemical-biological |
| CBR | Chemical, biological, and radiological |
| CDE | Chemical defense equipment |
| CECOM | Communications and Electronics Command |
| CENTCOM | Central Command |
| CFM | Cubic feet per minute |
| CINC | Commander-in-chief |
| CN | Chloroacetephone, tear gas |
| CPS | Collective protection system |
| CRDC | Chemical Research and Development Center |
| CRDEC | Chemical Research, Development and Engineering Center |
| CS | O-chlorobenzamalonitrile, tear gas |
| CSL | Chemical Systems Laboratory |
| CW | Chemical warfare |
| CWC | Chemical Weapons Convention |
| CWS | Chemical Warfare Service |
| DM | Adamsite tear gas |
| DoD | Department of Defense |
| DPG | Dugway Proving Ground |
| FFE | Flame field expedient |
| FORSCOM | Forces Command |
| GA | Tabun, nerve agent |

| | |
|---|---|
| GAO | General Accounting Office |
| GB | Sarin, non-persistent nerve agent |
| GD | Soman, semi-persistent nerve agent |
| GF | Cyclosarin, semi-persistent nerve agent |
| HD | Mustard agent, persistent non-lethal agent |
| HQ DA | Headquarters, Department of the Army |
| JACADS | Johnston Atoll Chemical Agent Disposal System |
| MOPP | Military Oriented Protective Posture |
| MRLS | Multiple Rocket Launch System |
| NCO | Noncommissioned officer |
| ODCSLOG | Office of the Deputy Chief of Staff for Logistics |
| ODCSPER | Office of the Deputy Chief of Staff for Personnel |
| ODCSOPS | Office of the Deputy Chief of Staff for Operations and Plans |
| OSD | Office of the Secretary of Defense |
| OSHA | Office of Safety and Health Affairs |
| OTSG | Office of the Surgeon General |
| PAO | Public Affairs Officer |
| PD | Program director |
| PM | Program/project/product manager |
| RCA | Riot control agent |
| R&D | Research and development |
| RDA | Research, development, and acquisition |
| RDD | Radiological dispersal device |
| RDI | Reconnaissance, detection, and identification |
| SBCCOM | Soldier and Biological Chemical Command |
| SCPE | Simplified collective protection equipment |
| STB | Super tropical bleach |
| TACOM | Tank and Automotive Command |
| TECOM | Test and Evaluation Command |
| TOCDF | Tooele Chemical Agent Disposal Facility |
| TRADOC | Training and Doctrine Command |
| USAREUR | U.S. Army Europe |
| VX | Persistent nerve agent |
| WMD | Weapons of mass destruction |
| WP | White phosphorus |

# PART I

# Demise of the Chemical Corps

The chlorine gas originally used was undeniably cruel, but no worse than the frequent effect of shell or bayonet, and when it was succeeded by improved forms of gas both experience and statistics proved it the least inhuman of modern weapons. But it was novel and therefore labeled an atrocity by a world which condones abuses but detests innovations.

—B. H. Liddell Hart, *A History of the Real War*, 1935

These steps should go a long way towards outlawing weapons whose use has been repugnant to the conscience of mankind. . . . Mankind already carries in its own hands the seeds of its own destruction. By the examples that we set today, we hope to contribute to an atmosphere of peace and understanding between all nations.

—President Richard M. Nixon, November 1969

# CHAPTER 1

# Swords or Shields:
# The Debate over WMDs

It is August 8, 1990, and the 82d Airborne Division is deploying to Saudi Arabia to draw "a line in the sand" against Iraq's invasion of Kuwait. Among the Central Command (CENTCOM) commander-in-chief's (CINC) concerns is that his soldiers have a limited capability to stand up to and defeat Iraqi armored brigades and even less capability to survive a chemical or biological weapons attack. The first brigade into theater has no chemical specialists to advise them on what to do, since Congress had disbanded the Army's Chemical Corps in 1972. There had been no improvements in the Vietnam-era M17 protective mask, and those masks that had not dry-rotted away had no filters in supply to make them functional. The soldiers had no chemical protective suits, since the last stores had expired years ago. The incoming British forces had protective suits, but none to spare to the much larger American force. Spare parts for the M8 chemical detectors had never been plentiful, and there were no industrial firms to produce replacements, since they had shifted to more profitable lines of work years ago. The CENTCOM CINC saw only one option; he would threaten massive retaliation against any Iraqi aggression that included the use of chemical-biological agents. Retaliating with U.S. chemical weapons was not an option. The only chemical munitions available were over twenty years old and were not compatible with modern artillery and aircraft delivery systems. He decided to request release authority for Air Force tactical nuclear weapons and waited for diplomats to deliver the warning message to Saddam Hussein.

As the lead brigade of the 82d Airborne Division landed at King Fahd International Airfield, they had only a few hours to reflect on how damn hot it was before air-raid sirens erupted with warning klaxons. Running toward the shelters, they had barely made it to safety as the incoming Iraqi jets released their munitions. The shock of explosions around them soon died off. It wasn't until soldiers noted their comrades stiffening in shock and grasping at their throats that they realized that the attack included gas weapons. While the brigade commander tried to assemble those soldiers left alive by the yet unknown chemical agent, the Marines landing at the port of al-Damman were suffering a similar fate. The Air Force's Air Expeditionary Force's (AEF's) wings stationed at air fields at Dhahran and Riyadh were being hit with multiple Scud missile salvos, spraying the airfields with a deadly mist. While inaccurate, the dozen missiles were enough to cause the air commander to order an immediate evacuation. The Air Force had even less protective equipment and detection devices than the Army. Naval forces and inbound aircraft were warned off from the chemically contaminated sites, as Iraqi armored divisions began rolling into Saudi Arabia's eastern peninsula toward the practically defenseless oil fields.

American reinforcements began building in western Saudi Arabia, as outraged Muslim clerics denounced the infidel presence so close to their holy cities while staying silent about Saddam's invasion. Airbases and ports in eastern Saudi Arabia were probably safe to enter, given the desert heat and the volatile nature of nerve agents, but no military troops, let alone civilian personnel, were brave enough to venture there without reliable agent detectors or specialists to assess the areas and declare them safe. Aircraft deploying to uncontaminated airbases in the west could only offer limited air defense, and without any organized ground resistance, the Iraqi columns had little difficulty advancing toward Riyadh, the Saudi capital. The American president now had to determine whether he wanted to negotiate with Iraq or be known in history for releasing nuclear weapons for only the second time in history. Anticipating this move, Saddam had already directed his allies to initiate cries of "JIHAD!" in Africa, Europe, and Asia, warning of the terrible price the coalition allies would pay if they devastated a Muslim capital with a weapon not used since Hiroshima and Nagasaki were flattened in 1945.

Unbelievable scenario? Maybe, but consider what might have happened if General Creighton Abrams had been successful in disestablishing the Chemical Corps in 1972. Without a dedicated force of full time chemical-biological (CB) defense specialists, how ready would our military force have been in 1990?

For many decades, CB warfare has been described as barbarous, a morally repugnant form of warfare, a "dirty" way to fight, and a particularly gruesome and painful way to die. The myths and misconceptions surrounding CB warfare have grown in number and in stature ever since the modern birth of chemical warfare on the French and Belgian battlefields in April 1915. Since the Cold War began, tactical CB weapons have been discussed in the same terms as strategic, megaton nuclear devices—as so-called "weapons of mass destruction" or WMDs. Our national policy of responding to enemy use of CB weapons has shifted over the years from one extreme to the other; from retaliation using similar CB weapons to massive conventional retaliation to (most recently) nuclear retaliation. Politicians, arms control proponents, and the media covering defense issues have so fixated on this topic that one might think the last great evil in the world is the threat of CB weapons. It is hard for laypeople and even military professionals to understand why the United States itself might have once invested in CB weapons, years ago, unless one faces what CB warfare really means in military, not emotional, terms.

Some critics of the military's CB weapons program dislike the nature of CB agents such as sarin nerve gas and anthrax spores because small quantities of lethal agents can cause such instantaneous harm and even death to many individuals in a given area, if properly disseminated (thus the WMD label). They often overlook the facts that many CB agents are nonlethal incapacitants, are difficult to disseminate over a large area, and often cover a comparatively small area of the battlefield. Historically, that has been why CB weapons employed alone have had a relatively minor effect on the overall conflict. As for casualties, counting all the deaths caused by CB weapons over the past eighty years still would not add up to the number of deaths caused by handguns in one year in the United States. Let's not even begin to count the deaths caused by two particular weapons: the M16-series and the AK-47 automatic rifles, which have probably caused the deaths of millions over the last thirty-plus years. For every time a news anchor solemnly states how an accident at a U.S. chemical weapons depot *could* kill 80,000 people (one drop of nerve agent dolled out to each individual within a hundred miles in all directions), you have to wonder why these anchors do not note that the amount of ammunition at one sports retail store could also kill tens of thousands (one bullet to the head of each victim). Shouldn't we reexamine the term "weapons of mass destruction" and apply the labels where they really belong?

Some believe that an international revulsion exists against the stockpiling and use of CB weapons, that the U.S. government recognized world opinion in 1969 and stopped their production. After all, we now have the Chemical Weapons Convention, signed by over a hundred countries, that should ensure that all industrial countries are discouraged from this line of warfare (Were we really worried about Micronesia's and Iceland's intents to develop chemical weapons in the future?) Then again, there are the statistics from intelligence agencies and arms control groups that point out how the worldwide proliferation of CB weapons and technologies has accelerated constantly over the decades. How can this rising proliferation be explained against the "universal abhorrence" of CB warfare?

Very easily, actually. Other countries can hardly afford to spend billions of dollars in the escalation of a conflict, with the current trend of rising weapon system prices and the cost of training. If a country allows itself to be completely vulnerable to a certain type of warfare to the point that a conflict would be very short and significantly less expensive (in terms of people and equipment), their enemies would have to be fools to ignore the opportunity. Countries invest in CB warfare for the very reason that CB agents disable and kill people, just as conventional high explosives and bayonets do, and thus constitute a tool of warfare. These countries are not fighting by the Queen's rules, they are fighting for their survival.

Last and perhaps most confused are those idealists who rail against the inhumanity of CB warfare, of a way of fighting that "treats humans like insects," that somehow CB warfare is dirtier than other ways of combat. Politicians love to pander to these people, playing on their emotional responses to the "horrors" of warfare. Even the History Channel, while regaling the power of combat aircraft and armored vehicles, calls chemical warfare one of the greatest evils of war. Other military scholars have already pointed out the obvious: how is it more humane to conduct strategic bombing raids against cities, killing civilians indiscriminately; to sink ships at sea, giving sailors the choice to burn or to drown; to use cluster bombs or antipersonnel mines that rip limbs from bodies; to bayonet an individual in the stomach and watch them slowly die? Is that more humane than nerve agents that kill quickly and surely? Find someone willing to fight a humane war and you'll see someone who will lose the same war. War, by definition, is not about humanity but against it.

## WHAT IS CB WARFARE?

This very technical field is confusing to laypeople who do not distinguish the fine details between the weaponization and the employment of munitions loaded with nerve gas, anthrax spores, napalm, CS gas, or tactical nuclear weapons. This has been aggravated by sensationalistic journalists, authors, and others who associate napalm and CS use during the Vietnam conflict as a violation of the Geneva Protocol of 1925, which tried to limit chemical warfare among its signatories to no first use. Sometimes the military and political leadership also forget to draw distinctions, which is why even these learned individuals often do not understand why a country would want to develop these weapons. The Army Chemical Corps once took a lead role in all these areas, but it defines napalm and CS gas as conventional munitions related to chemical munitions in design only, as opposed to chemical, biological, or radiological weapons, which are by definition unconventional munitions.[1] This book focuses on the military's views and decisions on the practice of nuclear, biological, and chemical warfare on the modern battlefield (and primarily only on CB warfare, for reasons to be explained).

This mission area is usually referred to as NBC warfare, or sometimes chemical, biological, and radiological (CBR) warfare. Since the end of the Cold War, the phrase CB warfare has become more predominant with the perceived lessened threat of nuclear attack. And of course, weapons of mass destruction (a favorite overused phrase) include all three threats plus conventional explosives that cause mass casualties (since the event of Oklahoma City's Federal Building bombing). Cyber attacks against computers that threaten the interests of a large number of people may join the WMD definition as well. On the surface, it might make sense to group these threats together, as they are "special" munitions that do affect a large area (as measured in square kilometers); create a persistent residual danger lasting hours to days to years; have a mass casualty potential; and share common defensive measures (special detectors, protective suits and masks, the need for decontaminants and collective protection shelters). The Chemical Corps used this commonality during World War II to assume control of the biological warfare program, and after World War II, it quickly entered the growing field of research on radiological contamination. If one looks at the military implications of NBC warfare, let alone the real distinctions, it quickly becomes apparent that tactical nuclear weapons, biological weapons, and chemical weapons have distinct and sharp differences.

Chemical weapons are the usually the first unconventional weapon researched and produced, because they are (comparatively) the safest to develop and produce; use technology modified from conventional artillery, aircraft, and other weapon systems; cause modest casualties without damaging buildings or equipment; and rarely affect more than a small tactical area (immediate battlespace).[2] The world first saw choking agents such as chlorine and phosgene gases in World War I, and then blood agents such as hydrogen cyanide gas (so called because they impeded the transfer of oxygen from the blood to vital organs). Germans, British and American scientists all experimented with other classic chemical gases, rising from their background in industrial sciences. Both choking and blood agents are generally non-persistent; that is to say, lasting minutes to hours prior to dispersing from the area. While the gases were toxic, they evaporated quickly and only attacked the soldiers' airways. As such, they were required in large quantities to overwhelm a force of soldiers in a militarily significant manner, and a simple mask could protect those soldiers from the vapors. The first primitive munitions were hundreds of gas cylinders in long rows; later, the cylinders were propelled into the air like mortar shells toward the enemy. These agents were not very effective in artillery or bombs unless one was prepared to use massive quantities of the shells or bombs to create a large lethal cloud. Very often, these agents were more of a harassing nature than a weapon system designed to kill thousands for tactical advantage on the battlefield. Still, non-persistent chemical warfare (CW) agents were and remain useful for offensive attacks, when the force using chemical agents intends to operate on the same ground that they just contaminated that morning.

Late in World War I and into World War II, countries invested in more persistent agents, those that would linger on the ground for days and weeks, depending on the climate and weather conditions. This included mustard gases and lewisite, the blister agents; they were not really gases, since they had a consistency similar to motor oil. These liquids were dispersed into the air as an aerosol mist by land mines, mortars, artillery shells, and aircraft spray tanks and bombs. While these chemical agents are not lethal in quantities less than very large doses, they disable unprotected troops by attacking moist areas of the body (eyes, throat, underarms, and groin), causing large blisters to rise after a few hour's exposure. Because of their persistency, these agents perform as invisible mine fields, protecting flanks, restricting enemy advances, and hampering rear-area supply functions and artillery positioning. Now soldiers had to wear protective clothing as well as masks and required detectors to identify where the threat existed.

Prior to the end of World War II, the nerve agents emerged. Initially intended as a pesticide, the first G-nerve agents were non-persistent (evaporating as fast as water), while the latter V-type nerve agents developed after the war were made more persistent. The current nerve agents are organophosphate compounds, odorless and colorless liquids.[3]    As they evaporate, their vapors can cause symptomatic reactions, starting with myosis and runny noses and leading to extreme muscle spasms and death.  Their relatively immediate effects on the body's nervous system called for increased reviews of defensive equipment (to create less risk, more warning).  Many people may not realize that, in their wars against Japanese beetles in rose gardens, they may be using dilute forms of nerve agents to get rid of the pests.  It is not uncommon for careless gardeners to suffer the same symptoms as exposure to low levels of nerve agents.  These symptoms, unlike nerve agents, may actually persist for a far greater period of time after exposure.

Since the development of nerve agents, there have not been many advances in the field of CW agents other than in how one delivers the agent.  CW agents can be delivered by artillery projectiles, land mines, aerial bombs and spray tanks, guided and unguided rockets, cruise missiles, spray generators in trucks, and a host of improvised devices (anything that sprays a liquid).  While some point to alleged new Russian nerve agents, supposedly more lethal and developed as binary munitions to avoid the Chemical Weapons Convention, they are still nerve agents and act in much the same fashion.

Biological weapons are the second technological advancement in developing unconventional munitions.  An offensive biological weapons program requires a steep initial investment in research, development, test, and evaluation but are much cheaper to produce (pound for pound).  They cause practically no collateral damage, may or may not cause large casualties (depending on the agent), and are generally seen as operational weapons (affecting the immediate theater of conflict).  In simple terms, biological warfare involves the use of living organisms and their by products to attack personnel, plants, and animals (and some would include anti-equipment).  These agents are not always lethal and they are not always living organisms (e.g., some are toxins from biological organisms).  To catch all the possibilities in this area of endeavor, CB experts often use the term *agents of biological origin* (ABOs).

One could point to three general categories.  There are those biological warfare (BW) agents that are contagious and possibly epidemic; there are biological agents that are not contagious or epidemic (content with attacking one host); and there are chemical toxins derived from organisms, plants, and animals that are much more deadly than CW agents (but in many ways are more limited in their possible applications).  One could also group BW agents by their structures: bacteria, single-celled, plant-like microorganisms that are environmentally sturdy and can reproduce almost anywhere (such as anthrax and cholera); viruses, very small microorganisms, obligate parasites unable to reproduce outside a living host and environmentally weak (such as yellow fever and Ebola); rickettsia, intracellular microorganisms shaped like bacteria but closer in function to viruses in their strict requirements for living host cells; fungi, relatives of yeast and molds; and last, chemical toxins derived from biological sources, such as botulinum toxin and snake venom.  A final way to categorize BW agents is by what they attack:

antipersonnel agents (salmonella and botulinum toxin), antiplant agents (wheat rust virus, rice blast), antianimal agents (sheep pox virus, swine fever virus).

Biological warfare is perhaps most feared because of its potential to spread beyond its immediate intended area of effect.  While this is not true for all BW agents, the ability to select a dangerous organism to target a country's crops, its primary livestock, or its civilian populace is the lure it offers.  This is also what fiction authors and Hollywood twist into story plots to convince their audiences that biological warfare is the "ultimate threat to mankind."  In reality, there is only a small percentage of the tens of thousands of biological organisms that exist in nature that can be utilized as BW agents.  To be effective, BW agents must be able to be weaponized: either by aerosol sprays, dispersed into the air by munitions without destroying the agent, or by "vectors" (animals or insects infected with the agent).  They should be effective in low doses and able to affect a high percentage of its intended target (human, crop, or animal).  If the organisms are to be inhaled rather than injected, the optimal size must be two to five microns in diameter.  Smaller than that and the organisms do not stay in the lungs; more than that and the organisms often fall to the ground before being inhaled and die.  Ideal BW agents should be highly infectious but not necessarily contagious.  These requirements do limit the list of potential BW agents, and they eliminate Ebola virus, for instance, as an optimal candidate.

Each category of BW agents has its strengths and weaknesses.  While anthrax is very lethal and persistent, it is not epidemic and will not spread through a community by contact of infected persons.  Most people can be vaccinated against most bacteria.  Viruses, on the other hand, are often epidemic and have no treatments after exposure; one can be treated only for the symptoms and wait to recover as the virus burns out.  On the other hand, viruses die out very quickly when exposed to sunlight or bleach, and most are not excessively lethal.  After all, the virus wants the host to live as long as it can to allow maximum reproduction.  There aren't many rickettsia or fungi that are practical biological warfare antipersonnel agents; often they are targeted against crops or animals.  As for toxins such as botulinum toxin, ricin, or saxitoxin, they make fantastic assassination weapons, but as "weapons of mass destruction," they don't make the grade, as they are basically chemicals and cannot spread over large areas.  Most toxins have to penetrate the skin and enter the bloodstream to be effective; they are often too heavy to enter the lungs, and unless ingested with food, they stand a poor chance of poisoning the host.

There is always speculation (by fiction authors as well as military analysts and arms control advocates) about the ability to manipulate biological organisms to make more threatening BW agents.  Could someone take Ebola virus and genetically alter it to survive sunlight and be airborne-transmittable, thus making it a "doomsday" agent?  Could someone take anthrax and alter it to be unaffected by anthrax vaccine?  The answers in both cases are, probably not, at least not today or even ten years from now.  The amount of funds and testing required to attain this sort of BW agent would be staggering for any major power, and why bother?

There are plenty of other available CB warfare agents for much less bother. If a country or terrorist group has that kind of money to invest, they'll no doubt be spending it on more affordable, equally lethal, and "legal" means of warfare.

Filling munitions such as spray tanks and artillery shells with BW agents is much more difficult and expensive than chemical munitions, given the greater threat to the weapons handlers and the people operating the planes and artillery systems who have to dispense the agent. Many biological agents require days or weeks to create numerous casualties, as opposed to chemical agents that can cause casualties very quickly. These constraints are why many military analysts often see biological warfare as more of a terrorist tool than a tool of modern, fast-paced warfare. On the other hand, if your enemy expects CW agents to be used, but they have no detection devices or protective gear against biologicals, what a great surprise to spring. Biological agents are less likely to be suspected until it's too late, and then the targeted force is incapacitated. Chemical weapons are much more quick-acting, but they do not normally affect a large area and can be detected more quickly. While CW agents tend to break down into products that are often associated with that agent in environmental samples, (most) biological agents degrade quickly and are hard to distinguish from the natural environmental background. Careful sampling with PCR type detection can identify these biological agents, depending on time and the degree of expertise of the sampler.

Tactical nuclear weapons require a great deal of technology and funding, can cause massive collateral and long-term damage, are certainly lethal to the majority of the target within a short time, and are generally seen as weapons with a strategic impact (that is, affecting national policies). For purposes of comparison, I discuss here tactical rather than strategic nuclear weapons, in part to keep a parallel focus on the limited (relative) effect primarily directed at military forces. As I will demonstrate later, the evolution of chemical and biological arms control closely followed tactical nuclear weapons policy. Tactical nukes focus primarily on explosive blast as their force (especially air bursts), with heat and gamma radiation (both initial and fallout-generated) as secondary casualty causes. There are also radiological dispersal devices (RDDs), which do not explode as severely but rather are designed to spread radiological contamination. Delivery systems include a variety of packages from man-packed atomic demolitions to artillery shells, aircraft bombs, and cruise missiles. In all, the threat of nuclear weapons (blast, heat, gamma radiation) has not generally changed as years go by; and as a result, the military is relatively prepared for responding to this scenario (or at least, they understand the threat well).

On a policy side, there are two schools of thought. Most people, to include the arms control community, feel that first use of tactical nuclear weapons in response to conventional attacks will inevitably lead to strategic nuclear releases. During the 1970s, there were quite a few military scholars that felt that the low-yield air bursts (thus limiting fallout) targeting military forces could play a role on future battlefields without raising the specter of nuclear holocausts against cities. Whether one agreed with one school or the other, it was expected that the United

States had to store and test nuclear weapons as a retaliatory measure in the event that any adversary would arm themselves with nuclear weapons. Executive policy in the White House once dictated that the United States could release nuclear weapons against an enemy that was just planning to attack with nuclear weapons, rather than to parallel a "no first use" policy as exists with chemical weapons. In any event, there is now a general perception that any nuclear use would have to be well justified prior to any release, but one of those justifications is an adversary's owning nuclear weapons.

History has recorded the pattern of major nations investing in chemical weapons first, biological weapons second, and nuclear weapons third (minimizing risk and maximizing investment with limited resources, while increasing technological capabilities at each stage). Each weapon system has particular characteristics, uses different delivery systems, and incurs different consequences to battlefield operations. Putting all three weapon systems into one common view is much like comparing an M1 rifle, a 203-mm mortar, and an 8-inch howitzer and deciding that a military force should use the same defense against all three because they all use ballistics as a principle of operation. While use of tactical nuclear weapons could be construed as mass destruction, chemical and most biological weapons do not make the same impact, despite fears to the contrary. The real evolution of the term "weapons of mass destruction" is more politically motivated than it is logical or reasonable, and is confusing since most people are talking about nuclear weapons when they speak about WMDs in the general sense. For this reason, we will abandon the term WMD in this analysis and focus on the two most similar unconventional styles of combat, chemical and biological warfare.

## HOW THE MILITARY VIEWS CB WARFARE

Our own military knows that there is a difference between nuclear, biological, and chemical munitions (for the most part). However, exposed to a litany of myths from arms control experts and media's talking heads, under knee-jerk reaction legal constraints from politicians, and without adequate explanations from its own chemical defense experts, the military has begun to believe the WMD propaganda. Because soldiers are told that CB warfare is such a great menace, they believe that it is an unstoppable and always lethal weapon. CB warfare conditions are not ideal for fighting soldiers in the first place; it creates an environment that is very confusing, that forces them to wear protective ensembles that slow down their reactions, that makes the simplest tasks such as using the latrine a life-and-death issue. CB warfare is hard to train against; if the agents are invisible, how do you know if they are in the area? Using riot control agents is one way, but the agent detectors do not respond with warnings to tear gas. Soldiers can judge whether their suits and masks work if they are using tear gases, but again one cannot tell whether decontamination exercises are successful. Soldiers understand a physical threat that they can attack or repulse. Invisible CB agents and radioactivity become enemies that seemingly cannot be stopped, poisoning the very environment in which soldiers are operating and making it unsafe to eat, sleep, or defecate without wearing protective ensembles.  It becomes a time- and resource-consuming drill that disrupts combat operations, making CB defense incompatible to normal combat operations.

Rather than confront the peril of a CB warfare environment directly, most combat leaders would rather take a simpler approach.  First they ask how they can prevent the enemy from using CB weapons at all—usually this can be done in the form of arms control agreements or threats of offensive retaliation, either in kind (chemical counterattacks against chemical attacks, etc.) or by massive conventional responses or even nuclear retaliation.   These deterrence efforts, called nonproliferation activities, are executed by politicians and military leaders often prior to and even during hostilities.  Second is the use of "active defense" (perhaps another military oxymoron), in which the one side actively identifies the CB agent production, storage, and delivery systems and attacks them with aircraft, missiles, and special forces to eliminate weapon systems that deploy CB agent munitions.  This is the first half of counterproliferation activities.  The second half is where CB defense comes into the picture.

In the event threats of retaliation fail to convince the enemy to abstain from CB warfare and active defense measures can't find the delivery systems, combat leaders must rely on "passive defense," which assumes that the enemy's offensive capabilities cannot be stopped.  In passive defense, they want to know where the agents are on the battlefield—in this step, usually through the use of CB agent detectors set as low as possible to allow the entire force to protect its soldiers.  Protecting the force usually takes the form of protective masks and suits, encapsulating the individual until the threat passes and the force can resume its conventional operations outside the contaminated area.  Command, control, and communication nodes and medical areas often receive collective protection shelters to enable soldiers to execute complicated tasks without protective suits and masks.

In addition to these requirements, combat leaders insist that their troops should pass through this special environment at "zero risk."  That is to say, they believe there should be an absolute minimal chance that their force strength will be diminished by CB agent casualties, so they can resume normal operations as quickly as possible in conventional modes.  If they cannot avoid contamination and casualties, they demand medical treatments that are quick-acting and safe.  Last, military leaders demand decontaminants to wash the equipment and troops off, as the fastest way to remove the threat of contamination.

It should be emphasized that military forces are expected to fight through battlefields, regardless of whether it is contaminated.  During the Cold War, this was true also for tactical nuclear warfare scenarios, but one could hardly blame troops that stopped or retreated from nuclear attacks or radiological fallout.  Because CB warfare agents are, by their physical nature, temporary barriers (as opposed to radiological contamination, perhaps excluding anthrax), soldiers were expected to "fight dirty" and continue the battle.  As long as soldiers had protective suits and masks, they were impeded but not stopped.  Nonetheless, the delay and impediments caused by wearing protective gear gives a potential advantage to the side using CB munitions (since they do not have to wear protective gear). In the history of U.S. military engagements, there is this "cowboy attitude" that our combat leaders would much rather prefer a "clean, honest fight"—defined as when American soldiers have overwhelming artillery and air support to back up their military operations and they suffer few to no casualties as a result. CB agents do not permit this scenario, which is why our civilian leadership hates the thought of training and fighting in CB warfare conditions.

This simplified view explains why combat arms leaders have, in the past, accepted the presence of U.S. chemical weapons as a retaliatory threat, to avoid having to deal with CB warfare conditions at all. Between 1941 and 1990, the U.S. military armed itself with "swords" of chemical (and for a while, biological) weapons to warn its enemies against using CB weapons. This view also explains the lopsided funding of CB defense programs, the military's "shields." CB agent detectors take up 50 percent of the nonmedical CB defense research, development, and acquisition (RDA) program budget, with protective suits and masks at 35 percent. The less appreciated decontamination devices and collective protection equipment make up 15 percent of the CB defense RDA budget. Most people focus either on the offensive weapon systems or the defensive equipment, neglecting to note that there is a huge doctrine, training, organizational structure, and leader development required for a successful defense program. The Chemical Corps's mission has been to develop that doctrine, training, organizational structure, leadership, and material to protect the force.

Some arms control proponents would have us believe that the only way to eliminate the threat of CB warfare is not just to eliminate one's weapons stocks, but also to refrain from defensive programs. If one side has a defense against particular CB weapons, then (the logic goes) the other side will develop alternatives to counter that defense, thus increasing the risk of CB warfare. For example, if the U.S. military has a chemical detector that detects only nerve agents, the adversaries may invest in producing blister agents that the detectors will not identify. Or if we inoculate our soldiers with anthrax vaccine, the adversaries will use cholera as a biological weapon. This theory argues for unilateral disarmament to convince the world to lay down its arms. This sets the stage for an unprepared military that faces adversaries that do not believe in turning swords into plowshares. Doctrine and training without effective defensive equipment is shear stupidity. The real debate has always been on the munitions—are they required to stop enemy employment of similar weapons, or do they encourage worldwide proliferation?

Politicians have focused on CB munitions as the source of ultimate evil, most vehemently since the 1968 event at Dugway Proving Ground. Because CB defense has never been a big-ticket defense area (as compared to bombers, submarines, and tanks), there were few supporters of CB agent detectors, protective suits, and other defense programs until the Gulf War. Despite numerous bad report cards issued by the General Accounting Office (GAO), Congress has never really involved itself heavily in this area of the military-industrial complex. Bottom line, as the DoD budget for CB defense programs amounts to less than one-half of 1 percent of the total DoD program, CB defense never got much attention until very recently (given the threat of domestic terrorism). But CB munitions (both within and outside the United States) are "A Bad Thing" that Congress does address with more tenacity, if not always with the best follow-through.

The military leadership used to believe that all one required was a big enough "stick" (a CB weapons stockpile of some size) and protective ensembles to deter its adversaries from investing in their own CB weapons. In the worst case, they would be prepared to stop, don protective gear, exchange a few CB munitions, and then return to conventional fire and maneuver operations. The Army Chemical Corps had a very strong view in the 1980s that the military required a strong retaliatory capability, an integrated defensive capability, plus a deterrence role to minimize the threat of CB warfare. The argument comes down to how much of a shield (defensive capability) and how good of a sword (CB munitions) the U.S. military required to protect its troops. What was the balance required to survive and sustain its forces on the modern battlefield?

Behind all the rhetoric of the arms control community, the military leadership, and the political leaders in Congress, there are strategies to deal with "weapons of mass destruction." Our military has had to deal with CB warfare for decades, and will continue facing this threat in the future decades as well. Both the military and the Army Chemical Corps have adapted to new weapons and new doctrine to cope with the threat. What is dangerous is allowing emotions and political soapboxing to override and overcome a responsible review of CB warfare concepts. The alleged Gulf War Syndrome has led our congressional leadership decide that sublethal levels of chemical agents are important enough to demand the Department of Defense develop protective gear and detectors that will ensure that soldiers on the battlefield are as safe from CB agents as the public in New York City. This decision was made as a knee-jerk reaction to ignorance over the source of Gulf War illnesses without understanding the fundamental reasons why CB detectors, protective ensembles, collective protection shelters, decontaminants, and medical defense items are employed.[4] First, who ever promised wars would be safe places to earn a buck, and second, is the measure of public safety in metropolitan areas really the standard we want our soldiers to meet? There is a cost to overprotecting our troops, and that cost may be an increased inability to operate effectively on a battlefield, not to mention the increased costs of operating on an actual CB-contaminated battlefield due to over-engineered equipment that hinders, rather than aids, our troops during combat. Military personnel cannot merely survive a contaminated battlefield, they must be able to sustain combat operations as well.

The Department of Defense in general, and the United States Army specifically, have a bad habit of allowing politics and emotions to overcome logic and the development of a real capability to survive and sustain combat operations on the modern battlefield. There is a history of this mentality documented since World War I, and there is a reasonable approach to designing defensive equipment that has adapted with the military's changes throughout history. This book is designed to address one of the most critical periods of the military's CB defense program: from 1968, when the Army began thinking about eliminating the Chemical Corps, to 1990, when the Army realized it was facing an adversary armed with a substantial CB arsenal and needed doctrine, training, smart leaders, dedicated specialists, and the right equipment to protect itself. The decisions and events during this period are illuminating and should be cause to us all to reflect on a path for the future.

# CHAPTER 2

# The Chemical Corps Enters the Cold War

Major General William Porter was appointed to the position of Chief Chemical Officer in mid-1941. At the time, the Chemical Warfare Service (CWS) was still a very small part of the U.S. Army. The War Department was busy with its Louisiana Maneuvers, testing concepts for tank, airplane, and paratroop employment that had been demonstrated so successfully in Europe. There was no foreshadowing of chemical warfare in U.S. military doctrinal development. The War Department had first made the decision to limit the CWS to laboratory and decontamination companies, but with some impassioned arguments, the CWS could keep its few chemical mortar units. It took a direct request to General George Marshall, the Chief of Staff of the Army, to approve the activation of new chemical mortar units armed with the new 4.2-inch chemical mortar. It would not be until after December 1941, combined with the fact that the Axis nations had been building up their chemical and biological warfare capability, that Major General Porter got the authorization to build up the offensive and defensive capabilities of the Army.[1]

As the war started, the War Department and Congress realized that the United States faced enemies on both shores—enemies that had stockpiles of chemical and perhaps biological weapons. Because the military's readiness was so low, there had to be immediate preparations to rebuild an offensive, and later a defensive, capability in chemical and biological warfare. Congress authorized special appropriations of over $27 million for construction and repair at Edgewood Arsenal, to include rounding out and adding chemical plants, depot construction, a cantonment hospital, and an incendiary bomb pilot plant. Another $41 million went toward a new chemical agent arsenal at Huntsville, Alabama, and $18.5 million for the building of an incendiary bomb filling plant at Pine Bluff, Arkansas (later to grow into Pine Bluff Arsenal). The CWS had received the incendiary mission based on prewar studies of aerial attacks on cities using high explosives, gas, and incendiaries, as well as reports of the destruction caused by the Battle of

Britain. A fourth arsenal was activated outside Denver, Colorado, during May 1942 (Rocky Mountain Arsenal).

On June 5, 1942, President Franklin D. Roosevelt issued the first U.S. administration policy on chemical warfare:

Use of such weapons has been outlawed by the general opinion of civilized mankind. This country has not used them, and I hope we never will be compelled to use them. I state categorically that we shall under no circumstances resort to the use of such weapons unless they are first used by our enemies. . . . Any use of gas by any Axis Power . . . will immediately be followed by the fullest possible retaliation upon munition centers, seaports, and other military objectives.[2]

While this was a bold and noble statement, the fact was that at the time, the United States had no credible CB defensive and retaliatory capability. Through the end of 1942, the U.S. military lacked a modern and robust stockpile of chemical weapons (and thus had no retaliatory capability). This kept the policy of "retaliation in kind" a very weak bluff, one that military planners prayed the politicians would not boast about and the Axis forces would not call. Neither Japan nor the United States had ratified the Geneva Protocol, and by that deliberate omission, neither was bound against initiating chemical warfare. This did not mean that the U.S. military was anxious to explore this option.

Protective clothing plants sprang up in Columbus, Ohio; Kansas City, Missouri; and New Cumberland, Pennsylvania. There were charcoal-filter plants built at Zanesville and Fostoria, Ohio, and impregnate factories at Niagara Falls, New York; East St. Louis, Illinois; and Midland, Michigan. Also in 1942, the Army began construction of a large-scale test installation encompassing over 125,000 acres near Tootle, Utah (Dugway Proving Ground).[3] CWS soldiers and units began training at the CWS School at Edgewood Arsenal, but due to the limited space and facilities, the school expanded its training facilities to Camp Sibert, built near Gadsden, Alabama, in June 1942.[4] In the fall of 1943, the CWS received permission to start a Chemical Warfare School on the West Coast to support Army, Air Force, and Navy forces deploying to the Pacific. Initially this school was at Camp Beale, California—it moved to Rocky Mountain Arsenal later that year due to limited facilities.

The United States' and Britain's biological warfare arsenals were not as publicized as the chemical warfare arsenals. Again, due to the concern over the Japanese biological warfare capabilities (and by inference, potential German capabilities), the U.S. military initiated its biological warfare (BW) program in the fall of 1941. In March 1943 the Army CWS formally acquired its center for BW research at Camp Detrick, Maryland, a former aviation field near to Edgewood Arsenal and Washington, D.C., yet remote from prying eyes. The level of secrecy was matched only by the Manhattan Project. Lieutenant Colonel Richard Clendenin commented:

Reasons for the stringent security were two-fold, not only to prevent the enemy from learning that work was being done in BW, but also to keep the public and even the Armed Forces themselves from becoming unduly alarmed over the possibility of BW.  The elaborate security precautions taken were so effective that it was not until January 1946, four months after VJ (Victory in Japan) Day, that the public learned of the wartime research in BW (at Fort Detrick).[5]

This cooperative effort resulted in the development of a four-pound anthrax-filled aerial bomb.  Anthrax had been tested at Gruinard Island in the summer of 1942, when it was found to be a very deadly and persistent spore ideal for dissemination from aerial munitions.  The island was subsequently quarantined and reopened only to the public in 1992.  The CWS built two pilot plants at Camp Detrick, one of which was designed for botulinum toxin, and the second manufactured an initial run of 5,000 four-pound anthrax munitions in May 1944.  These munitions were sent to England as a retaliatory capability in the event Germany resorted to biological warfare.  These munitions joined the 16,785 long tons of mustard gas, stored in 100-, 500-, and 1,000-pound aerial bombs, stored for similar reasons.  A larger plant was built in Vigo, Indiana, which was tested by producing harmless biological organisms but was never actually used to manufacture anthrax.[6]

At the war's end, the Allies discovered the German nerve agents tabun and sarin in their production plants.  The Soviet Red Army had overrun German chemical production plants near Berlin and discovered a third nerve agent, soman.  Other CW agent stockpiles and German scientists fell into American and British hands.  Overall, German stocks amounted to 78,000 tons of mustard, tabun, arsenic, chloroacetophenone, phosgene, adamsite, nitrogen mustard, and diphenylchlorarsine (as compared to 146,000 tons of American stock worldwide).  Other German stockpiles held another 50,000 tons of Italian, French, Greek, Polish, Hungarian, and Yugoslavian chemical munitions.  Although some hints of German nerve agent research had surfaced before 1945, Allied military leaders and scientists were shaken by the discovery.

## THE POSTWAR "BOOM YEARS"

As demobilization activities tore the huge wartime organization down, the Army reexamined its organization for areas to cut.  Huntsville Arsenal and Dugway Proving Ground were closed, along with other military installations.  Before Major General Porter retired in November 1945, he made a vigorous argument before the Army board about the distinctive character of the Chemical Warfare Service and the need to continue an offensive and defensive chemical warfare capability.  In light of the captured German nerve agent munitions, the Army leadership agreed that the CWS should continue its existence in the new peacetime Army.  Major General Alden H. Waitt, who had been a principal assistant to Major General Porter during the war, assumed the Chief Chemical Officer position.  His testimony before Congress in the summer of 1946, discussing the German nerve agent program and U.S. biological warfare program, would be key in mapping a future for the new "Chemical Corps."

In August 1946 Congress officially approved the Chemical Warfare Service to become the Chemical Corps. That same month, Edgewood's Chemical Warfare Center was renamed as the Army Chemical Center. Its production and manufacturing responsibilities halted, but work continued in the area of chemical warfare and medical defense research and development. American, British, and Canadian scientists formed a Tripartite Agreement in 1947 that allowed the three countries to share their resources and information. Their annual ABC (America-Britain-Canada) conferences combined British expertise, American resources, and Canadian testing grounds. Although Canada did not produce chemical munitions, it benefitted from the exchange of knowledge to develop their defensive program. The Canadian government also contributed a thousand-acre site near Suffield (located near Medicine Hat, Alberta) for open-air testing. With the cooperation of German scientists (transported to the United States under Operation Paperclip),[7] the Army had finally begun producing pure mustard agent and began researching nerve agents.

At Camp Detrick, George Merck, head of the giant Merck pharmaceutical company who had led the American biological warfare program during World War II, issued a press release in 1946. "Work in this field, born of necessity of war, cannot be ignored in time of peace; it must be continued on a sufficient scale to provide adequate defense," wrote Merck. "It is important to note that unlike the development of the atomic bomb, the development of agents for biological warfare could readily proceed in many countries, perhaps under the guise of legitimate medical or bacteriological research."[8] Not everyone was happy that Merck had announced the existence of the American biological warfare program. The new Department of Defense slapped a classified gag on the Army BW program that would stifle any official mention of this top secret program for the next three years. Secretary of Defense James Forrestal authorized the formation of a Special Operations Division at Camp Detrick in May 1949 that would engage in research and development in the field of special biological warfare operations. This was strictly laboratory-scale research and pilot plant development. No facilities existed for the production of BW agents, nor were any attempts made to produce biological agent munitions until 1950.[9]

The advent of the atomic age changed the mission of the Chemical Corps. As the technical scientists of the Army, the Chemical Corps included nuclear weapon effects into their charter and began the procurement of radiation detectors. The Army Chemical Center had organized a Radiological Division at Edgewood to concentrate on various hazards of nuclear war, specifically the effects of radiological fallout on ground forces. Instruments that assisted in determining the "**ra**dioactivity, **d**etection, **i**ndication, and **c**omputation" were named "radiacs" as a general term. While the Chemical Corps had the responsibility for identifying

Army defense requirements, the Signal Corps was given the responsibility to build the instruments, given the similar electromagnetic relationship of radiowaves to radioactive hazards. Since neither the Chemical Corps nor the Signal Corps had any experience in building radiacs, they chose to modify commercial radiation instruments used in physics labs into military hardware.

In 1947 the Chemical Warfare School initiated a six-week course in radiological hazards for all chemical soldiers. In 1950 the U.S. Army, Europe, began an Atomic Energy Indoctrination Training course at Kitzingen Training Center (Germany). This course gave a primer on nuclear physics, theory and use of radiacs, effects of atomic explosions, and medical aspects of radiological defense. This course was available to Navy and Air Force students as well.[10] The M9 protective mask, developed in 1951, would protect soldiers against biological agents and radiological fallout in addition to chemical agents; this demanded the official name change from a "gas mask" to a "protective mask."[11]   Other innovations in protective clothing, agent detection, and decontamination would follow. These changes in focus were reflected in a change of mission from being "chemical soldiers" to "chemical, biological, and radiological" (CBR) defense experts. Also seen was the grouping of "atomic, biological, and chemical" (ABC) weapons in discussions of future warfare.

## THE KOREAN CONFLICT

Military planners were concerned with the idea that the Soviets might either invade Europe while the United States was in Korea or directly assist the North Koreans' war efforts. This influenced the Truman administration to pursue the war while limiting the objectives and resources to be used, thus bringing about the first U.S. "limited" war—limited by executive policy, not by military capability. This limited war included a voluntary prohibition against first use of CB munitions, in line with Roosevelt's World War II policy.[12] At that time, neither North Korea nor China had CB agent weapons, but the U.S. government suspected that the Soviet Union might have provided the arms or technology to these countries to develop a CB warfare capability. When the North Koreans stormed over the border in 1950, only three chemical officers were stationed in Korea. The newly formed Department of Defense (DoD) responded by reactivating several chemical units (along with the combat arms). Several chemical decontamination, depot, technical intelligence, and smoke generator units deployed to Korea in November 1950. While the war would remain limited in its scope, the Army shipped several tons of phosgene and mustard agent munitions to depots in Okinawa and Japan beginning in 1951, in the event that a retaliatory capability was requested and authorized.[13]

While CB warfare never emerged, chemical units were key to smoke operations, supporting incendiary weapons use, and mortar operations, much as they had done in World War II. Decontamination units provided showers for the troops; assisted in smoke and flame-fuel weapons support; and provided chemical ammunition support and decontamination training for the South Korean Army. As in World War II, smoke generator units protected U.S. forces from long-range enemy artillery and air attacks through large area obscuration (though few air raids came over Seoul). Demand for the 4.2-inch mortar support would eventually lead to the Army's decision to transform the chemical mortar to an infantry weapon in 1953 and to change all chemical mortar battalions into infantry battalions.

Many combat units began using the napalm-thickening ingredients to develop their own incendiary weapons for defensive positions, termed *fougasse*. The technical military term was flame field expedients, or FFE. The soldiers began filling drums with twenty gallons of fuel and thickening the fuel with the napalm thickener (which resembled soap detergent). They placed a spiral of primer cord on the bottom of the drum, which led to a white phosphorus (WP) grenade tied to the top of the drum. This drum would be emplaced at an angle pointed away from the defensive position, toward the enemy's expected line of attack. When the primer cord was ignited, it propelled the thickened fuel toward the enemy, while the WP grenade ignited the mixture in mid-flight. The effect was much like a wave of pure flame rising over the attackers, guaranteed to freeze their hearts in their throats and initiate a hasty retreat (and also illuminated the battlefield to riflemen). Training demands grew so large that the Corps moved its unit training facilities from Camp Sibert thirty miles down the road to Fort McClellan, Alabama, on January 4, 1951. In 1952 the Chemical School and all training functions moved from Edgewood Arsenal to Fort McClellan.

With the onset of the Korean War, the Army CBR program grew in scope to develop both retaliatory capabilities and defensive equipment against potential Soviet-developed munitions. The Chemical Center accelerated work on nerve agent munitions and began preliminary research into new weapon designs (providing better battlefield efficiency through larger area coverage). The primary focus remained on investigating CB agents that were lethal in very low concentrations and rapid acting, circumventing the ability of targeted forces to take simple protective measures. This included researching medical countermeasures against the effects of nerve agents, designing protective masks and clothing that would protect troops against both chemical and biological agents, and detectors that would warn of their use against friendly forces. Dugway Proving Grounds reopened in 1950 and received an additional 279,000 acres of land for its use in large-area open-air testing of incendiaries and nerve agent munitions. This replaced Edgewood Arsenal's test fields as the primary Army CB warfare test and evaluation activity. On September 27, 1950, the Secretary of Defense formally authorized the Army to implement an offensive BW capability at Pine Bluff Arsenal. In early 1952 the Pine Bluff Arsenal BW antipersonnel plant was 40 percent completed, with production scheduled to begin in October. The facility was completed in November, with shakedown tests planned in December 1953, with a total cost of $90 million for the entire project.

To meet the need for chemical agent precursors, the Army built a government facility on 45 acres of land in Alabama, called the Muscle Shoals Development works.  Headquarters, Department of the Army (HQ DA) convinced DoD that the Army had no adequate lethal CW capability (World War II emphasized mustard gas, which is not immediately lethal); that the U.S. military had a need to produce more agents quickly and in quantity, given the suspected Soviet effort; that mass casualty weapons such as CW agents were essential for the defense effort; and that the U.S. government had the technical know-how to produce nerve agents.  The building of the facility was launched in 1950 for completion in 1951.  After a slight delay, this plant was producing dichlor in 1953, which in turn was shipped to Rocky Mountain Arsenal for finishing the chemical munition assembly.[14]  By 1954 both the United States and Britain had begun producing nerve agent projectiles and bombs.  While the nerve agent and biological agent weapons production effort had begun too late to support the Korean War, it remained a vital part of the Cold War arms race.

The Korean War had actually strengthened the Chemical Corps's position more than World War II had, considering the successful employment of the 4.2-inch chemical mortar and the growing suspicion that the Soviets could be building up a CB warfare arsenal in addition to nuclear weapons.  In February 1956 Soviet military leaders had publicly stated that chemical and biological weapons would be used for mass destruction in future wars.[15]  The term "weapons of mass destruction" to include CB weapons had been initiated, and the Chemical Corps took advantage of the news by pushing to accelerate their weapons production program.

While most chemical units left the active Army by 1958, Chemical Corps installations flourished.  Camp Detrick had been designated as a permanent installation shortly after World War II but did not have its status solidified until 1956, when it became Fort Detrick.  Dugway Proving Ground was confirmed as a permanent installation in 1954, with a mission of testing CB agent munitions.  Pine Bluff Arsenal also became a permanent installation in August 1954.  In 1958 the Joint Chiefs concluded that budget limitations had slowed U.S. offensive CB warfare capabilities.  One chemical officer commented that Joseph Stalin should have been recognized for his unique contributions to the growth of the Army Chemical Corps (a remark repeated about Saddam Hussein in 1991).

By 1959 the Chemical Corps had gone to considerable lengths to impress upon Congress and the military leadership of the value of CB munitions as a flexible weapon system suited for the "flexible response" posture that was replacing the strategy of massive retaliation.[16]  Public awareness of CB weapons grew stronger in 1960, in response to concerns of the vulnerability of U.S. cities to Soviet attack.  The *Baltimore Sun* commented that the development of a nuclear stalemate would resort in "some nations" resorting to weapons as effective or much more so than the atomic bomb, meaning germ and gas-filled munitions.  A three-piece exclusive in the *Baltimore News-Post* screamed "Gas, Biological Warfare Threat to U.S. NOW: Government Admits Incredible Danger"; "U.S. Wide Open to a Surprise Gas-Germ Attack: New Mask Rated High for Safety"; and "U.S. Has Few Ways to Spot Cloud of Death: More Work Needed on Detection Devices." In late 1961, articles in the *Baltimore News-Post* warned that if "World War III should come, the Soviet Union would probably turn it into a chemical and gas war and not an atomic conflict."

In light of the increased public concern, Edgewood Arsenal developed and produced a civilian protective mask (the M16 noncombatant protective mask) for the civil defense units who would require protection against these Soviet CB agent attacks.[17] This campaign convinced the public and many in the government that CB agent weapons were as deadly and effective as nuclear weapons were (an inaccurate, but highly stressed, government stance). The Air Force and Navy, recognizing that chemical weapons provided a flexible alternative to a nuclear response, demanded and received their own CB warfare funds for offensive and defensive programs. Now the Army had competition for CB defense programs and offensive weapons, but on the other hand, DoD had increased their funding fivefold.

## SUPPORT FOR THE VIETNAM CONFLICT

As U.S. government involvement in Vietnam increased, the Chemical Corps was once again called upon to support the troops. The lack of a CB warfare threat did not limit the employment of chemical soldiers. During the late 1950s and early 1960s, the Corps's scientists and engineers had turned their focus on incapacitants, nonlethal CB agents, to include riot control agents (RCAs or tear gases), psychological chemical agents (such as agent BZ), herbicides, and incapacitating antipersonnel biological agents. This was in part due to the graphic images of the Korean War and its high casualty rates on both sides, and senior leadership's desire to maintain American public support for the military. At the request of the South Vietnamese government, President John F. Kennedy authorized the beginning of Operation Ranch Hand in the summer of 1961. This began as an anticrop effort to deny food sources to the enemy. As U.S. military forces and defensive positions grew in strength, the effort shifted toward deforestation to expose enemy operations. On September 4, 1963, Lieutenant Colonel Peter G. Olenchuk headed the team to conduct an evaluation, whose report rated the military worth of the herbicide operations as high. Defoliation operations had made aerial surveillance much more effective, and thus diminished the need for ground surveillance troops. Defensive positions had much better fields of fire, with increased visibility of up to 80 percent.[18] River operations in the delta, once showing very high casualty rates, dropped directly in proportion to the increase of herbicides on the riverbanks.

While the American media and public did not see the use of herbicides as newsworthy at the time, the military use of RCAs and napalm was attracting more attention. In December 1964 American soldiers used CS grenades as part of a rescue operation. In February 1965 senior advisers began carrying CN, CS, and DM grenades and protective masks for self-defense. Reporters, to include Associated Press reporter Horst Faas and Peter Arnett, noticed the use of tear gas grenades and duly filed reports on their intended use in tactical situations.[19] The reports initiated a flurry of media headlines screaming "U.S. Using Gas Warfare in Vietnam!" The controversy swelled over the use of nonlethal gas in the war, especially as politicians in London, Paris, Moscow, and Washington compared use of CS gas with World War I gas attacks. Many questioned the "morality" of a military force that would stoop to using gas against its enemy. These critics chose not to differentiate non-lethal riot gases in use with police forces around the world from the more poisonous chemical warfare agents used in World War I.

In fall 1965 the Department of Defense requested an official opinion from the State Department on the legality of using irritant gases in combat. Since the United States was not the party of any international treaty that prohibited the use of gas, the State Department agreed that non-lethal gases could represent a "humane decision." Secretary of State Dean Rusk defended the use of RCAs, telling newscasters on March 25, 1965: "We do not expect that [tear] gas will be used in ordinary military situations [but] . . . in situations analogous to riot control." Deputy Secretary of Defense Cyrus Vance echoed this sentiment, writing "Riot control agents were employed in an attempt to subdue the Viet Cong without exposing the South Vietnamese civilians and prisoners . . . to injury."[20]   In November 1965 the Joint Chiefs gave permission to General William Westmoreland to use CS and CN at his discretion, which was further delegated to his major commanders.

When the military use of RCAs was continued in 1966, the United Nations took up the issue of whether such use was against the Geneva Protocols of 1925. Only the Soviet Union and its satellites actively took issue with the United States, claiming that the use of RCAs during wartime was prohibited by international law. American allies either supported the American view or abstained. American units continued to use CS grenades and powder against noncombatants to limit friendly casualties, and increasingly used in combat where its use would offer an overall tactical advantage (such as in flushing out caves and tunnels). This remained a controversial topic in the UN for the next three years.

The use of napalm, once a well-accepted munition used in both World War II and the Korean War, came under new scrutiny with live color news coverage of its use in Vietnam. The public was told by the media and critics of the war that the use of napalm was a new and frightening escalation and was excessively barbaric and inhuman (as opposed to normal bombing operations using high explosives?). Groups of citizens began picketing and filing lawsuits against chemical industries that were producing napalm, calling for referendums to prevent plants from manufacturing "flaming death." Over the years, these calls escalated to the point of college students threatening to "napalm" a dog in public to show their abhorrence of its use in Vietnam. While these threats were not carried out, the demonstrators used this example to emphasize the cruelty of using napalm against humans.[21]

This abhorrence was not echoed by the soldiers, who increasingly relied on their chemical soldiers' advice on emplacing drums of fougasse around their perimeters and on air-delivered napalm strikes to keep their positions from being overrun by overwhelming human wave assaults. An example of this was one Captain William S. Carpenter, Jr. (later Major General Carpenter, commanding general of the 10th Mountain Division), who called in napalm and high-explosive bombing strikes on his own base camp as it was being overrun by Viet Cong. This enabled him to save himself and what was left of his force from certain capture or death.[22] Nor were American soldiers upset about the ability to use CS in addition to napalm to protect themselves against adversaries. In the military's point of view, both napalm and CS gas were conventional munitions, to be used in normal combat operations to give U.S. troops an edge over high odds.

While the Chemical Corps's products of herbicides, napalm, and riot control agents came under fire, the Corps's scientists continued to apply themselves to other areas. Using their detector technology, the Edgewood engineers developed a helicopter-mounted electrochemical instrument that sampled the air for ammonia excretions (i.e., urine). The XM2 Airborne Personnel Detector (or "people sniffer") worked in the field but was not used extensively, as commanders relied more on visual sightings of the enemy than on this device. Smoke systems were modernized, both as hand-held colored smoke grenades and as helicopter-mounted smoke generators. Helicopter-mounted generators were used either to screen airmobile movements or to deceive the enemy about the exact landing zones occupied by U.S. troops. This novel employment of mobile smoke was not often used (due to higher priority missions involving helicopters), but when executed correctly, they proved very successful. Despite the lack of a CB threat, the Corps actively supported their combat brethren.

While the American public protested against Agent Orange, riot control agents, and napalm during the Vietnam conflict, events in the same period in the Middle East were slipping past on the world stage. In the Yemeni civil war (1962–67), Egyptian forces had been accused of using aerial bombs containing nerve agent and mustard agent against the Yemeni Royalists. Evidence collected by the Saudi government and International Red Cross seemed to support this use. This was the first strong evidence of Soviet chemical warfare efforts since World War II. The Soviet chemical weapons buildup had picked up momentum in 1958, after the Soviet military had increased their tactical and strategic nuclear weapon stockpiles (their first priority) and after they recognized the advantages (and American superiority) of nerve agent weapons. Sarin and soman (GB/GD) manufacturing plants soon sprang up, producing thousands of tons of chemical weapons. Parallel efforts in defense equipment development, offensive employment, and training followed. The Yemeni civil war offered an opportunity for practical tests in wartime conditions.

Egypt declared that its forces had never participated in gas attacks in Yemen—which, if Soviet pilots flew the Egyptian (Soviet-produced) bombers with Soviet munitions, would technically be true. With the ongoing use of Agent Orange in Vietnam, the Washington administration was not about to get into a frank conversation about the legalities of chemical warfare. As for Britain, it had been attempting to reestablish diplomatic relations with Egypt since the nationalization of the Suez Canal in 1956. Both deferred to the UN Security Council, where Secretary-General U Thant, on March 1, 1967, said that he was "powerless" to deal with the issue. U Thant added that "the facts are in sharp dispute and I have no means of ascertaining the truth." That summer, *U.S. News and World Report* published two IRC memos obtained by private sources, confirming the chemical attacks. Despite a brief respite while Egypt fought with Israel (Arab-Israeli War of 1967), the gas attacks continued through July. In August the two sides agreed to halt the civil war and called for the withdrawal of the British from Saudi Arabia and the Egyptians from Yemen by the end of the year. Altogether through the war, 1,400 loyalists were killed by gas, and another 900 became gas casualties.[23]

While the U.S. military would mostly ignore this backwater war, this was the first use of nerve agents in combat. Because of the remote location and scattered occurrences of incidents, it was next to impossible to identify witnesses and gather evidence of any attacks. There was no doubt in the Pentagon that the Egyptian nerve agent munitions had come from Soviet stockpiles. The Soviet actions against Hungary, the aggressive blockade in Berlin, and rumblings of a crackdown against Czechoslovakia made clear the importance of deterring further Warsaw Pact aggressions. In response, the Army began shipping mustard (HD) and nerve (GB and VX) projectiles and bulk agent to depots in West Germany in five shipments under Operation YZU. These shipments took place from July 25 through October 13, 1967, creating an in-theater retaliatory capability for U.S. forces in Europe. On the defensive side, the Yemeni Civil War emphasized the need for an automatic chemical agent detector that would detect agents at sublethal doses, alerting soldiers to a chemical attack. Edgewood Arsenal standardized the M8 Automatic Chemical Agent Alarm in 1968; four years later, it entered the Army inventory as the first field automatic chemical agent alarm for combat units.[24] Work began on an automatic biological agent detector, a much more difficult technical task. Unknown to the Chemical Corps, there were random forces in action that would cause all their efforts to come to a screaming halt.

# CHAPTER 3

# The Chemical Corps Begins Its Fall

On March 13, 1968, an Air Force F-4 aircraft released 320 gallons of VX from two TMU-28B spray tanks on a target area deep within Dugway Proving Ground (DPG), Utah. At least 80 percent of the two tanks emptied as the plane traveled at 150 feet from the ground on an azimuth of 315 degrees true. Five seconds after passing over the target, the plane dropped its tanks prior to its return to its airfield. On March 15, ranchers reported to Dugway officials that they had over 4,300 ill sheep, some dying, in Skull Valley, Utah, nearly thirty miles away. No conclusive evidence of nerve agent poisoning was apparent to state or federal officials first on the scene of the mysterious illnesses, nor were any humans affected by whatever was hurting the sheep. The Army later admitted to negligence and paid more than $376,000 in compensation for the sheep and an additional $198,000 for range damages.[1] Those are the reported facts. This story has been exaggerated for years as the ultimate example of a loosely-monitored weapons development program as well as the dangers of a military CB weapons stockpile.

Dr. C. Grant Ash, then scientific director of Deseret Test Center, Fort Douglas, Utah, recently returned to the "scene of the crime" to piece together the other side of the story of what had happened that spring in 1968. His investigations are related here, combined with details from the Army's official record of investigation, along with Major General (retired) John Appel's notes.[2] Then-Brigadier General John Appel was the new commander of Deseret Test Center, located next to Dugway Proving Ground. This was his first assignment as a general officer, literally the most junior flag officer of the Chemical Corps. He was told to stay out of the limelight, as the "new kid on block" and given his future command of Dugway Proving Ground later that summer (Deseret was integrated into DPG in July 1968). Nearly every day, Brigadier General Appel would discuss the latest political and scientific findings of the sheep illness mystery with Dr. Ash and the two deputy commanders at Deseret (an Air Force colonel and Navy captain).[3] As the Deseret Test Center personnel saw it, much of the investigation was political, not scientific. The desire to identify what had gone wrong was abandoned in favor of public demands, local political gain, and simple greed, combined with poor judgment on the part of the Army leadership. Although the Army had accepted the blame, there has been no conclusive evidence that it was nerve gas that killed these sheep, and more than enough evidence that there was a rush to judgement.

## THE OPENING ACT

Skull Valley lies twenty-seven miles northeast from Dugway Proving Ground, behind a mountain range 1,000 feet high, as shown in Figure 3.1. On March 14 Utah state officials and veterinarians had been called to the White Rock range on the west side of Skull Valley to investigate a report of thousands of dead sheep belonging to the Anschutz Feed and Livestock company of Denver, Colorado. The range supervisor, Mr. Alvin Hatch, claimed that at least 3,000 sheep were dead, with another 800 affected but recovering. The sheep were not insured, which the supervisor estimated would mean damages to Anschutz in the area of $200,000. Herds owned by D.S. Osguthorpe to the south, and Deseret Land and Livestock Co. to the north, both in Skull Valley, were not affected, nor were any cattle or horses near the affected herds. No one knew what to make of it, but some immediately began speculating that the Army's unpublicized and highly secretive open-air testing at nearby Dugway Proving Ground was at fault.

Some Dugway personnel were notified on the late afternoon of Friday, March 15, and invited to participate in the investigation. Over the weekend, Dugway investigators collected soil and vegetation samples from the area and placed the samples in deep-freeze to preserve them. The arid soil of the area would hold chemical traces for only a few days before all contaminants evaporated. The crews noted that no other animals (such as small rodents) or birds, normally much more susceptible to nerve agents, were sick or dying in the area. They did note finding large numbers of empty hypodermic needles and syringes among the dead sheep. The state veterinarians said they had injected the sheep with various vaccines, inoculations, and atropine, all with no effect. Many surviving sheep were lying still on the ground and not moving, nor were they eating, although their breathing was regular. Red urine and red teardrops spoke of some internal hemorrhaging. These symptoms were directly contrary to the effects of nerve agents, which would have caused shallow breathing and jerking muscles and no signs of hemorrhaging.

Colonel James Watts was the commander of Dugway Proving Ground at the time, and Dr. Mortimer Rothenburg was the scientific director. On Sunday afternoon, Colonel Watts called a general meeting of his staff to determine what they could do to assist in the problem. Clearly actions had to be taken to identify the culprit as soon as possible, if nothing else but to avoid a false charge of complicity. Guidelines limiting their direct public discussions of CB agents mandated a decision from higher headquarters. Sunday night (9:30 P.M. in Utah), Headquarters, Test and Evaluation Command (TECOM), at Aberdeen Proving Ground, Maryland, received notification that Dugway Proving Ground was potentially involved with the sheep sicknesses and deaths in Skull Valley.[4]

Figure 3.1
Dugway Proving Ground Test Site and Sheep Herd Locations

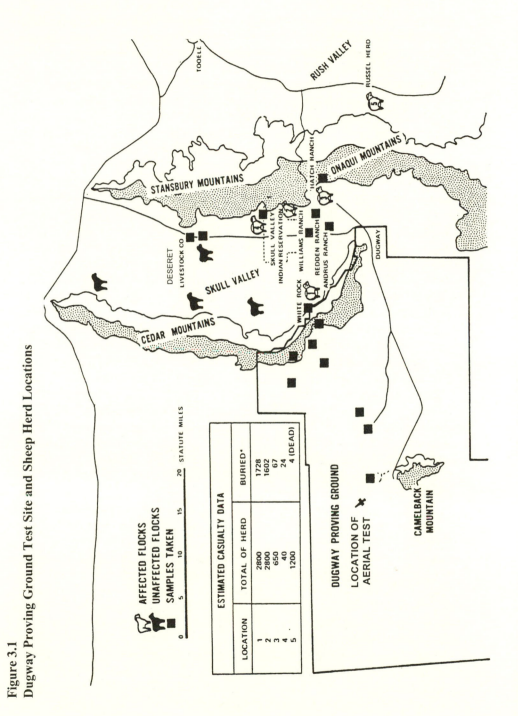

ESTIMATED CASUALTY DATA

| LOCATION | TOTAL OF HERD | BURIED* |
|----------|---------------|---------|
| 1 | 2800 | 1728 |
| 2 | 2800 | 1602 |
| 3 | 650 | 67 |
| 4 | 40 | 24 |
| 5 | 1200 | 4 (DEAD) |

AFFECTED FLOCKS
UNAFFECTED FLOCKS
SAMPLES TAKEN

0   5   10   15   20  STATUTE MILES

DUGWAY PROVING GROUND
LOCATION OF
AERIAL TEST

On Monday, March 18, Mr. Hatch arrived at Dugway to discuss his sheep's illnesses with the assembled scientists. He estimated that there were now 5,000 sheep down or dead. Because the sheep had not responded to atropine or shown signs of nerve agent poisoning, they were all unsure of what had affected such a large number of sheep and no other animal. The scientists agreed to support the investigation by running various analytical tests for trace chemical compounds in the sheep blood samples and stomach samples. Representatives from the U.S. Department of Agriculture, Utah State's Agricultural Department, and the University of Utah all joined in the investigation. Utah governor Calvin Rampton, a Democrat, and Senator Frank Moss (D-UT) called for full investigations.

The public began to hear news about the sheep deaths on Tuesday, March 19. Public affairs officers at Dugway Proving Ground told the press that tests at the proving grounds were definitely not responsible for the deaths. Meanwhile, an Army intelligence officer, a captain assigned to Dugway, initiated his own investigation. He discovered that Deseret Livestock Company ranchers had hired two spray planes to spray insecticide over lands where alfalfa was grown, about two to five miles north from the White Rocks sheep. He had obtained one pilot's name and the aircraft number and located two empty spray tanks. Eyewitnesses in the area were not sure whether the spraying had been conducted on March 13, 14 or 15, but it was in the right time frame. His second discovery was that the Fred Anschutz Livestock Company had possible financial ties to the Nevada gambling underworld. He reported his findings to Colonel Watts on Wednesday.

Wednesday morning, March 20, HQ Army Material Command (AMC) called. General Frank Besson (the commanding general) wanted a fact sheet on the situation in three hours (it was sent to AMC before noon). Word had finally traveled to the top that DPG might be involved in the sheep deaths. More tests continued throughout the day. Dr. Jordan Rassmussen, a state diagnostician to the animal health division of the U.S. Department of Agriculture, was quoted by the press as believing the problem was related to the feed on Wednesday. Disease had been tentatively ruled out, and people were gathering test animals and local poisonous plants to see whether they could replicate the illness. No one really knew what happened when sheep were exposed to nerve agent; there was no data to compare against the illnesses and to then declare the sheep were or were not exposed to Army tests. Meanwhile, Dugway personnel reported seeing national news reporters moving into the area. Because DPG information officers could not release information to the public about CB agents or weapons they were testing, they referred all queries to TECOM headquarters at Aberdeen Proving Ground, Maryland. Reporters began to take the delays in answering questions and the lack of any official information (due to the secrecy surrounding ongoing weapon system tests) as stall tactics and a cover-up.

On Thursday, March 21, Senator Wallace Bennett (R-UT) formally requested federal assistance into the sheep death investigation. As the event began drawing national attention, more Army officials in Washington, D.C., were getting involved. The Assistant Secretary of Defense for Public Affairs released a fact sheet on the situation through TECOM to Dugway for public release. It stated in brief that there was an ongoing investigation into the incident, that DPG personnel were assisting in the investigation, and that it would be speculative to suggest any specific cause of death, given the lack of hard evidence. The fact sheet was released at noon to the AP, the UPI, and television and newspaper reporters. The Utah congressional delegation (to include Representative Sherman Lloyd (R-UT), Senator Moss, and Senator Bennett), received a more detailed fact sheet. It stated that the cause of death had not been determined; that the ongoing investigation had ruled out bacterial or biological agents; and that they were still investigating organophosphate compounds, chlorinated hydrocarbons, and heavy metals as possible sources. It also listed three tests that had been conducted at Dugway on March 13. These included a 155-mm GB (sarin) artillery demonstration for the Army Chemical School (15-35 miles away from Skull Valley), disposal of 160 gallons of VX in an open burning pit (about 27 miles away), and an open-air spray trial using two 160-gallon tanks of VX on an F-4 jet.[5] Senator Moss promptly released the fact sheet to the press, despite the fact that it was marked "for official use only." Suspicion immediately fell upon the Army's tests. Newspapers began running stories that the open-air spray trials were now the number one suspect in the sheep deaths.

At Dugway, Colonel Watts had begun meeting with Governor Rampton daily and met with him that Thursday afternoon as the newspapers were writing their stories. He mentioned to him the investigator's discovery that the ranchers sprayed insecticides. The governor became infuriated that DPG officials had an ongoing investigation that he did not know about. He told Colonel Watts that the Army had killed these sheep, and the innocent ranchers and civilians of Utah would not be involved in this mess. He ordered Colonel Watts, and later Brigadier General Appel, to stop the probe immediately. Governor Rampton also called offices in Washington, resulting in the intelligence officer's transfer from the post within the next few days. Later that day, ten sheep were reported sick at the neighboring Skull Valley Indian Reservation and a dozen or more sheep ill at the Russell Herd in Rush Valley, nearly 80 miles from the test site. Was the epidemic spreading? Lab results were still inconclusive in identifying a culprit.

Things were getting tense. General Besson's office called for an update on the sheep kill Friday morning, followed by a call from TECOM's commanding general directing that DPG personnel offer all possible assistance to the state investigators. Colonel Watts initiated a twenty-four-hour operations cell to track events. Following Colonel Watts's one-hour brief to Governor Rampton at the state capital, the governor held a full press conference. He stated that, in his opinion, the Army's nerve agent was responsible for the sheep's injuries, but that there was no apparent threat to other animals or people in the area. This was despite the fact that the lab tests were still ongoing, no one had found any evidence of nerve agent in the area, and the DPG personnel had just initiated nerve agent trials on sheep in an effort to duplicate the illnesses. He brushed off the fact that no domestic animals, cattle, or horses had been affected by explaining that the sheep had probably used old snow for water requirements, which might be a source of contamination. The governor went on to tell the press that Colonel Watts had assured him that all Dugway testing had been halted until this matter was cleared up, and that Brigadier General William W. Stone, Jr., of the Army's research and testing laboratories in Washington, D.C., was flying out to take charge of the investigation. The governor had appointed Commissioner of Livestock Division David Waldron to lead the state's investigating team.

Part of the reason the DPG personnel were so confounded by the charge that the open air spray trials were the cause was the extensive operational procedures taken to prevent just this situation. Since 1953 they had conducted 170 nerve agent spray trials (87 volatile agents, 24 nonvolatile agents, 20 incapacitating agents, and 39 simulant sprays, to be exact). This number did not include the hundreds of mustard gas spray trials and biological agent trials conducted at Dugway. The point of designing delivery systems such as spray tanks was to enable a fast-moving plane to contaminate a large fraction of the target with a significantly lethal dose of agent, ideally using all its load. To ensure success, that called for a series of tests to prove the delivery systems would work in combat as planned, in a predictable, calculated fashion.

Operational guidelines mandated that initial tests using chemical simulants, nontoxic materials with physical characteristics similar to nerve agent, prior to any agent tests. This allowed weapon designers to identify how well chemical agent dispersal devices worked (in this case, the TMU-28B tank) without incurring the risk of exposure. The simulant used for VX tests was bis(2-ethylhexyl) hydrogen phosphite (or BIS for short). Preliminary tests had been conducted first with water-filled spray tanks and seven additional tests with agent simulant, prior to any flights. These tests identified the dispersive pattern of the liquid on the ground, as the simulant was chosen for its ability to duplicate the size of the droplets of nerve agent. The DPG trials included two single tank trials and one two-tank trial with simulant prior to moving on to nerve agent use. After months of evaluation, the nerve agent trial had been conducted (the first of three planned trials). Even at this stage, the nerve agent-filled tanks also held a chemical dye to more easily identify where it landed on the test grid within the proving grounds. This chemical dye had not been seen anywhere off the post.

VX agent is a thick liquid with the consistency of motor oil, but colorless and odorless. The airborne particles were not a gas but suspended drops of water, an aerosol that did not evaporate quickly. It was designed to contaminate ground and material for days to weeks in addition to killing exposed soldiers that were downwind of the release. In this case, this meant that the chemical agent had to land on the sheep's skin in drops that would kill or sicken them; it would not have been taken into their lungs because of the (relatively) large particle size. Sarin, a nonpersistent liquid with the consistency of water, was designed to evaporate and attack targets through the respiratory system much quicker than through skin contact. The alternate theory was that the sheep had drunk water or eaten food that the VX had landed upon. Yet somehow only the sheep in these particular areas had been affected, but not any human or other domestic animal or livestock.

This is a good point to puncture two myths in the popular media story. Some later versions of this incident say that one of the two spray tanks was faulty, stuck half open as agent dribbled out. In reality, each tank was separately controlled, with one open full for eight seconds, and the other half open for sixteen seconds, the better to test its control capabilities. There were three stages to the spray release: first, the initial eight seconds over the target at 150-240 feet; second, the next eight seconds as the plane climbed to jettison altitude at 1,535 feet, still trailing agent from the second tank (deliberately); and third, the release of the tanks and their plunge to the ground four miles from the target. Agent mass for each of these intervals could be determined and accounted for after the test. The second myth is that the wind changed to push the agent toward the valleys. Again, while the wind direction was different at higher altitudes (not an uncommon phenomenon), the predominant wind direction stayed steady from the southeast throughout the test. The wind did shift two hours after the tests were completed, but all the liquid agent should have been on the ground by then. The point to emphasize here is that it was a test of liquid particle dispersion, it was not a gas that drifted off post.

Chemical munitions test at the proving ground used droplet cards, cardboard cards on the site of the agent release, to record the exact amount and pattern of agent released. This data is valuable not just as evaluation of the weapon system, but in understanding the particle dynamics of chemical warfare agents. Army test data had shown that the VX spray of an average particle size of 100 microns in diameter covered an area two to three miles downwind of the spray line, as the delivery system had been designed to do. These relatively heavy particles, roughly the size of raindrops (0.01 centimeters wide), made up about 94 percent of the spray by mass and fell to the ground on the droplet cards. Smaller particles (50-100 microns) could travel downwind for further distances, but none had ever been detected beyond fifteen miles. Much of the smaller particles were identified at the test site on the droplet cards. To the best of the DPG scientists' analyses, the downwind spray should never have left federal grounds.

In the worst case, the spray tanks might have released some agent as smaller (50-100 micron) particles, 55.7 pounds of which were not accounted for in the target area. Of this amount, 36.1 pounds would have settled out within fifteen miles of the test site, leaving 19.6 pounds of agent unaccounted for. This leaves about 5 of the 320 gallons, or less than 2 percent of the plane's payload, as the candidate for drifting off the military reservation. The agent particles, had they traveled that far, would have dispersed over at least two hundred square miles. Imagine a cup of VX agent thrown up in the air inside a large room. People standing within that room would be at a terrible risk. Now imagine the cup of VX thrown up in the air inside a football stadium at the fifty-yard line. People in the stands might feel no effects as they calmly walked out the exit doors, as the small amount of agent disseminated into the large arena's air space. The dilution factor, assuming that five gallons could drift more than thirty miles over the mountain range, would have been so great that neither sheep nor man would have been affected by the stray molecules of VX landing on exposed skin.

What Governor Rampton was suggesting was that somehow an agent cloud had held together for 35 (Skull Valley) to 80 miles (Rush Valley) to deposit agent in that particular area, to the point that its toxicity would have killed the sheep. While VX is a particularly nasty chemical agent, even it can eventually be diluted to the point of ineffectiveness (at least undetectable to modern epidemiological methods). Last but not least, the health effects of VX on individual people was relatively well understood. No one understood what sheep could and could not tolerate as exposure to VX—thus the need for agent trials on test sheep. Army personnel would have to test the sheep's vulnerability to various amounts of VX by placing samples on the sheep's wool, on their exposed skin (nose and eyes), and by feeding them VX-treated food pellets prior to determining whether this was a feasible case. Only after these results were measured could anyone know for sure whether VX was a credible candidate. Yet here was the governor telling the press that he absolutely knew it was the Army's fault.

## WASHINGTON TAKES OVER

Brigadier General Stone was the chemical officer and assistant deputy for research and laboratories at Headquarters, Army Material Command, at Washington, D.C., and also a former Edgewood Arsenal commander (1966-67). He arrived at Dugway at six o'clock that evening. A public affairs task force, including HQ DA, AMC, and TECOM personnel, accompanied him to support the DPG information office. A team of Edgewood Arsenal scientists, headed by Doctor Bernard P. McNamara, also arrived to support the agent tests.[6] A local news anchorman and Army reservist, Arthur Kent, called Brigadier General Appel to alert him that the news media were not going to wait for any long tests and investigations. His boss had instructed him to attack the Army chemical weapons tests at Dugway as the cause of the sheep deaths. "The people want blood from the Army as the cause for the sheep deaths, and we are going to give it to them," Kent quoted his boss as saying. Local news estimates had rounded the Anschutz sheep herd size to 2,800 rather than the 4,500 sheep number quoted by the supervisor, but national news accounts used the larger figures.

Over the weekend, investigators from the National Communicable Disease Center from Atlanta, Georgia, arrived at Dugway. Furnished with vehicles and supplies, they immediately traveled to Skull Valley and Rush Valley to begin their own analyses. Dr. McNamara and his team also left for the valleys to collect dead sheep for pathological studies. While DPG epidemiologists had exposed sheep on Dugway to VX in an effort to duplicate the illness, Dr. McNamara wanted to examine sheep at the location of the illnesses to compare against healthy sheep deliberately exposed to VX agent and control sheep (unexposed) at Dugway. Photo surveillance runs were conducted over the valleys to begin documenting both the living and the ambulatory sheep in the area, as Brigadier General Stone began assembling information to take back to Washington. During the helicopter surveillance runs, Major Weldin from Dugway stopped at White Rock to talk to Mr. Hatch, who was engaged with a crew of men in killing sheep. Many were still alive, and about a third were healthy enough to run as the helicopter swooped over them. For the purposes of the brief, they estimated there was about 15,000 sheep in the immediate affected area, and between 5,000 to 7,000 that had taken ill.

On Sunday, Brigadier General Stone departed for Washington to brief General Besson at HQ AMC and the Utah congressional delegation. Colonel Watts was still fuming over the lack of any investigation into the possibility of pesticide spraying over Skull Valley. He called for the judge advocate's office to take statements from local personnel who witnessed the rancher's spraying operations and discussed the idea of bringing the Federal Bureau of Investigation into the incident. What became more important to resolve was the burial process for the dead sheep. Colonel Watts began talks with the ranchers to discuss authorizations and operating instructions to safely bury the potentially contaminated sheep carcasses.

On Monday, initial test results were coming in. The Department of Agriculture officials conducted a dozen autopsies at Logan, Utah, confirming that the sheep's cause of death had been ingestion of an organic phosphate. No poisonous plants were found in their stomachs, but the feed ingested by the sheep showed the chemical radicals. While organophosphates may have implicated nerve agents as a possible cause, it also would include at least a half dozen commercial pesticides and herbicides. There were no direct traces of nerve agent or any chemical pesticide found. Families living near Dugway Proving Ground and Skull Valley showed normal acetylcholinesterase levels in their blood, which would have been depressed had they been exposed to nerve agent. This included the families of military and civilian personnel living on Dugway Proving Ground, much closer to the test sites. Birds, rodents, and insects, usually more sensitive to nerve agents than other animals, were equally unaffected.

Dr. D.A. Osguthorpe, a veterinarian and member of the state investigating team, was a consultant to the Utah State Department of Agriculture (also a wealthy rancher and owner of the large sheep herd in Skull Valley) and was quoted often in the local newspapers. He felt that the presence of the organophosphate compound in the sheep's stomachs combined with the Army tests run on March 13 nailed down nerve agents as the definite culprit. Both Colonel Watts and Dr. Rothenburg objected to this opinion. They noted that their test sheep exposed to nerve agent at Dugway had shown labored breathing, convulsions, and excessive salivation, none of which had been seen in the Skull Valley sheep. In addition, the Skull Valley sheep had shown drooping heads and twisted necks and spines, symptoms not repeatable in the Dugway sheep. The Dugway sheep exposed to VX agent either quickly died or recovered completely, while the Skull Valley sheep had lingered for weeks and did not respond to atropine in the first few days of illness.

At the Pentagon on Monday morning (March 25), Brigadier General Stone briefed several officers and command levels at HQ AMC and the Pentagon on his fact-finding mission.   Air Force and Navy representatives, understandably concerned about events at the joint service test center, also participated at these briefs.  They called their respective deputy commanders at Deseret Test Center to give their counterparts a heads up on the briefing.  Brigadier General Appel and Colonel Watts had no such calls from their superiors.  The Army had decided to admit that the Dugway Proving Ground tests had probably killed the sheep, and that the government would compensate the ranchers for their losses.  Whether there was adequate evidence supporting the claim was immaterial.  The instructions were to complete the investigation, as quickly as possible, admit involvement, and return to a normal testing routine as rapidly as circumstances would allow.

Brigadier General Stone briefed Senator Moss, Senator Bennett, and the press later that day.  He opened his comments stating that they did not yet know whether Dugway tests were responsible for the death of the sheep.  The open air spray trials were the only test issue discussed (of the three events on March 13), now the clear favorite as villain of the story.  At 5:30 P.M., an F-4 jet had sprayed 320 gallons of VX nerve agents at a height of 150 feet on a heading of 315 degrees, and that at the time the wind was blowing from the west-southwest 5 to 25 miles per hour with gusts up to 35 miles per hour.  The spray tanks used had been factory-filled, sealed, and delivered to Dugway in approved shipping containers with technical escort and were free of contamination.

He described the general characteristics of the agent, the environmental conditions that existed, extensive testing conducted prior to agent trials, and how the test had been conducted.  In addition to the technical information about the tests and the weather conditions, Brigadier General Stone noted that Dugway had been home to over 100 spray trials since 1953.  While there had been accidental field crew exposures, none were serious and no effects were ever seen off post.  He then directed them to a map to show where the affected sheep herds had been located and where ground and water samples had been taken, and he stressed that all individuals who had submitted blood tests had shown no exposure to organophosphate poisons.  Brigadier General Stone stressed that they had no evidence at this point to indicate that insecticides had been used in the affected areas.  This was not exactly truthful; there were certainly suspicions on the part of the DPG personnel, later confirmed by lab tests, that insecticides had been used in the area.  Utah had no state laws against spraying insecticides at the time, although the investigating teams had been told by ranchers that no one had sprayed in those areas within the last two years.

In his summary statement, Brigadier General Stone told the audience

In our view this question [of the sheep deaths] has not been answered.  Although there is increasing evidence that an anti-cholinesterase material is involved, we do not, to my knowledge, have any evidence to tell us the actual chemical compound or to help us pinpoint the source and how it got to the sheep and not to humans or to the other animals.  We fully recognize, with this occurring right on our doorstep and probably involving a chemical similar to the materials we have been testing, that we are highly suspect. . . . In summary, gentlemen, although we already have a mass of information, the picture is not clear.[7]

Given that long and detailed report, all the news reports paraphrased the general the next day "Army says 'We're in the position of being highly suspect until we can prove otherwise.' " Brigadier General Stone returned to Dugway on March 26, where the sheep burials were well underway (over 1,200 estimated). A DPG military team of forty personnel and heavy equipment worked at the main burial site at White Rock. Prior to beginning work, all had blood drawn to monitor cholinesterase levels and donned protective clothing. Three alternative burial sites had been prepared, but the one site was adequate for all the carcasses. To address the local unfavorable editorial comments that had been written, the local media was invited to Dugway for an update on all available information. Brigadier General Stone in essence repeated his previous statement to the press (newspapers and television), which were probably more balanced in their presentations that night than the national reception in Washington had been.

Utah State Division of Health personnel visiting the Deseret ranch discovered empty cans of heptachlor pesticide. Upon questioning, the Deseret Livestock Company ranchers claimed they had sprayed heptachlor, a pesticide similar to DDT, on their alfalfa for weevil treatment on March 15 in the morning, as the winds were blowing from the south. Heptachlor is a hydrocarbon, not an organophosphate compound; to be safe, the investigators began tests of the pesticide against the sheep samples. This discovery confirmed the rancher aircraft spraying incident that Dugway's military investigator had originally discovered two weeks prior but which the governor had dismissed so casually.

The admission was not viewed as entirely forthcoming. No one in the many investigating teams looking at the sheep on March 15 and the following days had seen the company's planes; they had to have flown prior to March 14. That week, a team of DPG scientists was given access to two spray tanks used in insecticide operations by the ranchers. By that time, the tanks had been cleaned with a caustic solution, leaving no indications of what they had held. The ranchers showed the DPG scientists an unopened half-gallon can of heptachlor. This struck the scientists as surprising in that if the ranchers were going to fill the hundred-gallon tanks with pesticide, why had they ordered the pesticide in half-gallon containers? State Health Division tests confirmed the presence of heptachlor in the soil and vegetation, in particularly heavy doses on the Deseret ranch. Heptachlor, like DDT, is a very stable compound, decaying slowly over years. These samples could have resulted from past years of spraying just as easily as last month's.

Heptachlor and dieldrin, two chlorinated hydrocarbons commonly used as pesticides as DDT was, would not have been used on ground or forage crops used by animals. Both are not registered for these applications. If these highly stable chemicals are found in animals or dairy products, they are seized for destruction by the Food and Drug Administration. The findings of red teardrops and red urine were similar to a case in Colorado two years earlier, where sheep had also died in large numbers. One suspected culprit was an outlawed seed grain preservative manufactured in Turkey. The state team refused to pursue the issue. Further tests conducted by the Agriculture office at Logan revealed other discrepancies. Chromatographic comparisons of VX agent did not match against the sheep stomach samples of organophosphates. A year later, more sensitive testing measures at Dugway would confirm these same findings in the soil and vegetation samples they had collected.

Burial details continued work on Wednesday, March 27. The Dugway Safety Office attempted to count the dead sheep. Their count, still on hand today, was 3,843 dead sheep. One individual reported many live sheep still wandering unattended in the juniper-covered hills above the death scene at White Rock. Congressman Lloyd came out to Dugway the next day to inspect the investigations personally, where he toured the DPG labs and flew over the sheep kill areas. He was satisfied that there was no negligence on the part of the DPG personnel conducting the tests and that there was no cover-up underway, although he acknowledged the Army tests continued to be "a prime suspect."

Independent Army tests continued into April. DPG scientists took five sheep to the Skull Valley area, whereon four of the five sheep contracted the same sickness as the original group. These sheep died exhibiting drooping necks with similar twisted necks and spine injuries shortly after that. DPG scientists had been unable to duplicate the sheep poisoning with a larger test herd of 100 sheep fed VX-sprayed crops. Again, either the sheep died quickly exhibiting the more common signs of nerve agent poisoning or they recovered completely. Over one thousand samples of soil, pond water, vegetation, snow, wool, blood, and cotton swabs had been collected, both within the boundaries of DPG and at the herd locations. Early analysis showed the organophosphate peaks that might have been the decomposition products of VX in some of the snow samples and sheep blood, but there still remained more misses than hits and no clear evidence of what the material was. It didn't match any known pesticides, but it still didn't match VX or the simulant BIS either.

By the end of the month, things had settled down to routine testing and analysis without a completion date in sight, leading to more political posturing and media buzz. Nationally syndicated journalists Jack Anderson and Drew Parson claimed that three men that had been in the area on March 15 (a Basque sheep herder and two Logan veterinarians) had suffered ill effects after their exposure. The NCDC tested all three men and found them normal for cholinesterase depression (nerve agents would have caused some amount of cholinesterase depression) and more likely suffering from the flu or fatigue. The main show was over, though. Brigadier General Stone left for Washington on April 1, with the Edgewood scientists leaving the next day, and the NCDC team leaving on April 3. Tests continued, with DPG personnel stating that there were still no conclusive results, Brigadier General Stone acting as the Army's spokesperson saying they were "highly suspect" but not certain of the deaths, and politicians talking to the papers saying they were convinced of the Army's involvement.

The two senators from Utah had taken differing sides in the debate. Senator Moss thought that there was now positive proof that the nerve agent spray had killed the sheep. With no clear end in sight, he was pushing for quick resolution and payment to the ranchers. Senator Bennett had held back from rushing to judgment, warning against blaming the Army before having conclusive proof of any fault. His position began wavering as the media frenzy and public opinion mounted against the Army. On April 20 Senator Bennett announced his bid to run for a fourth term of office. Less than a week later, Governor Rampton announced his bid for a second term of office as the state governor, supported by Senator Moss. The combination of these announcements and the need to conclude the Army's role in the incident all but guaranteed nailing the coffin shut on the Dugway case.

## POST MORTEM

The numbers of dead and ill sheep were still ambiguous. Some 1,300 sheep from Skull Valley were still "surviving but suffering" to include thirty sheep at Utah State University campus undergoing various studies and tests by federal agricultural and state university officials. This meant that, combined with the earlier report of 600 sheep known to be shot and buried, there had been nearly 2,000 sheep still alive for weeks after the initial incident. This didn't seem to correspond with Mr. Hatch's initial estimates of 4,500 dead sheep in Skull Valley. Yet there would be no formal accounting. Ranchers from the three herds presented claims of a total of 5,727 ewes, 142 pure-bred Suffolk ewes, and 380 bucks, the overwhelming majority of which belonged to the Anschutz company. Of that total, 4,372 were claimed killed by nerve gas, and 1,877 disabled and shot by ranchers, who claimed that their meat and pelts could not be sold and were potentially hazardous. Army Claims Services approved the initial claim and forwarded the damages for $376,685 to the Secretary of the Army on July 10, 1968. Senator Bennett promised Utahans that he would do "all within his power to see that the claim is contained in a supplemental appropriations bill before Congress adjourns this year" (and before fall elections).

Test results over the next few months remained mostly inconclusive with some important exceptions. When the National CDC team returned to Atlanta, they continued their blood and tissue tests. While some tests seemed to confirm the presence of VX, many other tests failed to do so, resulting in the CDC's final report that their data were inconclusive. The Edgewood toxicologists said they believed they did find trace amounts of VX and BIS in the grass and snow, and their interpretation of the sheep trials (exposing sheep to VX and observing the results) was that the symptoms were in part similar to the sick sheep of White Rock. The DPG scientists disagreed vehemently, pointing out that the Edgewood tests had revealed only organophosphate radicals that could have been any chemical structure that decomposed down to organophosphates. The Edgewood tests had not definitively identified the chemical structure of VX in any of the environmental samples. At any rate, the Edgewood scientists could not say with certainty that they believed VX was the cause of death.

The test sheep that had been deliberately exposed to nerve agent had shown some of the same symptoms as the sick sheep, but again the sick sheep had significant characteristics that were not symptomatic of nerve agent exposure. VX was not producing the drooping neck effect, and the sick sheep were not suffering from muscle spasms one would expect from VX. The first ill sheep discovered on March 15-16 had not responded to atropine therapy and remained ill; the sheep deliberately exposed to VX became symptomatic, and upon receiving atropine injections, recovered fully. There didn't seem to be any evidence other than circumstantial, but that was enough to hang the blame on the Dugway tests.

As an alternative theory, a simple academic exercise, consider the following scenario. Some ranchers in the Skull Valley vicinity fly an airplane spraying a chemical insecticide on crops within a few miles of the sheep. They are spraying illegally, using Parathion or Malathion obtained from a cheap retailer that didn't say how pure or what quality of insecticide it is. They're not sure what's in the mix, not realizing how strong the organophosphate compounds are, but it was cheap and effective. They disregarded the need for local permits because they knew they were flying close to the herds; they weren't supposed to spray in areas where the livestock were feeding (Utah had lax laws on spraying, as did many farming states). An accident occurs, and the plane sprays prematurely over the sheep herds.

When hundreds of sheep become sick and start to die, the ranchers panic. Not only are they losing sheep that aren't insured, their illegal spraying activities are going to be found out. At first they haul sheep to the Hatch ranch headquarters where the sheep could receive veterinarian care, but that doesn't work. Then they learn that Dugway was conducting tests a few days prior. They haul a few sick sheep to the Indian Reservation and over the mountain to a Russell ranch in Rush Valley. The sick sheep mix with the healthy sheep, making any count of affected sheep or identification of where they were originally at the time of spraying impossible. What's the worst that could happen, they ask themselves? The Army takes some blame, pays for some livestock losses, the ranchers avoid legal problems, life goes on. No one expected the politicians and media to turn the event into a three-ring circus with national spotlights on the incident. When it gets out of hand, they are forced to see their lies through to the end.

Of course, maybe a dense "gas cloud" composed of five gallons of liquid VX agent traveled 35–80 miles over a mountain range to strike down thousands of sheep without affecting horses, cattle, domestic animals, or people, and then vanished promptly from the scene.

The Army public affairs offices observed the situation from a point of view that later seemed almost predictive. They saw three possible outcomes to the incident: either the Army caused the incident, the Army did not cause the incident, or no cause would be found.  If the Army did cause the incident, local interest would wane once the ranchers were paid and they were promised this would never happen again.  Nationally, CB warfare foes would take advantage of the news but it would not support interest forever.  If the Army didn't cause the incident, the news media might acknowledge they were wrong and the news would dry up.  If there was no cause found, local news interest would peak every time someone announced a new "conclusion."  On a national level, antimilitary groups would push the perception that even the Army didn't understand the inherent dangers of CB weapons.  Editorials and scientific theories would generate full congressional interest in the CB program by suggesting that the CB tests were as dangerous as nuclear testing.  Unfortunately, it appeared the last outcome would take place.

Stories throughout the summer and fall continued to play on the appearance of the Army's admission of guilt and the Chemical Corps's apparent refusal to admit negligence in the incident.  The three major networks all began intensely biased coverage over the Army's handling of the Dugway incident and on the Army's CBW program in general.  *Newsweek* printed a story in June asking whether chemical warfare was "Too Horrible to Use?" and detailing the Dugway story.  *Time* magazine ran an article "Toward the Doomsday Bug" in September. Many media sources referenced former AP correspondent Seymour Hersh, since he had released a book entitled *Chemical and Biological Warfare* that summer (focussing on the historical evils of CBW and the U.S. military's CBW program in particular).

New stories hit the press constantly, detailing the Army's CBW program, spreading and exaggerating the dangers of chemical agent disposal, the military use of herbicides and CS, and the immorality of the entire DoD CBW program.  This incident initiated Congressman Richard McCarthy's (D-NY) investigation of the Army CBW program, distorting the chemical munitions disposal program into another "uncontrolled, dangerous and poorly overseen" exercise.  This showed the real impact of the Dugway incident.  The actual event did not harm the Chemical Corps as much as the exaggerated and adverse publicity that took place after the incident.

# CHAPTER 4

# Bad News Gets Worse

Public scrutiny of the Army's CB warfare program grew louder and more abrasive, with national headlines tripling in 1969 as compared to the year prior. The Army Medical Unit at Fort Detrick was renamed the Army Medical Research Institute of Infectious Diseases (USAMRIID) in January 1969, which announced its intent to carry on the medical biological defense research in an open, unclassified scientific environment. In the middle of the month, United Nations Secretary General U Thant announced the appointment of a panel of fourteen experts to help him prepare a report on CB weapons, as directed by the General Assembly resolution in December 1968. The fourteen scientists, hailing from as many nations, were to examine the threat to the environment as well as to civilians created by CB warfare agents. No military representatives were on the panel to discuss why these weapons are used.

In February 1969 a former senator accused the Army of searching for a remote Pacific island for the purpose of continuing its CB weapons testing, which was denied by Army spokespersons. This statement is based on the "fact" that the Army sponsored a Smithsonian Institute study of wildlife in the Pacific, briefed to the Senate Foreign Relations Committee. In March, congressmen leaked the details of the annual Army budget for CB munitions production—$350 million a year—a previously classified figure released during a private meeting with twenty-four House members. Later that month, it was announced that U.S. and Soviet representatives were in Geneva, agreeing to work together toward the control of CB weapons.

In April the U.S. military sprayed 37,000 acres in Cambodia with Agent Orange, sparking an official letter of protest from its government to the United States and to the United Nations. Representative Richard McCarthy (D-NY) introduced a joint resolution to the House Committee on Foreign Affairs to study the use and effects of anticrop sprays and chemical defoliants in Vietnam.[1] At the end of the month, House Minority Leader Representative Gerald Ford (R-MI) reportedly suggested that Congressional critics of DoD CB warfare programs are advocating unilateral disarmament plans. Senator William Fulbright (D-AR) endorsed Representative McCarthy's call for President Richard Nixon to resubmit the Geneva Protocol banning CB warfare for approval by the Senate.

In early May 1969, several Congressmen (including Representative McCarthy) and mayors protested the Army's plan to sink ships filled with chemical munitions off the U.S. coast in international waters, fearing the possibility of contamination on the beaches (although there is no scientific evidence that this might occur). The Army had planned to move the older, outdated chemical munitions at Rocky Mountain and Edgewood Arsenals to the Naval Ammunition Depot at Earle, New Jersey. There, the chemical munitions could be loaded onto Liberty ships and sunk 250 miles at sea. This operation was part of an Army-initiated ammunition disposal program called Operation CHASE, for "Cut Holes And Sink'Em" (a Navy acronym), which was well underway before it attracted this attention. Three of the previous eleven operations already executed involved chemical agents (the other eight shiploads being conventional ammunition). The military had been dumping chemical agent-filled munitions and bulk chemical agents at high sea since March 1946 (mustard-filled mortar shells in waters off of New Orleans, Louisiana), and there had been no signs of contamination or complaints of illnesses from local beach walkers.

The first Liberty ship dumping of chemical munitions, CHASE VIII, involved 1-ton containers filled with mustard agent and GB-filled M55 rockets that had been placed in steel vaults and filled with concrete. These munitions had been dumped in May-June 1967. CHASE XI occurred exactly one year later, including bulk ton containers of GB and VX nerve, HD mustard, and more M55 rockets. CHASE XII dumped the same type of cargo in June 1968. All these dumps were off the East Coast over 200 miles from shore. Despite the absence of any evidence of danger to the public, the Army promised not to move any additional chemical munitions until the National Academy of Sciences (NAS) examined the plan. The NAS recommended incinerating the chemical agents, with sea dumping as a last resort. The Pentagon accepted the panel's recommendation on this plan of incineration and announced it would follow them to the letter.[2]

In May-August 1969, the Army also began efforts to sell its several millions of pounds of bulk phosgene to American plastics industries for conversion into harmless commercial products. These efforts ran into public concern over the safety of rail transport to the receiving companies, causing the Department of Transportation to block the transportation of phosgene by rail until all phosgene cylinders were inspected, repaired, or replaced. This order stranded 1,294 cylinders at Rocky Mountain Arsenal, although industry could continue to ship the same bulk phosgene by the tons in railcars as an industrial chemical.[3]

On June 18 President Nixon called for a "sweeping review" of CB warfare policies, including the U.S. position on arms control and the question of ratifying the Geneva Protocol. What later became publicized was that the U.S. military policy on CB weapons had been changed in 1960, in part due to recommendations from the Office of the Chief Chemical Officer in 1958. The "no first use" policy established by President Franklin D. Roosevelt in 1943 had been altered so that U.S. forces were not limited to retaliation only. It clearly implied that the United States would be prepared for CB warfare, and could use chemical or biological weapons in a general war under any circumstances where a military advantage could be foreseen, subject to approval by the president.[4] Between 1960 and 1969, the four services had submitted increased and urgent requirements for tactical CB munitions, to include artillery, missiles, drones, mines, and other delivery systems. The radical notion that CB weapons should be treated the same as conventional weapons, used to augment the total military capability of the armed forces, was not accepted well by the politicians or the public constituency in the summer of 1969.

July was a very busy month. United Nations Secretary General U Thant announced the results of his UN report, which identified the growing proliferation of CB weapons and warned that there was no secure defense against them "even for the richest countries." All the scientists on the panel agreed to one conclusion, prominently noted: "Were these weapons ever to be used on a large scale in war, no one can predict how enduring the effects would be, and how they would affect the structure of society and the environment in which we live."[5] To call this charge melodramatic is like calling the Titanic a little ship. The report derided the idea that any nation owning these weapons would gain any comfort of security, being constantly at threat from these "horrible" weapons, and that all the world would sleep easier if only every nation eliminated these weapons from their arsenals. As if this generic, naive statement wouldn't apply to any other class of weapons used in modern combat. President Nixon immediately welcomed the United Nation's report, and the Senate Arms Services Committee eliminated all funds for CB weapons development in the FY70 DoD budget.

When Army Secretary Stanley Resor told a House Government Operations subcommittee in May that open air tests of chemical weapons were still taking place at Fort McClellan, Aberdeen Proving Ground, and Dugway Proving Ground, word got into the newspapers on July 12. The chair, Representative Henry Reuss (D-WI), was probing about the health risks of open air testing and said he was "gratified that the Army has recognized the public interest by revealing the general extent of open air testing of poisonous compounds." Representative C.D. Long (D-MD) was not so gratified and called for immediate cessation of open air tests at Edgewood Arsenal, which was within his district (his request was granted). Fort McClellan's open air tests were also suspended, pending reviews of test safety data.

Days later, Representative McCarthy released the fact that the Army was developing binary nerve agent weapons; devices that mix two separate chemicals together to create nerve gas. Again, this information was discovered in Army briefs to House committees and immediately leaked to the press.[6] The Army, Air Force, and Navy were all interested in developing chemical munitions for their forces. Each service held the position that exclusion from this capability would mean one of the other services held the alternative to nuclear weapons employment, CB weapons being seen as a more credible and flexible deterrent. Edgewood engineers had researched binary nerve agent munitions in the late 1950s, under the desire to develop chemical munitions that would be safer to handle and transport. While the Army had not expressed much interest in binary chemical munitions, the Navy had. If the Navy was to safely carry out aerial chemical attacks from carrier forces, the service would have to refit each carrier for handling dangerous unitary chemical rounds at a tune of $10 to $12 million each. Obviously, this was not a cost-effective solution. The Navy approached Edgewood Arsenal in early 1961 with a request to develop a 500-lb binary VX chemical bomb, which would later be called the Mark-116 Bigeye. After initial research and development measures tested the feasibility of the weapon, the program moved to the Naval Ordnance Test Center at China Lake. Prove-out tests of the bomb and experiments for the dissemination patterns followed in the years of testing between 1965 and 1969. All aspects of the binary munition showed great promise.[7]

General Jim Hebbler, the Army Assistant Chief of Staff for Force Development at the Pentagon, completed a study titled "Mandrake Root." This study compared the logistical, tactical, and budgetary differences between a unitary and a binary munition. Its conclusions pointed out that a binary munition was safer to manufacture, store, and transport. Binaries were more effective than a unitary round, since the binary munition could use thin-walled shells rather than the current thick-walled unitary shells designed to prevent leaks. This meant that the same size binary round could hold more chemical agent, meaning one would fire fewer binary artillery rounds than unitary for an equivalent coverage. Operationally, the Army would use binary munitions the same way as unitary munitions. Cost savings equaled approximately $400 to $500 savings *per round*. These features convinced the Army to begin investing in binary weapons technology. With the increase of unfavorable attention on the Army's chemical warfare program, the Navy temporarily suspended the Bigeye program and withdrew their funding.

The Chemical Center at Edgewood Arsenal continued the binary weapon program and began research toward the development of a binary GB-filled 155-mm artillery projectile and a VX-filled 8-inch artillery projectile.[8] Production of any binary munition was not yet authorized by Congress. Nor, unfortunately, would any production be authorized in the next decade. True to form, the ill-informed media did not see binary weapons as a safer alternative to chemical weapons, one that would allow the armed forces to retain a retaliatory capability during the Cold War. Binary weapons became portrayed as a radical "new" nerve agent weapon, more dangerous than the nerve agents that killed the Skull Valley sheep, rather than as a safe and cost-reducing enhancement of an existing weapon system. This widely-portrayed bias resulted in the refusal to authorize production.

On July 19 news reports noted an accidental discharge of nerve gas at a depot in Okinawa resulting in the hospitalization of twenty-five American soldiers. The soldiers were part of the 267th Chemical Depot Company; they were stripping paint from depot walls when the leak was reported. What the papers did not report as prominently was that all twenty-five soldiers were back to work within six hours after the incident, without any apparent health risks from low levels of agent exposure. The incident led to the public revelation that chemical weapons had been stored at Okinawan Army depots since the 1950s. In addition to bad timing, this was an embarrassment to the pro-American Japanese government, which demanded the removal of the chemical munitions. Increasing public outcry over the Okinawa incident forced the Army to search for a new storage site for those munitions; in December, the Army announced that the nerve agents would be shipped to Umatilla Army Depot, Oregon.[9] Four days later, West Germany admitted that it had knowledge of nerve agent weapons in U.S. depots on its territory. All this publicity led the Senate to plan for legislation to restrict the use, transportation, and storage of CW agents as an amendment to the DoD military procurement bill. The proposed legislation would restrict the use, transportation and storage of CB warfare agents, specifically requiring Congressional approval prior to any movement of CB agent munitions. The U.S. nuclear weapons held in Okinawa and West Germany remained.

A cynic would think that members of Congress should hardly be "shocked, shocked to discover" the Army stockpiling chemical weapons overseas. The whole theory of discouraging potential adversaries from using CB weapons was based on the threat of retaliation in kind. This meant (1) the United States needed CB weapons in the form of modern munitions in a status ready to go to war; (2) they had to be geographically close to where U.S. forces were going to engage the enemy to enable a quick response; and (3) the stockpiles had to hold quantities that were militarily significant to give the enemy a reason not to use CB weapons. The military leadership, to include Defense Secretary Melvin Laird, still considered maintaining a retaliatory capability as the best deterrent, despite the administration review that was underway. Given that estimates were that the Soviet Union had much greater stocks and a more robust research and development effort ongoing, they saw two avenues—deter in kind, or escalate the conflict to using nuclear weapons in response. "As much as we deplore this kind of weapon," Secretary Laird said, "if we want to make sure this weapon is never used, we must have the capability to use it."[10] In Congress, public clamors and media stories were overruling politicians' better senses.

## EXECUTIVE ACTIONS

In June 1969 President Nixon ordered a thorough and complete Executive Branch review of the U.S. military's CBW policies and practices and directed the U.S. delegation to the Eighteen-Nation Disarmament Committee (ENDC) in Geneva to work on effective ways to control CB weapons. In July President Nixon praised the recently released UN report on CB warfare, and revealed that he was considering the question of resubmission of the Geneva Protocols to the Senate.[11] In August, the Senate unilaterally initiated a moratorium on the acquisition of chemical weapons and a policy of no first use of chemical weapons during wartime and de-emphasized the need for chemical warfare readiness. The amendment to the military procurement bill passed by a vote of 91 to 0, although some conservative members such as Senator Strom Thurmond (R-SC) admitted to "reservations."

The Nixon administration began intense debates over possible cutbacks in the CB munition stockpiles and possible adherence to the Geneva Protocol in September. In mid-October, the Army admitted to ownership of eight chemical weapons depots in the United States and its plans to manufacture binary chemical rounds. There was no danger to nearby communities, given the elaborate safety precautions afforded munition stockpiles; but all this did was resurrect the Dugway Proving Ground horror story again. Debates grew in volume in Washington, as even Republican members of Congress petitioned the president to consider scrapping all CB weapons in the U.S. stockpile. Their argument matched the UN report in surmising that ownership and potential use of chemical weapons undermined, rather than strengthened, the nation's security.

Public Law 91-121, passed on November 19, 1969, required an annual report on the funds spent on all lethal and non-lethal CB agents during the previous year. It mandated severe limitations on the transportation, open air testing, and disposal of CB agents; on deployment, storage, and disposal of CB agents outside the United States; and on human-subject and open-air tests in general. It also directed the U.S. Public Health Service's Department of Health and Human Services to provide the public health oversight of DoD's chemical weapons stewardship.[12] The last chemical agent trial in the open atmosphere was conducted at Dugway Proving Ground on September 16, 1969. In the preceding eighteen years, the Army had tested over 10,000 munitions in 1,200 chemical field trials for a total release of approximately 132,600 pounds of various chemical agents. Officials had disposed of an additional 36,000 M55 rockets for an additional release of 378,000 pounds of GB on the proving ground. All the bulk agent remaining at Dugway was moved to nearby Tooele Army Depot.[13] Although its primary mission of open-air testing would cease, Dugway Proving Ground would remain the site for continued CB agent testing of materiel and equipment within safe, contained facilities.

On November 25, 1969, President Nixon announced that the U.S. government would renounce the use of biological agents and first use of chemical agents, to include incapacitants. The U.S. government would destroy its stockpile of biological warfare agents and reconsider ratifying the Geneva Protocol. Nixon also announced movement toward a worldwide arms control agreement on the use of biological weapons, primarily through association with the British proposal submitted to the ENDC the year prior. Previously, only Canada had supported the British draft, which extended the Geneva Protocol's ban to BW agents and delivery systems. Reaction from the Senate and House was unsurprisingly positive, with further calls from Representative McCarthy to ban riot control agents, defoliants, and napalm as well.[14]

It is somewhat surprising that this drastic shift in policy takes up very little (if any) room in books covering Nixon's legacy and even less mention in arms control discussions. The complete and utter abandonment of an entire class of weapon systems with which the Soviet Union was still armed is unparalleled to this day. No responsible historian or researcher has ever clearly identified whether this was a deliberate and planned policy act, balancing military plans and options against diplomatic maneuvering, or merely partisan political hotdogging. Some scholars have pointed out the disparities in the views on "weapons of mass destruction" between the 1940s and the late 1960s, and President Nixon's (relatively) sudden decision that the U.S. government should give up the BW program with its "massive, unpredictable and potentially uncontrollable consequences," as he stated it. This decision to abandon the BW program was seen by some as strictly a political maneuver; cutting off bad baggage as it were, designed to placate the congressional, national, and international concerns, to foster progress in the arms control talks, and to draw attention away from the Vietnam conflict that had starred the use of nonlethal chemical agents.[15]

There is no evidence that this was the case, reviewing Nixon's actions today. In November 1969 President Nixon was enjoying high public popularity in his first year of office, and he had no need to distract the majority of the public from Vietnam (although unrest was building). He was trying to score early points in his first term against an entrenched Democratic majority in Congress, and he decided to do this through advances of an arms control agenda that included topics such as the Anti-Ballistic Missile (ABM) treaty and the Non-Proliferation Treaty (NPT). President Nixon knew that, once he proposed the unilateral elimination of biological weapons from the U.S. stockpile, no one from the Democratic ranks would dare vote against this action. Given the history of RCAs used in Vietnam and the Dugway Proving Ground incident, they could ill afford not to publicly support Nixon's speech.[16] The media, of course, chose to see Nixon's rationale as a sudden universal awareness that there were features of CB warfare so repulsive that its military effectiveness was insignificant in comparison to the moral consequences. Public perception that biological warfare was an uncontrollable, doomsday horror weapon was confirmed through his announcement and interpretation of events as filtered by the media.

This was of course incorrect. By 1969 the military had researched biological weapons for over twenty-five years, and chemical weapons for over fifty years. The Chemical Corps and Medical Corps understood the agents very well, understood what they could and could not do to human bodies, and knew they could employ CB weapons with predictable and measurable results. Military planning counted on offensive weapons and predictable results, and this included the BW program. The two main weaponized BW agents, anthrax and botulinum toxin, were antipersonnel agents that were not transmittable between infected and unexposed humans and therefore not epidemic. The possibility of epidemics precluded many BW agents from the U.S. stockpile. While Fort Detrick had studied contagious antipersonnel agents such as viruses for offensive and defensive programs, they had not been weaponized. The viruses were under study for the purposes of understanding what would happen if an enemy with fewer scruples used them—medics had to know what to look for, and they required vaccines and treatments ready for that eventuality. Testing protocols at Edgewood, Detrick, and Dugway were safe, effective and carefully followed, but the sheep incident and the UN report had called all this into question.

There were still questions about what exactly the president's declaration covered. As toxins were technically chemicals and noncontagious, some questioned whether his directive meant only "germ" weapons, i.e., living biological organisms as opposed to chemical toxins. Work continued on developing staphylococcus enterotoxin type B (or SEB toxin for short) as a weapon system, which caused severe short-term incapacitation similar to food poisoning. Fort Detrick labs had initiated work in 1964, and development of the agent for use in delivery systems appeared feasible. For several months, debate raged within the military over whether toxins were included in the president's order.

On February 14, 1970, President Nixon extended the U.S. administration's policy to include toxins in the biological agent destruction program. The Army developed demilitarization plans to dispose of all the BW agents and munitions then stored at Pine Bluff Arsenal, Fort Detrick, Rocky Mountain Arsenal and Beale Air Force Base between May 1971 and March 1973. These demilitarization plans were reviewed by the Departments of Health, Education, and Welfare, Interior, and Agriculture; the Environmental Protection Agency; and state and local officials. The antipersonnel agents were at Pine Bluff Arsenal; they were all destroyed by May 1972 and the facilities decontaminated over a three-year period. Anticrop agents such as wheat stem rust and rice blast were stored at Beale AFB and Rocky Mountain Arsenal. They had been grown at government planting sites, shipped to Edgewood Arsenal for classification, drying and storage until 1959, when Rocky Mountain Arsenal took the storage role. The majority of Fort Detrick's biological agents could be safely disposed of by standard lab practices because of the small amounts involved in laboratory research and development.[17] All these agents and munitions were destroyed by March 1973 and their facilities decontaminated (with the exception of small quantities of biological agent at Fort Detrick, used for development of vaccines and testing defense programs).

In the preceding twenty-eight years of the biological offensive program at Fort Detrick, the Army had documented 419 infections and three deaths.[18] Only fifty of these infections (and no deaths) were within the last ten years of the program. Representative J. Glenn Beall, Jr. (R-MD), stated that this record should be "praised rather than criticized." Dugway Proving Ground had a slightly better record, with 220 personnel exposed to chemical agents between 1952 and 1969 and only two fatalities.[19] Compared to the safety record of conventional explosives testing at any one military ordnance testing facility, these posts represented the safest records in the history of DoD's weapons development programs.

The only place that held filled BW munitions was Pine Bluff Arsenal, where spray tanks and bomblets stored there as the U.S. retaliatory capability had to be emptied and incinerated. The filled munitions had never been shipped anywhere else, except for test purposes. Most of the BW agents were produced and stored at Pine Bluff in bulk form. The military had developed ways to produce, fill, and store biological agent munitions as they had with unitary chemical munitions, but most organisms were live, unlike chemical warfare agents. Much of the combat arms leadership felt satisfied to be rid of the biological warfare program, having never seen a truly integrated concept on how they would actually employ biological weapons in combat. But they were still uneasy knowing that the Soviets had not abandoned their offensive program, and without a retaliatory capability and no detection systems, options to counter the threat on the battlefield were few.

Many arms control pundits thought that no government should undertake even defensive biological warfare efforts that might encourage other countries to initiate or accelerate their own BW programs. This theory assumed that other countries would suspect the U.S. government of using its defensive program to secretly keep its offensive program alive. They pointed out that retaining a biological vaccine capability might tempt the U.S. military into launching a first-strike biological weapon, once their own soldiers were immune. The existence of a defensive program would encourage other nations to develop more dangerous, more exotic biological agent weapons for which the American military had no countermeasures. Others questioned the effectiveness of any vaccine program, since it might well be impossible to inoculate one's soldiers against every type and strain of possible BW agents. As a result of these accusations, Nixon's announcement effectively stopped biological defense research and development programs. While such a halt would not measurably affect the chemical defense program, which had existed for over fifty years, it stopped the biological defense program before it began to mature.

On the other side, the Soviet Union scientists and politicians were convinced that Nixon's proclamation was a cover to move the U.S. biological agent stockpile and the offensive program deep underground. After all, the American BW experts had just all consolidated at Fort Detrick's USAMRIID—there was no doubt to them that the U.S. offensive program was still ongoing, and the Soviets correspondingly increased their activities. It was not until a Soviet delegation came over to inspect Fort Detrick, Pine Bluff Arsenal, Dugway Proving Ground and the Salk Center in early December 1991 that they saw the lack of equipment and resources necessary for an offensive BW program.[20]

The BWC had an unintentional collateral effect on the binary chemical weapons program. The U.S. government's policy of retaliation in kind had not changed, yet people had misinterpreted Nixon's statements. The Geneva arms talks that had begun in 1968 turned to examine the feasibility of a bilateral chemical arms prohibition. Many in the congressional halls thought that if the president had abandoned biological warfare, he would soon abandon the chemical warfare program. To some congressmen, modernizing the chemical weapons stockpiles would be detrimental to the spirit of the talks and to the president's intent. This began a trend within Congress to deliberately delay and refrain from maintaining and modernizing a viable retaliatory capability while arms control negotiations continued in Geneva (and while other nations continued to build up and modernize their CB agent munition stockpiles). Such being the case, Congress halted any further funding of the binary weapons production.

At the end of 1970, the Army announced that it would send the Okinawan chemical munitions from Chibana Army Depot to Johnston Island, two years after the initial public protests began. (The governor of Oregon had sought an injunction to stop the shipment of chemical agents to Umatilla, which had resulted in the decision to send them to Kodiak Island Naval Station, Alaska. Of course, the senators from Alaska had protested and passed a bill to stop that action. This had led to the final decision to ship the agents to Johnston Island in the Pacific.[21])

Because Johnston Island, one member of a three-island atoll, was 825 miles southwest from Hawaii, the military felt confident that the stockpile could be secured without endangering the public. The senior Army chemical officer, Major General John J. Hayes, planned and executed Operation Red Hat, moving more than 10,000 tons of chemical munitions from Okinawa to Johnston Island. His staff planned the construction of storage facilities on Johnston Island, identified numerous routes for the movement, trained personnel to accompany the munitions, and coordinated between the four services and government agencies to plan the move. The operation was executed between January and September 1971, in six separate movements.[22] Major General Hayes was later credited with overcoming adverse public opinion and heated national opposition to successfully transport the chemical munitions without any danger to the public and without any safety incidents.

President Nixon sent the Geneva Protocol to the Senate on August 10, 1970, with an added exception against the constraint on the use of herbicides and RCAs. This initiative, combined with the U.S. intentions to cease its offensive BW program, prompted the Soviet Union to begin bilateral talks in March 1971, with their submission of a revised draft convention to the Committee on Disarmament (the former ENDC), limited to biological weapons and toxins only. This led the Geneva diplomats toward the 1972 Convention on the Prohibition of the Development, Production, and Stockpiling of Bacteriological (Biological) and Toxin Weapons and on Their Destruction—or the Biological Weapons Convention, BWC for short.[23] The Geneva Protocol and BWC sat in the Senate Foreign Relations Committee for three years, while the Senate considered the Geneva Protocol and whether riot control agents and herbicides should be included. The Senate finally approved both the Geneva Protocol and the BWC on December 16, 1974. President Gerald Ford signed the documents of ratification on January 22, 1975, and the BWC came into force on March 22, 1975.

## THE CHEMICAL CORPS IS TARGETED

As the Vietnam Conflict wound down, the armed services were in strong need of modernization. President Lyndon Johnson had suspended most military modernization programs during his administration in favor of increased procurement of existing weapon systems to support the war effort. A number of newly designed weapons programs were ready for procurement in 1970, but funds were still supporting a force with 3.4 million military personnel and 1.3 million civilians, to include ongoing operations in Southeast Asia (up to 1973). One of the reforms would be a massive reduction-in-force of all the services and civilian force structure, cutting one-third of all Army units, Air Force units, and Marine Corps units, and about half the Navy surface fleet. Pentagon planners would address this sudden loss of capability by ensuring that the armed forces were complementary to each other; for instance, including Marine Corps units into European ground missions and using Air Force strategic units to augment naval aviation forces. In addition, they would place more reliance on nuclear weapons for deterrence.[24] This all led to the need to cut military and civilian personnel, most notably in areas the military felt it no longer needed to continue. Discussions began over whether the Army really needed a fully-manned Chemical Corps, as there had been no actual CB warfare against U.S. forces in World War II or the Vietnam or Korean conflicts.

Chemical Corps spokespersons continued to press the need to retain a strong defensive capability, which included the capability to retaliate against an enemy using CBW munitions. Most of this was the traditional litany of the need to protect civilian and military personnel from the dangers of massive Soviet CB weapons use on the battlefield and against the U.S. homeland. Unfortunately, these concerns over offensive chemical weapons employment were exactly what was driving public opinion and congressional views increasingly toward unilateral disarmament and against the Corps. Chemical Corps representatives increasingly lost credibility by exaggerating the Soviet threat and the corresponding importance of retaliatory CB munitions. At the same time, they neglected the importance of smoke and flame programs that combat units had appreciated during the Vietnamese, Korean, and World War II conflicts. This approach was not winning the Chemical Corps any new friends in the military or political arenas.

The flood of negative publicity against the Chemical Corps, combined with the Army's reform efforts, had generated a movement toward closing down the entire DoD CBW program, to include both offensive and defensive measures. In 1967 an Army Board of Inquiry on the Army Logistics System had concluded that the removal of supply and maintenance functions from the Chemical Corps (due to centralization efforts within the Army) would represent a "significant reduction in the responsibilities" of that branch. The board recommended that consideration be given to abolishing the branch and consolidating its remaining functions within the special weapons branch of the Ordnance Corps. HQ AMC had already begun redistributing the Chemical Corps responsibilities and assets to other agencies. The Deseret Test Center was disestablished in July 1968 and its territories merged with Dugway Proving Ground, which all fell under HQ TECOM. President Nixon's renouncement of BW and first-use CW in November 1969 caused an immediate shutdown and cessation of munitions development at Edgewood Arsenal, which included large cuts in funds and personnel. In 1971 the Army Officer Personnel Management office recommended disestablishing the Chemical Corps because number of positions within the Army was insufficient to support a viable chemical officer's career structure. Their analysis determined that 750 officers, trained in the chemical defense functional area and shepherded by another branch, would be sufficient to support the remaining operational and branch common positions.[25]

In July 1971 Edgewood Arsenal was discontinued as a separate installation and merged with neighboring Aberdeen Proving Ground, which was run by the Ordnance Corps.[26] The Intelligence Division of Edgewood Arsenal was transferred to the Army Intelligence Agency in 1972 and joined the intelligence technical services of the Signal, Ordnance, Quartermaster, and Engineer Corps to become the Army Foreign Science and Technology Center (FSTC). AMC's Munitions Command (MUCOM) decided to separate biological programs from the chemical community in its entirety and transferred Fort Detrick and the Army Biological Defense Research Center to the Office of the Surgeon General in April 1972. One month later, the Army turned over the X201 biological agent plant to the Department of Health, Education, and Welfare, which became a National Center for Toxicology Research. In July 1972 Pine Bluff Arsenal and Rocky Mountain Arsenal were transferred from the command jurisdiction of Edgewood Arsenal and assigned directly to MUCOM.[27] Many of these actions may be considered the Army's consolidation effort as the post-Vietnam downsizing began, but the net effect was that the Chemical Corps lost much of its post-World War II infrastructure and self-direction.

In June 1972 President Nixon announced that his selection of a new Chief of Staff for the Army would be General Creighton Abrams, Jr., formerly commander of U.S. Military Assistance Command, Vietnam. The designated Army Chief of Staff moved into the Pentagon's E-ring prior to confirmation, bringing a host of sharp field grade officers to study ways to reform the post-Vietnam Army. On the top of their list was the development of a concept to reduce the Army force structure by a third. Abrams's approach was to change the structure of the active duty divisions; each would have two active duty combat brigades and one National Guard combat brigade. By this measure, any action requiring a military response would force the political process to commit itself fully by activating the Reserves (which had not occurred during Vietnam). His goal was to develop three additional Army divisions from the current thirteen active divisions, instead of cutting three divisions from the force as directed. To meet manpower requirements, this plan would still call for additional manpower cuts and transfers of active duty combat support and combat service support units to reserve unit status.

The Senate confirmed General Abrams's nomination on October 12, 1972. On the same day that he was sworn into office, October 16, 1972, the new Chief of Staff fired off a memorandum ordering the Deputy Chief of Staff for Personnel (DCSPER), Lieutenant General Bernie Rodgers, to chair an ad hoc study group with the purpose of developing an implementation plan to consolidate the Chemical Corps with other branches of the Army, with a deadline of November 30, 1972. On the next day, the Chief was off to Vietnam to tour the troops he had just left. This initial memorandum went to all Army staff agencies, AMC and Continental Army Command (CONARC), *but not* to the Chemical School and senior ranking chemical officer, the Chief of Staff's own chemical adviser in the Office of the Deputy Chief of Staff for Operations and Plans (ODCSOPS), Major General John

Appel.[28]    All subordinate commands (with the exception of CONARC) nonconcurred, most notably General Henry Miley (commander, AMC) and Lieutenant General Joseph Heiser (Deputy Chief of Staff for Logistics, or DCSLOG), who voiced the need for a focal point on the DA staff for chemical, biological, and radiological (CBR) warfare expertise. CONARC had concurred on the Corps's consolidation largely because overall military manpower would be reduced (in line with the downsizing initiative), allowing them to save other desired military slots.

The study group, chaired by DCSPER and later including Major General Appel, met between October and December to evaluate where they would transfer the chemical personnel to other branches; how they could ensure that a level of CBR defense expertise was maintained to protect the national defense; and where to move the Chemical School and the Combat Developments Command CBR Agency.  Notably absent was any effort to identify possible negative results of eliminating the Chemical Corps.  The group recommended moving the entire Chemical Corps CBR functions into a single branch in order to retain a consolidated position, with the least turmoil.  Moving into one of the combat arms was rejected immediately; the group similarly rejected the combat support branch (such as the engineers) because the skills and functions were still not quite similar enough.  The combat service support seemed ideal, with the similar emphasis on materiel life cycle management and technical staff duties.  The Ordnance Corps was the closest branch in comparison and was already overseeing Edgewood Arsenal.[29]

Three Chemical Corps functions—smoke and flame weapons, protective clothing, and technical escort responsibilities—were seen as incompatible with the Ordnance Corps's role.  The Engineer Corps was assigned responsibility for flame weapons and smoke generators.  The function of processing protective suit clothing was transferred to the Quartermaster Corps.   While the Chemical School downscaled into a department under the Ordnance Corps School, the Explosives Ordnance Disposal, Technical Escort, and Senior Chemical Accident/Incident Control Officer Courses would move to the Army Missile and Munitions Center and School at Redstone Arsenal, Alabama.  The Chief of Staff accepted the final plan on December 15, 1972, which was presented to Army Secretary Robert Froehlke on December 29 and accepted by him on January 8, 1973.  Three days later, the announcement was made public in what the Army called its most sweeping reorganization since 1962.  The  Army had created the Training and Doctrine Command (TRADOC—replacing the Combat Developments Command) and Forces Command (FORSCOM—replacing the Continental Army Command).  TRADOC would begin the reform of the post-Vietnam Army and direct all future individual training, education, organizational developments, materiel developments, and military doctrine.  The announcement also noted abolishment of Third Army headquarters and disestablishment plans for the Chemical Corps.[30]

This came as a complete shock to most of the rank and file in the Corps, who had no idea that this top level review had been underway.  Although the chemical soldiers were assured that the Army still required a chemical defense specialty, unfilled chemical positions in combat divisions and corps in Europe, Korea, and the United States continued to increase. Chemical officers who thought they were en route to Europe or Korea were held back in state-side assignments. Chemical defense companies were disbanded or relegated to the reserves. About a third of all chemical officers dropped out of their branch in favor of joining the Ordnance Corps, Transportation Corps, or other combat support units with more of a future. It seemed destined that the Chemical Corps would slowly wither away, with its functions transferred to other parts of the military.

Since the Chemical Corps had been established as a basic branch by an act of Congress in 1920, the Army had to bring the disestablishment recommendation to Congress before acting upon it. When the measure to disestablish the Chemical Corps was presented to Congress in May 1973, Congress decided not to act on the recommendation and held no disestablishment hearings. Although not many records exist on their reasons, perhaps some politicians recalled the chemical warfare threat and lack of preparations during World War II and the Korean War, the stories about Soviet-backed Egyptian forces using chemical weapons in Yemen in 1968, and the continued threat of Soviet CB weapons in Europe. Congress returned the decision to DoD a year later, deciding that the Secretary of Defense had the authority to abolish the Chemical Corps if he felt it was required. In the interim, General Abrams issued a freeze on recruiting new soldiers into the Chemical Corps, reducing the Corps to its lowest manpower and funding levels since the end of World War II. The Chemical School at Fort McClellan closed and moved to become trainers for a specialty function (special weapons) under the Ordnance Branch at Aberdeen Proving Ground in June 1973. The Army CB warfare community had been completely dismantled and dispersed.

Major General (retired) Gerald Watson recalled a visit by General Abrams in late 1972, then a colonel commanding the Rocky Mountain Arsenal. After a tour of the plant and lunch, Colonel Watson asked the general why he felt it was necessary to disestablish the Chemical Corps. General Abrams's reply was short and simple: the combat arms were the ones that had to live and die on the battlefield, and it was their responsibility—not some technician's responsibility—to make sure they had a defensive capability against CBW agents. This struck to the heart of the matter. The Chemical Corps had been too technical, focused on developing new munitions and ensuring its specialists were the experts on CB weapons use and had not become a true partner with the combat forces as the Engineer Corps and Aviation Branch had.

Some chemical officers felt that the animosity ran deeper than this statement. General Abrams had been the deputy commander-in-chief in Vietnam and at one time had ordered Operation Ranch Hand halted. He thought the Chemical Corps was the purveyor of the program, rather than it being a necessary program to support combat operations. When his field commanders came back with emphatic support for the herbicide program, he relented and resumed the program. When the Senate confirmed General Abrams's appointment as Army Chief of Staff in 1972,

Agent Orange health issues had steadily been growing in number and in visibility at the VA hospitals. He may have harbored self-recrimination for not stopping the herbicide program earlier; more important, he may have never forgiven the Chemical Corps.[31]

General Abrams did not leave an oral history, as he died of cancer on September 4, 1974, still in office. In reviewing the interviews with people who knew him, this act could not be contrived as malicious. Lieutenant General Dan Cowles recalled him as not an intellectual, but as extraordinarily wise and sensitive to the soldier's needs. When Abrams decided to reorganize the Army, he did what was necessary to save an Army that was losing divisions, funds, and personnel at a rate that would make it unviable. He took care of his people, which probably explains why he decided to consolidate the chemical soldiers into the Ordnance Corps rather than eliminating their jobs. None of the twenty-plus oral histories on General Abrams's career elaborate on why the Chemical Corps was singled out for disestablishment. Since most of the decision makers of the time are dead or not talking, there are perhaps three theories why this might have occurred.

- President Nixon, in the midst of arms control talks with the Soviet Union, may have told Army Secretary Froehlke and General Abrams to disband the Chemical Corps in his zeal to promote the appearance of progress. General Abrams met with President Nixon at the White House on the day prior to sending out the memorandum announcing the disestablishment plans. While the meeting could have been pro forma, there is no record of what was discussed.

- Reorganization plans begun under former Army Chiefs of Staff (General William Westmoreland and General Bruce Palmer) and Secretaries (Stanley Resor and Bob Froehlke) and briefed to the Secretary of Defense in February 1972 may have included the recommendation to disestablish the Chemical Corps. There is mention of a "Fitzhugh study," which is alleged to be a DoD procurement and reorganization study commissioned by President Nixon but never released. This study could have held recommendations for eliminating the Chemical Corps. Their concepts may have been swept up and refined as General Abrams's reorganization plans took hold.

- General Abrams's staffers included visionaries such as Lieutenant General Bill DePuy and Major General Jim Kalergis. In briefs to the Secretary of Defense in November 1972, they noted the special concerns over CB warfare at the national level beginning in 1969, the decreased emphasis on CB warfare within the military, and the need to consolidate personnel management activities where similar skills existed (i.e., the smaller pool of chemical officers into the larger Ordnance branch). While their later interviews do not mention any bias, it may be that they simply did not see any need for a specialty branch for CB defense, given the lack of CB warfare (not of a CB warfare threat, but rather of actual use) against U.S. soldiers since World War I.[32]

I believe that the third theory is the most likely. General Abrams was driven to reform the Army while maintaining readiness, but he did not tolerate anything that in his view constituted a lack of professionalism. In the annual State of the Army testimony to the House of Representatives in February 1974, he stated "My job is to produce an efficient Army." Nearly a year and a half since his appointment, he was still pushing for eliminating Army headquarters overseas and converting military positions to civilian positions in an effort to streamline the Army into becoming a more effective fighting force.[33]

If he thought that the Chemical Corps had not done a thing since World War I, that made them a liability to his Army. His thoughts may have been that while the Army needed chemical weapons specialists to maintain the existing chemical weapons stockpiles, they were not needed for combat operations. While General Abrams did listen to those that argued against his positions, it does not appear that he was swayed by any argument from the Chemical Corps's leaders against disestablishment.

At least one chemical officer of that time has pointed out that the problem was that none of the Chemical Corps leadership could talk in the language of combat arms, since precious few actually served as division and corps chemical officers (to include Major General Appel). They did not have the knowledge, background, credibility, or experience in Washington to fight for the Corps's survival. Most chemical officers pursued positions in logistics (arsenals, ammunition plants), research and development centers, West Point faculty, aide, and executive support-type jobs.[34] Little wonder that the combat arms and combat support arms considered CB training and operations as a tax on their time and patience, if it was never seen as credible in the first place.

During all this debate and dramatics over the DoD CBW program, the combat arms community remained silent. Many had never seen a chemical soldier through much of their military career, as there were no longer chemical defense companies in the divisions. There seemed to be no reason to defend one small combat service support branch, when deep cuts were being made throughout the military. Given the choice, better they lose chemical soldiers than infantry and armor soldiers. Because the Chemical Corps had remained a technical support service, with most of its personnel in depots, laboratories, and testing grounds, they had been alienated from their combat arms brothers. The increasingly hostile public reaction to the military's use of riot control agents and napalm (and later, Agent Orange) in Vietnam fostered an environment where no military leader was willing to stick his neck out for the Chemical Corps. That, combined with the lack of evidenced chemical warfare in any U.S. conflict since World War I, the lack of any concrete threat from the Communist Bloc countries, and the strong nuclear capability of the armed forces gave for precious few military supporters.

# CHAPTER 5

# Regaining CB Defense Capabilities

General William DePuy, the first commander of TRADOC, began a series of meetings and workshops intended to break the Army of their Vietnam malaise. He instituted new training at all levels of the Army, with the slogan, "An army must train as it fights." He took a personal, intense interest in the reform of tactics and training in line with the tactical lessons of the Arab-Israeli War in October 1973. The Middle East War had shown the new lethality of modern weaponry and suppressive fire, the use of terrain (even in the desert), camouflage, routes of advance, and combined arms coordination. In particular, the outstanding performance of tank guns, antitank and antiaircraft missiles, and the consequences of their use on combat operations had impressed him. General DePuy's intent was to rewrite the manuals (now sporting a camouflaged cover instead of the traditional tan color) to enable the Army to fight and win a European conflict against a larger Warsaw Pact force.[1]

The Arab-Israeli War of 1973 was the first real test of American conventional weapon systems against their Soviet counterparts, although neither side was directly involved. While the Air Force had proven its tactics over Vietnam, theories of ground maneuver warfare were yet to be tested with new armored systems, antitank guided missiles, and supporting systems. No one had expected the Arab forces to use anything but conventional weapons, although there was evidence that Egypt might have nerve and blister agents (based on evidence from the Yemeni Civil War). The Soviet Union had continued its chemical warfare research during the period between 1967 and 1973, initiating production of persistent nerve agents (V-agents). Anwar Sadat had publicly boasted of the Soviet-backed chemical weapons capability. Prior to the conflict, the Israeli Defense Force (IDF) had not taken these claims seriously and had little chemical defense training at the war's outbreak. During the 1973 war, however, the IDF captured large stocks of Egyptian and Syrian chemical defense gear, including protective masks and clothes, nerve agent antidotes, decontamination kits, and air filtration systems in the armored vehicles. One Israeli officer was quoted as saying

"We captured many Egyptian soldiers without their rifles, but never without their gas masks."[2]

While there are some indications that the Arab forces may have just deployed with standard-unit equipment from the USSR, the IDF felt that the threat was more serious. Individual chemical defense training became mandatory, and IDF forces started chemical defense training for brigades, divisions, and air bases.[3] With the advent of more accurate and lethal munitions, smoke and obscurants played an increasingly obvious role in combat. The Syrian army had used smoke to impede Israeli artillery observers on the Golan Heights, and the Egyptians had used smoke screens to conceal their crossing of the Suez Canal from Israeli forces. The use of smoke screens also greatly reduced tank fatalities caused by antitank guided missiles.

These events did not immediately register with the U.S. military until further studies examined the potential roles of CB warfare and smoke on future global battlefields. As these military officers devised combat scenarios and strategies, they began to recognize the weakness in their CB defensive and smoke capability, as opposed to the growing Soviet CBW capability within the Warsaw Pact. The U.S. military leadership had little concept of CBW operations, having professionally developed through the ranks without much practical exposure to chemical defense units or specialists. Recognizing that Soviet chemical munitions were employed in Middle East wars led to a reassessment of the wisdom of eliminating the Chemical Corps. As Congress returned the recommendation to disestablish the Chemical Corps to DoD in 1974, the new Army Chief of Staff (General Fred Weyand) stopped the action until the Army could reexamine the issues.[4] TRADOC analysts began to reevaluate the CW threat and the Army's capability to meet that threat.

The Army continued to press for modernized tactical nuclear capabilities to make up for its numerical inferiority, caused by the post-Vietnam drawdown. The debate over whether nuclear weapons should have been used in Vietnam had been ongoing since 1965. As late as 1973, the administration would not rule out nuclear bombing in Vietnam if the peace negotiations in Paris were to break down.[5] In April 1974, Major General Frank Camm (Atomic Energy Commission, assistant general manager for nuclear security) testified before Congress on the need for future subkiloton weapons, especially in the event of a European battle against the Soviet Union. This debate had begun in response to the "hollow" Army, which, as in the pre-Korean War days, argued that a small ground force required a nuclear deterrent against larger enemy forces. Major General Camm argued that the development of 155-mm and 8-inch nuclear artillery shells would give the Army the option of highly controlled, tailored nuclear effects. If exploded as airbursts, the physical and biological damage due to radioactivity would be minimal, allowing the armed forces to operate through the affected areas immediately after the blast. This led to a debate over whether the use of subkiloton devices would escalate to large-scale nuclear war. The limited nuclear war view won out, leading to a renewed interest in chemical weapons modernization as well. Tactical employment of unconventional weapons was in vogue.

The Army began to lobby for a revitalized binary chemical program, using a similar argument that the best defense lay in a strong and flexible retaliatory capability. A request to authorize funds for binary weapon production beginning in FY75 was thrown out by later congressional committees. NATO commanders and their staff remained concerned over the possibility that they would have no way to counter the Soviet's expected use of chemical weapons in Europe. They had no faith in the aging unitary munitions held in West Germany and pressed for the modernization program as a more viable and credible retaliatory option. The past decade of publicity on chemical weapons production, however, tainted their arguments to Congress.

At a Moscow summit meeting from June 27 to July 3, 1974, President Nixon and General Secretary Leonid Brezhnev agreed to formulate a joint initiative on chemical weapons for presentation to the forty-nation Conference on Disarmament (CD) in Geneva. The former ENCD had been discussing a chemical weapons ban since August 1968 but had gotten nowhere. With the two nations that owned the largest chemical stockpiles in the world joining for bilateral talks, there was new hope that there might be progress. President Gerald Ford and General Secretary Brezhnev reaffirmed this agreement in November 1974, and in August 1976, bilateral United States-Soviet Union talks began again in Geneva on the subject of a global chemical weapons ban.[6]

On December 17, 1974, the Senate ratified both the Geneva Protocol of 1925 and the 1972 BWC to become U.S. law, with President Ford's final signature of the ratification on January 22, 1975. With all forces out of Vietnam, the U.S. government no longer had to worry about charges of chemical warfare against the North Vietnamese forces. Executive Order No. 11850, signed by President Ford on April 8, 1975, changed the US policy on herbicides and RCAs. Hereafter, the U.S. government renounced the first use of herbicides in war (except for the use under regulations for controlling vegetation within U.S. bases and installations, or around their immediate defensive perimeters); and first use of riot control agents (except in defensive modes to save lives such as controlling rioting POWs, reducing civilian casualties, rescue missions, and protecting convoys in rear echelon areas).[7] This did not stop the continued procurement of CS agent for traditional riot control purposes, such as for the National Guard and police forces (and later, military NBC defense training).

Between 1975 and 1977, Congress continued to reject all Army requests to fund the building of a production facility for binary weapons. Part of the impetus behind these rulings was pressure from the State Department and Arms Control and Disarmament Agency (ACDA) as arms control talks continued with the Soviet Union in Geneva. To ensure that the Army had abandoned the biological and binary agent programs, Congress passed Public Law 93-608, which required the Secretary of Defense to submit annual reports on expenditures of monies for research of lethal and nonlethal CB agents.[8] Chemical Corps military strength hit its post-World War II low in 1975 at approximately 2,250 personnel, with a DoD NBC defense budget of $38 million. Talks continued in Geneva without much progress, but they gave Congress reason to deny any binary munitions funding until their conclusion.[9]

## REDEFINING THE ARMY'S CONCEPTS OF NBC WARFARE

The Military Personnel Center (MILPERCEN) forwarded a decision memorandum titled "Disestablishment of the Chemical Corps" in June 1975 through HQ DA in an attempt to bring the issue of the Chemical Corps's disestablishment to closure. At that time, momentum for disestablishment was still there, chemical specialists were deserting the Chemical Corps, and morale was at an all-time low. Chemical officers within MILPERCEN and ODCSOPS were lobbying for another hearing. The chemical officers at the Ordnance School had sponsored two studies reexamining the need for chemical defense, in light of the Arab-Israeli War lessons. These studies were titled "Improved Chemical Defense System for Battalion-Sized Units" and "Chemical Defense at Division and Echelons Above Division," due to be completed in 1976. They provided recommendations on the type of organization required to provide the Army the necessary capability to operate in a chemical warfare environment, and to assure the availability of chemical warfare expertise throughout the Army. Since TRADOC was still conducting studies on chemical warfare vulnerabilities, the Assistant Chief of Staff for Intelligence and the DCSOPS both nonconcurred with the MILPERCEN action.

Once the Army leadership was ready to listen for a case of the need for a Chemical Corps, the next logical step was to reinstate a team at MILPERCEN to take responsibility for the chemical force structure (previously run by the Ordnance Corps). This team put together a concept paper that looked at the requirements necessary to bring back a robust capability that would serve the military as a deterrent against chemical weapons systems. This included two aspects: developing the force structure (soldiers) and developing new materiel systems (new defensive equipment). While both were important, the team concentrated on developing a force structure plan that would get chemical commissioned and noncommissioned officers into the combat units as soon as possible. Even without state-of-the-art equipment, chemical soldiers could, at the least, train and advise their combat units in the event of NBC weapons use.

Before General Ed "Shy" Meyer had moved from his position as DCSOPS to the Army Chief of Staff position, Colonel Watson had discussed with him the number of chemical soldiers necessary for a future force. Because the Army was still coming out of the "hollow Army" era, the numbers were at first deliberately kept low, focussing on technical positions and brigade and division positions. This would build an infrastructure of chemical expertise into the fighting arms of the military at a cost of an additional 208 officers and 2,250 noncommissioned officers.  General Meyer saw the need for a chemical noncommissioned officer in each infantry and armor company and artillery battery, and a chemical officer in every combat arms battalion, which would escalate the number higher.

Over at MILPERCEN, General Doty (DCSPER) was a bit more skeptical about where to find the authorization and positions for all these new soldiers.  The Chemical Branch at MILPERCEN had worked for over a year to develop the slots within all the combat units to support General Meyer's plan.  Lieutenant Colonel Bill Cook and Lieutenant Colonel Hugh Stringer were the nucleus of the team, which later included Major Bob Orton, Major Walt Busbee, and Captain Rick Read.[10]  Lieutenant Colonel Cook had staffed and forwarded all sorts of studies and justifications supporting the increased numbers, to no avail.  Finally, Lieutenant Colonel Cook appealed to General Doty's love of coin collecting.  One day, General Doty appeared at the Chemical Branch's office, just as Lieutenant Colonel Cook was polishing up his personal mint collection of 19th century silver dollars (one of the larger collections on the East Coast).  The door closed, and half an hour later, the general left a broadly smiling Cook and smaller stacks of coins.  A few weeks later, the larger option for the personnel force structure for the Chemical Corps was approved.  Rumor is that the new Chemical Corps force structure had been paid for with those silver dollars (combined with excellent staff memorandums).

The effort to reinitiate the defensive program was a bit fuzzier, since basic research and development had been virtually halted for any NBC defense equipment for nearly a decade.  In coordination with the Edgewood labs, chemical officers developed an initial plan to develop new protective masks, new overgarments, gloves, boots, agent detectors, and so on, using both programs from other nations and programs that had been in long hibernation.  Congress assured the Army of increased procurement funds for NBC defense equipment (among other programs), despite the past years of low defense spending.

The last major decision needed prior to the planned May 1980 systems program review was the new location of the school.  Brigadier General Watson and Colonel Walt Phillips (the current commander of the Chemical Course under the Ordnance School) saw three options available: remaining at Aberdeen Proving Ground, collocated with the Ordnance School; moving to a major combat arms school, such as Fort Benning, Fort Sill, or Fort Knox; or returning to Fort McClellan, where the Military Police School had taken up residence in the Chemical School's prior residence.[11]  They used two requirements for the selection: to execute large-area smoke training missions and to train chemical soldiers with toxic chemical agents.  Smoke operations, traditionally a chemical mission, would require open ranges and maneuver room.  Training with toxic agents had been a Chemical Corps soldier's rite of passage from 1917 to 1973, disrupted only by the attempted disestablishment of the Corps.  The senior leadership of the Chemical Corps saw this training as vital toward maintaining credibility and high training standards for its subject-matter experts.

Aberdeen Proving Ground could not support either smoke operations or toxic agent training, due to its small training areas. Between 1972 and 1979, chemical specialists had traveled to Fort Indiantown Gap in Pennsylvania to train with smoke generator systems. Given the Edgewood community's sensitivity about chemical agents, toxic agent training was not included. With no combat arms schools volunteering their posts for candidates, they looked south to Alabama. At the Missile Munitions Center and School (Huntsville Arsenal), the Explosives Ordnance Disposal school used toxic agents to train their Technical Escort soldiers on making discovered chemical munitions safe. As the Chemical School investigated this option, the Huntsville community reacted with alarm over the news of toxic agent training and promptly requested that the Army discontinue that training.[12] That left Fort McClellan as the best option. Fort McClellan had the room for smoke operations and the sites available for toxic agent training. The Chemical School returned to Fort McClellan on December 14, 1979, with newly promoted Brigadier General Watson as its commandant.

In 1976 the U.S. government began receiving intelligence reports about the Vietnamese using chemical warfare against Hmong tribes in Laos. Intelligence agencies suspected Soviet backing, especially considering the high level of technology involved in certain laboratories built and manned by Soviets in Vietnam. The reports of the size and depth of the Soviet CB weapons program prompted some military leaders to reexamine the capability of U.S. and NATO combat units to survive and sustain a war in an NBC environment.

A battalion led by a young Lieutenant Colonel Barry McCaffrey participated in six weeks of intensive training involving protective equipment and large-scale decontamination training exercises in Europe, demonstrating how soldiers might operate on a chemical warfare battlefield. McCaffrey realized that the more proficient his unit became in operating in a chemical environment within the constraints of protective gear, the more capable his unit was when they operated in a conventional environment (as well as in a contaminated environment). If soldiers trained for NBC warfare, they could retain their combat lethality, instead of becoming operationally degraded. He wrote up his findings and forwarded the report to his division commander, who was so impressed that soon all the unit commanders in Germany had picked up on the chemical weapons threat and its consequences.

FORSCOM headquarters concurred and forwarded their comments on how several factors had contributed to degrade the Army's NBC defensive posture. These factors included the public outcry over herbicide and napalm use in Vietnam, the Dugway Proving Ground sheep incident, President Nixon's 1969 announcement banning first use of chemical weapons and eliminating biological offensive capability, closing the Chemical School and transferring the responsibilities to the Ordnance Corps, and losing all but one company-sized chemical defense unit in the active force. The question was, how would the Army develop the personnel, doctrine and equipment to regain that capability.

The Chemical School (now as part of the renamed Ordnance and Chemical School and Center) presented the study on "Improved Chemical Defense System for Battalion-Sized Units" to General DuPuy on May 4, 1976. He called it "the most outstanding [study] I have seen since being at TRADOC." Among other recommendations, the briefing called for a new study of the chemical defense function; new chemical defense units; a stronger combat support role (as opposed to a combat service support role); and a need to include a chemical focal point within TRADOC. Army Secretary Martin Hoffman formally withdrew the earlier recommendation to disestablish the Chemical Corps. In October 1976, the Chief of Staff of the Army, General Bernard Rodgers, authorized the resumption of commissioning officers in the Chemical Corps.

General Rodgers commented to (then) Colonel Watson how concerned he was about how in the world the United States Army could make such a dumb decision as abolishing the Corps. General Rogers realized that it had been done in good faith, thinking that, as many did at the time, it was the right thing to do. The general had been the DCSPER between 1972 and 1974, and had overseen the diminishing of the Chemical Corps's personnel at the time. Many other senior combat arms officers realized that they had been wrong in abolishing the Chemical Corps without understanding the consequences of a world abounding with CB weapon-armed nations.[13]

Elsewhere, the NBC defense community began to emerge from its isolation. The former Chemical Center's Medical Research Division became the Army Surgeon General's Medical Research Institute of Chemical Defense (USAMRICD), where it would continue its medical NBC defense research under the Army Medical Research and Development Command (MRDC). Edgewood Arsenal was renamed, in light of its revitalized mission, as the Chemical Systems Laboratory (CSL) in March 1977, under the equally new U.S. Army Armament Research and Development Command (ARRADCOM). HQ DA redesignated the U.S. Army Nuclear Agency under ODCSOPS to become the U.S. Army Nuclear and Chemical Agency (USANCA) in May 1978, adding CB contamination survivability to its charter of ensuring Army weapon systems were nuclear survivable. DoD modified the responsibilities of the Assistant to the Secretary of Defense for Atomic Energy (ATSD[AE]) on August 10, 1978,[14] to coordinate issues related to chemical and biological defense between the Joint Chiefs, Office of the Secretary of Defense, and other government agencies. The Army Medical Intelligence and Information Agency (AMIIA) moved to Fort Detrick in an effort to work more closely with the medical community's biological defense agencies.

## THE ARMY REVISES ITS DOCTRINE

By 1977, many military theorists had read the TRADOC studies showing that NATO's NBC defense capability had eroded to a point where a chemical attack would devastate the NATO forces, or at the least offer a strong advantage to an attacking, protected Warsaw Pact force. Details of the large, modern Soviet chemical defense units, the Red Army toxic agent training, and scenarios of CW use against NATO airfields and depots initiated a debate in military circles over rearming the NATO forces for chemical offense, as well as increasing its defensive programs. More important, the U.S. armed forces realized that the proliferation of weapons of mass destruction had changed the nature of the threat, from one coming solely from the Soviet Union to a threat from a number of smaller countries, within and outside of Europe. The new term emerging to describe this was "horizontal proliferation" among other nations, as opposed to the "vertical proliferation" of chemical warfare stockpiles within the Soviet Union alone.

No more would the Big Five (United States, United Kingdom, France, China, Soviet Union) monopolize the NBC weapons field. The U.S. government had tracked the proliferation of nuclear arms from five countries in 1964 to seven countries confirmed/suspected in 1980 (20 countries confirmed/suspected in 1991). In 1980 the U.S. government reported thirteen countries as confirmed or suspect in developing chemical arms programs. In 1985 the Chemical Warfare Review Commission would tell the President and Congress that sixteen countries, including the United States and Soviet Union, were known or probable owners of chemical weapons. In 1991 the official government count was twenty-five confirmed and suspect countries. Biological weapons had a similar, if smaller, rise from two in the 1960s to three in 1980 (and seventeen in 1991). There was a definite trend in growing proliferation of these weapons. This was a view held by other NATO countries as well, as the British, French, and Germans began modernizing their respective chemical defensive capabilities.

The size of the Soviet chemical troop strength, estimated at 80,000 personnel, numbered one-tenth the size of the entire U.S. Army. This strength was compared to the less than 2,000 chemical personnel in the U.S. Army structure. Critics pointed out that the Soviet buildup of chemical specialists, chemical weapons, and chemical defense equipment (as found in the Middle East) could very well represent Soviet concerns over the U.S. military's buildup of CB agent weapons in the 1950s and 1960s. This was partially true; the Soviets had acknowledged CB agent munitions as a potential threat. At the same time, they also viewed it as an option and an asset in achieving their military objectives in time of war. As military professionals and observers of history, the Soviet Army understood that the correct response to a weapon system was to develop defensive tactics and equipment to counter its use, and to use that weapon system offensively if it could defeat an enemy's vulnerabilities. If your enemy had 105-mm main guns on his tanks, you developed armor that stopped that caliber and upgraded your gun to 120-mm to defeat his armor. The solution was not to stick one's head in the sand and ignore it or to hope treaties would stop that weapon system's use. You made sure you would win.

Because of the more candid appraisals of the Soviet NBC threat in Europe, tactical nuclear and chemical warfare reemerged as topics of discussion. The Field Artillery School proposed a new operational concept termed the "integrated battlefield." This meant integrating tactical nuclear support with conventional fire support; integrating maneuver and fire support; and integrating air and land operations. In this scenario, the corps would use tactical nuclear weapons to disrupt enemy follow-on echelons, or if necessary, to destroy first echelon divisions. While chemical weapons might be utilized in a like role, they were seen as primarily defensive in nature. Their best employment was to deny the enemy rapid passage through an area or to intercept and stop his approach. First use of chemical weapons remained excluded because of the national policy set by President Nixon—but first strike with tactical nuclear weapons was a possible scenario. The new integrated offensive strategy required a similar integrated defensive strategy against the enemy's expected use of nuclear and chemical weapons. The Field Artillery School volunteered to lead the effort in developing binary weapons, but it was reluctant to pursue the issue before Congress. This was reflected in their development programs, which placed developmental high explosive and antitank munition programs high in priority over the binary chemical munitions program.

The late 1970s and early 1980s also saw a stronger effort to standardize military operations within NATO. The fifteen member nations created a multinational group known as NATO Panel VII, which was tasked to develop a number of standardization agreements (STANAGs) in NBC defense that, in time of war, would give them a common reference in operations, medical aspects, and research and development. These STANAGs include an NBC Warning and Reporting System (NBCWRS), with its six standard NBC reports (STANAG 2103), and Medical Aspects of NBC Defensive Operations (STANAG 2500).[15] These STANAGs are still in use today to provide NATO partners a common understanding of NBC principles and notification of NBC attacks.

DoD attempted to rebuild its NBC defense program management structure. A Joint Service Agreement (JSA) for Chemical Warfare/Chemical-Biological Defense Research, Development, Test and Evaluation (CW/CBD RDT&E) named the Army as the DoD Executive Agent for NBC defense on March 30, 1976.[16] This JSA would subordinate Air Force and Navy research and development (but not acquisition) to the Army, who had retained the subject matter experts at Edgewood Arsenal. Procurement of NBC defense equipment was left to the prerogatives of the individual services. The important fact was that CB defense funds were immediately increased. The U.S. military dedicated funds for purchases of thousands of British protective suits for forces in Europe. Research funds were also made available for operational testing of Soviet CB defense equipment captured during the Arab-Israeli War.

Congressional committees had discussed the military's observations of the Arab-Israeli war of 1973, including details on the collective protection of the Soviet combat vehicles and corresponding lack in American systems. In response, Congress passed Public Law 95-79, which required the Secretary of the Army to submit a plan for funding and scheduling the incorporation of collective protection systems in all armored vehicles by 1991.[17] President Jimmy Carter, meanwhile, directed an executive review of the Army's chemical warfare policy and posture. The review resulted in a presidential decision that directed that the U.S. chemical weapons stockpile be maintained without improvement. President Carter made a policy decision throughout his term of office to deny funds for binary production facilities because of still ongoing U.S.-Soviet efforts to control chemical weapons.[18] However, Defense Secretary Harold Brown had managed to raise CB defensive RDT&E funds about one-third higher than the 1972–76 levels to begin the four services' modernization (see Figure 5.1). This included plans to submit funding requirements for a binary weapons production facility. This funding request would be included in the FY80 budget, and was expected to be less than $15 million for the facility with some long-term funds for actual production.[19]

TRADOC proposed to undertake two major systems program reviews, one for tactical nuclear systems in December 1979, and a second for chemical warfare operations in May 1980. This was TRADOC's first attempt to undertake a front-end analysis of specific battlefield functions to identify and address future warfare concerns. For the Chemical Corps, this was their chance to show how the new chemical defense units could augment and strengthen the Army in its new joint battlefield concept. This was their opportunity to rebuild the collapsed NBC defense program and win back a position within the Army as a respected combat support branch.

The net effect of this last decade had severely disrupted the nation's NBC defensive and offensive capability. Perhaps the most severe loss was the disruption to the formerly centralized command structure of the CBW commodity centers. Where there had once been a sole command that controlled all four services' medical and nonmedical NBC defense programs and offensive weapon capabilities, there were now over a dozen independent agencies with loose DoD oversight capability through the Assistant to the Secretary of Defense (Atomic Energy). This collection of agencies practically guaranteed an uncoordinated, underfunded, and unprioritized defense effort. Ironically, the Army would be routinely criticized by Congress, the GAO, and other organizations for this unorganized and unfocused effort in the DoD NBC defense management for years afterward.

While the Chemical School was under the Ordnance School, the Chemical Corps lost its general officer advocacy for the branch, both within TRADOC and the Pentagon's Army staff. As the Army was reforming its post-Vietnam military force and doctrine, Ordnance generals saw no need to address CBW doctrinal concerns. The average officer loss across the Army between 1973 and 1976 was 15 percent, compared to an attrition of 27 percent in the Chemical Corps, a small branch even prior to the disestablishment attempt.

There were no champions to remind TRADOC of the threat of global CB weapon proliferation, and that the Army had to maintain an ability to operate effectively in such an environment. As a result, Army NBC defense doctrine and training had remained stagnant for several years (with some exceptions). As the

**Figure 5.1**
**CB Defense Expenditures in Relation to DoD Budget**

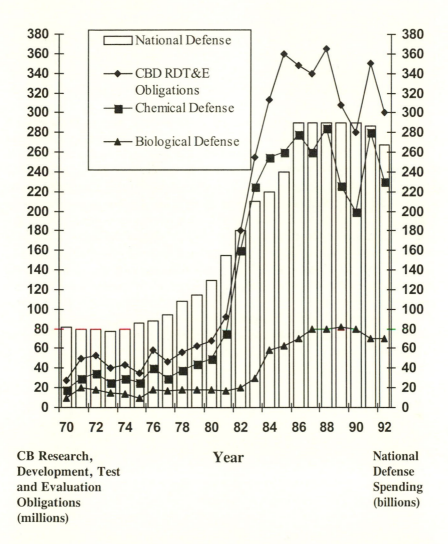

CB Research,
Development, Test
and Evaluation
Obligations
(millions)

**Year**

National
Defense
Spending
(billions)

1980s began, a revitalized Chemical School began work to develop modern tactics for chemical defense units to employ in emerging Army doctrine. While there would never be another Chemical Corps general officer on the Army staff, at least the Chemical School commandant would be able to lead at the same level as other combat support branches.

The quality of chemical personnel suffered over the years as well. The generation of young chemical officers and noncommissioned officers that progressed up through the Corps in this decade had no experience as troop commanders or as leaders of decontamination, smoke, or NBC reconnaissance platoons or companies since none existed!  The Ordnance School had never invested in Chemical Corps training, since it appeared that the chemical officers would all be forced into the "flaming cannonball" ranks as chemical munition specialists.  The Chemical Corps's ranks, heavy with senior chemical officers and noncommissioned officers, required transfers from other Army branches to fill its depreciated ranks with new blood.  It would be years before every company, battalion, and brigade in the Army force would actually see their allocated chemical specialists.

When the Chemical Corps emerged from its isolation, it found itself a generation behind its international allies and the Soviet Union in equipment modernization.  The lack of program funds through the years had dried up the industrial base.  Industry was skeptical about reentering the NBC defense sector, given its poor public reputation and their uncertainty whether the Army was serious about keeping the Chemical Corps.  The Army's first biological agent detector, standoff chemical agent detectors, NBC reconnaissance vehicles, collective protection systems, and a new protective mask to replace the aging M17-series protective mask had been lost to budget cuts and kept in limbo for ten years.  In addition to the traditional NBC defense equipment programs, the Army's smoke and flame programs had never progressed, due to lack of interest in the Engineer and Artillery branches that had held proponencies for those areas.  Riot control agents, no longer a military option without presidential approval, would never recover and would eventually be replaced by other nonlethal programs.  There was a lot of work ahead with little time to waste.

# PART II

# The Renaissance Years Begin, 1979–84

Since the original decision to disestablish the Chemical Corps was made . . . circumstances have changed. . . . A review of U.S. Army Chemical Warfare Posture . . . revealed our military needs to improve its capability to conduct CW operations and operate in a CW environment.

—Lieutenant General John Vessey, DCSOPS, 1976

I regret, then, to report that chemical and toxin weapons are nevertheless being used today in Laos, Kampuchea, and Afghanistan by the Soviet Union and their allies. . . . The use of chemical and toxin weapons must be stopped.

—George P. Schultz, Secretary of State, November 1982

# CHAPTER 6

# Changes in Doctrine
# and Training

With the changes in military philosophy after Vietnam, the Chemical Corps leadership soon realized that it had to change with the Army to remain a valuable supporting asset. The attempt to disestablish the Corps in 1972 prevented the Chemical Corps from effecting any significant changes in Army doctrine, training, leader development, or organizational units. With the Dugway sheep incident in 1968 and the BWC's initiation in 1975, the visibility and political pressure was just too intense to expect anyone to change their minds about the fate of the Chemical Corps. In addition, the "Chemistry Corps" image persisted among the military leadership, biasing the judgment of the "war-fighters" (infantry, armor, artillery, aviation) that CBR defense was not really an important issue. Important indicators such as the use of nerve agents in the Yemeni Civil War were ignored or dismissed summarily as not representative of future war. With the Chemical School under the Ordnance branch, there was no "official" general officer proponent to champion the cause. As a result, the threat of chemical-biological warfare was not considered as the other Army branches began their post-Vietnam reforms. It took the combined effects of the Arab-Israeli wars, the Sverdlovsk accident in the Soviet Union, and reports of chemical warfare in Laos, Afghanistan, and the Iran-Iraq war to allow the Corps to initiate its reform efforts into the new AirLand Battle philosophy.

Once these reforms began, they took shape in four areas of emphasis. First, the Army had to upgrade its training programs for chemical warfare significantly, both for its specialists and for every individual soldier. This was a quickly implemented, low-cost investment. Second, the armed forces had to procure available defense items (masks, protective clothes, etc.) immediately and in quantity, with the understanding that while limitations existed, there was time later for improvements through research and development. Third, the armed forces needed to improve the credibility of their retaliatory capability, which was deemed both quantitatively and qualitatively deficient (and therefore not credible). Last, the DoD had to deal with the problems of an aging chemical weapons stockpile and how they would demilitarize the aging and leaking munitions in a safe, method-efficient and cost-efficient process.

## REEXAMINING OFFENSIVE CHEMICAL PROGRAMS

In April 1979 reports of an anthrax outbreak in Sverdlovsk, Soviet Union, caught many governments by surprise. The Soviet news agency, *Tass*, claimed that the thousand-plus civilian casualties had died because of intestinal anthrax resulting from spoiled sausage. Later investigations led others to believe that the deaths were a result of an explosion at a nearby suspect biological weapons factory. Although the USSR had signed the BWC in 1972, there were no provisions to inspect suspect biological agent facilities in other countries without their permission.[1] Later that year, reports came out of Soviet-invaded Afghanistan, which stated that Soviet chemical companies had prominently deployed with the divisions rolling into the country. Eyewitnesses spoke of seeing Soviet soldiers preparing and wearing protective suits and masks, and not because Afghanistan had any chemical warfare capability. News videos showed Soviet TMS-65 decontamination vehicles rolling in behind the tanks. In 1979–80, the National Security Council publicly recognized the growing threat from the Soviet Union and other countries seeking a "weapon of mass destruction" capability and obtained a presidential direction to modify the national policy with respect to chemical warfare. This new approach encompassed a two-prong effort with the goal of reducing the military advantage of potential opponents employing chemical weapons: (1) an intensive diplomatic effort in a multinational forum to complete a chemical arms elimination treaty; and (2) a revitalization of the chemical warfare capabilities of the armed forces.[2]

The four years of chemical arms control discussions (1976–80) between the United States and the USSR had not been fruitful. Negotiations broke off over verification issues and in response to the Soviet invasion of Afghanistan. The Conference on Disarmament in Geneva established an Ad Hoc Working Group on Chemical Weapons on March 17, 1980, to begin multilateral discussions toward a Chemical Weapons Convention (CWC). Congress came back to the side of the Chemical Corps in 1980. Senator Howell Hefflin (D-AL) presented a stirring speech on June 30, 1980, in which he identified the growing Soviet threat as a juggernaut poised to invade Europe, using "chemical weapons to provide a breakthrough in the NATO defenses or to seal off important areas such as NATO airfields, command centers, and nuclear weapon sites."[3] He called on Congress to provide the necessary funds and force the DoD to use the funds both to provide a defensive posture superior to the Soviets and to present a substantial chemical warfare deterrent through the production and deployment of binary weapons. Many other members of Congress agreed, citing the years of stalled negotiations with the Soviet Union on the subject of chemical warfare disarmament. After the Soviet invasion of Afghanistan, Representative Richard Ichord (D-MO), chair of the Research and Development Subcommittee of the House Armed Services Committee, led a successful initiative to approve an initial funding of $3.15 million for the construction of a binary weapons production plant at Pine Bluff Arsenal.

Congress subsequently passed Public Law 99-145, with a Senate amendment that directed the accelerated replacement of current old, deteriorating, and largely obsolete chemical weapons with safer, more efficient munitions compatible with modern battlefield systems. This authorized the reemergence of the Army binary program, beginning with the construction of a productions plant for the 155-mm binary projectile (but no funds for actual manufacturing), further field tests of the Bigeye bomb, and development of the Multiple Launch Rocket System (MLRS) chemical warhead in 1981–82. Under President Ronald Reagan's FY81 supplemental request, another $19 million was added to equip the facility. President Reagan announced the production of the "neutron bomb" in August 1981, initiating the development of a weapon system that had been debated and postponed for over two decades. This would add to the commander's tactical options in fighting on an NBC battlefield. Although these programs would cause no end of controversy, it displayed the serious intent to develop a tactical retaliatory capability in both nuclear and chemical warfare.

These actions triggered a Senate Armed Services Committee hearing on chemical warfare on September 4, 1980. Defense Secretary Harold Brown, accompanied by Lieutenant General Eugene Tighe, Jr. (director of the Defense Intelligence Agency), briefed the committee (presided by Senator Gary Hart [D-CO]) on why the military required binary weapons. At that briefing, Secretary Brown used the reports of chemical agent use in Laos and Afghanistan and the anthrax incident in the Soviet Union to press for an effective CW retaliatory capability combined with a viable defense.[4] The main arguments for binary production included the need to present a credible retaliatory capability that did not rely on pre-1969 munitions; the lack of success in arms control talks with the Soviets; and the need for chemical munitions that were safe to manufacture, transport, store, and demilitarize.

The binary facility would eventually include modules for three chemical weapons (155-mm GB projectile, the Bigeye bomb, and the 8-inch VX projectile), with the MLRS warhead deferred to a later date. Total cost of the program was estimated at $156 million from start to finish. The committee reviewed the existing stockpile figures, military contingency plans to use chemical agents in Europe, and the possible political and military repercussions that might result because of reinitiating chemical weapons production. During the brief, Senator Hart reminded Secretary Brown that the president had not yet complied with Public Law 94-106, which required the president to certify to Congress that the binary chemical munitions production was essential to the national interest.[5]

## THE RENAISSANCE ERA BEGINS

With the Chemical School's return to Fort McClellan in December 1979, the staff began preparing for a Chemical Systems Program Review. Brigadier General Gerald Watson, the new commandant, was the host for this meeting on May 28–29, 1980. Over fifty flag officers and eighty-six additional personnel from the four services attended, including representatives from TRADOC, Combined Arms Center at Fort Leavenworth, and the Pentagon. The first day's agenda included discussions on the emerging NBC weapons threat, the Army and Air Force proposed NBC defense programs, and TRADOC's assessment of the readiness of the U.S. forces. The second day reviewed future materiel programs: chemical weapons employment procedures and requirements, NBC defense training, sustaining the combat force, and smoke operations. This two-day review resulted in the draft of a Chemical Program Action Plan in June 1980, which gave the Army a roadmap to integrating NBC defense and offense into the Corps/Division 86 plans. Included was a concept for a six-platoon NBC defense company at division level, and an overall 36 percent increase in chemical personnel in combat arms units. In addition, they pushed for a smoke generator company to be stationed at the National Training Center (NTC), with the mission of integrating smoke operations into the combat operations training. Unfortunately, they had to settle for a smoke generator platoon attached from Fort Lewis. As more chemical soldiers entered the new Chemical Corps, more combat arms companies and battalions would receive their own NBC warfare specialists to coordinate training, requisition supplies, and offer subject-matter expertise in operations that included the threat of NBC munitions. The SPR also produced a Binary Munitions Modernization Action Plan to rebuild the military's retaliatory capability.

Chemical officer education had to change from its roots. Major Dan Shea, a former infantry officer turned chemical, brought a new training concept entitled "platoon trainers" from the Infantry School. Instead of large single classes numbering over one hundred, chemical soldiers would train as thirty-person cells. This enabled a closer trainer-student ratio and emphasized a level of excellence in small unit operations based on the Infantry School model., Since the school was just getting under steam, field units still had to rely on senior NCOs and officers that had either returned to the Chemical Corps or had remained during the lean years. Many battalions and brigades would remain without officers until 1985, units that had not seen chemical officers since the Vietnam years. Slowly, the level of expertise was rising.

The years since TRADOC was formed had seen vigorous debates within the Army over what its new doctrine should look like. In 1981 the new Army Field Manual 100-1, *The Army*, formally defined the new goals and strategy of a ground force, thus abolishing the atomic battlefield and Pentomic Army concept forever. One of the new ideas was the adoption of an operational level between tactics and grand strategy. In 1982 General Don Starry released his AirLand Battle concept, based on his 1976 TRADOC Pamphlet 525-2, *Operations*.[6] On July 30, 1982, the

Chemical Corps released TRADOC Pamphlet 525-20, *U.S. Army Operational Concept for Individual and Collective Measures for Chemical, Biological and Radiological (CBR) Defense*. This concept stressed a three-tiered approach of contamination avoidance, protection, and decontamination, which was the first time the tenets of the Chemical Corps had ever been outlined as a concept for combat forces (as opposed to specialists). A series of interim field manuals followed to implement the guidelines as new doctrine.[7] The new trend emphasized continuing the mission even if contaminated with NBC agents. This was a major change from the past, when the combat units expected to be completely decontaminated before continuing operations. Other changes emphasized the tenets of AirLand Battle (agility, initiative, depth, and synchronization), and the need for the Army to accept NBC warfare as an environment or condition, not as a separate mission. The changes can be summarized in Table 6.1.

**Table 6.1**
**Changes to Chemical Corps Doctrine**

|  | Old | New |
|---|---|---|
| **Doctrine and Training** | Chemical Corps concern | Army-wide concern |
| **Operational Emphasis** | Minimize chemical casualties | Minimize mission degradation |
| **Degree of Risk** | Zero-risk | Take intelligent risks |
| **Control of Chemical Defense Operations** | Centralized under division NBC element | Decentralized, flexible down to brigade level |
| **Decontamination Operations** | Complete decontamination of troops and equipment | Partial decontamination —enough to continue the mission |

Early in the Chemical School's organization in 1981, the training staff began to examine options for conducting training exercises during which the instructors would use minute quantities of U.S. military standard chemical agents. Live agent training had been a part of the Corps for all its soldiers from its inception up to 1973. Between 1973 and 1987, several generations of chemical officers and NCOs entered the military without really understanding the mental and physical stress suffered by ground soldiers caused by the necessity to continue combat operations in a toxic environment by wearing protective gear. There was the question of credibility—how could these chemical soldiers unquestionably support the use of NBC defense equipment to continue the mission if they were not absolutely sure that the equipment would work in combat? It was like asking a soldier who had never attended Airborne School to trust in his parachute as he/she was exiting the door of a C130 transport from a few thousand feet in the air.

There had been an early decision not to conduct the toxic agent training outdoors as had been done in years past, in order to avoid a lengthy environmental battle in court.  The School completed an environmental assessment for the Chemical Decontamination Training Facility (CDTF), as it was first known, in October 1981.  The actual building was designed by July 1982, and the Chemical Corps sought military construction funds to begin work.  Congress approved the military construction funds for 1983, and after approval of the site safety plan, the engineers began working on the Army's first toxic agent training facility.

There was still resistance to the idea of toxic agent training within the Army.  General John Wickham, Army Chief of Staff, failed to see why soldiers could not learn just as well with chemical simulants as with actual nerve agents.  He wanted proof from Major General Alan Nord, the next commandant of the Chemical School (1982–85).  Major General Nord had just arrived from commanding the White Sands Missile Range and would carry through Brigadier General Watson's plans for a CDTF and other initiatives.  Under Major General Nord's direction, the Chemical School established a protocol with the Army Surgeon General's assistance that would allow them to measure the stress, in terms of blood pressure and several other medical parameters, of the soldiers training in the facility.  The baseline assumed that chemical agents were not necessary, and the soldiers trained in the facility performed NBC defense-related tasks knowing that chemical simulants were being used.  This was compared to a second group of soldiers, performing the same tasks, who went in with the understanding that there were actual chemical agents used.  The Surgeon General's report confirmed the added stress caused by the chemical agents, and the post training interviews verified the tremendous increase in respect and credibility that the soldiers had for their own equipment.  Once General Wickham saw this report's findings, he reversed himself and authorized the CDTF to resume its construction.

In an effort to educate the Army's senior leadership on NBC defense and offense, the School began a biannual Senior Commander/Chemical Officer course.  This course was geared primarily at general officers from all services, which allowed them to review the current doctrine and equipment for NBC defense and smoke operations.  Many of these officers had developed their military experience during the "Dry Years," when chemical defense units and CBW doctrine were not present and being exercised in the Army.  The course highlighted major Army programs and plans for improvement, with emphasis on NBC defense applications toward TRADOC's Integrated Battlefield operations concept.

Another early School initiative had been to relate the new doctrine being developed to actual benefits to combat power of the maneuver forces, or to the support and service support units.  The 1980 Defense Science Board documented that the use of full chemical protection clothing imposed significant costs in terms of operational performance.  They recommended that there was an urgent need for realistic field exercises to evaluate the impact of individual protection equipment on military operations.  This led to the development of a training evaluation plan conducted in coordination with the combat arms branches to identify the real differences between normal combat operations and combat operations in a nuclear or chemical environment. In 1983 the Chemical School began a series of training evaluations through the Combined Arms Center to examine the effects of a nuclear/chemical environment on current military operations. These exercises were called CANE, or Combined Arms in a Nuclear/Chemical Environment.

By comparing the performance of units of various sizes in a simulated nuclear/chemical environment against their baseline performance in a conventional combat environment, the evaluators could quantify, for the first time in history, the actual degradation of the soldiers' actions. All exercises would simulate battle against an opposing force representing an enemy using nuclear/chemical munitions, conducting both offensive and defensive missions. The first trial, CANE I (completed in May 1983), focused on a mechanized squad and platoon. Some military leaders criticized the CANE tests as too small-scale to predict effects on divisions and corps accurately. CANE IIA stepped up the tests to a tank company team in April 1985. CANE IIB examined an armor-heavy battalion task force in March 1988, and light infantry forces were examined in the fall of 1992. These tests provided TRADOC, for the first time, with quantifiable data and specific recommendations for improving soldiers' performances in a contaminated environment. For instance, some initial results detailed that:

- Direct fire engagements dropped 52 percent, and friendly fire incidents rose 360 percent
- Battle intensity dropped 46 percent, and troops engaged the enemy 25 percent less
- Threat forces killed by offensive attacks dropped 22 percent, by night defense actions dropped 25 percent, by day defense actions rose 11 percent
- Volume of radio message traffic rose 47 percent, and took 53 percent longer to be understood
- Calls for indirect fire support rose 209 percent in the offense, and dropped 11 percent in the defense
- Time to replace the chain of command rose 340 percent

Most of these statistics can be explained by the psychological isolation and physical degradation felt by troops fighting in protective clothing and masks and the poor level of training among the leaders and the troops. There is an instinct to "huddle down" and ride the battle out, relying on fire support rather than by aggressively attacking while wearing protective suits. While these indications were generally understood, this was the first time the Army had made the effort to truly quantify the effects of protective clothing on soldiers in combat operations. Besides adding to the understanding of NBC agents on combat operations, these tests refocused the need to develop and build equipment that could survive the physical effects of NBC agents and the caustic decontaminants developed by the services. People began to see that CB warfare was a definable and manageable challenge, rather than an issue to be ignored because it was too immense.

Obviously, the CANE exercises were presenting a macro-level overview of the issues involved in combat operations within an NBC-contaminated environment.

Each branch of the Army began to wonder what specific issues could be discovered in relation to their equipment; for instance, what were the exact causes and effects of wearing protective clothing and masks while operating trucks, tanks, and helicopters and operating equipment within these vehicles? The newly named Chemical Research and Development Center (formerly Chemical Systems Laboratory)[8] began work with the Armor School on the physiological and psychological effects of operating armored vehicles in an NBC environment. These were later turned over the Chemical School as the proponent TRADOC center, and named P2NBC2 (physiological and psychological effects in NBC contamination). Eventually this work would expand to investigate several different operational issues in other branches of the Army. These studies focused on very specific issues, such as the extent of contamination that might seep into helicopters hovering above a contaminated area with its doors closed.

## INTERNATIONAL EVENTS AND ARMS CONTROL

Reports began publicly surfacing in 1981 on the alleged Soviet use of new, third-generation chemical agents in Afghanistan and Indochina, which only fueled the U.S. military's desire to rebuild a chemical warfare program. On March 22, 1982, Secretary of State Alexander Haig presented a special report to Congress on alleged chemical warfare in Southeast Asia and Afghanistan. In his report, he acknowledged that the U.S. government had been receiving information on the use of lethal weapons in Laos beginning in 1975. Some samples analyzed were identified as trichothecene mycotoxins (T2 toxin) or yellow rain. In Afghanistan, much of the information came from mujahedin fighters' accounts and reports from Afghani deserters. In both cases, physical evidence was difficult to collect due to the remoteness and isolation of the suspected sites, and much of the evidence gathered came from eyewitnesses and survivors of the chemical attacks. The United States accused the Soviet Union of developing the agent-filled munitions, transporting them to the field, filling the munitions, and loading the munitions on aircraft. *"There is no evidence to support any alternate explanation, such as the hypothesis that the Vietnamese produce and employ toxin weapons completely on their own"* (italics as in report).[9]

In Laos, reports from Hmong tribes identified 261 attacks causing more than 6,504 deaths between summer of 1975 and fall of 1981. Vietnamese and Lao forces used Soviet AN-2 and captured American L-19 and T-28/41 aircraft to disseminate sprays, rockets, and bombs containing riot control agents, nerve agents, and T2 toxin. The agents were delivered separately and in combinations. In nearby Kampuchea, 124 attacks over the same period caused more than 981 deaths, again with riot control agents, chemical warfare agents, and the T2 toxin. The Soviet support included building the chemical storage sites, giving advanced training in chemical munitions handling and offensive use, and accompanying the troops on the ground and in the aircraft as the attacks took place. Sterling Seagrave detailed his trip to Laos to investigate these claims in his book, *Yellow Rain*. His interviews with doctors, French mercenaries, and the survivors in Laos led him to believe that the Hmong were being wiped out with a chemical compound besides the use of nerve agent and mustard gas, whose signs were evident on the victims' bodies.[10]

In Afghanistan, the first clues of potential chemical warfare were the chemical decontamination companies, chemical defense battalions, and special NBC defense logistics rolling behind the Soviet divisions in 1979. Certainly Afghanistan had no chemical weapons of their own. The U.S. government received reports of 47 attacks in twelve provinces between the summer of 1979 and summer of 1981, with over 3,042 deaths. The bulk of these attacks were against mujahedin hideouts in the mountains in areas of Soviet combat operations. Again, fixed-wing and rotary-wing aircraft delivered chemical agents from rockets, sprays, and bombs. Again, both single and combination attacks of nerve agents, T2 toxin, and riot control agents were reported. In addition, some reports of hallucinogenic and incapacitating agents surfaced.[11]

According to most reports, Soviet use of chemical agents declined sharply after 1982. The press pointed out the increase of international condemnation as having an effect; that or the Soviets were striking more remote areas where the press wasn't present. Soviet chemical weapons appeared to be used in a strategic supporting role (bombing villages and terrain denial missions), rather than in a tactical role, supporting the combined arms offensive against the guerrilla forces. As has been seen in cases since World War I, chemical agents do little to advance strategic gains and have always been better applied to tactical operations. Thus the Soviet use of chemical agents was not helping the tactical battles, which is where their forces needed the support. Last, using chemical munitions restricted Soviet troop movement in already restricted terrain. Other weapon systems, such as fuel-air explosives, incendiaries, and antipersonnel mines proved much more effective against the rebels.[12] These reasons, and not those of morality, were the more likely causes of the end of Soviet chemical weapons use.

Many skeptics did not believe that "yellow rain" existed; that it was a fabrication to justify the U.S. military's growing binary weapons program. Chief among these naysayers was Professor Matthew Meselson and his colleagues, who discounted the laboratory evidence of the T2 toxin. For instance, the T2 toxin had been collected in samples that included yellow bee feces and pollen. After Professor Meselson's trip to Southeast Asia, he concluded that the yellow feces droppings, which indeed had been dropped by mass groups of bees on "cleansing flights," had been confused as a chemical warfare agent. The university laboratories that had confirmed the Army's findings of mycotoxins probably had "erroneous findings." As for the symptoms of chemical warfare on the Hmong victims, he found only 8 of the 217 people interviewed as suffering all three symptoms of bloody vomiting, bloody diarrhea, and rashes or blisters. Therefore, in his mind, there was inconclusive evidence of Soviet-backed chemical warfare.[13]

To the military, at least, there was sufficient evidence that the Soviet Union had used traditional chemical warfare agents in Afghanistan and Laos. Most felt that the Soviets had been experimenting with new "third generation" CBW agents, hoping that these agents were the next step past nerve agents. Perhaps because of the inconclusive results of T2 toxin on the civilians in these theaters, the Soviets did not pursue further development. This case showed the extreme difficulties in proving any chemical agent use and evidence of proliferation. Not only were better intelligence sources required, better laboratory procedures were needed to keep these CBW agent samples viable until they reached accredited laboratories.

It became obvious that the United States required a dedicated intelligence agency to investigate and compile information on the growing proliferation of CB weapons. DoD established the Armed Forces Medical Intelligence Center (AFMIC) in 1982, replacing the Army's Medical Intelligence and Information Agency, due to general dissatisfaction with the medical intelligence efforts at Fort Detrick. Part of their new charter was to assess all foreign biomedical R&D, as well as produce medical, scientific, and technical intelligence on biological, chemical, psychological, and biophysical areas. Much of their direction came from the Defense Intelligence Agency (DIA). Later, AFMIC and the Foreign Science Technical Center (FSTC) would come to an agreement on the division of biological warfare intelligence (AFMIC's bailiwick) and chemical warfare intelligence (FSTC's area).

In addition, DoD established a Deputy Assistant to the Secretary of Defense (Atomic Energy)(Chemical Matters)—ATSD(AE)(CM)—under the Assistant to the Secretary of Defense (Atomic Energy) to provide oversight over chemical matters within the Department of Defense. This would include oversight of the DoD NBC defense program, the binary chemical weapons program, and the chemical demilitarization program. It enabled a new focus on the DoD NBC defense program from the top levels, as this deputy provided DoD representation on all joint-service NBC defense programs. This included a chair of the DoD CB Defense Steering Committee, created to advise the ATSD(AE) and the Secretary of Defense on CB defense matters.[14]

## BINARY WEAPONS

As was noted earlier, the Carter administration and the Democratic-dominated House had consistently blocked the reinitiation of building the binary production facilities, hoping that the Soviets would return for chemical arms talks in Geneva. The House now decided to include funding to proceed with the construction of a facility at Pine Bluff Arsenal capable of manufacturing 155-mm binary chemical artillery rounds at a cost of $3.15 million in the FY81 military construction appropriations bill (against the Carter administration's desires). The Senate approved this appropriation by a narrow margin (52–48), with the agreement that for every binary munition produced, one older chemical munition had to be destroyed. In February 1982 the DoD began to seek funds for binary production, in light of President Reagan's declarations that the production of binary weapons was in the national security interest.[15] However, while seeking $54 million for procuring the binary weapons for FY93, the program was frozen by the full House voting to delete the entire funding (against the recommendations of its Armed Services Committee). On the other hand, the House retained the request for nearly $700 million in NBC defense equipment funds.

Four senators were especially vocal against the production of binary weapons. Senators Mark Hatfield (R-OR), David Pryor (D-AR), Gary Hart (D-CO), and Thad Cochran (D-MI) summarized their objections in a "Dear Colleague" letter. It focused on four major points: (1) that the Army could not afford to spend billions of dollars on the production, storage, and demilitarization of chemical rounds over the years; (2) that the production of new chemical weapons added nothing to the overall national security; (3) that the production of binary rounds might initiate a new arms race, which was counter to the arms control agenda; and (4) most chemical weapons would be stored in the United States, instead of in Western Europe where the Army stated they would be employed, which made little sense.

The counter argument from the Defense and State departments did not address program costs, since no one could realistically identify the life cycle costs of the entire binary program. They pointed out that the Soviets retained both an extensive chemical offensive capability and well-trained troops that could fight in an NBC environment.[16] The resulting advantage would have degraded NATO soldiers' performance as they stayed in protective posture all the time, while the Soviets could minimize their degradation by picking the time and place of the chemical weapons attacks. At the worst, restarting the binary program kept the sides equal as far as the threat of NBC warfare stood. It was expected that the Soviets, understanding the limitations on combat forces caused by chemical agent employment, might restrain their forces from using such weapons if they thought U.S. forces could retaliate in kind. Therefore the buildup of chemical weapons was in line with improving the nation's security. As for an arms race, the Soviets were reported to have ten times the stockpile that the U.S. military had, and their troops actually fired the munitions in training.

The last point, where the chemical weapons were stored, depended more on diplomacy than on military plans to get the munitions where conflicts might start. After all, chemical munitions were already in U.S. depots in West Germany. The administration's point was that they would be replacing the older, dangerous rounds with modern binary (safer) rounds, and it would improve European security by lessening the threat of chemical warfare. If there were retaliatory chemical munitions that meant less reliance on nukes, and the West Germans liked the idea of nuclear weapons employment in their country much less than the possibility of chemical weapons employment. In order to effectively deter chemical warfare, U.S. forces required diplomatic efforts, modern chemical defense readiness, and a retaliatory capability.

The Chemical School's argument for the development of chemical weapons was based on what they saw as a logical extension to achieve the administration's policy of deterrence. For effective deterrence, Brigadier General Watson argued, the military needed three things. First, one required a capability to use chemical weapons in an attempt to deter the escalation of chemical weapons use. If there was no capability, all the posturing in the world would not deter chemical weapons use by a potential enemy. One could argue that threatening retaliation with tactical nuclear weapons might deter enemy use of chemical weapons (as Britain did), but wouldn't an enemy such as the Soviet Union escalate from tactical nuclear use to strategic nuclear response? In the case of threats of a massive conventional attack in response to a chemical attack, again, against an equal or superior enemy, one has to question if one could afford the cost of a massive conventional retaliation that would be taken seriously, considering the increased chance of friendly casualties that might result.

Second, the military needed a policy in place at the national level that would allow it to use chemical weapons if necessary. The resulting confusion over a national CB weapons policy during debates between 1958 and 1968 had resulted in a great deal of confusion over what the military could and could not do regarding CB weapons employment. How would theater-level commanders get permission to employ chemical weapons in time to stop enemy use of such weapons? The threat had to be credible.

Third, the enemy had to be convinced that the U.S. military had the capability and that administration policy allowed such use. If the enemy knew the U.S. military's CB weapons capability and policy to be a fraud, it would not deter enemy use of CB weapons. Once all three of these points were in place, the United States could rest assured that it had a credible means of deterrence in place. The problem was that while the Soviet Union was producing chemical munitions, the U.S. military was still relying on an aging, deteriorating stockpile of bulk chemical agents and chemical munitions that were not compatible with modern delivery systems.[17] There was no current deterrent against Soviet chemical weapons use.

There was also the issue of safer and less expensive storage of binary munitions. Over the years, Congress had placed heavy restrictions on the military's storage and transportation of chemical munitions. These measures had been above and beyond normal safety precautions, driving up the storage and transportation costs of chemical munitions. For example, in 1981, moving 888 Weteye VX nerve agent bombs from Rocky Mountain Arsenal to Tooele Army Depot cost the government approximately $3.2 million. If the munitions had been binary VX chemical bombs, the same transportation would have cost $170,000.[18]

From February through November 1983, the U.S. government presented their requirements for a verifiable prohibition on the production, stockpiling, and transfer of chemical weapons to the Conference on Disarmament (CD) in Geneva. This entailed declarations of plans for the destruction of stocks and vigorous on-site inspection standards. The United States sponsored a Chemical Weapons

Verification Workshop in November at Tooele Army Depot, Utah, to allow the CD representatives to examine a U.S. chemical weapons destruction test bed facility. The Soviet Union and Romania declined the invitation.[19]  In Washington, the Republican-dominated Senate supported the production initiative (twice only by Vice President George Bush's vote to break a tie), while the Democratic-dominated House firmly opposed any additional funds.  This did not stop Congress from finding the time to fund further development and production of the nuclear-armed ground-launched cruise missiles (GCLMs) and Pershing II missiles.  After all, there were Soviet SS-20 MIRVs in Europe to counter.  The Strategic Arms Limitations Talks (SALT) in 1972 did not cover MIRV warheads, allowing the Soviets to deploy the SS-20s in 1976.  The Reagan administration responded by deploying the Pershings and GLCMs to Europe in 1983.  Again, the development of tactical nuclear weapons closely paralleled the increased discussions on binary chemical weapons.  The only difference was that politicians evidently liked nukes better than chemical weapons.

Events in the Middle East were again calling attention to the proliferation of chemical weapons.  On the request of Iran, the UN Secretary General sent a special commission to investigate the claims of chemical weapons use by Iraq on March 13–19, 1984.  The four-man mission, staffed by experts from CBW centers in Australia, Spain, Sweden, and Switzerland, concluded that Iraq had clearly violated the 1925 Geneva Protocol through the use of chemical weapons and that Iraq had obtained much of the materials for its chemical warfare program from the international chemical industry.  Their report stated:

The following are our unanimous conclusions:

a.  Chemical weapons in the form of aerial bombs have been used in the areas inspected in Iran by the specialists.

b.  The types of chemical agents used were bis-(2-chloroethyl)-sulfide, also known as mustard gas, and ethyl-n, n-dimethylphosphoro amidocyanidate, a nerve agent known as tabun.  The extent to which these chemical agents have been used could not be determined within the time and resources available to us.[20]

One result of the escalating Iran-Iraq war and the use of chemical weapons was the reinitiation of the quadripartite conferences between America, Britain, Canada, and Australia (ABCA Conferences).  These conferences revitalized the old technical community links established during the Vietnam years, with the new purpose of modernizing NBC defense equipment and discussing issues of NBC contamination survivability of equipment on the battlefield.  The Chemical Defense Establishment at Porton Down had gone through similar political controversies over the intent of their research, despite the United Kingdom's abandonment of offensive chemical weapons in the late 1950s.  Bringing the four countries together would help coordinate the future of joint NATO members' NBC defense measures.

The downing of KAL 007 in September 1983 brought a newfound hawkish mood into the Congress, which began to translate into action toward a binary chemical weapons program. Combined with the reports of chemical warfare in Iraq-Iran's war, the push began gaining momentum. The traditional doves in the Congress moved to stop the program's funding before production was initiated. On April 4, 1984, a controversial report, prepared by the Congressional Research Service, reached the House Foreign Affairs Committee. The Subcommittee on International Security and Scientific Affairs had requested this comprehensive study of the administration's plan for binary chemical weapons production to identify possible implications for chemical weapons proliferation. This study pointed out that a decision to modernize present U.S. offensive chemical warfare capability by producing binaries "undermines a variety of military, technical, political, psychological, and moral constraints that to date have generally inhibited countries from producing or using chemical weapons."[21]

This report suggested that binary chemical weapons were not as effective as unitary chemical weapons; that resumption of chemical weapons production would spark horizontal proliferation in other countries; increase vertical proliferation of the Soviet chemical stockpile; increase the production of defensive chemical programs, thus increasing the likelihood of the use of chemical weapons during a conflict; and result in greater terrorist access to binary chemical munitions. The language of this report led the readers to believe that U.S. troops would be more vulnerable in CB warfare conditions with binary weapon production than they would be without a retaliatory capability. What they avoided noticing was that global proliferation of CB weapons was going on with or without the U.S. binary chemical weapons program's assistance.

President Reagan stated his position on the chemical weapons modernization program to rebut the report's conclusions. He announced that the U.S. administration would present a draft chemical weapons ban treaty in Geneva but simultaneously called for congressional support for modernization of the chemical stockpile. He stated:

The United States must maintain a limited retaliatory capability until we achieve an effective ban. We must be able to deter a chemical attack against us or our allies. And without a modern and credible deterrent, the prospects for achieving a comprehensive ban would be nil. . . . If we're going to have a chemical warfare ban or treaty banning them, we've got to have something to bargain with. They [the Soviet Union] must know that the alternative to banning them is to then face the fact that we're going to build a deterrent.[22]

That same month, Vice President Bush presented a draft treaty that provided for a worldwide ban on the development, production, stockpiling, transfer, and use of chemical weapons to the CD in Geneva. The Soviet Union dismissed the treaty immediately, continuing to push their stand on voluntary disclosures and invited on-site inspection teams, modeled much after the BWC language. This continued to be the main sticking point between the United States and the Soviet Union positions over the next year, as the two nations' representatives debated over exactly how verification of chemical weapon sites in each other's countries would take place.

## CHEMICAL CORPS RESURGENCE

The deployment of active duty chemical units continued at an unprecedented rate, as every active division in the Army continued to receive chemical soldiers and equipment (see Table 6.2, Figure 6.1). This capability greatly increased the opportunity for combat units to include chemical defense units in their field exercises and deployments to the National Training Center. Prior to 1979, this was possible only for short durations as reserve chemical units went through their two-week active duty annual requirements, and then only for certain active duty units whose training schedules could take advantage of those reserve units' training cycles. Initially, there were problems developing commanders of these new active duty chemical defense companies. Junior officers and noncoms were inexperienced in commanding the chemical defense units to fully support combat operations and lacked knowledgeable senior leaders. Many of the new officers had served in transportation, military intelligence, or other specialties and were rebranched and retrained to supplement the Corps. In the same vein, brigade and division commanders had no feel for how to incorporate the units into their operations. Most had never seen chemical officers, let alone chemical defense units, making it difficult to develop realistic training for nonchemical soldiers.

The first batch of chemical defense units were division-level chemical decontamination companies. Since no practical methods of simulating CB agent attacks during training exercises existed, decon units were often used as military car washes. While it could be argued that this was good training for the chemical decon units, it had no value added to train the combat units about how decontamination operations would really occur in wartime. The mechanized smoke companies, when they joined the force, were often broken into separate platoons and sent to other posts to ensure all divisions had a mechanized smoke capability. The 172d Chemical Company (smoke) (mech), stationed at Fort Carson, had one platoon at Fort Riley. The 164th Chemical Company (smoke) (mech), stationed at Fort Lewis, had a smoke platoon at the National Training Center. These smoke units often had to fight the combat arms operations cells to be used as tactical smoke units rather than being used as artillery smoke simulators. The School had to adapt its training to develop leaders that would proactively use chemical units in the best possible way, supporting combat operations. Simultaneously, the School would develop a course for senior leadership to learn about NBC defense operations and chemical defense unit employment.

In June 1984, the Chemical School held a functional area review for the Army DCSPER to examine how chemical personnel would fit into the ranks. In August, the Army Vice Chief of Staff, General Max Thurman, called for a functional area assessment to reconsider the future role of the Chemical Corps. That September,

**Table 6.2**
**Active Duty Chemical Units (Re)Activated 1979–90**

| Division | Chemical Unit | Date Activated |
|---|---|---|
| 1st Cavalry Div. | 68th Chem. Co. (Hvy Div) | Jul. 1, 1979 |
| 82d Airborne Div. | 21st Chem. Co. (Smoke/Decon) | Sep. 16, 1979 |
| 3d Armored Div. | 22d Chem. Co. (Hvy Div) | Sep. 21, 1979 |
| 8th Infantry Div. | 25th Chem. Co. (Hvy Div) | Sep. 21, 1979 |
| 1st Armored Div. | 69th Chem. Co. (Hvy Div) | Sep. 21, 1979 |
| 3d Infantry Div. | 92d Chem. Co. (Hvy Div) | Sep. 21, 1979 |
| 101st Airborne Div. | 63d Chem. Co. (Smoke/Decon) | Mar. 1, 1980 |
| 1st Infantry Div. | 12th Chem. Co. (Hvy Div) | Mar. 1, 1980 |
| 2d Armored Div. | 44th Chem. Co. (Hvy Div) | Mar. 1, 1980 |
| III Corps | 181st Chem. Co. (Corps/TA) | Sep. 1, 1980 |
| V Corps | 10th Chem. Co. (Corps) | Sep. 16, 1980 |
| VII Corps | 11th Chem. Co. (Corps/TA) | Sep. 16, 1980 |
| V Corps | 95th Chem. Co. (Corps/TA) | Sep. 16, 1980 |
| III Corps | 172d Chem. Co. (Smoke) (Mech) | Mar. 1, 1981 |
| 9th Infantry Div. | 9th Chem. Co. (Motorized) | Sep. 1, 1981 |
| 4th Infantry Div. | 31st Chem. Co. (Hvy Div) | Sep. 1, 1981 |
| III Corps | 46th Chem. Co. (Smoke) (Mech) | Sep. 1, 1981 |
| III Corps | 84th Chem. Co. (Smoke) (Mech) | Sep. 1, 1981 |
| 24th Infantry Div. | 91st Chem. Co. (Hvy Div) | Sep. 1, 1981 |
| I Corps | 164th Chem. Co. (Smoke) (Mech) | Sep. 1, 1981 |
| XVIII Abn. Corps | 101st Chem. Co. (Decon) | Aug. 16, 1983 |
| 5th Infantry Div. | 45th Chem. Co. (Hvy Div) | Sep. 1, 1983 |
| I Corps | 813th Chem. Co. (Corps/TA) | Oct. 1, 1984 |
| 10th Mountain Div. | 59th Chem. Co. (Smoke/Decon) | Mar. 16, 1985 |
| 25th Infantry Div. | 71st Chem. Co. (Smoke/Decon)* | Oct. 16, 1986 |
| V Corps | 13th Chem. Co. (Decon) | Sep. 16, 1987 |
| 7th Infantry Div. | 761st Chem. Co. (Smoke/Decon) | Oct. 1, 1987 |
| 8th Army | 23d Chemical Battalion (HHD) | Sep. 20, 1988 |

* Actually the first smoke/decon unit. Other dual units activated prior to 1986 were decon units refitted as dual-purpose (S/D). "Lineage and Honors," Army Chemical Journal, Spring 1986, p. 15.

**Figure 6.1**
**Growth of the Army Chemical Corps versus the Total Army, 1968–90**

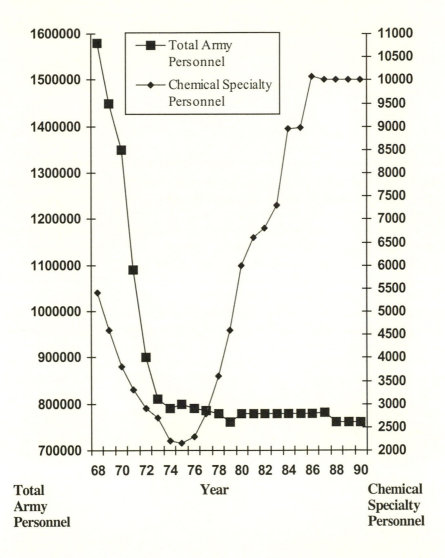

the Army conducted another Chemical System Program Review, a total analysis review to consider every chemical unit in the force structure. This review provided approval for a Table of Operations and Equipment (TO&E) for a heavy division chemical company, which included the mechanized smoke platoons, dual purpose smoke/decontamination companies for "light" infantry units, and an NBC reconnaissance company for the heavy division cavalry squadron HQ unit. These organizational changes were based on the new smoke generator system (the M157) that allowed smoke on the move, the Army's acquisition of the HMMWV, and the NBC reconnaissance vehicle (still under development). They also recommended adding two M17 Lightweight Decontamination Systems to every Army battalion.[23]

The Chemical School released several new doctrinal publications in 1984, reflecting the official adoption of new doctrine developed over the years since 1979. This included a draft FM 3-5, *NBC Decontamination*, in January (final in November); FM 3-100, *NBC Operations*, and FM 3-4, *NBC Protection* in March; FM 3-87, *Chemical Units* in June; and FM 3-3, *Contamination Avoidance* in September. These documents represented strong, field-oriented use of NBC defense doctrine, heavy in operational language and less focused on technical matters. With this new doctrine and new chemical units in place, and new equipment due out to the Army, the Chemical Corps was ready to stand up once again as a full branch of the military. Not everyone was celebrating. Many critics saw the old specter of unrestrained NBC warfare research and development funds rising, and they were very vocal in expressing this view. Rather than acknowledging that the Army was correcting a dangerous weakness, they chose to see this effort as increasing the chance of chemical warfare.

Despite the naysayers, the Chemical Corps was firmly on its way toward a new position in the Army. It now had the correct force structure, backing from the combat arms branches on how NBC defense should be integrated into military operations, and a strong equipment modernization effort underway. There were continuing challenges ahead; Congress had not yet authorized binary chemical weapons production; the combat divisions still were feeling their way into the new NBC defense doctrine, training, and organization; and the ongoing defense program had yet to produce a new protective mask, new chemical detectors, and new decontamination devices. And speaking of dreams of all the new equipment, designed to make CB warfare irrelevant to the soldier, where were all the promised technological miracle cures?

# CHAPTER 7

# Reconnaissance, Detection, and Identification

> Avoidance is the most important fundamental of NBC Defense. In addition to the casualties an attack can cause, the contamination that may come with an attack also causes casualties and produces long-term hazards that can interfere with the mission. Overcoming these hazards can tie up tremendous amounts of labor and equipment. Finding the clean areas when the mission allows reduces casualties and saves resources.
>
> —FM 3-100, *NBC Operations*, 1985

In January 1981 the Defense Science Board released a report on the status of chemical warfare readiness in the armed forces. They recommended that the Joint Chiefs of Staff form a task force to develop joint doctrine for conducting operations in a contaminated environment. There was an urgent need, in their estimation, to evaluate the impact of individual protective equipment on military operations. They also recommended that the Undersecretary of Defense, Research and Engineering develop a prioritized list of R&D defense programs for acceleration and review and report on the four services' NBC research and development efforts to remove needless impediments.[1] Specific recommendations of their report emphasized the need to develop a chemical monitor to determine the extent of equipment/personnel contamination; to develop a program that could test water and food for contamination; to address a lack of fixed, semifixed, and tactical collective protection systems; and to ensure effective patient decontamination. Special emphasis was needed to develop more sensitive chemical agent detectors that detected all agents and false-alarmed less often, which would provide soldiers with a more sufficient warning time to allow for donning protective suits.

Detection devices have always played an important role in the Chemical Corps's history, as one of the two most demanded functions of chemical defense (the other being individual protection). The ability to determine whether an area is clear of invisible CB agents could mean the difference between a fully capable force and a combat-ineffective force. Obviously, a good mask and protective suit are no good if one is not warned in time. Equally important is identifying what exact CB agent was used and if it still remained, so soldiers could get out of protective suits after the agent dissipated.

Between 1917 and 1968, this field of expertise was reserved for the specialists of the Chemical Corps. After the disestablishment proceedings settled, the Chemical Corps leadership pushed to develop detection devices that all troops could use with little training, thus reducing the chemical specialist manpower requirements and as well as giving every soldier an ability to determine his or her own risk. Detection and identification equipment became more simplified, while chemical specialists focused on reconnaissance and monitoring roles. The budget for reconnaissance, detection, and identification (RDI) programs quickly grew to over a third of the total program budget. Developing CB agent detectors was not without some rancor, as the desire to meet high technical requirements (highly sensitive equipment that had zero false alarms) ran counter to operational field demands (such as ruggedness, low weight, and low cost).

Chemical and biological agent detectors use similar principles of operation. A military force benefits the most from identifying the agents that are being employed against them, either before these agents cause casualties or immediately after (hopefully before). If one knew what CB agent was being used, one could predict the duration of the hazard and take appropriate actions. At first this was done by using the human nose. Since chemical agents were often impure and had to be used in large quantities for lethal effect, soldiers literally smelled low levels of phosgene (fresh-mown hay) or mustard (garlic) and were able to raise the alarm before lethal levels swept in. The M1 gas alarm was a hollow horseshoe-shaped tube hung from a wire that was rung like a dinner bell (but requiring far more urgent actions than arriving for dinner on time). Chemical specialists determined type and quantity of agents remaining after an attack, usually through manual chemistry kits, and could announce the "all clear."

As the major chemical warfare agents became relatively well understood (into World War II), soldiers used manual measures such as the M4 mustard vapor kit and M6 liquid vesicant detector paper to quickly identify the liquids and gases. Chemical specialists used M7A1 vesicant detector crayons and paint that turned color when liquid chemical agent splashed on it (both used at chemical weapons depots to detect leaks). Ideally, automated air samplers should be able to provide more protection in a small area, and a network of detectors could provide even more warning than individual soldiers with kits. Because they are more sophisticated and expensive (and therefore fewer), automatic point detectors and detectors that can identify agents at a distance (standoff detectors) became the specialist's tools. Last, CB agent monitors determine when soldiers can remove their protective masks, when they can safely cross formerly contaminated terrain, and when soldiers can verify that decontaminated equipment is clean without fear of further casualties.

As one can see, there are a number of different requirements for detection, to include early warning detection, reconnaissance, identification, and monitoring post-attack presence of solid, liquid and vapor chemical and biological warfare agents.  Some of these requirements required a great deal of precision (for specialists) or they demanded a cheap and easy solution (for non-specialists).  As it is impossible to design one detector for so many technical and operational requirements, this meant there would be demands for a large number of programs.  As a result, the budget associated with this commodity area accounts for nearly half of the entire CB defense program.

## RDI PROGRAMS PRIOR TO 1975

Before 1945, the most accurate warning of chemical agents still came from an individual's physical senses.  The smell of garlic during an artillery attack indicated mustard agent, geraniums lewisite, and fresh-mown hay, phosgene, warning soldiers to mask.  Identification kits used after an attack were largely manual chemistry sets that required a trained operator to test for a variety of agents.  The chemical agent detectors, for instance, relied on a trained human operator manually pumping air through several silica gel-filled glass tubes, each one filled with a specific reagent to detect different chemical agents.  The wax from a chemical agent crayon would change color if it touched chemical agent leaking from a munition.  Detector paper, similar to litmus paper, changes color when contacting chemical agents.  These were considered adequate until nerve agents and biological agents arrived, which called for early preattack warnings before lethal levels overwhelmed the fighting force.

Initial efforts focused on three areas: improving detector paper, developing specific 1½-inch long glass detector tubes with silica gel absorbents, and developing enzyme tickets.  Most of these yielded a color change when exposed to agent.  This technology led to the M9A2 chemical agent detector kit (a lightweight kit for chemical specialists in the field), the M10A1 chemical agent analyzer kit (a suitcase-sized field lab for technical intelligence personnel), and the M12 agent sampling kit (to take soil and water samples for detailed analysis).

There was a long debate in the late 1950s in the CB defense community about whether common soldiers (the nonspecialists) should have any access to automatic chemical vapor detectors.  Scenarios of Soviet bombers and artillery laying down massive clouds of nerve agents drove two differing views.  One side thought that soldiers needed a capability to detect the relatively new nerve agents in concentrations low enough that would allow them to mask, prior to their suffering any casualties, and that would allow them to unmask and resume combat operations once agent vapors dissipated.  This was the instinctive thought of most military analysts.  Others warned that, if soldiers could not determine the difference between false alarms and real alarms, their confidence in all chemical defense equipment would ebb.  Soldiers might ignore automatic alarms after hearing a few false alarms, making them more vulnerable to real chemical agent attacks.

Doctrine during World War II had specified the responsibilities for gas sentries based on experiences of the Great War. These included "not passing on alarms arising in other areas, but will give the alarm only when he himself detects the presence of chemical agents. A false alarm in many cases may be worse than giving no alarm at all."[2] It might be better that only specialists make the determination of whether there were CB warfare agents present. After all, the first warning of an enemy machine gun nest was often casualties falling from a hail of bullets. Given scenarios envisioning heavy clouds of nerve agents sweeping the battlefields, the first school of thought won out—but not much more thought was given to balancing soldiers' reactions to false alarms versus how sensitive the detector should be, given the strong desire for minimal casualties.

The last general chemistry kits developed prior to 1973 were the AN-M2 water testing and screening kit and M18A1 chemical agent detector kit, type-classified in 1958 and 1964 respectively.[3] Both required a relatively moderate amount of training, both were used to identify the agent after it was employed, and both took up to half an hour to determine results (testing for all agents). They were very sensitive and detected low levels of all the chemical warfare agents, but what the common soldier required was a simpler and quicker method of detection. Initially, this was provided by chemical agent-sensitive paper such as M6A1 paper. This used a basic litmus test approach of observing a color change upon contact with liquid chemical agents. M6A1 paper turned color when contacting liquid nerve or blister agents (same color for both agents, good for warning but not identification). In January 1964 the United States, Canada, and the United Kingdom developed a book of M8 paper to identify liquid contamination. One book of M8 paper held twenty-five slips of 4-inch by 2.5-inch dye-impregnated papers. Red colors indicated mustard agent; yellow meant G-nerve agents; and blue indicated V-nerve agents. This was not foolproof, however; other chemical liquids, such as acids, antifreeze, and insecticides could cause similar color changes. In addition, soldiers required detectors for gaseous agents as well as liquid agents.

Beginning about 1963, Edgewood Arsenal began work on a simpler vapor detection kit that would identify chemical agents at low dosage levels, primarily to replace the M18A1 detector kits. The design focused on developing a disposable sampler/detector that would use color-change indications to identify nerve, blood, and blister agent vapors in the air. The kit consisted of a small plastic box containing a dozen expendable vapor sampler/detectors and M8 paper. Each sampler was a plastic five-by-eight-inch card with four exposed filter paper areas, and sealed ampules of various liquid chemical reagents channeled to flow onto the paper areas, once broken by the operator. This became the M256 chemical detection kit program, type-classified in June 1977.[4] Still, the M8 paper and M256 kit were manually operated, meaning the soldier was verifying the presence of chemical agent (or lack thereof), rather than providing early warning indications.

With the increased lethalities of nerve agents, commanders wanted to minimize any chance that their force would be affected, since any moderate exposure would now kill rather than incapacitate (as with mustard agent or phosgene). They wanted 100 percent of their force prepared for combat, and any decrease in their force meant a drop in the odds against the enemy. Because chemical vapor clouds could be as large as miles or as small as a hundred yards (but as lethal), every squad and company in the Army wanted a chemical detection capability. Obviously, there weren't that many chemical specialists. The optimum solution was a continuously sensing automatic point detector for the field units to operate as they maneuvered against the enemy, always sniffing the air, protecting them from invisible threats before they struck.

The problem in developing the ideal automatic agent detector was the degree of confidence and risk to which the combat and materiel developers were aiming. Automatic detectors manned by front-line units had to be hand-carried and thus portable (the lighter the better), and run on batteries rather than an electrical generator, which eliminated more sophisticated devices. Ideally, a detector would alarm to sublethal levels of CB agents 100 percent of the time and would never false alarm when CB agents were not present. The degree of risk to the soldier, combined with the technological limitations of detection equipment, determined the low end of this detection range. The guidance for developing an automatic chemical agent point detector, then, might be to alarm to vapors at a certain toxic level, allowing all soldiers within 150 meters to mask and suffer no ill effect other than some stinging to the eyes. This might correspond to an incapacitating dose level that would affect less than 5 percent of the force, or an $ICt_5$ level. This level of risk was much lower than the amount of chemical agent required to create 50 percent casualties ($LCt_{50}$). Last, as there had to be tens of thousands of these detectors across the battlefield, they had to be relatively inexpensive.

The Edgewood developers tried to accommodate all these operational requests. Technology simply would not allow the best of all worlds; zero risk to soldiers, zero false alarms, low weight, low power requirements, detection on-the-move, low cost, and ruggedness. There had to be a compromise, either in technical or operational requirements. The challenge with a zero casualty-risk approach is that the detector must be very sensitive to identify trace levels of chemical agents. Because the chemical detector must alarm within seconds, it usually does not key on the exact chemical structure of the warfare agent; rather, it focuses on some physical property such as organophospate radicals on nerve agents, the weight of the chemical molecules, or the breakdown products of blister agents. As a result, it might alarm to any chemical vapor with a similar physical pattern. This might include purple smoke, burning gunpowder, diesel fumes, and organic compounds (such as those found in field hospitals).

To avoid the interferent problem, the labs had to call for the combat developers to raise the level of risk or raise the cost of individual detectors. Expensive detectors were out, competing against the big five modernization programs (Abrams tank, Bradley vehicle, Blackhawk helicopter, HMMWV, and MLRS). Another alternative was fielding lots of inexpensive detectors that positively identified a heavy chemical agent concentration prior to warning troops to avoid false alarms. Allowing detection at higher agent concentrations meant increased risk to some proportion of the soldiers and certain casualties, but every time that detector sounded, the alarm was *real*. On the other hand, emphasizing zero casualties as a priority called for sensitive detection of trace agent levels, which meant more false alarms but time for everyone to mask. Since the combat leadership refused to accept any increased casualties due to CB agent attacks and refused to fund expensive detection systems, the Chemical Corps made the decision that combat units would have to accept a certain number of false alarms. This solution caused frustration as the soldiers had to mask up and get into protective clothes for both real and false alarms.

The Edgewood labs had produced an automatic alarm system for G-agents called the M5 automatic alarm in August 1958, used strictly at the chemical weapon depots and stockpiles. This device drew in air through a wetted tape and identified changes in reflectance (this was called the Shoenemann Reaction), noting G-nerve agents down to 0.4 milligrams per cubic meter. It was not rugged or lightweight enough for general field use by combat units (the M5 weighed 725 pounds and stood 79 inches tall). Developing a practical field automatic alarm had become feasible beginning in the mid-1960s and was spurred by the use of nerve agents in the Yemeni Civil War in 1967–68. By 1969 Edgewood Arsenal had developed and type-classified a rugged, lightweight automatic chemical agent point detector. The M8 Automatic Chemical Agent Alarm was a two-piece system composed of an M43 agent detector, which used a wet-chemistry electrolysis reaction to detect nerve agent, choking agent, and blood agent vapors at levels under human threshold.[5] This reaction would electronically trigger an M42 audio and/or visual alarm, giving a soldier between 15 and 90 seconds to don a protective mask before dangerous agent levels built up (depending on the agent and wind speed). With its battery, the M8 alarm weighed twenty pounds.

The M8 chemical agent alarm wasn't perfect—it false-alarmed to gunpowder, purple-smoke grenades, diesel fuels, and other battlefield interferents. Because it relied on a wet chemistry reaction, it could not be relied on in climates under 32°F unless a winterization kit was used. Its M229 liquid chemical cell and BA3517/U battery required replacement every twelve hours. Yet it was the first point detector that could alert field troops to sublethal chemical agent levels while running automatically and unmanned. The basis of issue was roughly one per squad or section, allowing a platoon or company to string several around its perimeter to account for changes in wind direction. It could be strapped to a rucksack frame and carried by soldiers on foot, or mounted on vehicles and run off the vehicle's battery power.[6] Chemical weapon stockpile sites began using the M8 alarm in 1969, and combat units began receiving the system in 1972. The chemical weapon stockpile sites did not stop using rabbits in cages as the ultimate sensitive detector, however, until the early 1980s (rabbits were more sensitive to potential low-level agent leaks and required less maintenance).

Many thought more was required than the one minute of warning given by these point detectors. Standoff detection was the ideal solution to a true early warning requirement. If a chemical reconnaissance team could spot a chemical or biological agent cloud miles away but moving toward friendly forces, they could warn troops far in advance of its arrival. By "seeing" where the CB agent clouds drifted, maneuver forces could avoid contaminated ground. The difficulty was in the ability to discriminate between a CB agent cloud and the normal environmental background. For chemical agent standoff detection, Edgewood scientists used active infrared sensors to identify and categorize potential chemical vapors against the horizon. This technology could confuse smoke clouds or dust clouds with chemical agent vapor, if the data were not screened carefully. It also could not detect liquid agent contamination on the ground, or give an estimate of the distance of the vapor cloud (only a compass bearing).

This led to the development in the early 1950s of the Long Path Infra-Red (LOPAIR) chemical agent detector; a tripod-mounted, generator-powered, active infrared scanner. It detected chemical agents by bouncing infrared light off a reflector and reading any changes in spectral patterns; it also required a stationary point to operate. This made it potentially valuable for depots and rear area detection, but not the battlefield. Getting this detector to reliably discriminate between chemical warfare agent vapor clouds and normal gases in the atmosphere kept it in research and development for a decade, and estimated costs grew rapidly from $25,000 to $45,000 per detector. The Army produced sixteen LOPAIR systems for testing and use at the chemical munitions depots before they stopped the program in 1966. The standoff program continued as the XM21 Remote Sensing Chemical Agent Alarm (RSCAAL). To discard the reflector requirement (impractical for battlefield applications), the Edgewood scientists developed a passive infrared scanner rather than LOPAIR's active infrared scanner. This would eventually mature into a similar tripod-mounted detector, weighing nearly seventy pounds and requiring a generator for power consumption of over sixty watts. As the funds dried up after 1973, the program slowed to a grinding halt.

Interest in biological detection programs was accelerated after an Army briefing to the Assistant Secretary of Defense in the early 1960s reported that there were no biological agent detectors, primarily due to technical challenges of the time. Before this, only Fort Detrick was conducting some in-house biodefense work. It was not the lack of a known threat that was retarding progress; biological warfare agents were known to be weaponized since World War II. The challenge was that there were so many distinct and different biological warfare agents, as compared to the (relatively) few and well-understood classes of chemical warfare agents. Chemical agents attacked within seconds to minutes; biological agents took hours or days to weeks to indicate their presence. It was impossible prior to 1970 to develop a "real-time" field biological agent detector similar to chemical agent detectors, either as a point or standoff detection system, so very little effort was being put into this particular R&D program area.

Biological agent detection is much more difficult than chemical agent detection, requiring different technical and doctrinal approaches. With the exception of the flu and cold season, few people appreciate how much organic material is in the air normally, such as pollen, not to mention the thousands of different viruses, bacteria, and rickettsia. Most of these biological organisms are harmless to humans, but any biological detector must sort through the harmless organisms and the harmful organisms prior to alarming. Because of the variety, the accepted doctrine for biological agent detection was to collect samples of dead animals, food, and water, or blood samples from soldiers (friendly and enemy) for tests by medical specialists. Detection and identification could be performed only after an attack, often requiring transportation to a sophisticated laboratory and 24–48 hours time to culture the samples. Up to 1968, the goal of fielding a battlefield-survivable, automatic biological agent detector was just too difficult, and therefore it was not attempted until inquiries into the lack of such detectors initiated stronger actions.

A point or standoff biological agent detector must establish a background signature for that particular environment (wherever it is employed in the world), monitor for a sudden increase in organic material (ideally both dry and liquid biological warfare agents), identify it as a potential biological warfare agent, and then sound its alarm. More difficult was the operational requirement to conduct this testing quickly with a small number of organisms, prior to that biological agent's ability to infect a host. The minimum time to run this cycle in the late 1960s was forty-five minutes to an hour. If the chances for a false alarm were high for chemical agent detectors, they were downright astronomical for early biological agent detectors. There were just too many different biological warfare agents with unique characteristics that made it very difficult, if not impossible, to develop a generic automatic biological agent detector. This philosophy can be summarized as "detect to treat" as opposed to "detect to warn" the soldiers; not an optimal arrangement but a very practical and executable option.

Edgewood Arsenal began investigating a number of technologies to start this development, to include protein detectors, fluorescent antibody staining techniques, chemiluminescence, and ultraviolet fluorescence. Of the many methods, chemiluminescence proceeded out of research into advanced development (prototype hardware in 1970–71). With the halt in 1972, all efforts were stalled. The Chemical Corps issued manual biological sampling kits to field units, which allowed soldiers to take samples of suspected contaminated water and soil. These samples would be tagged and transported to forward laboratories for further culturing and identification. This, combined with medical evaluation of environmental hazards and troop fitness, would constitute the sole biological agent detection program for decades. At the time the Army leadership didn't see any real threat emerging other than the Soviet Union. Some probably thought (along with naive politicians of the time) that since the United States had abandoned BW agents, the Soviet Union had abandoned that course as well.

## RDI PROGRAMS, 1975–85

After receiving much-needed funding boosts in 1976, Edgewood's Chemical Systems Laboratory (CSL) worked hard on producing the M256 detector kit (fielded in 1977), and developing requirements for a new point chemical agent detector and a biological agent detector program. CSL had begun plans in 1975 to develop a prototype field automatic biological agent detector by 1977. The Biological Detection and Warning System (BDWS) was a two-piece system, consisting of an aerosol sampler (XM2) and an automatic protein-sensing detector (XM19). The technical approach taken used chemiluminescence to detect possible biological agents in a liquid sample, requiring approximately forty-five minutes to process and identify biological agents per sample. Operational tests demonstrated a poor reliability, a very limited detection capability to detect more than a few known biological warfare agents, and a high false alarm rate. The system had to be hauled in a trailer due to its size, weight, and power requirements (one 110 volt, 60 Hertz generator), and it required high maintenance. Although there was no fielded biological agent detector at the time, the Chemical School decided to terminate the program in May 1983, rather than to let a potentially faulty system enter the field. The Edgewood lab was instructed to examine different technical approaches consistent with a reevaluation of the biological threat and concept of operations, such as mass spectroscopy.

HQ AMCCOM called for a replacement to the high-maintenance, inconsistently alarming M8 automatic chemical agent alarm. This requirement became one of the first joint service NBC defense programs in November 1978, calling for a man-portable detector with a surface-sampling capability, detecting nerve, mustard, and lewisite agents. The joint service program evolved into the XM22 Automatic Chemical Agent Detector and Alarm (ACADA), which the Army planned to field to its units in 1989. In the meantime, the Edgewood engineers would have to improve the M8 detector.

In their efforts to improve the M8 detector's specificity and maintenance issues, Edgewood engineers modified technology from the Air Force ionization detector set (IDS) and developed the M43A1 chemical agent detector (fielded in 1984).[7] This interim measure replaced the M43 detector's wet chemistry cell with a dry americium-241 (beta emitter) radioactive isotope. The detector cell identified chemical warfare agents by electric current changes caused by ionized molecules; this was much easier to maintain and much more reliable with a higher sensitivity and quicker response time. The M43A1 detector was approximately the same size and weight as the M43 detector it replaced and used the same M42 visual/audio alarm (the two creating the M8A1 alarm system). The new M43A1 agent detector would still not detect mustard agent, since the main intent of the detector was to redesign the maintenance requirements, not redefine the original operational requirements.[8]

To detect liquid persistent chemical agents (both nerve and blister agents), CSL developed the XM86 Automatic Liquid Agent Detector (ALAD) detector unit and XM85 central alarm unit in 1980. The detector unit's major component was a number of four-inch-diameter disks with an electrical current running through them, mounted to a rectangular casing. Chemical agent drops, as small as 400 micrometers, vaporized on the disk and caused a unique physical chemical reaction with a special resin on the disk. The electronic disturbance would cause the alarm to sound and sent a radio signal to the main central unit. Initial tests were very positive, to the extent of discriminating chemical agent liquids from both natural and man-made liquids in a combat environment, even during wet weather conditions.

M9 paper was a spinoff of the M8 paper concept. M9 paper was a 30-foot long roll of two-inch wide dye-impregnated sticky paper that also acted as a litmus test for liquid chemical agents. Its adhesive backing allowed soldiers to rip off sections of the paper to be stuck to vehicles, wrapped around one's arms or legs on the uniform, or on a radio antenna. It provided a quick, inexpensive first indication of liquid mustard or nerve agents. When the green-dyed paper contacted a liquid chemical agent (nerve or mustard), the detector paper would turn from green to pink or red. It was not foolproof—as with M8 paper, diesel fuel, insecticides, and polyethylene glycol (antifreeze) could also cause a similar indication. It was, however, a very visible indication of whether soldier had walked through contaminated terrain.

Edgewood engineers obtained the British Chemical Agent Monitors (CAMs) for test and evaluation in 1982 (the United Kingdom Ministry of Defense R&D program was initiated in 1979). This device drew vapors into a chamber, ionized gas molecules, and measured the time required for clusters of molecules to drift across the chamber (ion mobility spectroscopy, or IMS).[9] A simple computer memory would match this against mustard and nerve vapor signatures and could quantify the relative amount of vapor in bars (one bar being low, eight bars being high). As a lightweight, hand-operated detector that identified very low levels of nerve or mustard vapors within seconds, it seemed an ideal tool for monitoring personnel and equipment for residual contamination. Its only drawbacks were that it was not an automatic detector; had to be manually switched from nerve to mustard agent detection (i.e., it could only sniff one agent or the other); had a potential for being overwhelmed by excessive vapors, flooding its sensitive detection cells; and utilized a nonstandard nickel-lithium cell battery. After nearly two years of operational testing and evaluation, the Chemical School decided that it was interested in pursuing the program.

Edgewood scientists worked to improve the 1970s-era M256 chemical agent detector kit. The M256A1 kit, fielded in 1985, had ten times the sensitivity of its predecessor for nerve agents, which made it more sensitive than even the new M8A1 alarms. Each small box held twelve samplers and a package of M8 paper, like its predecessor. Using the M256A1 kit became the absolute indicator for clean air used by soldiers prior to taking off their masks. These three items (M8 paper, M9 paper, and M256A1 kit) constitute the primary manual detectors used by the common soldier even today for immediate warning and identification of chemical warfare agents. Also in the works was a new water-testing kit to replace the AN-M2 water-testing kit, titled the XM272 water test kit. Program goals included increasing the reliability and breadth of detection capabilities for waterborne chemical agents, to include hydrogen cyanide, mustard, lewisite, and all the nerve agents. Medical units and water purification units would use the kit to test and monitor water sources after chemical attacks. Initial incompatibilities with detecting lewisite and VX in chlorinated water slowed the engineering tests, delaying the release of the kit to the mid-1980s.

The Army continued to test and evaluate the XM21 RSCAAL. Developers continued to hit technical problems of discriminating chemical agent vapor from other interferents, such as direct heat from the sun, smoke, fog, sandstorms, etc. The detector could not determine whether an agent cloud was one hundred yards away or two miles distant. It could not operate in a moving vehicle, requiring a stable tripod mount. Since the program's reinitiation in 1978, it continued to be plagued by limited successes in overcoming these technical issues. The weight (over fifty pounds), power requirements (separate generator), and inability to detect on the move made some question its effectiveness for combat units and suggested redirection to a fixed site concept. These issues threatened to stop the program in 1982. The Army ordered the development of a special project office to provide intensive management to accelerate the program, but not before the program undertook a severe funding cut in FY83. In response, the project office presented a special field demonstration to the Assistant Secretary of the Army for RDA and key members of the House Armed Services Committee staff. Based on this demonstration, Congress reauthorized funds for the program in FY84.

The XM21 RSCAAL had initiated thoughts about standoff biological agent detection. All biological material contains the amino acid tryptophan, which, when irradiated by an intense source of electromagnetic radiation, fluoresces. This fluorescence would be captured by a remote monitor or signal processor. The problem was selectivity—if all biological organisms had this amino acid, how would one identify just the biological warfare agents? Scientists initiated tests with infrared or ultraviolet light detection, both as light detection and ranging (LIDAR) technologies, programs then under review at Los Alamos National Laboratory and Southern Research Institute (SRI) International.

The search for a modern NBC reconnaissance capability received strong support throughout the Army, especially from combat units in Europe. Chemical personnel in jeeps performing reconnaissance on the front lines was definitely not the optimal solution. M151 jeeps and M113 Armored Personnel Carriers (APCs) could not perform NBC reconnaissance on the move, did not have collective protection for their crew, and did not incorporate the necessary equipment for detection and collection of samples. In short, it amounted to vulnerable vehicles carrying specialists that were forced to remain in full protective gear for hours, stopping occasionally to allow personnel to step out with M8 paper on a stick to check for contamination.

The Armor School helped draft the requirement for an NBC reconnaissance vehicle in 1982, as the proponent for the armored cavalry reconnaissance squadrons. The Army began an evaluation of a customized M113A2 APC coupled with the German MM-1 mass spectrometer detector, a collective protection system, and assorted NBC agent sensors. Another option was the German Fuchs NBC reconnaissance system (an armored, six-wheeled troop vehicle) under development in the German Army. The Armor Center (and some in the Chemical School) disliked the concept of a wheeled armored vehicle, and argued forcefully for the APC-tracked option. In 1982 the Chemical School recommended the German Fuchs to the TRADOC commander, General William Richardson, who approved the Fuchs concept. In 1984, after his retirement, the requirement reverted back to the M113A2 option as the XM87 NBCRS program. The plan was to field a number of these APC versions by 1989, and improve the capability by transitioning to a Bradley Infantry Fighting Vehicle or HMMWV M998 chassis in 1992.

Table 7.1 summarizes and compares the detection levels of the various detectors developed over the decades. It should be noted that while the detectors may not be sensitive enough to sample at the permissive exposure limits for nerve and mustard agents (allowable exposure for peacetime), they all meet the requirement to sense agents prior to reaching the incapacitating and lethal agent levels. With the help from Britain, Canada, and other friendly countries, the United States was catching up on a decade of neglect in detection technology. While the automated CB detectors may not have been ready, any individual soldier could now detect and identify chemical agents in his/her vicinity. Combined with the NATO Warning and Reporting System, these individual soldiers would generate the data for division and corps chemical cells to identify and plot the extent of enemy chemical attacks.

The trick was knowing which detector to use and when to use it; vapor detectors and liquid detectors were required for early warning, and soldiers had to use manual M256 kits to double-check the automatic alarms against false alarms. Reconnaissance required different detectors, biologicals required different detectors, and to compound the difficulties, the four services were all using different systems for the same purposes. Very quickly, the number of CB agent detectors available in the inventory began to overwhelm even the specialists' knowledge and the ability of logistics centers to support them.

**Table 7.1**
**Chemical Agent Detection Equipment Limits**

| | GB nerve agent | VX nerve agent | HD blister agent[10] | AC blood agent | Response Time |
|---|---|---|---|---|---|
| Permissive/airborne exposure limit | 0.001 mg-min/m³ | 0.00001 mg/m³ | 0.003 mg/m³ | 10 mg/m³ | |
| Incapacitating dose | 35 mg-min/m³ | 25 mg-min/m³ | 2,000 mg-min/m³ | 1,500 mg-min/m³ | |
| Lethal dose (inhalation) (skin) | 70 mg-min/m³ 1,700 mg-min/m³ | 30 mg-min/m³ 10 mg/70 kg man | 49 mg/70 kg man 10,000 mg-min/m³ | 2,500–5,000 mg-min/m³ | |
| M8 paper | 0.02 ml drops* | 0.02 ml drops* | 0.02 ml drops* | Does not detect | under thirty seconds |
| M9 paper | 0.01 ml drops* | 0.01 ml drops* | 0.01 ml drops* | Does not detect | under twenty seconds |
| M18A2 detector kit | 0.1 mg/m³ | 0.1 mg/m³ | 0.5 mg/m³ | 8.0 mg/m³ | 4 minutes per agent |
| M256 detector kit | 0.05 mg/m³ | 0.1 mg/m³ | 3.0 mg/m³ | 9.0 mg/m³ | under 15-20 minutes |
| M256A1 detector kit | 0.005 mg/m³ | 0.02 mg/m³ | 2.0 mg/m³ | 9.0 mg/m³ | under 15-20 minutes |
| M272 water test kit | 0.02 mg/liter* | 0.02 mg/liter* | 2.0 mg/liter* | 20.0 mg/m³ | 7 minutes per agent |
| ALAD | 0.02 ml drops* | 0.02 ml drops* | 0.02 ml drops | Does not detect | under 10-35 seconds |
| M8 detector | 0.5 mg/m³ | 0.5 mg/m³ | Does not detect | 9.0 mg/m³ | under two minutes |
| M8A1 detector | 0.1-0.2 mg/m³ | 0.4 mg/m³ | Does not detect | Does not detect | under two minutes |
| CAM | 0.03 mg/m³ | 0.01 mg/m³ | 0.01 mg/m³ | Does not detect | under one minute |
| ICAD | 0.2-0.5 mg/m³ | Does not detect | 10.0 mg/m³ | 50.0 mg/m³ | under two minutes |
| M21 RSCAAL | 3.0 mg/m³ | 3.0 mg/m³ | 150.0 mg/m³ | Does not detect | under one minute |
| MM-1 (M93 Fox) | 62 mg/m³ | 0.01 µg/liter* | 0.001 µg/liter* | 46 mg/m³ | under 45 seconds |

*Note:* Asterisk denotes liquid measures; all other measures are gaseous measures. mg - milligram, ml - milliliter, min - minute, m - meter, µg - microgram

*Source:* GulfLINK case narratives and other government sources.

# CHAPTER 8

# Individual Protection

Protecting yourself and your equipment is needed if contamination avoidance is not possible or practical. If the enemy can use NBC weapons, you must be prepared to protect yourself. You may become contaminated because you are directly engaged with NBC weapons, or your mission may require you to cross a contaminated area. Therefore, NBC protection must be an integral part of all operations.

—FM 3-100, *NBC Operations*, 1985

Because Edgewood Arsenal had been out of business for ten years, the Air Force, Navy, and Marine Corps took the opportunity to build up their own CB defense materiel programs. With the flush defense funds of the 1980s and emphasis on the Soviet threat fresh in their minds, all the armed services began producing their own unique protective masks, suits, agent detectors, collective protection systems, and decontamination programs. The Air Force Systems Command's (AFSC) Human Systems Division performed technology base research at Brooks Air Force Base (AFB), Texas, while their Aeronautical Systems Division completed the research through advanced development programs at Eglin AFB, Florida. Once the Air Force CB defense equipment was ready for production, the Air Force Logistics Command (AFLC, headquartered at Wright-Patterson AFB, Ohio) requisitioned and distributed the equipment to Air Force wings. Kelly AFB, near Brooks, and Warner-Robbins AFB, Georgia, conducted most of the maintenance work.

The Naval Surface Weapons Center at Dahlgren, Virginia, had the lead for most Navy technology base CB defense programs. Three systems commands (Naval Sea Systems Command—NAVSEA; Naval Air Systems Command —NAVAIR; and Naval Facilities Engineering Systems Command—NAVFAC) carried out their respective program management as their programs enter advanced development. NAVSEA carried the majority of Navy CB defense programs, to include individual protection and decontamination programs. NAVAIR focused on both Navy and Marine Corps aviator individual protection and aircraft CB defense programs (detection and decontamination). NAVFAC had responsibility for CB defense at ports and other ground facilities but often relied on Army collective protection and decontamination programs due to low funds and lower priority in comparison to its Navy siblings.

The Marine Corps Research, Development and Acquisition Command (MCRDAC) was responsible for overseeing all Marine CB defense programs, from technology base through production and fielding, through the Program Manager for Combat Service Support. While they were the least funded in comparison to the other services, their small staff of three began reviewing Army programs for applications to their needs and made their dollars stretch. Where the Army was not meeting their needs, they made it clear in no uncertain terms and pushed for their modifications. All these organizations competed with the Army's Chemical Research and Development Center's (CRDC) traditional CB defense systems (CSL was renamed to CRDC in 1983) for the sparse DoD funds.[1]

There were numerous examples of unnecessary duplication of effort about which people (to include the GAO) were commenting. The services claimed they could not count on the Army to develop their "service-unique" programs, while the Army retorted that the other services wouldn't pay their way for joint cooperation on Army programs. Both sides had their issues and non-issues. For example, the other services, lacking a full-time proponent such as the Chemical Corps, would not pay for a research and development program the size of the Army's, preferring to spend their funds on other major defense systems. This resulted in underfunded programs in the other services that detracted from Army and other limited joint service funds that were available. On the services' side, the Army often ignored their unique customer needs if this funding wasn't available. Also, the services complained that the Army testing and evaluation process was overly complicated, creating unnecessarily long delays in fielding equipment.

The four services attempted to bring their program efforts closer, without having to relinquish any control over their individual NBC defense equipment funds. The Joint Logistics Commanders (JLC), a group of four-star flag officers who headed their respective logistics branches, ran many joint service committees that worked throughout the year on bringing similar service programs together. In June 1984, a JLC action group headed by Colonel Pete Hidalgo (then AMC's top chemical officer) proposed that several chemical defense programs, to include collective protection systems, decontaminants, protective gloves, masks, and similar programs could be combined as joint programs. The action group, the Joint Panel on Chemical and Biological Defense (JP-CBD), became more involved as a forum for joint service discussions on development issues.[2]

That same summer, the Army DCSOPS approved a new Joint Service Agreement (JSA) on NBC defense research, development and acquisition, based on the DoDD 5180.2. This JSA was the charter for a second joint service group, titled the Joint Service Review Group (JSRG), which would discuss medical and nonmedical CB defense doctrine and program requirements. These groups set out with ambitious plans to move the DoD CB defense program forward as service partners. Without any incentives other than the spirit of teamwork, these joint panels often did not accomplish much. This can be seen most clearly in the area of individual protection programs, where the services tailored their protective suits and masks specifically to what they saw as service-unique mission requirements.

Individual protection programs include research and development into those devices that protect one's eyes and respiratory system (protective masks), and textiles that protects the skin (protective clothing). Ever since World War I and the use of mustard agent, this program area has always been near and dear to the common foot soldier. While they might not understand the nuances of automatic point detectors versus standoff detection systems, everyone understands that wearing protective ensembles means immediate survival on the contaminated battlefield. This was especially true all those who had taken a visit to the CS chamber to test their masks (note: we don't call it a gas chamber exercise anymore, it is politically correct to call it a "mask confidence exercise"). While CB detection programs account for half the R&D budget (largely because of the cost of technology), protective suits accounted for about a third of the overall DoD CB defense program. This wasn't because it was less important, just that the technology was simpler.

During World War II, a large number of the Chemical Warfare Service's field units focused on the maintenance and delivery of impregnated protective suits, as each suit had to be manually "laundered" to apply the impregnate. In addition to impregnated suits, there were impregnated underwear, gloves and socks, depending on the level of protection desired. Gas masks were often made of canvas fabric with glass lens, and their canisters were designed to filter mustard, phosgene, and cyanide-related compounds. After World War II, with the arrival of radioactive particles, nerve agents, and biological agents, everything had to be redesigned. Masks had to filter all CB agents and radioactive fallout. Protective suits had to resist liquid nerve agents, which were expected to arrive in overwhelming quantities, delivered by massive Soviet artillery and air barrages. This scenario drove a very robust program over the decades that focused almost entirely on the soldiers' survival, but not necessarily their ability to continue operations at full capacity in this lethal environment.

While combat arms leaders feel very strongly about minimizing risk to their troops, this is one time when they chose an increased risk of chemical agent exposure rather than an increased burden and decreased operational capability. Soldiers have always tried to minimize their combat load, for obvious reasons. You move slow, you become a better target. Hauling an oxygen tank around for CB agent exposure would have been too much weight, thus the negative pressure approach. Firefighters aren't being shot at (usually), and because of their much higher and more frequent exposure to dangerous fumes, they take the extra precautions. The same goes for protective suits. Wearing impermeable suits would be more protection against liquid nerve agents, but the soldiers would be able to run across a battlefield only for maybe a half hour before collapsing. Therefore, the combat arms demand a compromise; maximize the duration of use while minimizing the risk to acceptable levels, without causing their troops to become combat ineffective due to heat stress and overburdening. Still, the current compromise is no picnic. Soldiers still suffer physical and physiological stress when isolated in protective masks and suits, despite recent advances in technology.

As mentioned in chapter 6, the CANE and P2NBC2 studies measured the difficulties soldiers faced as they tried to carry out combat missions while wearing protective suits and masks. Protective suits and masks have always caused a sense of isolation from one's unit, dampening the individual's senses and ability to proactively execute offensive actions. It may be that this effect will never be overcome entirely, which is more the shame, as it probably is the number one reason why combat soldiers react so poorly when they face dealing with CB warfare. Many of them recall having to unmask in the CS gas chambers, or how hot they were wearing protective gear during military exercises, or how they couldn't talk over radios or even to individuals more than five feet away. Priorities in designing protective suits and masks, however, have always been on emphasizing protecting the individual soldier and still allowing the soldier to operate in a CB-contaminated environment with some impediments. Ideally, these suits should be manufactured within the cost restraints of equipping a force that potentially requires millions of suits during wartime.

## PROTECTIVE MASKS AND SUITS PRIOR TO 1975

Most military masks operate on the principle of negative pressure. When you inhale, the valves close and air comes through the canisters or filters into the mask, with some resistance caused from the effort to pull air through the filters. When you exhale, the air escapes through valves in the mask out into the environment. In addition, military masks have to be designed so that the lenses do not fog (reduced visibility being an obvious hazard). This is accomplished by deflecting inhaled air over the lenses to sweep away moisture before it enters the nose and mouth. Moist exhaled air is directed out through the outlet valves without coming into contact with the lenses. Office of Safety and Health Affairs (OSHA) regulations for firefighters and hazardous material (hazmat) technicians call for positive pressure ventilation, which is when air is forced to the individual's mask by pressure of compressed air. This principle is used for self-contained breathing apparatuses, which ensure that no contamination is drawn into the mask from any breaks between the mask seal and skin, as well as eliminating the fogging concern.[3]

One of the drawbacks of negative pressure masks is that, while they do filter many industrial gases, they do not filter carbon monoxide or allow personnel to operate in an oxygen-deficient environment. Given that the alternative is to wear an oxygen bottle for the few times this situation might occur, the military chose to accept the risk of negative pressure filtration.

Edgewood Arsenal has traditionally developed protective masks for the Army, Navy, Marine Corps and Air Force since American involvement in World War I. After the M2A2 service gas mask, M3 lightweight mask, M5 gas mask, M1A2 and M2 noncombatant masks for civilians, and the M6-12-8 dog gas mask, all developed during World War II, the M9 gas mask was fielded in 1947. In 1951 Edgewood type-classified the improved M9A1 protective mask. Note the change from a "gas mask" to a "protective mask," as the Chemical Corps had designed a mask with canisters that would filter out biological organisms and radiological particles as well as chemical agent vapors.[4] This had been accomplished by developing a two-part filter canister, including a particle filter that stopped 2–5-micron particles, and a carbon filter that absorbed any vapors. This mask was a rubber-molded facepiece with two eye lenses and an external round filter canister. There were several mask sizes and configurations to allow left- and right-mounted canisters, designed to permit shooting rifles while wearing masks without the canister causing obstruction. The M9A1 mask remained the primary ground troop protective mask through the Korean War into the 1960s and survived well into the 1980s as a civil defense mask. The M10 mask for acids and organic vapors was fielded in April 1951, the M11A1 all-purpose mask in December 1953, the M12 ammonia gas mask in 1953, the M14 tank crew member mask (adding radio compatibility) in September 1954, and the M16 noncombatant mask (for civil defense) in December 1957. There was a mask for every purpose and trade.

One of the oldest and most venerated NBC defense systems still in use in some reserve units and police forces is the M17 field protective mask. The M17 protective mask was type-classified in 1959 and sent to most units during the Vietnam War beginning in 1966. This butyl rubber mask featured a larger field of vision, better speech transmission, more size choices, and lightweight internal filters that reduced breathing resistance (as compared to the M9A1) and eliminated the need for special facepieces to favor left-handed shooters. The M17 came in only four sizes, which further reduced the logistics of stocking nine sizes of masks. At the time, this mask's technology represented a quantum leap over the M9A1 mask used during and after the Korean War. The Navy chose to adopt the Mark V for shipboard protection in February 1959.

The M18 headwound mask followed the M17 mask in September 1959. It resembled a large plastic bag with a filter, allowing patients with head injuries a protective breathing environment. The M21 rocket propellant handler's mask (for ground-launched rocket crews) was fielded in April 1960. An improved civil defense protective mask, the M22, followed in September 1960, just in time for the Cold War's heating up. Edgewood Arsenal released two new masks, the M24 aviator mask and M25A1 tanker mask, in December 1962 and May 1963 respectively. These masks were intended to connect with collective protection systems on tanks and aircraft, primarily through a gas-particulate filtration system.[5] These masks went back to a single lens piece on the faceblank, a microphone for plugging into the communications system, and a filter canister at the end of a hose. Both masks used the M10 filter canisters when employed outside the vehicles. The hose permitted crewmen to plug into the gas-particulate filter system of the vehicle, or in the case of the M24, the oxygen system of the aircraft, as the primary source of their protection.

Army leaders later changed their minds on incorporating a filtration system on the M113 APC and M60 tank, which killed the original intent of the M25 mask. Modifying the M113 APC and M60 tank for power and size requirements of integrated vehicular collective protection systems was too difficult, and the requirement remained delayed for the next generation of armored vehicles. The Army chose not to incorporate the filtration system in its fixed-wing or rotary-wing aircraft as well. As a result, these vehicle and air crews relied on standard protective masks alone. Air Force, Navy, and Marine aviators intended to use the M24 protective mask for their aviators, until they realized that it was not designed for high altitude and multi-G force maneuvers. The other three services developed their own protective masks more in line with high performance requirements. In the Air Force's case, this turned out to be the MBU-13/P, fielded in the late 1970s.

Given the heavy use of riot control agents beginning in 1965 (both in domestic situations and in military conflicts), the M17 mask soon became a standard issue for all soldiers. Because soldiers in Vietnam's hot tropical climate found the M17 mask too bulky, heavy, and difficult to carry in the jungle, Edgewood Arsenal developed the M28 riot control agent mask. This mask, produced in limited numbers beginning in August 1968, weighed less than 22 ounces and featured a silicon rubber facepiece (instead of butyl rubber) with plastic eye lenses that permitted folding into a small bundle. It was not designed for long-term durability or to handle CB warfare agents, but it could filter out CS gas adequately. The Army produced 270,000 of these masks before the war ended.

The only improvement made to the M17 over the next decade was the incorporation of a resuscitation device and a drinking tube, creating the M17A1 mask around 1972. The resuscitation tube allowed a soldier to perform mouth-to-mouth resuscitation on another soldier while keeping his own mask on (the idea originated in 1966 as a standalone component for the M17 mask). A drinking tube was added because of the dehydration caused by extended periods of remaining in protective clothing and mask. This tube connected with a specially designed canteen cap, which allowed for limited quenching of one's thirst without contaminating the water within the canteen. This feature was not incorporated into the M24/25 masks.

In May 1974 the Chemical School developed a new mask requirement, calling for greater visibility and a return to the external canister, to permit quicker and easier replacement of filters. The silicone-rubber facepiece would feature a capability to mount the canister on either side of the mask. Different modifications of this mask would also replace the M24/25-series masks. The Army wanted one universal facepiece that would accommodate most users, to include ground forces, tankers, and aviators, in just three sizes. The initial laboratory response was the XM29 CB protective mask, featuring a large one-piece lens to permit maximum field of vision, an external canister, and improved voicemeters (the component through which the soldier spoke—voices are often muffled and nearly incomprehensible while wearing masks). The sparsity of Army NBC defense program funds in the mid-1970s prevented this prototype from being developed further.

Between 1945 and 1967, the standard protective clothing ensemble depended on the chemical agent one expected to face; impregnated permeable clothing for a soldier's typical exposure to liquid agents, and an impermeable suit such as the M3 protective outfit (M4 butyl rubber suit, M2A1 boots, and M4 gloves), for specialists engaged in decon operations or weapons handling. This created a continued demand for chemical processing companies to reimpregnate the clothing, just as they had in World War II. Into the 1960s, most of these chemical processing companies were retired or in the reserve component. Impregnated suits remained the state-of-the-art technology through the 1960s and into the 1970s. Combat units during the early 1970s, such as the 101st Airborne Division, had reimpregnation kits for their protective suits. There were rumors of a new chemical protective overgarment in research but no production funds were made available. When DoD demanded new protective suits in the mid-1970s, there were no domestic textile firms set up to address the government requirements.

Chemical protective garment development had moved to the Natick Research, Development, and Engineering Center (NRDEC) in Natick, Massachusetts, since the 1973 disestablishment process. Direction from politicians and combat unit leaders to the Chemical Corps has always been to minimize casualties to a zero risk, which calls for increased levels of protection, which in turn calls for increased heat stress. There were additional requirements to protect against biological agents and radiological fallout, as the masks had. Since most biological agents and radiological particles cannot penetrate the skin physically (as chemical agents can), any light clothing that encloses the body can meet the challenge. There was still a need to abandon contaminated clothing and don clean clothing, but the test for biological and radiological contamination is more on the flaps and seals of the protective suits (rather than the fabric's absorptive qualities). The high bar for protective clothing, then, has always been how it withstands the challenge of liquid chemical agents. If the suit can keep mustard and nerve agents off the soldier's skin, it will most likely protect against biological and radiological contamination.

Obviously, soldiers could not minimize their risk to liquid agents by donning rubber suits and running around on the battlefield without quickly becoming combat ineffective. If the body is prevented from releasing its heat because of the suit's impermeability, it will shut down. Even commercial hazmat technicians cannot operate for more than a few hours without relief from the suit. Researchers attempted to model the chemical agent threat, worst-casing the situation to the chances of a soldier being near the detonation of several chemical-filled artillery projectiles. They decided that 10 grams of nerve agent per square meter of ground would represent a fairly typical exposure (near the ground zero of the chemical artillery barrage). Therefore, every soldier's protective suit is designed to that worst-case level. To balance operational capability with the least risk possible, combat arms leaders stressed the need for a permeable suit that offered at least six hours of protection prior to liquid agents permeating to the soldier's skin.

Protective gloves and boots followed a pattern of development similar to that of the suits. Initially, there were two sets of chemical gloves and boots: one set for blister agents and a second for nerve agents. Along with the new suit, the Army developed protective gloves made of 25-mil-thick butyl rubber. The Air Force preferred thinner gloves, offering more dexterity, at 7 and 14 mil thicknesses. In 1973 the Army and Air Force decided to adopt the British-designed wraparound, lace-up "fishtail" butyl rubber boots. Their design makes them very easy to strip off in a decon line, but soldiers almost immediately noticed "significant problems in operational effectiveness"—translation, the one-size-fits-all boots fit most soldiers like clown boots, and the outer laces got tangled in everything. Soldiers could not walk easily with the fishtail boots, let alone run during combat situations.

If combat units would accept an increased risk as a way to increase their performance, they could request a protective suit that does not build up such a high heat level—but they must understand that a few more soldiers exposed to higher levels of agent may become casualties as a result. Then again, those soldiers at ground-zero of a chemical agent barrage have other things to worry about than the agent concentration. British Mark III protective suits, for instance, are designed with a lower agent challenge of 2–3 grams per square meter, but they are much lighter and cause less heat stress. They are less durable and require replacement sooner, but they allow troops more freedom, or at least the perception of less burden. Since combat leaders have never backed off the zero-risk desire, they accepted (by default) the burden of heavy and hot protective suits.

## PROTECTIVE MASKS AND SUITS, 1975–85

After R&D funds began to increase in the late 1970s, the XM29 protective mask became the keystone NBC defense program. It was formally adopted as a joint service program between the Army and Air Force in October 1978 and renamed as the XM30. This mask, scheduled to replace the M17A1 by the mid-1980s, featured a silicon rubber facepiece with an in-turned peripheral faceseal (giving a superior and more comfortable fit), improved front and side voicemeters, a cheek-mounted (left or right) NATO-compatible impregnated carbon external canister, and a rigid one-piece polymer eyeshield. The side voicemeter allowed easier and more legible communications with radio and telephones. The XM33 and XM34 would use the same facepiece and canister design as the XM30 to replace the M24 aviator and M25A1 tanker masks, respectively. Among the reasons for the return to the external canister was the need to quickly change the canister, much as the British S-10 mask featured. It also aided logistics by standardizing the mask canister with the NATO countries, much as ammunition had been standardized among NATO countries.

Industry had difficulties developing the one-piece eyeshield; the plastic had to be resistant to scratches but not rigid (allowing some give rather than breaking under stress), while retaining a tight bond to the facepiece.  The chemically bonded curved plastic facelens would not stay attached to the facepiece, breaking from the faceblank like a compressed spring.  It simply would not retain its integrity under rough treatment.  Because of this program issue, a special Army In-Progress Review (IPR) in January 1982 concluded that the XM30 was unacceptable and ordered the project to be terminated by 1984.[6]

Once the Army decided that the XM30 mask would not fit their needs, they moved to a new mask design.  The new mask had to incorporate a minimum amount of change and a minimum amount of technical risk to quickly transition the program from the XM30.  The mask program was designated the XM40 (for normal ground use), XM41 (aviators), and XM42 (vehicle crewmen).  The one major change was its mechanically mounted two-lens facepiece.  The XM41/42 would use the same facepiece as the XM40 but would use a hose assembly to plug into ventilated facepiece systems (the M113A2 APC and M60A3 tank had now incorporated collective protection systems in their modifications).  They also included communication links, as their predecessors (the M24/25s) had.  The XM40 would come in three sizes (small, medium, and large), replacing the four sizes of the M17-series masks and the six sizes of the M9A1 mask.

Since the XM30 program had been set back by at least five years, Chemical Systems Laboratory continued modernizing the M17 mask.  In May 1983 the Army type-classified and began producing the M17A2 protective mask.  This version removed the resuscitation hosing of the M17A1 mask, which had never been seen as adding much value.  All other features, including the cumbersome internal filters, remained basically the same.  Because of a serious reliability issue involving the original M17 masks, AMCCOM initiated a major effort from 1980 through 1983 to equip all Army units with the M17A2 model.

The Army's aviation community required a special mask for its new Apache helicopter because of the need for compatibility with its Integrated Helmet and Display Sighting System (IHADSS) and Optical Relay Tube (ORT).  This highly engineered, close-fitting mask would develop into the XM41 general aviator mask and the XM43 Apache protective mask, first designed in 1983.  This mask had motorized air flowing into the facepiece to avoid fogging, and the eye lenses were so close to the pilot's eyes that some pilots had to use special contact lenses and clip their eyelashes to fit within the facepiece's lens.  The Air Force finished development and began procurement of a mask more suited for high-altitude performance, called the MBU-13.  There were a number of complaints about the MBU-13, to include limiting the pilot's field of vision and hampering the ability to eject while wearing the mask.  The Air Force initiated a joint Air Force/Navy Aircrew Ensemble Respiratory Protection (AERP) program, which would replace the current MBU-13 aviator protective mask.

After 1974, the Army cast about for a protective suit that would not require a special impregnating process or the manpower-intensive units that had to prepare the suits.  In particular, the U.S. forces in Europe demanded a very near-term solution, given their proximity to the Warsaw Pact, and they required millions of suits, not merely thousands.  In 1977, the 200th Theater Army Materiel Management Center in Europe had the responsibility to hold all chemical defense equipment in war reserve stocks for the U.S. Army Europe (USAREUR).  They had formal war requirements for 16 million overgarments.  Initially, they had to activate reserve component laundry units to keep impregnated suits viable and ready for war, but they were not enough to meet the requirements.

The Army CB defense community turned to the British military for a solution.  The British military had a chemical-protective permeable overgarment called the Mark III, which used an activated charcoal-impregnated inner layer of nonwoven fibers to capture liquid chemical agents that penetrated the suit's outer liquid-resistant layer.  The fabric allowed water vapor and air to pass through, allowing for low and medium work with some discomfort and little heat exhaustion.  Because of congressional trade restrictions, this suit could not be purchased off the shelf for U.S. forces in the United States.  Because of the urgent need, U.S. forces in Europe were the only units allowed to purchase the British Mark III suits.[7]

Based on the British design, the Army labs developed a uniform that offered a six-hour protection against liquid agents, up to an expected 10 grams of agent per square meter.  This suit featured a liquid-resistant outer nylon cotton shell and a carbon-impregnated polyurethane foam bonded to a nylon tricot inner fabric.  If the clothing was not wet or used in a chemical attack, it could last for fourteen days before requiring replacement.  This achieved two goals within the logistics community—it eliminated the need for two sets of protective clothing and did away with the chemical processing companies of World War II and Korean War vintage.  This protective clothing was termed the chemical protective overgarment, or CPO.  These came in eight sizes, were stored in airtight packages, and had a shelf life of five years (extendable based on lot samples).  The problems with the foam were that if it got wet, it became very heavy; it was always hot with its extra layer of clothing; and the activated carbon in the foam often shook loose onto soldiers' clothing, covering them with black carbon and creating the impression that the suit was losing its protective capability.

As U.S. companies responded to the DoD funding for millions of CPOs, the new protective suits replaced both the U.S. impregnated and British suits in the war reserve stocks.  Between 1977 and 1980, over 2.1 million overgarments were added to the European war reserves, with another 400,000 residing within the combat units' supply rooms.  By 1985, nearly 8 million suits were in the worldwide military inventory.  As for the 16 million requirement, the USAREUR Deputy Chief of Staff for Logistics, Brigadier General David Watts, sent a message to the Pentagon logisticians stating that USAREUR would not accept any more overgarments on the basis that they had no warehouse room available for more suits and they couldn't consume enough suits in training to justify the high requirement.  The last of these suits were consumed during the 1990 Gulf War.

In May 1984 the Program Manager for Clothing and Individual Equipment (PM-CIE)[8] began fielding the Overgarment Concept 1984 (OG84), which would evolve into the Battledress Overgarment (BDO). It utilized the same basic carbon-impregnated foam approach that the older CPO had, with an outer nylon cotton fabric that better resisted liquid penetration. This protective clothing increased protection against a liquid chemical agent threat from six hours to twenty-four hours. Service life after the shipping bag was opened (barring contamination) was similarly increased from fourteen days to twenty-two days, and had a five-year shelf life (extendable based on lot samples). The Air Force and Marines agreed to procure the suits as well, with the Navy choosing the Mark I suit (a protective suit designed after the British Mark III suits).[9]

Two other specialized suit programs bear mention. As noted, chemical specialists involved in decontamination operations and chemical weapons handling used special suits for the increased hazard of contact with CBW agents. The solution developed in the 1960s was improving the butyl-rubber impermeable suits, resulting in the M3 toxicological agent protection (TAP) suit and M2 TAP apron. When the explosive ordnance disposal (EOD)-trained specialists wore the M3 tap suit with impregnated undergarments and the M9A2 mask, it was equivalent to what civilian hazmat specialists would call modified "Level B." The M2 apron, combined with TAP boots, gloves and hood, impregnated undergarments and M17A2 mask, gave chemical specialists an increased protective factor and lower heat stress levels (as compared to the CPO) while decontaminating equipment (a very wet operation involving hundreds if not thousands of gallons of water). This was considered modified "Level C."

Aviators and tankers requested a special protective suit as well as a special protective mask. They pointed out that the carbon-impregnated suits were a hazard in an environment where fires might flash through their vehicles, possibly igniting the suits. Natick began investigating flame-retardant coatings for the outer shells. In addition, aviators saw the BDOs as too bulky and incompatible with their flight operations (although cynics thought that aviators just wanted to retain their cool image of a one-piece suit). Air Force pilots and Navy/Marine aviators adopted a three-piece CB protective aircrew ensemble that was worn underneath their flight suits. Their respective R&D communities began investigating the costs and benefits of a one-piece protective suit that could be used for daily operations as well as protective use.

The Air Force and Army agreed on a standard set of protective gloves, at the 7-, 14-, and 25-mil thickness, later adopted by the Navy.[10] The Chemical School pressed Natick labs to investigate the Canadian-German MULO as the design for a chemical protective boot to replace the "fishtail" boots. NRDEC tried incorporating CB agent protection into its next generation of standard combat footwear, rather than developing a new disposable overboot. In the meantime, the military was stuck with the fishtail concept. Many units unofficially switched to the green vinyl overboots (GVOs) used for raingear as the preferred chemical protection boots. These boots would protect as well as the fishtail design (if new and not punctured), but they were more expensive and would have to be discarded after contamination; but, on the other hand, the soldiers could run much more easily in them. After some discussion about the boot's liquid resistance, the Army officially authorized the GVOs as a substitute for the fishtail boots.

In an effort to reduce the physical degradation associated with wearing protective suits, the Chemical Corps developed a flexible clothing arrangement that offered different degrees of protection at the discretion of the combat leader and his/her interpretation of the threat. This was called the "Mission Oriented Protective Posture" or MOPP status. Wearing part of the clothing would reduce the heat stress without the risk of leaving soldiers unprotected against surprise chemical attacks. There are five MOPP levels as shown in Table 8.1.

**Table 8.1**
**Mission Oriented Protective Posture (MOPP) Levels**

|                | Overgarment           | Overboots             | Mask/Hood | Gloves                |
|----------------|-----------------------|-----------------------|-----------|-----------------------|
| **MOPP Zero**  | Readily Available     | Readily Available     | Carried   | Readily Available     |
| **MOPP One**   | Worn Open             | Carried               | Carried   | Carried               |
| **MOPP Two**   | Worn Open             | Worn                  | Carried   | Carried               |
| **MOPP Three** | Worn Open             | Worn                  | Worn      | Carried               |
| **MOPP Four**  | Worn Closed           | Worn                  | Worn      | Worn                  |

The theory was that soldiers in a low-risk environment would just keep their suits within reach and the mask around their waists. At a slightly higher risk level, the soldiers would don the suits but keep them open to increase ventilation and don the boots as the risk rose. The suit and boots took the longest to don, therefore having them on reduced the risk but allowed some flexibility. MOPP Three added the mask but kept the hands free to allow dexterity. Ideally this might be seen in a non-persistent vapor-only threat environment. Finally, MOPP Four was the highest level of protection, resulting in a completely enclosed body.

Everyone understood the need for suits, and they trained as individuals to don them and to wear them during combat operations—to a degree. Sustained unit operations in protective suits were always draining, physically and psychologically. Soldiers throughout history have complained about the heat stress and difficulty in carrying out manual operations while dressed in protective gear. Ideally, soldiers required a place to relax, a protected area where groups of people could unmask, work, and sleep at ease. This was the concept behind collective protection shelters, the next area of CB defense programs.

# CHAPTER 9

# Collective Protection

Studies on the effectiveness of collective protection in the M1 tank indicate a significant increase in the life expectancy of the vehicle. This increase is due to the increased effectiveness of the crew which can operate in a lower level of MOPP. In addition, hybrid collective protection and overpressure can prevent vapor contamination of the vehicle interior, thereby increasing the amount of time a crew can remain unmasked.

—FM 3-100, *NBC Operations*, 1985

Collective protection programs are the bastard stepchildren of the CB defense community, which may seem a strange statement to make, since the concept of collective protection is to allow groups of individuals to avoid dressing up in protective suits and masks. Operating inside a shelter that provides clean air in an otherwise deadly environment seems like a preferred option. The down side is that collective protection shelters take time to set up and take down, demand dedicated power sources, rely on huge filters that are expensive and difficult to replace, and are not well integrated into conventional shelter and vehicle design. CB detectors, protective ensembles, and decontamination systems are all unique, stand-alone systems that do not require integration with someone else's programs.[1] When one pushes the requirement of collective protection onto another military defense program, what one must recognize is that one is asking another R&D program manager to make room in their tank/airplane/GP medium tent/shelter system/van/armored personnel carrier/ship for something that is large, power-draining, and hardly ever used in the grand scope of its life cycle. This is a prime reason why there are so few fielded collective protection systems and why, when troops go to war, the stores of large filters are so low (no one's ordering them).

The Army and Marine Corps use collective protection for two distinct functions. The older function is as shelters that exist to provide safe agent-free havens for personnel that may have to operate in contaminated environments for extended period of time and that require freedom from protective suits and masks to function fully. These include communications, command and control (C3) units and hospital units. Various configurations exist for both fixed sites (buildings) and mobile shelters (general purpose [GP] small, medium, and large tents).  The second function is aimed at providing armored vehicles and certain vehicles with hard shelters (vans) with integrated collective protection systems.  This creates a safe environment within the vehicle (as long as the hatches are secure), in which the troops can operate unhindered from protective ensembles (timing being vital for fire direction centers for artillery/air defense units and tank crews).  Studies have shown that reaction times are much shorter if the soldiers can operate with a lower heat burden and unrestricted from gloves and masks.

The Navy worried about contamination issues on their ships during World War II for a while, but it passed once they saw the Germans and Japanese were not using chemical munitions.  After World War II, the preferred solution was tightening down the hatches and turning on the internal air circulation system.  After all, the ships were expected to keep water out, so the ship's features (hatches and air circulation) could keep CB agents out (at least in theory).  The Air Force rarely considered collective protection at the air bases prior to the Arab-Israeli wars, preferring to stop the threat from reaching the air base in the first place by direct engagement.[2]  Since 1972 all services have understood the practical requirement for collective protection, but the technology has limited the systems to big, bulky, expensive programs that no one really wants to purchase or maintain until time of war.

Field units in World War I had jury-rigged collective protection systems (CPS) together to protect their trenches against gas attacks.  The most sophisticated they got was hanging an impermeable blanket over the shelter entrance and weighting the blanket down so that it didn't flap in the wind.  This was still the accepted tactical design for troops in World War II.  Many true collective protection systems developed during and after World War II were designed for buildings at fixed-site installations and were installed into the air handling equipment.  These systems were large, power-draining systems, pushing from 200 to 5,000 cubic feet of purified air per minute (CFM), designed more as civil defense shelters against the expected mass bombings of mustard gas munitions that never came.  Although the M3 Sherman tank was outfitted with a prototype CPS late in the war, it did not become a standard fielded item.  It was not technically practical to integrate collective protection systems into vehicles and shelters prior to 1950, and the lack of tactical collective protection systems was not seriously addressed until after the Arab-Israeli War in October 1973.

All collective protection systems have a set of common components.  First, they use an enclosed area that is to be protected, not necessarily air-tight, but with a minimum of openings (a large plastic liner within a tent, a room on a ship or airplane, the shelter on back of a truck, etc).  They have a protective entrance, an airlock if you will, which allows individuals access into and out of the shelter.  They have a power source (usually a small generator) and air blower unit that forces air into the enclosed area.  And last but not least, they have one or two large filter units attached to the air blower unit's intake.  These filter units are often in pairs: one filter blocks large particles from entering the system (a particulate filter) and one activated-carbon filter absorbs the gases that pass through the particulate filter. The hardware (controls and hoses) plus the filters are referred to as a gas-particulate filter unit (GPFU). The size and number of the filters vary depending on the size of the area to be protected; therefore a tank may have a pair of 200-CFM filters, while a ship may have four to six pairs of such filters, and a fixed-site installation may have several 2,000-CFM filters. The basic technology is simple, not much more complicated than air conditioning systems. The problems occur as one tries to shrink the collective protection system down in size and power and still retain its ability to ensure a clean environment.

Communications vans and fire direction vans for artillery and air defense units were the first vehicles protected, as these systems (holding sophisticated computers and radios) were seen as critical nodes that required an ability to work unimpaired by masks and protective suits. The air blowers and filters were mounted on the outside over the driver's cab, and the protective entrance was on the rear. By using positive pressure, contaminated air is kept out as long as the positive pressure is maintained and no contaminated personnel and equipment enter the vehicle. Of course, if the occupants need to relieve themselves or change shifts, they would have to mask up and rotate through the entrance. Troops that were contaminated and wanted into the van were expected to strip their suits outside the entrance, step into the airlock with their mask on, let the air cycle through, unmask, and enter the van. Not very tidy, but it made for a safe environment—but we're getting ahead of ourselves. Very few people were taking collective protection seriously until they saw that the Soviets were taking it seriously.

## CPS PROGRAMS PRIOR TO 1975

As mentioned, the Army had experience in fixed-site collective protection programs, many of them springing up from the requirements of civil defense. These included the M9-series collective protection system (fielded between 1959 and 1965, 600 CFM capability); the M10-series collective protection system (fielded between 1958 and 1965, 1,200 CFM capability); and the M11- and M12-series collective protection system (fielded between 1958 and 1965, 5,000 CFM capability), used for Nike-Hercules systems in the United States. These were massive systems weighing up to 4,000 pounds, not something meant for the field. In 1965 another series of fixed site systems emerged, the M14 through M17 systems, ranging from 600 to 5,000 CFM capability, but with reduced weights (400 to 2,500 pounds, respectively). These systems used the existing building as its shelter and power source, largely by sealing the windows and installing protective entrances at the doors.

Also in 1965 the Army detailed a requirement for a self-contained mobile field shelter that would allow protection for up to twelve occupants against all CB agents. The XM51 Collective Protection System (CPS) was type-classified in July 1971. This was the first mobile NBC shelter designed for the Army; double-walled, air-inflatable, and self-supporting with an airlock for entry and exit into the clean interior environment. They could be used for a number of purposes, the major one being medical care of casualties in an NBC-contaminated environment. It could also be used for a safe command and control radio site (continuous communications in battle being a vital capability), or to provide a temporary respite for soldiers who had been in protective clothing for extended periods. Its major drawback was that it required a separate generator to power the filtration, pressurization, inflation, and environmental control unit for the system. It also required a dedicated vehicle to move it and its accessory equipment around the battlefield (it weighed approximately 5,400 pounds). The cost ran to $43,500 per unit (FY80 dollars). The lack of available five-ton trucks to move the system and the high cost delayed its fielding to European-deployed units. Before procurement could begin, the funding ax dropped the program, leaving the Army with no mobile collective protection shelters prior to 1978.

Edgewood Arsenal had developed gas-particulate filtration systems for vehicles beginning in the early 1960s. Field artillery fire control vans were the first to receive vehicular CPSs, due to the high value of those units. Tanks, armored personnel carriers, and combat aircraft were another story. The Army accepted the concept of collective protection for shelters and vans, but the combat arms community did not want to trade off engine power and space used for ammunition and radios against a threat they did not expect to encounter. Still, there was an Army requirement to protect all vehicles from expected chemical agent attacks, but obviously it would be cost-prohibitive to refit all the vehicles to be airtight.

The compromise was to develop a ventilation system that would force clean filtered air into the crew's protective masks, reducing breathing resistance and providing some relief from heat stress. This was termed a ventilated facepiece system. Soldiers would still have to wear protective suits, as the vehicles were not airtight and there was still the chance of internal contamination if the hatches were open. Edgewood Arsenal developed a number of filter units, ranging from 300 to 5,000 CFM, for the M551 Sheridan tank, M48 Patton tank, M60 tank, the M113 armored personnel carrier (APC) chassis (to include variants such as the armored ambulance), and the Army's Mohawk aircraft by the early to mid-1960s, only to see the Army change its mind on the merits of CPS. Basically, the designers for armored vehicles had built upon past designs that emphasized space for ammunition, engine, radios, and fuel, and not for filters and allocated power for the CPS, despite the known threat of CB warfare. To be fair to the vehicle designers, the CPS was bulky, calling for the installation of an air blower, two large filters with dust separators, the ventilated facepiece interface, control module, and installation kit, and it ran off the vehicle battery power. It added thousands of dollars onto the unit price of the vehicle. As a result of the lack of Army senior leadership endorsement, no vehicles or aircraft had incorporated any CPS by 1972, and by then there was no Army CB defense program to push the requirement.

## CPS PROGRAM DEVELOPMENT, 1975–85

Interest in vehicular CPS came back as a result of the 1973 October War and the discovery of Soviet vehicles with integrated CPSs. Responding to the obvious implication that Soviets were planning to operate in a CB environment, Congress passed Public Law 95-79 in July 1977. The law tasked the Army to come up with a plan to integrate CPS into all armored vehicles under development. This reenergized the collective protection program area, initiating a number of shelter and vehicular configurations using similar large filters and air blowers. The former R&D efforts found their way into artillery fire direction control centers, such as the TACFIRE shelter requirement starting in March 1976.

In 1976 the Headquarters, U.S. Army Europe (USAREUR), and Seventh Army identified a requirement to transform rooms of buildings into collectively protected shelters. Two years later, Edgewood initiated a feasibility program to demonstrate a concept. The concept used vapor-impermeable plastic liners, an air blower with a 200-CFM gas-particulate filter unit, and an protective entrance to allow the conversion of any tent or interior room of a building into a positive-pressure clean environment. Again, this was focused on the impression that most of the fighting would be in urban (i.e., European) scenarios. As military units moved through heavily urban Europe, they could convert rooms in city buildings into safe, clean areas with a quick and flexible CPS. Instead of a tent or shelter with a rigid skeleton, the XM20 Simplified Collective Protection Equipment (SCPE) resembled an airlock attached to a large plastic bubble, which could fill a small room. By taping liners together, the dimensions of the shelter could expand to almost any size within larger rooms. Its only limitation would be the time necessary to inflate the liner (up to 30 minutes) and the need to keep the SCPE under cover, since its liner would be very susceptible to shrapnel and bullets. The Chemical Corps anticipated fielding the system by 1984.

The Army fielded 112 M51 Shelter Systems beginning in June 1980, with several hundred more planned for the following years (637 systems by the close of 1984). Despite the lack of any other protective shelters, no branch of the Army (or any other service) was asking for the shelter other than the Medical Corps. The system's weight and high cost kept its operational benefits from being exploited. The Air Force decided to invest in fixed-site protection, largely for air base survivability improvements. The KMU-450 shelter modification kits were able to transform permanent facilities into CPS. Most of the 160 KMU-450s that were made in 1979 and 1980 went to European air bases for command posts and squadron operations facilities. This was only a partial solution, since the shelters did have some operational features that caused Air Force personnel to be less than thrilled with them (lack of toilets, lack of ability to cook meals, etc.). The Navy began investigating the feasibility of installing CPS on ships, in the event that their air-handling equipment on the ships might become contaminated.

Given the traditionally high cost of collective protection systems, the Chemical School approved a requirement for NBC protective covers for supplies and equipment in December 1984. Both the Quartermaster and Field Artillery Centers stressed the need to offer a quick protective capability for supplies and ammunition stored outside structures. Originally, this was to be a number of covers measuring 20 meters by 20 meters, providing 48 hours of protection against liquid agent contamination. Natick labs estimated the cost to run $3,000 per cover (1985 dollars). Upon reevaluating the requirements, the Chemical School requested that Natick evaluate other candidates and sizes in an effort to lower the cost.

Chemical Systems Laboratory prepared a plan to comply with Public Law 95-79, which required CPS integration in all armored vehicles, specifically those in development or procurement in FY81. At the time, this included the M60A1/A3 tank, the XM1 main battle tank, the Infantry Fighting Vehicle/Cavalry Fighting Vehicle (IFV/CFV), the General Support Rocket System (GSRS), the Improved Tow Vehicle (ITV), the M577 command post carrier, the M109 self-propelled howitzer, the U.S. Roland air defense system, and the Division Air Defense (DIVAD) gun. CSL had two options to propose; a ventilated facepiece and a positive pressure system. The ventilated facepiece program consisted of a main filtration unit for the tank, which the crewmen could plug their M25 mask hoses into, providing fresh air for their masks. The positive pressure option would force air into the vehicle through a 400 CFM filter, and assuming the hatches were closed, would keep CB agents, both liquid and vapor, out of the compartment. The options included using one of these two systems, or incorporating both into a hybrid CPS.

The positive pressure option was attractive, since it would allow the crew to forego any protective clothing—until the hatches opened, or the overpressure system failed. At the least, it appeared advantageous to include the ventilated facepiece option as either the primary or the backup for all these vehicles. The XM1 program office did not like the concept of fighting with closed hatches, nor sacrificing room in the vehicle used for ammunition for the system. The U.S. Roland, since that chassis had been selected, had no room for the filter; operationally, it could allow a closed-hatch operation. The other systems all required rapid and frequent entry and exit for personnel, which voided the operational effectiveness of the positive pressure design. Based on this analysis, CSL and TARADCOM (Tank-Automotive Research and Development Command) proposed to incorporate only the ventilated facepiece options on all vehicles save the Roland, if Congress would authorize funds and extended time to design the hybrid system into the Roland program. The system would use 100, 200 or 400 CFM filters, depending on the requirements of the vehicle.

In June 1982 CSL completed the Modular Collective Protection Equipment (MCPE) for the AN/TSQ-73 (air defense control and coordination facility) and TACFIRE (computerized fire support command and control) shelters, giving artillery units a clean operating environment to plan and conduct fire support operations. These systems relied on a positive overpressure system alone, since they were primarily closed-hatch operations, with the standard M17 protective mask as a backup (the shelters were not armored vehicles, so no requirement existed for the ventilated facepiece). They used the M56 gas particulate filter unit, blowing 200 CFM into the vans, which had the protective entrance standing out like a blister on its rear end (M10 protective entrance for TACFIRE, M12 protective entrance for AN/TSQ-73). There was a similar program in place for the Patriot surface-to-air missile system at the same time, but its program kept slipping to adjust to the Patriot's system test delays.

Believe it or not, that was it. Collective protection is not a very high technology area, and there are only so many ways to install air conditioning. The focus remained on providing integrated vehicular protection, primarily for armored vehicles and fire direction center vans, and shelters for field hospitals and the SCPE for buildings in Europe. The power demands, weight of the systems, and the logistics and costs related to the large filters remained limiting factors in selling the program to the combat arms. As a result, CPS did not resonate with the combat arms, especially when the light infantry phase took hold. Holes in protection remained, especially with the M557 command vehicles and other variants of the M113 APC; howitzer systems; large fixed-wing aircraft such as the C130, C141, and C5; and Navy ships, especially the Merchant Marine fleet. No one was addressing the real weakness, that being the threat of CB agents in the rear logistics area. Supply and maintenance areas, requiring a lot of terrain to deploy and hauling the beans, bullets, gasoline, spare parts, and medical supplies that enabled the force to sustain combat operations, had no CPS or protective covers to protect their material.

The next area, decontamination, received more attention not only because it was a true survival skill but because it was an immediate precursor to unmasking and taking protective suits off. Decontamination systems were incorporated into the field training exercises and made more of a known presence than CPS ever would. After all, the equipment and troops needed a good washing every now and then; "real men" didn't need air conditioning in the field.

# CHAPTER 10

# Decontamination

Decon often is needed because avoidance is not always an option. By making it possible to lower MOPP level, decon supports protection. Combat power is restored and improved—certainly over what it would have been in full MOPP gear.

—FM 3-100, *NBC Operations*, 1985

Decontamination is not a difficult concept to understand. People that work with hazardous chemicals, in laboratories or in hospitals, understand that there is a risk of contamination by some foreign chemical or organism. First rule of lab safety is that one should be protected with adequate suits and masks, but one may require a process to clean off hazardous materials from personnel or equipment. The fastest way out of protective masks and suits is by verifying that you are clean of contamination, and you can either allow the weather to remove contamination (very slow) or accelerate the process with decontaminants. The $64,000 question becomes, how clean is clean?

As usual, the limiting factor was how well one could decontaminate chemical agents. Radiological particles and biological organisms could be washed off with soap and water, eliminating the threat to soldiers with the very low technology approach of hot water and soap. Non-persistent chemical agents, by their nature, are not around long enough to require decon operations. That led to persistent chemical agents such as mustard, thickened soman, and VX, which called for thorough decontamination processes during recovery and restoration phases to completely eliminate the threat.

The challenge is how much time and resources one has to pull troops and equipment off line to clean themselves up before they are thrown back into battle. No combat leader appreciates having less than 100 percent of his force on the line, but not being able to relieve the troops while they're in MOPP suits and dropping from heat stress is a sure recipe for disaster. As long as the unit is in MOPP gear, they are fighting at less than 100 percent and deteriorating quickly. If troops and equipment remain contaminated, they will spread it across clean areas of the battlefield, increasing the hazard. Somewhere along the line, the commander has to determine whether to decon, whom to decon, and when to decon.[1]

In military concepts, the ability to carry out combat operations while wearing protective suits and masks is clean enough; this is colloquially termed "fighting dirty." As long as the CB agent is not causing a life-threatening situation and soldiers are not spreading contamination around the clean areas of the battlefield, the battle can go on. The basic philosophy of decontamination is to do it as soon as possible (as extended operations in MOPP gear fatigues your troops), as far forward in the battlefield as possible (limit the spread of contamination), by priority of importance (clean the shooters before supply trains), and only what is necessary (because decon operations take time, people, and resources). The only way a field soldier could tell the job was done was by using chemical agent monitors, which were sensitive, but not to the degree of ensuring 100 percent safety as interpreted by OSHA. For wartime operations, that was adequate—until nerve agents came along. Aviators in particular cannot fly if their eyesight is affected, for obvious reasons, and low, less-than-lethal levels of nerve agents caused myosis, pinpointed pupils that would inhibit their ability to get the first sighting of enemy air targets. This was the beginning of new unanswered requirements.

As for what one decontaminated, the obvious answers were personnel and equipment exposed to CB contamination. However, to successfully eliminate CB agents, very caustic solvents and bleaches were used that could destroy the material that was contaminated. Metals and glass were usually no problem, except for the nooks and crannies within equipment that might harbor liquid contamination or biological organisms. Fabrics, wood, and rubber were usually thrown away, since they absorbed chemical agents and often disintegrated under treatment from caustic decontaminants. The issue of how to decontaminate delicate electronics and avionics equipment was a relatively new requirement, one that remains unanswered today.

Impregnated chemical protective clothing was steam-cleaned for decontamination and reissued between 1943 and 1975. Small areas of terrain and buildings that were going to be reused might need decontamination (such as landing areas on beaches, roads, headquarters buildings, depot areas, etc.). Large area decontamination requirements, such as ports and airfields, called for great stores of decontaminant, creating major logistics challenges. Very often the only solution is to decontaminate specific buildings and equipment and require everyone to wear masks until time and the weather eliminated the threat.

## DECONTAMINATION PROGRAMS PRIOR TO 1975

During World War I, decontamination was not a major issue, as the majority of war gases used were non-persistent industrial chemicals. The exception was mustard agent, which arrived later in the war; at the time, the interim solution was to mark off the contaminated area and avoid it. If equipment was contaminated, it was abandoned and replaced. As World War II arrived, there was an increased desire to avoid the loss of contaminated areas and equipment if at all possible. Because the labs had had time to study mustard agent (the only persistent threat at the time), they had some solutions. The two standard decontaminants were chlorinated lime (bleaching powder), which could be used dry or as a liquid slurry mixture (mixed with equal volumes of water), and Decontamination Agent Non-Corrosive (DANC), which was a powder that was added to gallons of acetylene tetrachloride (1:6.4 mixture).

Decontamination companies had five main systems at their disposal. For metal surfaces such as aircraft and tanks, they would use the three-gallon M1 hand-pump decontamination apparatus and the 1½ quart M2 hand-pump decontamination apparatus. The M1 used the DANC formula to break down the mustard agents and water to flush the surfaces, while the M2 could be filled with either DANC or chlorinated lime slurry. For larger operations, to include terrain decontamination, they had the 400-gallon M3A1 truck-mounted and M4/M4A1 skid-mounted power-driven decontamination apparatuses. These systems used the chlorinated lime slurry to decontaminate terrain or to clean the exteriors and interiors of buildings, or they could be filled with DANC to decontaminate vehicles. The M3 was mounted on the back of a 2½-ton truck and featured two hoses, which could discharge 22–35 gallons per minute at a working pressure of 400–700 pounds per square inch. This made it ideal for rapid decontamination of roads, airplane runways, or exterior surfaces of buildings.

Skin decontamination focused on the exposure to vesicants only. To this purpose, the Army issued tubes of emergency M4 ointment that had to be applied prior to exposure. Other than washing with hot soapy water, that was the extent of personal decontamination through World War II. Because of the longer time required for mustard to act on its targets and its (generally) nonlethal nature, treating blister agent patients was seen more as a medical responsibility rather than an action that required immediate attention from the individual. The troops counted on protective masks and suits to keep mustard agents off their skin.

The Korean Conflict, with the potential capabilities of the Soviet- and Chinese-backed North Korean Army, saw a strong presence of chemical decontamination companies, using the improved M3A3 decontamination apparatuses (same design, better engine reliability). After the Korean Conflict, the M8A2 decontamination apparatus and M9 power-driven decontamination apparatus replaced the M3A3. These systems incorporated a pump, heater, and 400-gallon tank of water to provide streams of hot water to wash off DANC solution, which was applied to vehicles by hoses. It still required soldiers to scrub the vehicles or buildings clean with mops and buckets. They were large pieces of equipment, requiring a dedicated five-ton truck to move one apparatus around.

In 1962 the Army developed a more multi-purpose decon unit, the M12 Power-Driven Decontamination Apparatus (PDDA). The system was actually three pieces of equipment; a 200-gallon water tank (later increased to 500 gallons), a water heater, and the engine pump and hose unit. It also came with a personnel shower assembly and fire hydrant adapter rings. The standard operating procedure calls for four men to set up and operate one M12 apparatus. Two or three of these units would be included in a standard vehicle decontamination line, to present a sort of "car wash" as military vehicles drove through. The 500-gallon tank held decontaminant STB slurry to neutralize CB agents (see next paragraph). When not in use for decon operations, it could be used for fire fighting, pumping water-based solutions (such as pesticides), or field showers. This 1960s-era veteran basically followed the principles demonstrated in World War II. It performed well in unit reconstitution roles, although it remained dependent on a large nearby water source.

Super-Tropical Bleach, or STB, is a mixture of chlorinated lime and calcium oxide in a white power form, replacing the World War II bulk packages of chlorinated lime in September 1950. This decontaminant is still used as the military's main multipurpose decontaminant, packaged in fifty-pound drums. It can be used in a dry mix with earth or dirt, or in a wet mixture called slurry. The dry mix is used in personnel decontamination lines, in the shuffle pit to decontaminate footwear; dry STB mix could also be used to decontaminate terrain, buildings, and concrete. The wet slurry is used by the M12 apparatus to decontaminate vehicles. The high bleach content of STB makes it a potent decontaminant for both chemical and biological agents. The main drawback for STB is its tendency to catch fire if in contact with DS-2 (the next generation decontaminant).

The Chemical Corps experimented with specific biological decontamination, developing the M10 ethylene oxide dispenser in the late 1950s. Ethylene oxide was used in hospitals to sterilize operating instruments. While it did destroy biological organisms, it was not a practical field application and did not live long in inventory. It had a problem of persistence, and its residue could cause blisters on contact.[2] What was required was a decontaminant so caustic that it would destroy chemical and biological agents in the same application. That decontaminant was on the way.

Edgewood Arsenal formulated and packaged Decontamination Solution-2, or DS-2, in February 1961 after two decades of research and development. This clear liquid concoction was 70 percent active agent (diethylentriamine), 28 percent solvent (ethylene glycol monomethyl ether), and 2 percent active agent booster (sodium hydroxide). DS-2 was superior to DANC (which it replaced) largely because it did not have to be premixed immediately prior to use. DS-2 was more of an all-purpose decontaminant, neutralizing nerve and mustard agents quickly, as well as most biological organisms. Although DS-2 is flammable; corrosive on aluminum, cadmium, zinc, and tin; softens rubber, leather and paint; and is a potential carcinogen, it was considered safer to handle than DANC and less damaging to the decontamination systems that utilized it. Once DS-2 was applied and washed off, it removed most if not all of the chemical or biological agent contamination. Its success is similar to aspirin; had the FDA been required to review aspirin prior to its marketing, it would have never been approved. Such is the case with DS-2 and the EPA; since DS-2 was developed in the less stringent years, people cared more about positive results than inconvenient side effects.

DS-2 comes in either a five-gallon drum or a 1 1/3 quart container. The latter container was designed to fill the 1½ quart M11 Decontamination Apparatus, Portable (DAP), a hand-held portable device resembling a small fire extinguisher. The only feature distinguishing the M11 DAP from its World War II predecessor was the nitrogen cylinder that replaced the hand pump. Charged with nitrogen to propel DS-2 out in a fine mist, it could decontaminate a small surface area such as a driver's area in a vehicle. This device was designed during the same time as DS-2 and released to the field in 1961. It replaced the three-gallon M4 decontamination apparatus, which had been using DANC since 1958.

Edgewood Arsenal released the ABC-M13 individual decontaminating and reimpregnating kit in June 1965.[3] This kit contained a pad of Fuller's earth powder for dabbing liquid nerve or mustard agent off the skin, two cloth bags of chloraamide powder for decontaminating clothing, and a razor to cut away contaminated clothing. In addition to deconning equipment and skin, soldiers could use the kit to reimpregnate the permeable outer liner of the older version protective suits. In a pinch, soldiers could also use gasoline, soap and detergent, and high-test hypochlorite (HTH—calcium hypochlorite) to augment their decon needs.

## DECONTAMINATION PROGRAMS, 1975–85

When Chemical Systems Laboratory decided to redesign the M13 individual decontamination kit in the mid-1970s, they examined the Soviet skin decontamination kits brought back from the Middle East (1973 October War). These kits used an alcohol-based solvent to neutralize the liquid agents instead of Fuller's earth. The Army promptly copied this approach, almost down to the alcohol vial's dimensions, and resurrected the kit as the M258 skin decontaminating kit. This kit included four gauze pads, two plastic capsules containing a caustic solvent, and two scraping sticks in a plastic carrying case. While Fuller's earth would continue to play a role in large-scale ground decontamination (an Air Force observation), the new M258 skin decon kit showed a more rapid neutralization of nerve agents.

CSL began redesigning the Soviet-style M258 skin decon kit in 1978. They repackaged the skin decon kit to hold three sets of two packets, each packet holding a small damp towelette. A soldier would use the towelette from decon packet #1 (marked in big, bold letters) to blot the liquid agent-contaminated area, then use the second towelette (marked with a #2) to wipe off the residue. This offered the soldier a capability to decontaminate small areas of flesh or individual equipment exposed to persistent chemical agents. M258A1 skin decontamination kits were available to the Army by 1981.

The Army TRADOC study released in 1976 called for improvements in the decontamination equipment and methods used in battalion-sized units, noting the inadequate volume provided by the 1 1/3 quart M11 decon apparatus. The Chemical School developed a requirement for a fourteen-liter disposable container with a manual pump, brush, and hoses, which would permit a vehicle operator to decontaminate all areas of the vehicle (wheeled or armored) that was required for normal operation and maintenance. This could fit roughly in the same bracket as a five-gallon liquid container and would eliminate the need for nitrogen cylinders to charge the apparatus. Again, this was not a new idea—it basically was the 1940s M2 decon apparatus with a somewhat larger capacity. Because the container was prefilled with DS-2, soldiers would not need to fill the containers prior to use. While it would not decontaminate the entire vehicle, the XM13 Decontamination Apparatus, Portable (DAP), would reduce the threat from CB agent contamination, allowing the soldier to continue his/her mission perhaps with a mask only instead of full protective posture. After suffering a number of delays due to missed test windows, equipment failures, contractor delays, and fielding issues, CRDC finally type-classified the M13 in August 1983, with production beginning in 1985.

In 1978 the Air Force obtained a number of Norwegian Sanator decontaminating apparatuses for test and evaluation. They saw these systems as a potential replacement for the bulky M12A1 decon system fielded by the Army. This pump, heater unit, and collapsible water tank offered a substantial size and power reduction over the older M12A1 system, with the limitation of only using hot water, not decontaminant, against contaminated equipment. The Air Force bought 750 systems and titled them as the A/E-32U-8 in 1983. The Army bought a limited number of these systems for test and evaluation, based upon an operational assessment conducted by Lieutenant Colonel Jan Van Prooyen. He had purchased a number of the decon systems in Europe for the Berlin Brigade in the early 1980s as the Berlin Brigade's chemical officer and later did the same for the 3d Infantry Division.[4] The Norwegian Sanator underwent some changes in engine design and power and was type-classified (limited procurement) in February 1984 as the XM17 Lightweight Decontamination System (LDS). CRDC unilaterally decided to stop the program a short time later, stating its failure to meet requirements on reliability of the engine, water pressure, and the overall limited decontaminating effectiveness of the system.

In January 1980 the Army decided it would not be cost-effective to try to improve the M12A1 Decon Apparatus. The XM14 truck-mounted DAP, designed to replace the aging M12A1, promised a vehicle rinse rack subsystem, increased pressure output, and increased engine reliability. However, it also faced several challenges (missed test windows, equipment failures, contractor delays, etc.), and died in 1987. The XM18 program replaced the XM14 program, again stressing the requirements of continuous mobility, a more reliable power source, steam-cleaning capability, and a vehicle rinse rack. It would use a new decontaminant, which had to be much less corrosive and less hazardous in handling than DS-2 and STB, but as effective or better. The Improved CB Agent Decontaminant (ICBAD) would be chosen from one of three candidates, the front runner being a German decontaminant called C8 emulsion, which was a special calcium hypochlorite mixed with tetrachloroethylene, a phase transfer catalyst and water.

Because C8 had to be added to water, either mixed into solution or injected into a water spray, it would not replace the DS-2 in M11 and M13 DAPs. The Chemical School developed a requirement for an end-state objective decontaminant, which would be used against all CB contamination on vehicles, supplies, facilities, aircraft, ammunition, and other military material without the adverse and corrosive effects associated with DS-2. This improved decontaminant was called the Multipurpose Chemical-Biological Decontaminant (MCBD). While there were no known technical candidates for this requirement, several research contracts were initiated to find them.

There were three efforts aimed at nonaqueous decontamination. The Chemical School was searching for a way to liberate chemical defense units from the intense logistical burden of water-hauling. The XM15 Interior Surface Decontamination System (ISDS), initiated in February 1980, was under development to decontaminate interior surfaces that could not be exposed to standard decontaminants, such as electronic components within aircraft, with hot air. This program had an element of technological risk associated with it, due to the lack of test data on how effectively hot air would decontaminate actual toxic agents to safe levels for humans. It was terminated after completing advanced development in 1985, partly because the system could not decon large surface areas quickly enough, and partly because the Army Aviation Center and Air Force decided that their decontamination requirement did not permit reliance solely on hot air.

The XM16 Jet Exhaust Decontamination Smoke System (JEDSS), a copy of the Soviet truck-mounted jet engine decontamination device (TMS-65), was initiated in July 1979. The Army system mounted a J60 jet engine, control cab, and modular control unit on a five-ton truck, which would vaporize or blow away contaminants on the exterior of large vehicles with high-velocity hot exhaust gases. It had two nozzles leading into the engines, one for decontaminants and water, the other for a liquid chemical to create smoke. However, when the jet engine was activated, the 5-ton trucks seemed to wanted to take off into the "wild blue yonder." This program was officially terminated in March 1984 in favor of directing the nonaqueous program toward "more versatile, more cost-effective, and less logistically burdensome alternatives." The Special Applications Decontamination System (SADS), later to be designated the XM19 Non-Aqueous Equipment Decontamination System (NAEDS), resembled a commercial glove box chamber. It used recycled freon-113 solvent issued from a spray gun to wash off NBC agents from sensitive equipment, such as communications gear. It showed potential for rear-area maintenance operations, but there were concerns that the military had not really asked for such a system. The operational needs for a NAEDS had not been fully investigated with TRADOC.

The Navy chose to rely on the on-board salt water fire extinguisher system on ships as its primary decontamination system. While not as effective as decontaminant DS-2, the Navy could not afford for its ships to lose all their paint at sea because of the effects of the corrosive decontaminant. The Air Force and

Marines relied on Army equipment to a large degree. The Air Force augmented their decontaminants with Fullers earth, a dry absorbing powder. Their concern remained focused on decreasing air base contamination and relied on the aircraft design and the high skin temperatures of flying high to destroy contamination on aircraft. They could hardly use corrosive DS-2 or STB on their aircraft without worrying about what cables or electronics the decontaminant was eating away. The Marines improved upon the Army's M11 by increasing the volume of the container to two quarts, almost doubling the surface area that could be decontaminated (creating the stretch M11 DAP).

As part of survivability studies conducted to see how military equipment stood up to CB agents and decontaminants, scientists had observed that oil-based military paints had the tendency to absorb chemical agents, holding them in the paint and extending the normal contamination times. To combat this problem, Chemical Agent Resistant Coating, or CARC, was developed in early 1980. By utilizing an alkaloid-based polyurethane paint instead of an oil-based paint, military equipment could resist chemical agent absorption, making decontamination easier. The program successfully passed its agent tests and a final in-progress review in 1981. This feature was instituted as Army policy in 1983 for all equipment.[5]

While decontamination systems had not made great leaps in the 1980s, the progress was evident. By keeping the decontaminants and improving on the delivery systems, the Chemical Corps was able to design equipment that complemented the Army's goal of retaining the maximum fighting force on the field. DS-2, STB and the decon delivery systems did not match high speed military requirements perfectly. They did ensure that combat units would be able to fight in a contaminated environment, exit a hazardous area to restore their personnel and systems and later, return to battle. The most evident weakness was the continued inability to identify a decontaminant for electronic and other sensitive systems, a requirement that remains unanswered today. The standard of "how clean is clean" meant fighting dirty for ground troops until the fight was over, but the aviators had higher standards (requiring protection against myosis, which would impair their flying ability) that weren't being met.

The M8A1 Automatic Chemical Agent Alarm is made up of the M43A1 detector and the M42 alarm. Courtesy of the U.S. Army.

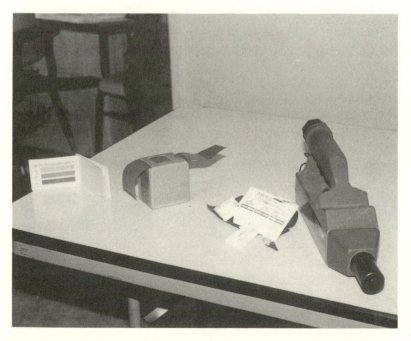

From left to right: a book of M8 paper, a roll of M9 paper, the M256A1 Chemical Agent Detector Kit, and the M1 Chemical Agent Monitor. Courtesy of the U.S. Army.

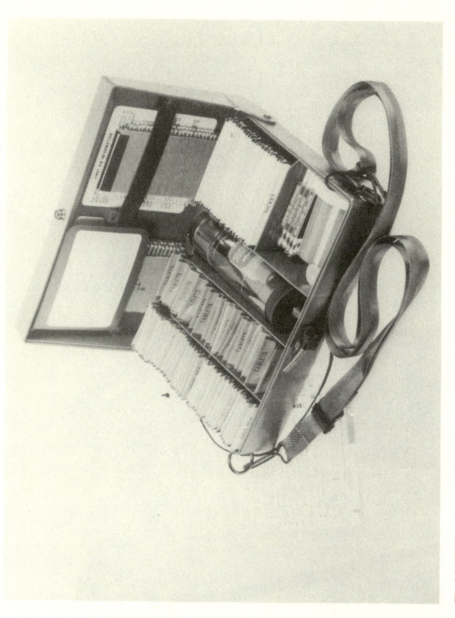

The M272 Water Testing Kit will remain one of the few "chemistry kits" still in the Army inventory until an automated water detector is fielded. Courtesy of the U.S. Army.

A 1980s soldier stands ready with his M17A1 protective mask, the Chemical Protective Oversuit, butyl rubber boots and gloves, and M9 paper adhering to his arms and leg. Courtesy of the U.S. Army.

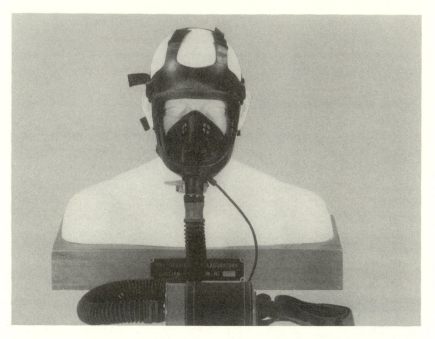

The M24 Aircraft Mask featured a full on-piece clear lens to allow unimpeded vision in all directions. This design was not sturdy enough for ground troops, thus the two-lens approach of the M17A1 mask. Courtesy of the U.S. Army.

Army troops in Vietnam use the M28 mask, a lightweight version that filtered only riot control agents. Courtesy of the U.S. Army.

Top view

Left front three-quarter view

M51 SHELTER
SYSTEM

Right front three-quarter view

The M51 Shelter System, seen here with its trailer-mounted generator, used inflated airbeams to maintain its structure. Courtesy of the U.S. Army.

The M12A1 Power-Driven Decon Apparatus is normally mounted on a 5-ton truck, as seen here.

The XM16 Jet-Exhaust Decon Smoke System, modeled after the Soviet TMS-65, was not the Army's best example of re-engineering. Courtesy of the U.S. Army.

M1059 mechanized smoke generator system rolls through the National Training Center, Fort Irwin, California. Courtesy of the U.S. Army.

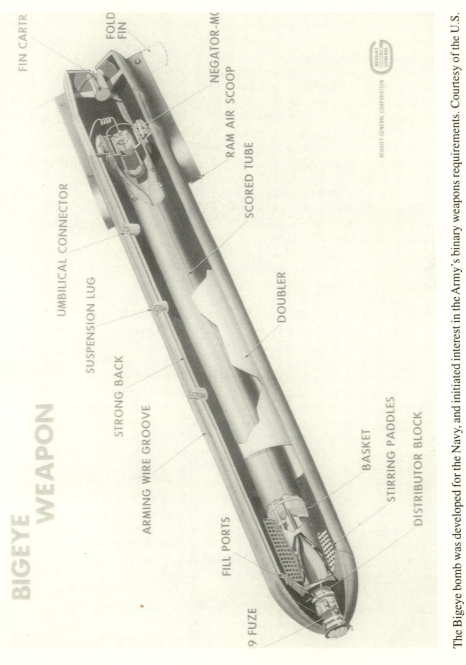

The Bigeye bomb was developed for the Navy, and initiated interest in the Army's binary weapons requirements. Courtesy of the U.S. Army.

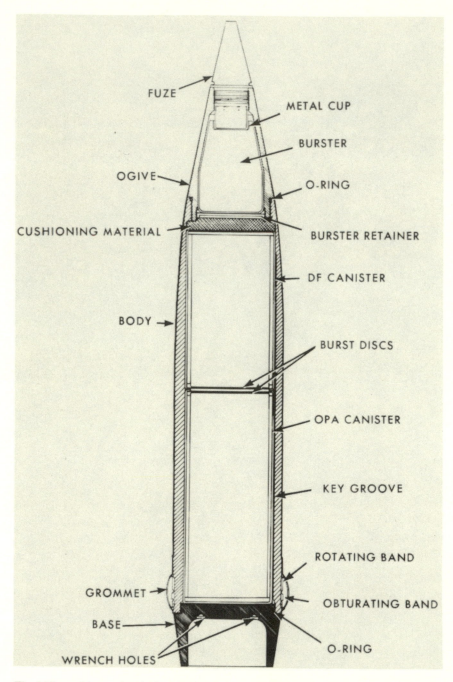

The 155-mm binary chemical projectile kept its two canisters separated prior to ignition. Courtesy of the U.S. Army.

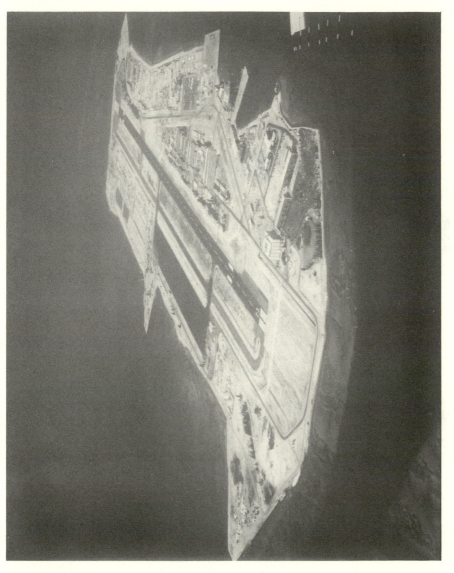

Johnston Island is a man-made formation built off the surrounding atoll. The incinerator is on the projecting land mass on the left center of the island. Courtesy of the U.S. Army.

An SBCCOM instructor trains Atlanta emergency medical technicians on how to use the M256A1 detector kit.

# PART III

# The Renaissance Years Fade, 1985–90

Progress has been made in some areas [of the DOD NBC defense program]. It is lacking in other areas, but DOD has ongoing efforts to make the necessary improvements.

—General Accounting Office report, 1985

After all, any country with a petrochemical, pesticide, fertilizer, or pharmaceutical industry has the potential in terms of equipment, raw materials, and technical expertise to produce some chemical warfare agents. Without direct access to such facilities, it is nearly impossible to know whether activities being undertaken are of a commercial or military nature.

—CIA Director William H. Webster, October 1988

# CHAPTER 11

# Politics of Chemical Arms and Chemical Defense

The latter half of the 1980s saw an increased emphasis on developing binary weapons, now that it appeared more feasible to resurrect the idea of retaliatory measures as a part of the military's counterproliferation program. Training at the School would include live agent training, for the first time in decades. This brought valuable lessons home in a realistic training environment. Developing chemical defense equipment continued as a well-planned modernization effort. The bywords became defense, deterrence, and retaliate! All three capabilities became vital interconnected legs of the military's ability to survive and sustain combat operations in a military environment. Without one leg, military vulnerabilities begin to show. Without two legs, the military force becomes too busy performing a balancing act to consider performing its mission. While the Army maintained a three-legged chair in the 1980s, it was clear to many that not all the legs were equally strong or of equal length.

## BINARY WEAPONS BUILDUP

While the Chemical Corp's defensive capabilities were improving, there was a chorus of calls from both the chemical and combat arms branches (as well as theater commanders) to restart the binary program. Many felt the existing chemical weapons stockpile was obsolete, and without a serious retaliatory capability, the European forces would have to endure a one-sided battle against the Soviets. Congressional funds had permitted the development of the Integrated Binary Munitions Production Facility from 1980 through its finished construction in April 1985. Before the binary program could be reinitiated, Congress would have to approve the production phase of the program. Although the Reagan administration had advocated a binary program since 1982 with the Senate's approval, the heavily Democratic House kept rejecting its return, the only major weapon system denied to DoD in Reagan's first term. Slowly, opinions were changing. There were several reasons offered for the change in climate. The Soviet conflict in Afghanistan provoked some to search for a way to bring the Soviets to arms control talks. The airliner KAL 007, shot down in 1983, provoked the need to "get tough" with the USSR. Some felt that conservative Democrats wanted to join the pro-military mood sweeping the nation. The chemical accident at Bhopal, India, made some representatives realize the increasing danger of storing deteriorating chemical munitions that were pushing fifteen years or more in age.[1] Yet the Iran-Iraq war had shown the need to maintain some type of active deterrence to discourage those nations with offensive stockpiles. If the military eliminated its current chemical stockpile, what could be used to maintain a retaliatory capability against future foes? Tactical nukes and neutron bombs were out. Obviously, a replacement program was needed.

President Reagan appointed a Chemical Warfare Review Commission (CWRC) in January 1985 to comply with congressional requirements, which had called for an executive review of the proposed production of binary munitions to reaffirm the national interest involved.[2] The commission was chaired by Walter Stoessel, Jr., former ambassador and Under Secretary of State. Other members of the commission included Philip Bakes, president of Continental Airlines; Zbigniew Brzezinski, former assistant to the president for National Security Affairs; Richard Cavazos, General, USA, Ret.; Barber Conable, Jr., former representative from New York; John Erlenborn, former representative from Illinois; Alexander Haig, Jr., General, U.S. Army, Retired and former Secretary of State; and John Kester, an attorney from Williams & Connolly. This panel, aided by a small staff of military and civilian government workers and two consultants, reviewed the existing NBC program in both offensive and defensive capabilities. After three months of meetings with academic, military, and political subject-matter experts and field visits to military bases in the United States and Europe, the commission released its report in late April 1985.[3]

The report included a review of chemical warfare history, the U.S. policy on chemical-biological warfare, the nature and condition of the stockpile, the current chemical weapon threat, proliferation of chemical weapons, and the proposed modernization program. Perhaps not surprisingly, they endorsed the binary modernization program. The final report, issued in June 1985, concluded that (1) modernization of the U.S. chemical weapons stockpile would not impede and would more likely encourage negotiations for a multilateral, verifiable ban on chemical weapons; (2) only a small fraction of the current stockpile had deterrent value, while the bulk of it was militarily useless and should be destroyed; (3) the proposed binary program would provide an adequate capability to meet the present armed forces' needs and was necessary; and (4) any expectation that protective measures alone could offset the advantages of the Soviets from a chemical attack was not realistic. It also added that the defensive research and development programs should be better funded; that the intelligence on CW programs in other countries be improved; and that the United States continue to work toward a solution to the proliferation of materials and equipment exported to countries for the purpose of supporting CW programs.[4]

On June 19, 1985, the House voted to authorize resumption of production of chemical weapons, reversing years of resistance. The vote was 229 for and 196 against. The House bill authorized, but did not provide the funding for, the FY86 binary program. An amendment to the House bill called for three conditions prior to production: certification that the Bigeye bomb's technical problems were solved; a commitment from DoD to store the separate parts of the binary weapons in different states; and a formal agreement from the European allies to a forward deployment of the weapons on their soil. The Senate had voted for the program's reinitiation in May.

The Army had fully come on board with the Chemical Corps on the issue of binary weapons, at least in theory. Combat leaders may not have known exactly how to employ them, but they did see retaliatory chemical munitions as the key to keeping their units out of CW scenarios. General John Wickham addressed the House Armed Services Committee in the Army's annual justification for the next year's budget on February 6, 1985. During his statement on the modernization initiatives for the Army, he emphasized the need to focus on chemical capabilities:

We lack a credible chemical warfare deterrent. Our nation's defense posture and the recent improvements in our total military readiness could be jeopardized by this single factor on the modern battlefield. We must modernize our deterrent stockpile with binary munitions and rid ourselves of the obsolete and potentially hazardous chemical munitions we currently store.[5]

Part of this plan meant developing a means of disposing of the older, aging unitary chemical weapons. The Army began building an incineration plant at Johnston Atoll, where a good quantity of the stockpile already existed, based on lessons learned on the Chemical Agent Munitions Disposal System (CAMDS) at Tooele Army Depot. Since the Hawaiian islands were over eight hundred miles away, there was no concern over accidentally releasing chemical agents near public population centers. This distance from the public did not sway the Army from emphasizing safety and environmental issues, given the number of military troops and government civilians stationed there. Being that this was the first large-scale attempt at chemical weapons demilitarization, this was an ideal spot for such an attempt. It would take five years before the incineration plant was accepted by Congress and ready for testing.

## CHEMICAL CORPS AND INTEGRATION INTO THE ARMY

On June 19–20, 1985, Major General Alan Nord hosted a second Chemical System Program Review. This event was initially planned after the last CSPR in September 1984. The preliminary panel meetings in April 1985 drew twenty general officers, their action officers, and a host of technical and subject-matter experts to form four expert panels. These panels included doctrine, chaired by Major General Robert RisCassi (commander, 9th Infantry Division); training, chaired by Major General Frederic Brown (commandant, Armor School); force structure, chaired by Brigadier General John Greenway (director, Force Programs, ODCSOPS); and materiel, chaired by Major General Vincent Russo, ADCSLOG. After these panels convened, they met again on May 13 to brief the commander of TRADOC, General William Richardson.     Based on General Richardson's guidance, the panel fine-tuned their brief and hosted General Max Thurman, Vice Chief of Staff of the Army, thirty-six other general officers and civilian equivalents, and close to two hundred other officers from all branches and commands.

The topics covered every field of the four panels. The host of generals debated the issues of the NBC threat to the Army, chemical weapons employment, the new shift in doctrine to contamination avoidance, the CANE tests, smoke doctrine and materiel programs, chemical warfare training at the National Training Center, training conducted at division and higher levels, logistical NBC defense issues, reserve training, modeling support for NBC environments in computer simulations, personnel restructuring in the many units of the Army, and, of course, extensive briefs on more than fifty programs in detection, decontamination, individual, and collective protection that had been initiated in the previous few years.

After the summary was presented to General Thurman, he emphasized the need for a "robust" concept of smoke employment and countermeasures for the Army. He also advocated a more defined "balanced and proactive" concept for NBC intelligence and reconnaissance for the AirLand Battle concept, and increased emphasis for NBC survivability of fixed sites (such as ports, air bases, supply areas, hospitals, and maintenance centers). At the conclusion of the two-day meeting, the Chemical School had a new action plan to chart its reemergence into the new AirLand Battle Army.[6]

The GAO returned to assess how effectively the armed forces had integrated these new programs and equipment into their training and doctrine. The House Foreign Affairs Committee had asked for a review of the modernization program, based on the GAO's last report in 1982. If grades had been given, the Army and Air Force might have received C pluses. While both services had rewritten most of the doctrine and training had improved measurably, the forces might not react automatically and precisely in a contaminated environment. The GAO cited lack of realism in training and the lack of readiness among combat support units as main reasons.     Medical doctrine for chemical warfare was specifically named as inadequate, although ongoing attempts were being developed. The GAO described the chemical warfare doctrine as being in transition.

The Army's active chemical force structure had grown from 6,800 soldiers in 1982 to 9,000 soldiers in 1985, with plans to expand to 24,000 by 1987. This significant increase, combined with the return of two-week NBC schools to augment the force structure, had improved the Army's effectiveness. Some units in Europe were even asking for more decontamination and smoke companies. The acute shortage caused by the disestablishment had still caused significant gaps in the ranks, notably in senior chemical NCOs and officers. The GAO did not believe the Army and Air Force's personnel plans for 1987 to be feasible, considering service personnel ceiling limits (nor would the Chemical Corps ever grow much beyond 10,000 soldiers).

Modernization efforts were good but inadequate in several areas. The Vice Chief of Staff for the Army was quoted as saying that the Army NBC defense program had failed to bring more capable technologies and systems to the field. The main objection was the Chemical Corps's consistent failure to "deliver X by date Y." In two cases, this had been due to delays in congressional budget actions. In other cases, DoD contractors and officials blamed a lack of urgency at CRDC both to finalize R&D contracts and get testing and field placement accomplished quickly. The developers at Edgewood blamed the Chemical School for "only wanting what's perfect." Program dates cited for the 1982 report had been too optimistic. A third delay cited was the difficulties working with the other branches of the Army to integrate NBC defense requirements into their weapon systems and platforms, such as collective protection into combat vehicles, which was actively resisted. DoD officials expressed their concerns that industry was still wary about getting into the NBC defense market, which was seen as too small for many companies and not enough profit to attract high-tech firms. Steady growth of NBC defense requirements since 1982 had made some firms more confident that it was not such an unstable market as had been feared. In general, major increases in defensive capability was seen as several years from realization.[7]

On March 3, 1987, the Chemical School officially established and opened the Chemical Decontamination Training Facility (CDTF). Training featured the introduction of actual nerve agents into various rooms, where students garbed in full protective clothing and masks practiced the use of agent detectors and walked through decontamination processes of equipment and vehicles. The facility operates on a 24-hour-a-day negative pressure system, which sucks air into the building and through an extensive ventilation filter bank, powered by multiple backup generator systems to retain a safe outside environment under any circumstances. Students give blood samples before and after their exercises to monitor the acetylcholinesterase levels in their system, which are kept on file for twenty years. The training process includes a detailed brief on the facility to its trainees, stressing its safety features, the training program, and emergency procedures in the event that a mask or suit is compromised.

The first line of training for most of the students begins with the training bays outside the building. Here, students brush up on their skills using training devices and simulants. Once they are ready to enter the facility, instructors lead the trainees to the red-roofed building (red for "hot"), where they sign into the facility. Students then swap their clothes for Army-issue underwear and clothing, protective suits, masks, boots, and gloves and enter the facility's inner training rooms. Contract employees pass nerve agent into the rooms from their laboratory (manufacturing only one liter at any one time), and instructors apply the nerve agent onto surfaces in the training rooms with syringes. While two of the training rooms hold individual equipment, four hold an M151 quarter-ton vehicle (jeep) to allow students to practice individual decontamination skills. The largest room holds a Sheridan tank to practice team decontamination skills. Training is completed once students decontaminate themselves by stripping and dropping the clothes into disposal carts, ending with a trip through the shower room.

This facility proves invaluable as a confidence builder and trainer for chemical defense personnel, learning the effectiveness of their equipment and training in an actual toxic environment. Major General Watson, as the school commandant, was one of the first "students" of the facility. This course is mandatory for all chemical soldiers attending training courses at Fort McClellan and now includes the Air Force, Navy, and Marine personnel at the base. In addition, inspectors involved in chemical arms control inspections use this facility to train their personnel. All senior commanders in the Army are encouraged to take the training, especially those attending the Senior Commanders Course at Fort McClellan. The course was expanded to include Army reservists and soldiers from Canada, Britain, Germany, and other countries. The CDTF (later renamed the Chemical *Defense* Training Facility) passed the 30,000-trainees mark in the summer of 1994 and the 40,000 mark in late 1995, without one accident to trainees or accidental agent release.

The Chemical School picked up the P2NBC2 program in October 1987. This program had begun 1984 in the Armor School, because military doctrine and training developers at Fort Knox were concerned over the degrading effects of protective clothing on an armor crew's effectiveness. This program expanded to include evaluations of several vehicles and individuals' abilities to cope with the physiological and psychological stress of long-term wearing of protective clothing. Between these two programs, the Army's knowledge of combat operations in an NBC environment began to blossom. The only difficulty that remained was distributing the information to the various training and doctrine centers in the Army and allowing them to digest the information to transfer its findings into their doctrine and training. Over the three years between the CDTF's opening and P2NBC2 program and the beginning of Operation Desert Shield, the knowledge and embedded training slowly began to take effect, educating the Army's soldiers on the real effects of NBC agents on combat operations.

## ARMS CONTROL ISSUES REVISITED—SUCCESS THROUGH STRENGTH

Late in 1985, President Reagan and General Secretary Gorbachev agreed to intensify bilateral discussions on all aspects of a CW ban and to initiate a dialogue on preventing CW proliferation. This agreement would begin a series of meetings between U.S. and Soviet arms control experts to stem global CW proliferation.

The deployment of Pershing II missiles in Europe in 1983–85 had given NATO forces the first opportunity to strike with tactical nuclear weapons at operational military targets deep within the USSR. These Intermediate Range Ballistic Missiles (IRBMs) had the effect of bringing the Soviet Union to the bargaining table in good faith. The result was an agreement between the U.S. and USSR to eliminate and ban all ground-launched ballistic and cruise missiles with a range capability of between 300 and 3,400 miles (500 and 5,500 kilometers). The agreement, titled the "Treaty between the U.S.A. and U.S.S.R. on the Elimination of Their Intermediate-Range and Shorter-Range Missiles," or Intermediate-Range Nuclear Forces (INF) Treaty, was signed December 8, 1987, and entered into force June 1, 1988. The U.S. Pershing II and GLCM missiles and Soviet SS-20 missiles were removed from European soil by the end of 1991.[8] This practice of negotiations through a strong retaliatory stance spread to the chemical munitions side of arms control.

In the late spring of 1986, the Army formed an office for managing the binary munitions program. After project funding and organizational funds were procured, the Office of the Program Manager for Binary Munitions (OPMBN) was provisionally chartered to begin operations under the supervision of the Office of the Program Manager for Chemical Munitions. This office did not gain permanent staff until July 1987, given the Army discussions on creating a Program Executive Office for Chemical and Nuclear Matters.[9] Beginning in December 1987, the nineteen-year moratorium on chemical weapons production was ended as the completion of low rate final assembly of M687 projectiles (155-mm) entered the stockpile. The OPMBN continued plans to complete testing for the BLU-80/B Bigeye bomb and to award contracts for the construction of facilities for the Bigeye bomb and XM135 MLRS binary warhead.

The 155-mm projectile was the first binary weapon system developed largely because the Army knew how to make artillery shells better than bombs or rockets, and it directly supported tactical operations. The M687 projectile is composed of a steel casing, two canisters (M20 and M21) each fitted with a polymer lining, and a point-detonating fuse. Each canister has a very thin steel burst disk on one end. When the canisters are placed in the casing, the two disks face each other. Upon firing, the disks collapse and allow the agents to mix en route to the target. When the shell bursts over the target, it releases the lethal GB nerve agent.

The Bigeye bomb had suffered technical problems in the past and was not especially well received by the Air Force and Navy, who were looking for a "smarter" munition. The BLU-80/B bomb, in the 500-pound range, has a similar two-canister setup (one canister within the other). The actual mixing occurs after release from the aircraft. A fighter-bomber such as the F-111 would "lob" the bomb toward its target, allowing the bomb to glide a few miles prior to releasing its agent. The bomb sprays VX from a dissemination port rather than by exploding, and the start of the agent release depends on a proximity fuse. This design minimizes the chances of contaminating the aircraft.

The Artillery School was more enamored with the idea of a chemically filled MLRS rocket than with an artillery shell. Their artillery battalions wanted to shoot Copperheads and dual-purpose improved conventional munitions, not hazardous liquids. There were fewer MRLS battalions, and sealed rockets would reach impact over thirty miles away. The MLRS warhead operated similarly to the 155-mm projectile, mixing en route to the target and releasing semi-persistent GB agent on a proximity fuse setting. All munitions relied on the premise that the two binary chemical agent components would be stored and shipped separately and assembled only immediately prior to use.

The Army Source Selection Authority chose Pine Bluff Arsenal in Arkansas as the site for the main production of binary agents for the 155-mm binary round, the Bigeye chemical bomb, and the MLRS binary chemical warhead. In keeping with the desire to manufacture and store these chemical weapons more safely, Pine Bluff Arsenal developed only one of the two binary components, while an industry contractor developed the other at a different location. The three sets of completed binary components and canisters were to be stored at three different sites. Pine Bluff Arsenal would store the M20 component of the 155-mm round and the M227 MLRS assembly. Tooele Army Depot in Utah would store the second MLRS rocket pod component, the M21 component of the 155-mm round, and the Bigeye bomb minus its second component. Anniston Army Depot in Alabama would store the second component of the Bigeye bomb.[10]

The initiation of the binary program did have the effect of bringing the Soviet Union back to the Conference on Disarmament in Geneva. Soviet and U.S. representatives met three times (March 1986, September 1986, and October 1987) to discuss efforts to stem CW proliferation. The meetings were closed sessions, reportedly involving discussions on intelligence indicators of countries initiating CBW programs, and on chemicals that should be placed under export controls. While not entirely successful, it marked a beginning of mutual understandings. Meanwhile, at the Tokyo Summit in May 1986, President Reagan continued playing hardball. He made an agreement with Chancellor Kohl of the Federal Republic of Germany to remove all U.S. chemical weapons, roughly 100,000 rounds, from West German soil by 1992. In return, Chancellor Kohl would support the president's goal of replacing the unitary rounds with binary chemical munitions, as long as the binary chemical weapons production began in December 1987 as planned.[11]

In October 1987, Reagan officially certified the need for retaliatory capability against the potential use of chemical weapons to Congress. Sixty days later, the binary production facility at Pine Bluff began its production of 155-mm binary chemical projectiles, ending a nineteen-year moratorium on chemical weapons production. Plans for reinitiating the Bigeye bomb production began to solidify, although some operational testing was still in the schedule. The Carter-Burgess Company was awarded a contract to begin the construction of the binary facility for the MLRS warhead. The need for a flexible retaliatory capability had become more evident with the recent displays of chemical munitions by Libya against Chad that summer.[12]    This progress in the U.S. binary production had not gone unnoticed by the Soviets.  In March 1987 Mikhail Gorbachev publicly acknowledged for the first time in history that the Soviets did possess chemical weapons (although he denied any were in East Germany).  In August 1987 Soviet Foreign Minister Shevardnadze addressed the Conference on Disarmament, accepting the principle of mandatory challenge inspections without the right of refusal.  He invited the CD delegations to the Shikany military facility (their version of Edgewood Arsenal, Pine Bluff Arsenal, and Dugway Proving Grounds combined) to visit their CW destruction facility under construction near Chapayevsk.  The CD delegations accepted that invitation, and viewed Soviet munitions and a mobile destruction site at Shikany on October 3–4, 1987.  Later that year, Gorbachev brought up the topic of binary weapon production in his talks with Reagan in Washington, D.C. (just as the 155-mm binary shell production line went active).

On September 26, 1988, President Reagan called for a conference of the Geneva Protocol signatories in an address to the UN General Assembly.  President Francois Mitterrand of France offered to hold the conference and opened it to all nations wishing to attend.  The Paris Conference of 1989 (January 7–11) became the first strong step toward the Chemical Weapons Convention, which would not be signed until 1993.  Syria, Algeria, Egypt, and Iraq all defended the right to produce chemical weapons, citing them as a necessary counterbalance to the nuclear weapons of other nations (notably, Israel, the United States, and the Soviet Union).  The Council of the League for Arab States called for a linkage between chemical and nuclear weapons disarmament before they would participate in any serious efforts.  The 149 participants, over half which were foreign minister-level politicians, did agree to restore the authority of existing constraints (such as the Geneva Protocol), to condemn chemical warfare generally and to reaffirm the worldwide political commitment against the illegal use of chemical weapons.[13]

President George Bush's administration continued the bilateral talks in Geneva as the binary production efforts continued at Pine Bluff.  For perhaps the first time in history, the Joint Chiefs at the Pentagon, the State Department, and the Arms Control Disarmament Agency all agreed that the route to deterrence lay through the development of binary weapons.  Once a credible (but small) stockpile had been prepared, the Soviets would come to the negotiating table in earnest.  The production of the 155-mm projectiles had hit an unfortunate and unexpected snag.  While Pine Bluff had produced 4,000 M20 canisters (half the binary compound), and Munitions Command had produced 17,000 projectile bodies, the Marquardt Company at Van Nuys, California, had yet to make one M21 canister by the end of 1988.  They had failed to obtain the necessary environmental permits from the state of California to paint and fill the canisters.  The company found that the manufacturing line had defective equipment, which caused additional delays.  The Army continued operational and hardware tests of the Bigeye and MLRS systems, with no problems emerging to stop their future production.  By 1988 the services were testing the Bigeye bomb for final approval, had initiated production of the 155-mm binary round and awarded a production contract for the MLRS binary round.

The House of Representatives again began to debate the "hypocrisy" of continuing negotiations directed toward banning chemical munitions while simultaneously producing them. Nonetheless, President Bush held firm to the intent of securing a chemical weapons treaty before announcing any plans for halting binary production. In March 1989 Secretary of State Jim Baker announced the goal of removing the U.S. unitary munitions from Germany by 1990, to accelerate negotiations in Geneva. Both Defense Secretary Dick Cheney and Army Chief of Staff General Carl Vuono opposed this accelerated schedule, considering the difficulties on the 155-mm binary production line. They knew that there would not be a modern chemical weapons stockpile to take its place before 1990. The announcement, while perhaps planned as a gesture of good faith, failed to impress or accelerate the Soviets. The initial production of 155-mm binary artillery projectiles, though unfilled, represented a genuine threat that had impressed the Soviet military.[14]

In February 1990 Secretary of State Baker and Foreign Minister Edward Shevardnadze agreed on a framework for action to hasten the Geneva negotiations. One condition of the Wyoming Agreement was the cessation of the U.S. binary program. Baker returned to Moscow in May with that concession. At the Bush-Gorbachev summit meeting on June 1, 1990, the two leaders signed the U.S./Soviet Agreement on Destruction and Non-Production of CW and on Measures to Facilitate the Multilateral Chemical Weapons Convention, or the Bilateral Destruction Agreement for short. The key provisions of the accord are

- cessation of CW production to begin upon entry into force and destruction of the vast bulk of declared stocks to start by the end of 1992; down to 5,000 metric tons of agent by 2002
- on-site inspections during and after the destruction process to confirm destruction
- development and use of safe and environmentally sound methods of destruction[15]

The Office of the Under Secretary of Defense (Acquisition), Donald Yockey, stopped all further acquisition and test efforts on July 12, 1990. All production base activities were terminated, and the binary facilities at Pine Bluff Arsenal were mothballed. The Army halted its testing of the Bigeye and MLRS warhead. No Bigeye or MLRS warheads had ever been produced (excepting Bigeye test prototypes). All products and chemical agents produced to date were to be destroyed in accordance with the bilateral agreement and future Chemical Weapons Convention. The only caveat was an option to retain 5,000 agent tons of chemical agent eight years after the multilateral ban took effect. As part of the instructions to the services, Defense Deputy Undersecretary Yockey requested that the Army and Air Force submit plans for retaining the unitary chemical weapons. These plans would identify type and quantity of unitary chemical rounds that would still function with modern weapon systems. He also asked the services to give chemical defense special emphasis during future program and budget reviews, considering the need for increased reliance on chemical defense without a retaliatory capability.[16]

## OPERATION STEEL BOX

One of the follow-on results of the Bilateral Destruction Agreement was the actual removal of U.S. chemical munitions from Germany. The original agreement between the United States and West Germany rested on the principle that the unitary rounds would be disposed of once an adequate binary capability existed. President Reagan's agreement with Chancellor Kohl had opened the door for the storage of binary rounds in Germany, contingent upon the removal of over 100,000 unitary rounds (both 155-mm and 8-inch projectiles, GB and VX). They had been stored near Clausen, a small town of about 1,600 people, since 1968. With the agreement in place, there was no further need to wait. In July 1990 Defense Secretary Cheney announced that there was room at Johnston Island for the munitions. This led to the initiation of Operation Steel Box.

This operation would entail the transport of steel military ammunition shipping containers (MILVANs) by truck, train, and ship. DoD planned to move the loaded MILVANs from the storage site near Clausen to the U.S. Army depot at Miesau, then by rail to the port of Nordenham, and by sea to Johnston Island. The planning and preparation for this event included cooperative measures between many Army and Navy agencies, U.S. Army European Command, U.S. Army Pacific Command, the Navy Military Sealift Command, and the Department of Transportation's Maritime Command. AMCCOM designed the secondary steel containers in which the rounds would be shipped, while the Military Traffic Management Command provided, inspected and repaired the MILVANs for transportation. The Naval Surface Weapons Center designed and emplaced a collective protection system on the two Ready Reserve Fleet ships involved, while CRDEC provided M8A1 chemical agent detection systems, CAMs and mini-CAMs to ensure early warning if a leak occurred. U.S. Navy Atlantic and Pacific Command arranged for naval escorts for the sea voyage.[17] This course of action could not occur without debate, even given its noble cause to rid Europe of chemical weapons. The German Green Party rallied against the movement, unsure about the safety of moving the old munitions. Representatives from American Samoa, the Republic of the Marshall Islands, the Federated States of Micronesia, the Cook Islands, New Zealand, the governor of Hawaii, and environmental groups all protested against the plan. They contended that the trip was hazardous and that the new $240 million incinerator on Johnston Island might not be ready to handle the disposal task safely—not that they had any credible evidence to support these claims.

The movement of the munitions to the Army depot took place from July 26 through September 1, 1990. Ordnance soldiers used electric forklifts to remove the munitions from the storage bunkers. Chemical experts from the Technical Escort

Unit packed the munitions in the secondary steel containers and then blocked and braced them in the MILVANs. Each steel container held either three pallets of 155-mm projectiles, or two pallets of 8-in projectiles. Ten containers were packed into each MILVAN. More than eighty U.S. Army, West German Army, and West German police vehicles moved the MILVANs to the railhead at Miesau. Over two-thirds of the vehicles were for security and emergency response. German and American officials went to great lengths to inform the public about exactly what was occurring and how safe the operation would be, especially in the states where the trucks and trains would be passing through. One example of this was a 24-hour telephone hotline established by USAREUR and German officials.

The railhead holding area had undergone extensive security upgrading before the MILVANs appeared at the station. Two specially configured ammunition trains then moved the MILVANs from Miesau to Nordenham between September 12 and 19. Police, military personnel, and civilian contractors totaling over 10,000 personnel provided extensive security, agent monitoring, medical, and firefighting services for the entire land movement. Air traffic was restricted over the trucks and trains at all times. Decontamination teams, medical teams, and casualty evacuation helicopters were positioned along the route all the way to the port.[18]

The two loaded ships left port on September 22, escorted by a Navy guided missile cruiser, and sailed around South America by Cape Horn to Johnston Island. They were refueled three times, and throughout the trip, there were no chemical agent leaks detected. The ships arrived on November 6 and were unloaded by November 18. The entire effort cost $53 million from start to finish, an overrun of only 26 percent. The planning, pre-mission training, preparations, public relations, and precautions had paid off by ensuring the 100 percent safe removal of all munitions. This successful operation marked the end of the overseas chemical offensive capability of the U.S. Army.

The Army had completed its building of the $240 million incineration plant at Johnston Island in 1990 and began to slowly shake out the system before embarking on the demilitarization program. Johnston Island now held 6.6 percent of the U.S. chemical weapons stockpile. Some obstacles remained. Governor John Waihee of Hawaii argued that the Johnston plant should first complete a sixteen-month test period. Other critics feared that its emissions would contaminate the ocean food chain. Over three years of compliance testing and tweaking would take place before the work of chemical weapons disposal could take place in earnest.[19]

The offensive chemical program, the binary program, had begun and ended without any effort from the military leadership to examine the aspects of a chemical retaliatory capability. The entire binary program had been more of a political gambit than a piece of the military arsenal. The Reagan and Bush administrations used the arms control community to disarm the Soviet chemical weapons capability, without considering the need to retain that retaliatory capability for deterring other hostile nations. There had been no effort and no desire from the Artillery Branch to calculate the new dispersal properties of the new weapon systems, or any effort from any of the DoD agencies to identify the tactical use and effects of employing chemical weapons. The Army leadership and the Reagan and Bush administrations saw the binary weapons program as a political deterrent, not as a weapon system ever intended for use.

This agreed with the odd history of the U.S. military as it accepted the use of tactical nuclear weapons, incendiary and cluster bombs, antipersonnel and antitank mines, guided high explosive missiles, and other weapon systems into their tactical and operational plans, while excluding chemical weapons. While some may argue over the positive points of this unwritten exclusion policy, it retained the faulty notion that chemical weapons were somehow dirtier than other weapons. This mindset kept professionals from seeing that CB warfare was just another aspect of the total battlefield, which in turn, stopped them from identifying how military forces were expected to fight in such an environment.

# CHAPTER 12

# Reconnaissance, Detection, and Identification—Part 2

The Army's new resurgence of interest in NBC warfare meant more funding and manning for those NBC defense programs, smoke programs, and chemical munitions research and development approved in the 1985 Chemical System Program Review. In June 1986 CRDC was renamed the Chemical Research, Development and Engineering Center (CRDEC). This change emphasizes HQ AMC's view that all their laboratories should include engineering expertise with their normal scientific research, thus decreasing (in theory) the time of developing and producing Army material programs by executing both functions within the same center. Program management within the Army was changing, and that meant changes in how CB defense equipment acquisition would take place.

The Goldwaters-Nichols Defense Reorganization Act of 1986 had created a change in program development, where program executive officers (PEOs), usually general officers, resided over a general program area; for instance, heavy tactical vehicles. PEOs had a number of product managers (colonel PMs) and project managers (lieutenant colonel PMs) working under them. The difference between the two was that the product manager might have a number of different (but related) programs, whereas the project manager would have only one type of system to manage. PM Abrams reported to PEO Heavy Tactical Vehicles, for instance, and the PEO reported to the Assistant to the Secretary of the Army for RDA, who was the Army Acquisition Executive. The senior leadership in the Army chemical defense community, concerned that chemical defense would lose visibility (and therefore funds) against the Army's major programs, proposed to create a PEO for Chemical and Nuclear Matters (PEO-CN) with associated PMs.[1]

The first Product Manager for Smoke and Obscurants (Colonel Henry Shelton), formed earlier in 1977, initially fell under the PEO-CN. In 1987 the Army created a Product Manager for NBC Defense Systems (Colonel Jan A. Van Prooyen) and a Program Manager for Binary Munitions (Colonel Bob Orton), both of which joined the PEO-CN. The Product Manager for Clothing and Individual

Equipment, responsible for protective suits, did not fall under the PEO-CN due to their wide range of products other than chemical protective suits. Traditionally, the PEO-CN position would go to a general officer; in this case, Brigadier General Pete Hidalgo, the commander of CRDEC, was the likely candidate. Unwilling to relinquish command of the Center, he recommended Mr. Billy Richardson (former Technical Director, CRDC) as PEO for Chemical and Nuclear Matters.

In theory, CRDEC would conduct initial research and development until a prototype piece of equipment was ready for advanced development. Either PM NBC Defense, PM Binary, or PM Smoke would then take over, completing the program development and fielding the system to Army units. In reality, the transition of releasing program controls from CRDEC to a PEO was rocky and ill-defined, and because of this, it ultimately crumbled. The PEO-CN dissolved in March 1989, as it was seen as not accomplishing the intent of the PEO-PM relationship. PM Smoke took over smoke generator programs (smoke pots, grenades, and munitions remained under CRDEC); PM Binary took over the three binary munitions programs; and PM NBC took over radiac programs (directed through CECOM), the XM21 RSCAAL, the NBC Recon System, the M40 mask, and CAM program. All other programs remained under CRDEC's directorates.[2]

The Army had approved a requirement for the Chemical Agent Monitor (CAM), leading to formal negotiations between the contractor, Graesby Dynamics, and the U.S. government in July 1984 to initiate an accelerated R&D program. Later that year, the U.K. Ministry of Defense would award a production contract for the same device. Before the Army could request full CAM production, the U.S. government required a domestic company to produce the CAMs under the Graesby contract. Army developers also required that the CAM be powered by a standard U.S. battery. Further testing of the CAM led some to doubt its logistical reliability, leading to more scheduled operational tests and evaluation. After several years of negotiations and further testing, the M1 CAM was finally type-classified in December 1988. The U.S. contractor had some initial difficulties setting up the production line but soon had produced the first CAMs in September 1989. They did not meet the production volume requested, due to the intense concentration on producing high-quality CAMs, and produced only a little over 2,000 in the following year. About 5,000 CAMs were produced prior to August 1990, delivered to U.S. forces in Europe, the XVIII Airborne Corps and certain TRADOC units (for training purposes).

In September 1985 the Army fielded its first M43A1 chemical agent detector. The Army Acquisition Executive decided that the number of M8A1 systems procured should be limited to 60 percent of the Army's stated requirements for point detectors, in part due to the expected procurement of the XM22 ACADA, the next generation chemical agent detector (expected to begin fielding in 1987). The ACADA would replace the M8 and M8A1 alarms on a one-to-one basis; that is, whenever it was released to the field. Balancing the increased sophistication of the new detector, which would detect both nerve and mustard agents nearly simultaneously, against power and weight considerations had led to complications. In an effort to meet the weight requirements, the designers had tried plastic tubing instead of metal for routing vapors through the detector's interior. While this did make the detector lighter, the plastic tubing leaked, resulting in a failing mark for its initial production tests in 1985 and forcing a return to the design boards. The resulting shortage of M43A1 detectors (and no promise of a future system) left some active duty and many reserve units without an adequate number of reliable chemical agent alarms. These units would have to use the older and more unreliable M8 detector for the rest of the decade.

The Army had abandoned the Automatic Liquid Agent Detector (ALAD) project. In a 1985 decision paper, the Chemical School pointed out that the benefits of a liquid agent detector might be small for combat units, since, as the liquid agent hit the detectors, it would also be hitting the nearby troops (thus without the desired early warning). That did not reduce the program's potential for fixed sites such as air bases and ports; by remoting the detectors outside of buildings, the inhabitants would have benefited from the device's warning. Regardless, the Army decided to kill the program in 1986, due to the perceived lack of direct benefits to ground combat units. The radio links that connected the ALAD detectors to its central control module were spun off into a new program the next year called Chemical Agent Detector Network (CADNET). CADNET would create an electronic link from CB agent detectors to radios, decreasing the response time between higher and lower units in reacting to local alarms. Because the CECOM labs thought this was still a chemical agent detector in principle, they declined to develop the program, and the CADNET program stayed at Edgewood.

Once again, the other services interpreted these actions as the Army refusing to fulfill its joint service obligations. As the time increased and costs spiraled higher on the ACADA program, the Air Force began researching alternatives, to include improving the M8A1 agent detector with a mustard agent detection module. The Air Force also continued developing the ALAD, seeing its benefits to air base survivability operations. The Navy claimed that they didn't like the ACADA's technical approach and began their own unique chemical agent detector program, using the same technology in a different package (the Improved Point Detection System, or IPDS). The Marine Corps looked at the weight of the ACADA and its battery (increased from twenty to twenty-five pounds because of the failure of plastic tubing), and bolted to ask industry if there were a way to return to the concept of a lightweight, individual detector. This led to the development of the Individual Chemical Agent Detector (ICAD), based on the wet-chemistry concept of the original M8 detector, and therefore subject to its limitations of high agent concentration limits and interferents. ICAD promised a disposable, inexpensive, and—most important to the Marine Corps—a lightweight detector/alarm package. It was about the size of a pack of cigarettes, had a fourteen-day chemical module life, and included a visual and audible alarm. The Marines began testing and acceptance of the ICAD in early 1990.[3]

Seeking a lightweight individual detector was a typical combat arms requirement. Special Forces wanted a small, lightweight chemical agent detector that was more reliable than the M8A1 system, had a silent alarm (light only), and was equipped with a communications module that would alert nearby Special Forces operatives with similar detectors upon alarming. This was the Special Operations Forces Chemical Agent Sensor, or SOFCAS. Air Force pilots wanted a similar small and sophisticated detector to wear in their planes, which had to be sensitive enough to detect very low levels of nerve agents, below that which caused myosis (blurred and dim vision caused by pin-pointed pupils). This was the Individual Vapor Agent Detector (IVAD). All three programs shared practically identical requirements with some minor distinctions; the Marine Corps was willing to accept a higher exposure risk to their soldiers at the cost of less burden to the soldier, while the Special Forces and Air Force programs were more demanding on their lower detection and false alarm rates. Yet no one (to include the Pentagon's Joint Staff) could force the three programs together as one joint service research and development program. Of course, the requirements to miniaturize what was then state-of-the-art technology into a pocket-sized detector that detected submyosis levels of agent with minimal false alarms was an extreme challenge. The Army Infantry School liked the concept but never pushed for a requirement for an individual detector, so the Chemical School ignored the three programs (as did the Edgewood scientists, amused at the seemingly impossible goals outlined in the requirement documents).

## THE FOX HUNT

Due in part to pressure from the Armor School, the 1984 NBC reconnaissance system requirements document called for an M113A2 APC chassis. Officially, this was to reduce the chance that its signature could be confused with a Soviet vehicle (the BTR-60 silhouette looked similar to the Fuchs), as well as to ensure a common logistics source for spare parts. Later operational testing showed that the APC model, designated as the XM87, had difficulties meeting the requirements of on-the-move reconnaissance. Because of stability problems, the chassis would have to be made from scratch (as opposed to using a standard M113A2 chassis) to accommodate the sensitive German MM-1 sensor and the standoff detector. Each chassis would incorporate a collective protection system and a sampling system was built to enable detection on the move. The technical challenge, driven by the desire for a tracked system, could not be overcome and the program slumped. In 1986, because U.S. forces in Germany demanded an immediate reconnaissance capability, the Army ordered a task force (composed of Chemical Corps' leaders Brigadier General Walt Kastenmeyer, Major General Gerry Watson, and Brigadier General Bobby Robinson) to evaluate the option to lease or buy forty-eight Fuchs (a six-wheeled armored recon vehicle) from the German government, as an interim capability and while development of the XM87 continued.[4] Based on the task force's recommendation, the Undersecretary of the Army and Vice Chief of Staff of the Army officially killed the XM87 program in July 1988 and ordered the Chemical Corps to buy the Fuchs. The PM NBC Defense office purchased five German Fuchs vehicles that month under the Nunn-Lugar legislation (authorizing DoD to acquire allied military equipment for test and evaluation), since known as the "Nunn" NBCRS vehicles.

General Motors immediately protested the decision to Congress, stating that there had been inadequate consideration for U.S. companies that could meet the requirement. This led to a shoot-off in May–July 1989 between the General Dynamics Land Systems/Thyssen-Henschel team's German Fuchs (translated as "Fox") and the TRW/General Motor team's Light Armored Vehicle (LAV) NBC reconnaissance systems, using a "plain vanilla" M113A2 APC with chemical soldiers using M256A1 kits and M8 paper as a baseline NBC reconnaissance system.[5] The German Fuchs won the competition, leading to a contract award to General Dynamics Land Systems (GDLS), the U.S. producer, and Thyssen-Henschel (the German partner) in March 1990. Since it would take years to develop the full capacity NBCRS, the Army decided to procure forty-eight vehicles as an interim measure (enough for forces in Europe and the Chemical School). The initial forty-eight XM93s would be "Americanized" German Fuchs vehicles, beginning deliveries in 1992. These Fuchs would be "Americanized" in Germany by building them to U.S. specifications, including U.S. Army radios, NBC defense equipment (CAM, AN/VDR-2 radiac, and M8A1 chemical agent alarm), a U.S. 7.62-mm machine gun, U.S. smoke grenade launchers, and an air-conditioning system. A second contract award (awarded the same day) would pay for the development of the full-capacity Fox with remote detection, a meteorological sensor, digital communications, organic maintenance, and a reduced crew (from four to three). The second contract also provided for the purchase of ten prototype objective systems, the XM93E1 NBCRS. After successful development, a second production contract would fill the full Army force requirements as the M93A1 NBCRS.

After the shoot-off, the PM Office asked the user community for message support and to support the quantity of NBCRSs the Army would procure. Only two "users" responded: the commander-in-chief for Army forces in Europe (CINCEUR) and an obscure commander from something called CENTCOM. Although CENTCOM's commander-in-chief, General Norman Schwarzkopf, had acknowledged the need for an NBCRS in his area of responsibility, he didn't have any divisions under his command, and his name wasn't immediately recognized. The Air Force showed interest in the NBCRS for reconning air bases but did not forward any procurement money. The Marine Corps flatly rejected the NBCRS, noting that it was too heavy and too wide to deploy with their initial battle groups. They began pushing a study for the same type of equipment in a HMMWV (the "light" NBCRS).

Long-range standoff detection had sparked more interest among the services, looking for a long-promised (but undelivered) early-warning capability in the

XM21 RSCAAL.  Because of the heavy investment of research funds and technical expertise required, the other services had let the Army spearhead the stand-off detection effort.  Its unit cost had climbed to $80,000 per detector (1985 dollars). CRDEC had been unable to reduce the weight under fifty pounds, could not enable detection on the move, and the detector could still not determine how far away the chemical agent cloud was.  It still had interferant and reliability issues that the Army wanted to iron out, which moved the type-classification date to much later in 1991.   Yet the RSCAAL's passive infrared sensor represented the best opportunity to give combat units a long-range early-warning capability.

The Marine Corps joined the Army program as a joint service effort as it came closer to its expected type-classification date in 1989.  The Army, Air Force, and Navy all wanted this kind of a standoff capability, but the lack of ranging information made the Air Force and Navy hold back their blessings.  Given their limited numbers of chemical specialists and the large, lucrative targets that ports and airfields made, the Air Force and Navy wanted to know precisely where the threat was and where their resources had to be allocated.  All three services began to independently investigate lasers as an option, a technology that had matured since the initiation of the standoff program in the 1970s.  Optical instruments could detect laser scattering against the agent clouds, which would give the ranging information that battlefield commanders desired.  Power requirements, identification of chemical agent signatures, safety issues associated with laser technology (developing eye-safe lasers), and competing programs with less technical risk would keep this program from maturing quickly.

There were a number of biological detection programs still ongoing up to 1980, mostly as lab-bench prototypes, none funded very highly.  CRDEC fostered an effort to combine chemical agent detectors with biological agent detectors, in an effort to save overall costs by developing one detector that filled two functions. The two main programs, the Chemical-Biological Mass Spectrometer (very sensitive and large for fixed sites and reconnaissance) and the Biological-Chemical Detector (a relatively man-portable field detector), were examples of this strategy. They used different scientific approaches, both commonly used in commercial laboratories, and were placed in a ruggedized frame that could communicate with military systems.  There was a great deal of undeveloped information, however; where would these devices operate on the battlefield, what military units would operate them, and what specific agents should they detect?  Should they detect all potential biological warfare agents (and there are many different types) or just the more common warfare agents?  Last, how does one incorporate chemical agent detection alongside the biological agent detector?  Do chemical and biological detectors even belong side by side on the battlefield?

The Chemical School knew there were serious doctrinal implications involved with the equipment requirements.  Because of the diverse characteristics of biological agents, Edgewood scientists warned that no one detection technology would be adequate.  Detecting bacteria was different from detecting viruses, and even different viruses required different procedures. Because many biological agents were dangerous in small quantities and could not be identified by automatic detection, Army personnel would have to collect soil and water samples, establish procedures on how to safely transport the samples back to forward laboratories, culture the samples, and inform political and combat leaders on what the results were. The School kept studying these issues, with little input (or interest) from the other Army branches. The Air Force and Navy had funded their own "service-unique" biological detection programs but had made even less progress than the Army, due to lack of funds (and a corresponding lack of interest among their combat warriors). This situation is why some people called the NBC defense program a small "n" small "b" big "C" (nbC) program, as the program was practically all chemical detection programs. Because of the difficulty in addressing these operational and technical issues, the biological detection program continued to limp along, underfunded and understudied—until August 1990, when the Army was forced to face the threat head-on. Figure 12.1 summarizes the equipment developed prior to 1990, with associated costs and density within the force.

## Detection in the Field

As the Chemical Corps was revamping doctrine and pushing a modernization program along, the combat units were just getting used to the idea of chemical detection capabilities. As the Army emerged from its post-Vietnam slump and decided to get serious about the potential for war in Europe, chemical specialists trained individual soldiers and squads repeatedly on how to use M8 paper to identify liquid chemical agents, how to wear strips of M9 paper on their uniforms, and how to interpret the M256A1 kits. Trainers would place antifreeze liquid or spray insecticide (to cause color changes) or water (no color change) on the paper to test their soldiers' understanding of their use. The M256A1 kit also had an associated training set. The training kits simulated the presence of different chemical agents with dyes mixed into the liquid vials in the card; the instructor could then judge to see if the trainee had identified the agent correctly.

There was one training system that simulated a wide area liquid agent attack, the Simulant, Projectile, Airborne Liquid or SPAL. This was basically a simple mortar, featuring a cardboard tube with an explosive charge in the base and a plastic jug filled with polyethylene glycol with an explosive charge in the bottle. Upon ignition, several jugs popped into the air and exploded, spraying a mist downwind that could cause a color change on M8 and M9 paper. It was difficult to emplace (because of safety issues) and surprise soldiers with this device, and tightened environmental concerns soon relegated this system to retirement. These manual detection methods were basic skills everyone understood along with wearing protective masks and clothing, easily trained across the board. More difficult was the concept of employing the M8A1 detector and CAMs.

Because the M8 and M8A1 detectors required some training to operate and maintain, very often two soldiers in the squad or company became the primary and

**Table 12.1**
**Representative Recon, Detection, and Identification Equipment**

| Nomenclature | Intended Use | Basis of Issue | Unit Cost* | DoD Inventory* |
|---|---|---|---|---|
| M8 Paper | Post attack identification, liquid only | 1 per soldier | $0.85 | 2,700,000 |
| M9 Paper | Attack indicator, liquid only | 1 roll per squad | $4.30 | 1,000,000 |
| M256A1 Detector Kit | Identification and all-clear indicator, vapor only | 1 per squad | $45 | 108,000 |
| M18A2 Detector Kit | Identification, vapor or liquid | special units only | $321 | 130 |
| M272A1 Water Test Kit | Identification, liquid only | 1 per company | $194 | 9,000 |
| M1 CAM | Identification and monitoring, vapor only | 2 per company | $6,000 | 13,000 |
| M8A1 Alarm | Early warning detection, vapor only | 2 per company | $2,500 | 30,000 |
| M21 RSCAAL | Standoff detection and warning | 6 per division | $175,000 | 200 |
| M93 "Fox" NBCRS | Reconnaissance & identification | 6 per division | $1,700,000 | 60 |
| M274 Marking Set | Marking contaminated areas | 1 per squad | $135 | 47,000 |
| DT-236 Dosimeter | Total radiation dose | 1 per soldier | $21 | 800,000 |
| AN/VDR-2 | Radiation dose-rate and monitoring | 1 per platoon | $635 | 40,000 |

* - FY98 costs and inventory figures, to give the reader a measure of the costs and DoD requirements

alternate designated operators. Their responsibility was to set up the detector and alarm in the field, to ensure it was running correctly, and to attend to its alarms. By doctrine, M8A1 detectors were supposed to be placed in three and four units across the company's front (or upwind), each one about 150 meters apart. Because of the shortfall mentioned earlier, many companies had only one or two units each and did the best they could to spread them apart.  It was more difficult to realistically train with these systems.  While there was an electronic trainer developed in the late 1980s, not many units had access to the system.  Having a soldier standing next to an M8A1 detector with insect spray or triggering the self-test alarm was a sure way to warn nearby soldiers that a mask drill was about to take place.  This was hardly realistic, and unit training and basic understanding of employing detectors in the field suffered as a result.  Since unit training often included only a few hours of chemical defense training (or maybe a whole day if fortunate), companies and larger units rarely realistically employed these systems and as a result failed to fully understand the concept.

Not many units had the CAM prior to 1990.  While the basic operation of the system was simple, it was a fussy instrument to maintain.  Poorly trained soldiers waved it over vehicles and personnel like a magic wand, expecting instant results like the M8/M9 paper.  It took some skill to learn how to operate the sensitive instrument without flooding its chamber with too much vapor, which made it inoperative for a few minutes until it cleared.  It false-alarmed to interferents such as organic-based solvents, hospital supplies (limiting its usefulness to medics), and fire-fighting foam (limiting its use on ships and airfields).  It required constant maintenance and nursing to ensure it would work on demand, which meant two soldier in the company became the "CAM team."  While the Chemical Corps had tried to get away from specialists operating the equipment, it was easier for combat arms units to designate teams to maintain/operate the equipment.  This worked in principle, but it limited the knowledge of employing the devices to a few personnel that very often rotated out of the unit, calling for new training for a new team.

As regards biological detection training, that was nonexistent.  Given that there were no detectors, no warning would take place other than a sudden increase in the sick call roster.  While chemical specialists were trained to collect samples, it was expected that the Army medics would make the call.  Except no one really told the medics this—the medical community acknowledged the mission of health promotion, but they were not set up to collect field samples, analyze them, and tell commanders when there was a biological warfare agent present.  No one in the combat arms really cared enough to face this threat other than ensuring their soldiers' shot records were up to date.  To them, this was a diplomatic function; if the politicians didn't stop the threat of biological warfare, there were always tactical nukes.  The concept of biological warfare just didn't seem viable enough to worry about, despite intelligence indications that more and more countries were developing BW munitions.

NBC reconnaissance was alive in a sense, as the division armored cavalry regiments had assigned chemical specialists that drove around in HMMWVs or APCs, fully dressed in protective suits and masks brandishing sticks with M8 paper stuck on the end. They were all waiting for the M93 NBCRS and CAMs to execute their mission, but in the meanwhile, they were glorified scouts augmenting the division scouts. Because there were no large area simulants, they received little training. More critical was the fact that combat leaders in the brigades and divisions had no sense of how to use chemical reconnaissance troops. At the National Training Center, these recon troops might stumble upon a marked "contaminated area" (with ersatz Warsaw Pact–marked signs), radio its location into headquarters, and the troops would avoid the area like the plague. Anything but the hassle of going through a decontamination line.

Standoff detection remained a dream just out of reach through the 1980s. The vision of using standoff detection to detect clouds of chemical vapors on the battlefield fueled the continued research in the M21 RSCAAL. Given the shortage of M8A1 chemical detectors, a few strategically placed standoff systems could cover square kilometers of the vulnerable rear supply areas, or screen the front areas for contaminated routes. Concepts of the laser-based system that would indicate distance as well as type of contamination remained just concepts. No one in the combat arms was really pushing for this capability, so there was little pressure on the Chemical Corps to deliver. There was the desire to ensure continued funding of the programs and therefore, there was the need to show progress. The problem was that the date to complete the project kept slipping a few years further down the road.

Given that the Army's chemical defense community was literally shut down for nearly a decade, they had made impressive strides in developing and fielding a robust chemical reconnaissance, detection and identification program. There was a clear transition from a limited spectrum of detection by specialists to a wide and diverse array of detection capabilities by both nonspecialists and specialists. What was lacking was a sense of familiarity by the military community (outside the Chemical Corps) with how to exploit this capability, and how to best integrate chemical doctrine and equipment into combat operations. Too many combat leaders still relied on the retaliatory threat of chemical weapons to bluff their opponents to not employ chemical agents against U.S. forces. In many minds, chemical detectors were just a warning to don protective masks and clothing, at which time their forces would stop operations until the chemical attack was over and assessed. Chemical detection and force reaction was never actually practiced in large-unit (battalion and brigade) training exercises, in part due to a lack of effective training devices and an overall shortage of detectors themselves (in particular, the M8A1 alarms). They knew that the chemical detectors meant there was something out there—but then what?

The M1 CAM, the XM93 NBCRS, the XM21 RSCAAL, the XM22 ACADA and a near-real-time biological agent detector were detection systems that could have had a great impact—had they ever been issued to the Army in quantity as intended during the mid-1980s. Instead, these programs were not fielded, due to a number of technical, programmatic, and political reasons. The Edgewood engineers blamed the Chemical School for program delays resulting from constantly changing requirements from the office of Directorate of Combat Developments. While combat units clamored for new equipment such as the M1 CAM, the M17 Lightweight Decon System and the NBC recon system, the Army military leadership took no action to encourage or penalize the Chemical Corps as programs failed to meet their schedules year after year. While the Air Force, Navy, and Marine Corps bemoaned the lack of compromise and overly long testing requirements by the Army, they refused to commit serious funds or personnel from their non-CB defense programs to joint CB defense programs. The Chemical School could not adequately communicate between the combat arms and the CB defense technical community to resolve conflicts between the ideal operational end-state and what was technically feasible. If one were looking for only one guilty party, there were too many accomplices, which is why the GAO reports on CB defense programs throughout the 1980s read so scathingly.

# CHAPTER 13

# Individual Protection— Part 2

In 1985 the Air Force announced it was procuring and fielding the former XM30 mask as the MCU-2/P protective mask, with a softer one-lens facepiece and a harder, clip-on protective shield. All Air Force ground personnel would use this mask. It was also adopted by NAVSEA, NAVAIR, and Marine Corps aviation crews, given its superior field of vision and better fit (as compared to the M17A2 mask) and its immediate availability (as compared to the M40 mask). Marine Corps ground forces and NAVFAC continued to procure the Army's M17-series masks for their ground personnel. Other government agencies, specifically law enforcement and the Secret Service, began requesting the new MCU-2/P masks as well, admiring the larger field of vision, more comfortable fit, and external canister. The Air Force's success with the MCU-2/P raised eyebrows at the Army's continuing difficulties with the M40 mask program.

M40 mask production had continued to hit delays due to difficulties designing the masks for industrial production and related testing issues. While it is one thing to produce a few hundred masks with trained industry personnel, it is something entirely different to produce tens of thousands of protective masks that would all pass quality assurance testing. The rubber facepiece molds for masks and the industrial presses, in particular, are critical to the process and are very difficult to design. Complicating the issue was a change in contractors, due to the military's requirement to open-bid each stage of R&D and production, and the practice of awarding contracts to low-bidding firms over higher quality (and more expensive) firms.

Although ILC Dover had conducted a large portion of the R&D on the mask, the production contract was awarded to Scott Aviation after the mask's type classification in May 1987. Scott Aviation delivered only 3,358 masks out of a contract target of 300,000, which initially resulted in a stop-work order in 1988, and eventually the contract's termination for the convenience of the government in January 1990. In September 1988 AMCCOM awarded Mine Safety Appliances (MSA) and ILC Dover with short-term M40 production contracts (120,000 each by September 1989) in an effort to get masks out quickly to the major Army units. Both firms faced technical and production start-up problems, such as difficulties in developing the proper tools and molding. This prevented either company from producing masks prior to August 1990. Because of the M40 mask's expected fielding date of 1988, the Army had stopped M17A2 and M25 mask production in 1986 and 1988, respectively. To offset the absence of new masks coming into the logistics system, Pine Bluff Arsenal established a mask refurbishing capability to refurbish and repair worn-out and broken M17-series and M24/25 masks.

On the aviation side, the Army decided that the Apache helicopter could not be fielded without a protective mask that permitted use of the Optical Relay Tube. In March 1985 the Aviation School asked the Chemical School to kill the XM41 program in favor of accelerating the XM43 to field it by 1986. In September 1986, the M43 aviator protective mask was type-classified limited-production-urgent, with a first unit issue date of July 1987. A follow-on production effort fabricated enough systems to test the concept thoroughly during REFORGER 87 (Return of Forces to Germany exercise). The M43 contractor, Scott Aviation (again), was terminated due to production problems in March 1990. A new contract was awarded in June 1990 to Mine Safety Appliances for 3,150 M43s to meet AH-64 battalion readiness requirements.

The Air Force ran into difficulties in its AERP program, the planned replacement for the current MBU-13 aviator protective mask. In 1985 the Air Force announced it was canceling the program after seven years of invested time and resources. They had not overcome the ejection compatibility, among other vital issues of aircraft compatibility and operator use. The Navy decided to continue developing a new aviator mask and began work on adapting the British AR-5 aviator mask. The AR-5 allowed clear visibility and night vision, provisions for drinking, and a comfortable portable blower/filter unit. The Air Force resumed its AERP program in 1988, after successfully addressing many of its prior problems. The Navy had already decided to commit to the modified AR-5 design for its next aviator protective mask and chose not to participate in the Air Force's restarted program.[1]

Other specialized mask programs rose and fell with the desire for an improvement over the M17/M40-style field protective mask. Both the Air Force and Special Forces put out feelers for a Disposable Eye/Respiratory Protection (DERP) mask (the Air Force term); essentially, they desired a mask that they could fold up and keep in their pocket, then whip it out and it if they ran into a chemical threat. The emphasis was on a lightweight throw-away mask, but the technical challenges were too great. True to the zero-risk desire, proponents for a light-weight mask wanted it to be as capable as the full-sized masks, without additional cost or risk. During the 1980s, the carbon-based filter canister were the only technology that could filter out all CBW hazards without increasing breathing resistance (making it too hard to breath). There have been similar masks marketed that claim a quick-donning capability, but they resemble a plastic bag sporting a thin carbon-impregnated fabric over the mouth area, a soft plastic visor over the eyes, and a less than perfect fit around the neck. This concept may be good for saving one's life and about fifteen minutes of breathing, but not for continuous combat operations. As in the case of the ICAD/IVD/SOFCAS, the Infantry School was happy with its M17A2/M40 masks and saw no real advantage to a lightweight mask that increased the risk to their soldiers.

## SAME OLD SUITS

In the protective clothing arena, the Marine Corps decided that the high heat stress, lack of launderability, and flammable nature of the BDOs were not suitable; moreover, they did not intend to wait until 1990 for the Army's follow-on protective suit. The German military's Saratoga suit used what was called "von Blucher carbon spheres" instead of carbon-impregnated foam that allowed laundering the suits. Its outer shell was flame-resistant, and Marines perceived it as more lightweight and cooler than the BDO. The Marines liked the parka hood it featured, which would eliminate the requirement for a hood on the mask. The Army disliked the parka hood, which they saw as allowing large gaps around the neck when the soldier twisted his/her head. The Saratoga also was roughly twice as expensive as the BDO and did not significantly lower heat stress in moderate to hot climates. The Marine Corps was convinced that this was their suit and pressed for its procurement as their primary protective suit, with the BDO as a backup.

Since it would not be seen as cost-effective to have two different chemical protective suits for DoD ground forces, the Marine Corps and Army began attacking each other's programs, largely by questioning data from tests and evaluation of clothing swatches. Soon, Congress stepped in to referee and requested a technical comparison between the Army BDO, the German Saratoga, and the British Mark IV protective clothing. The Army eventually won by stressing the need to meet the ten-gram-per-square-meter challenge and lower unit cost of the BDO, but they promised to form a joint working group with the Marines on the next generation of chemical suits. This resulted in the formation of the Joint Lightweight Integrated Suit Technology (JLIST) program.

The Air Force had quietly followed up on the von Blucher spheres as well and developed a new one-piece groundcrew ensemble, the CWU-77. Their flight suit version, called the CWU-66, would replace the current flight uniform of chemically impregnated underwear that the Air Force, Navy, and Marine Corps pilots wore. The costs of the CWU-66 and CWU-77 were considerably higher than the BDO and offered a lower degree of protection; but again, they were cooler than the BDO, and launderable, allowing reuse as long as it was uncontaminated. The Navy was investigating a new flight suit and new groundcrew suit, but it had no real candidates other than the British Mark III and Mark IV. The Army aviation community had been successful in pushing their own two-piece flame-resistant protective suit (the Aircrew Uniform Integrated Battlesuit [AUIB]) to type-classification by 1990. The Air Force's one-piece design was seen as overly expensive as compared to the two-piece, without any added operational values that would justify the cost. At least the AUIB had pockets for aviators to hold pens, notebooks, and sunglasses as their conventional flight suits did.[2]

The special forces community was seeking a lighter suit, similar to their requirement for a lightweight mask. Patterned after the aviator undergarment protective suits, Natick labs designed a lightweight one-piece suit to be worn under the soldier's uniform. It did not reduce heat stress by much, however. The Marine Corps pushed for a similar capability where a marine could tailor the clothes to the threat, using chemical protective socks, a protective undergarment, and a boot dressing to increase resistance to mustard agents.

Natick engineers were often frustrated by the combat arms' demand for a suit that didn't increase heat stress. In any geographical areas that had warm to hot climates, any addition of clothing, be it a tee-shirt, rain poncho, British Mark III suit, Army BDO, or Marine Corps Saratoga, was going to increase heat stress. There was not that much difference between the heat stress levels caused by a soldier wearing a normal uniform and a soldier wearing only underwear and the BDOs. The protective suit the combat arms really wanted was something out of "Starship Troopers," integrated protective suits-and-helmet systems that were resistant to ballistics (bullets), kinetic energy (blasts), flame, and CB agents, were air conditioned, augmented the soldier's strength with a powered exoskeleton, and had integrated communications systems in the helmets that connected everyone on the battlefield. In the 1990s, this concept took real form, becoming the "Land Warrior" program.[3]

To permit EOD specialists a full Level A equivalency (totally enclosed suit with breathing apparatus under the suit), Natick researchers initiated the Suit, Toxicological Environment Protective Overgarment (STEPO). The STEPO was initiated as a joint service program, but the Air Force and Navy later pulled out of the program, stating they did not see their service-unique requirements being met. The Air Force wanted a Level A suit that one could wear within the engineering vehicles used to clear damaged airfields, and the Navy had similar concerns with fitting through ship hatches. The bulk of the suit, with its self-contained breathing apparatus and body-cooling system, was not designed for tight spots. There were also complications in tests and evaluation, which was peculiar for a protective suit that was modeled directly after a commercially available item. This suit was not available in production quantities prior to the Gulf War.[4]

Natick was still undecided on the new design for the Multipurpose Overboot (MULO) boot. The emphasis remained on an all-purpose boot with protection against petroleum, oil, and lubricants as well as flame-resistant and NBC agent resistant. The protective gloves issue was still unresolved as well, with a number of new fabrics under consideration. Ideally, the soldiers wanted a more tactile sensation while wearing gloves, with no loss in protection as compared against butyl rubber. Testing appropriate fabrics for both sensation and protection while retaining durability kept the lab busy examining many alternatives for years.

There was no real pressure from the combat arms or chemical defense community, as there were literally millions of excess butyl-rubber gloves and boots in the inventory, along with the millions of protective suits stored in warehouses. By 1990 the new candidates had been selected, but none were in production. This left soldiers with the green vinyl overboots and heavy butyl rubber gloves, and no real advances in protection after ten years of research. Figure 13.1 summarizes the equipment developed prior to 1990, with associated costs and density within the force.

## INDIVIDUAL PROTECTION IN THE FIELD

Protective suits and protective masks have an interesting history from the standpoint that they are designed to protect individuals from the same CB agents and radioactive particles; yet there are multiple designs based on one's specific operational mission. Regular infantry get standard permeable suits, special forces want lighter suits, chemical specialists want impermeable suits, pilots want one-piece suits. The underlying technologies (absorbent fabrics, negative pressure face masks, and carbon-based filters) have not changed, just the forms have. Since the Chemical Corps' disestablishment process in 1972, the other services responded by initiating their own programs designed for specific applications. Some of these programs could have been joint, without the interference of interservice politics and dueling test and evaluation committees.

Soldiers in the field hated wearing protective suits and masks, even as they understood why they were being trained to use them. That should be no great surprise, as infantry soldiers have hated wearing protective masks since World War I. In the late 1970s and early 1980s, there was a great push to familiarize everyone with procedures to operate in a chemical environment. Soldiers had to fire their weapons on training ranges while wearing their protective masks. Army regulations called for each soldier to spend at least six hours training in protective suits each year. Everyone had an annual appointment with the gas chamber, that is to say, the "mask confidence" exercise. The infantry badge test called for donning the mask in nine seconds, fifteen seconds if it had a hood, and get into the suit in two minutes. Everyone knew the Mission Oriented Protective Posture (MOPP) levels—MOPP zero, have the suit nearby; MOPP one, wear the suit only; MOPP two, wear the suit and boots; MOPP three, add the mask; and MOPP four, add the gloves.

For individual survival, it wasn't that tough. Hold your breath, pull out the mask, put it on, seal it. Get the suit out of its bag, pull it on, zip up, call in the chemical attack to higher headquarters. It was trying to carry out the combat missions in the suit that was the task. Wearing the suit and mask, a group of soldiers suddenly all look alike. No one knows who the leader is, because the mask is muffling everyone's voice and they all look like green clones of the Michelin man. The CANE briefings didn't tell the Army anything new when it spoke of the isolation felt by individuals in MOPP gear, it merely quantified it in terms combat

**Table 13.1**
**Representative Individual Protection Equipment**

| Nomenclature | Intended Use | Basis of Issue | Unit Cost* | DoD Inventory* |
|---|---|---|---|---|
| M17A1 Mask | General purpose field mask | 1 per soldier | $90 | 756,000 |
| M13A2 Filter Element | Filters for M17A1 | 1 pair per mask | $19.40 | 410,000 |
| MCU-2/P | General purpose field mask | 1 per airman | $140 | 620,000 |
| C2 Canister | Filters for MCU-2/P | 1 per mask | $9 | 5,300,000 |
| M43 Apache Mask | Rotary wing aviator mask | 1 per pilot | $2,000 | 3,100 |
| AERP Mask | Fixed wing aviator mask | 1 per pilot | $680 | 20,000 |
| BDO | General purpose ensemble | 1 per soldier | $100 | 6,000,000 |
| Saratoga Suit | General purpose ensemble | 1 per Marine | $190 | 630,000 |
| CWU-66 Suit | Aviator ensemble | 1 per aviator | $400 | 165,000 |
| 7, 14, 25 mil Gloves | Liquid-repellant gloves | 1 pair per soldier | $8 | 13,300,000 |
| CP Footwear Covers | Disposable rubber footwear | 1 pair per soldier | $6.45 | 1,300,000 |
| Green Vinyl Overboots | Liquid-repellant boots | 1 per soldier | $14 | 6,000,000 |
| SCALP | Liquid splash protection only | 1 per crewman | $18 | 30,000 |

* - FY98 costs and inventory figures, to give the reader a measure of the costs and DoD requirements

arms leaders understood.  The optimal thing to do would be to "train as you would fight" as the motto went.  Major General Barry McCaffrey, as the commander of the 24th Infantry Division, understood that to make his troops more effective while in protective gear, they had to practice with protective gear.  They soon understood the limitations involved and overcame the sense of isolation.  Soldiers marked their helmets with their ranks, and taped their names on their suits.

This seems intuitive, but it is not.  Most infantry units decided that chemical defense training was something done as extra training on the side, something they should not allow to distract them from conventional battle training.  MOPP training was often executed in garrison; six hours of walking around the buildings, rather than in the field.  Another variation was MOPP athletics; playing MOPP soccer and MOPP volleyball, or walking a road march in protective masks.  While this may have toughened up their bodies or made them familiar with the suit and mask, it didn't train soldiers to attack the enemy in MOPP gear.  Because of the difficulty of operating in MOPP and the perception that chemical warfare was not as certain as had been thought, combat arms leaders increasingly neglected integrating chemical defense training into field exercises.  It was seen as an individual skill, not as a unit skill; and at the National Training Center exercises, when companies and brigades came under simulated chemical attacks, they inevitably failed.  The bad part is that they weren't penalized for poor performance if it was as a result of chemical warfare—that performance was excused, it wasn't what "really" would happen in combat.

Two short stories will illustrate.  Every good chemical lieutenant and NCO has tried using "training lanes," in which a platoon will split up its three squads into three lanes and have each squad train on some particular function as a team.  They rotate from one lane to the next, saving time and maximizing training resources.  NBC training lanes might have a movement to contact in which the squad runs into a contaminated area (mask up and identify the contamination); assault the enemy while in MOPP suits (fire and maneuver in masks); and then conduct hasty decontamination in order to get out of MOPP gear and move on.  Each time, the same incidents occurred.  In the contaminated area, troops would mask, and impatiently await the 15–20 minutes for the M256A1 kit to register (they had no idea it took that long, having never practiced the full operation).  During the assault, they tripped over logs they didn't see, couldn't yell to each other through the masks, and were out of breath at the end of the thirty-yard sprint.  At the decon area, they were so happy to get out of the "contaminated" suits, very often they never thought about the problems of resupplying extra suits that they would require to continue the mission (in the event there was more contamination ahead).

At a mask confidence exercise I held at Fort Benning in 1987, a sergeant called me over to inspect a soldier's mask.  This soldier's eyes were red and tearing, and he insisted his mask was broken because every time he masked in the chamber, the CS gas came in.  As I flipped the mask over and inspected it, I noticed the outlet valve was missing (normally this valve permits exhaled breaths to escape the mask and then seals during intake of breath).  Some soldiers, because their leaders made them road march with the masks on, had removed the outlet valves to enable them to breathe easier. As I pointed out to him the error of his ways, I also tried to convince him that this was the whole intent of the mask confidence exercise. You had to know how to properly use a mask if you intended to enter a toxic environment and keep on walking. Those soldiers that maintained their masks in good condition were not suffering any effects of CS exposure. He grinned and shrugged, saying he had no idea how that valve disappeared.

The logistics of purchasing, storing, and issuing protective suits remains a critical issue, more so perhaps here than in the other sectors of CB defense (save medical, which is very logistics-oriented as well). The standard issue of protective suits for military personnel ranges from two to four suits per individual, depending on which military command the troop belongs to. During the 1980s, the total number of suits required was felt to be between eight and twelve million (depending on who you talked to and what risks they were willing to take). This was seen as a heavy investment for a situation that was not seen as the standard model for war fighting. While having modern protective suits in quantities to support a world conflict against the Soviet Union was a big issue in the late 1970s, the situation had changed in the mid-1980s. The influx of new doctrine and new equipment competing with CB defense training and equipment had relegated protective suits to the sidelines. They became supplies everyone knew were necessary but no one wanted to invest in because of the costs of purchasing and storing millions of suits, boots, and gloves.

Since the suits were in airtight bags, the services began sampling from the lots to determine whether they were still resistant to chemical agents. The results of these annual tests extended their shelf lives from five years, the original lifespan, up to fourteen years. Butyl rubber boots and gloves were similarly tested and extended. Every soldier had at least one training protective suit with a pair of protective boots and gloves, often drawn from the wartime contingency stocks, for the annual MOPP training and occasionally for field exercises. While these suits would in theory be replaced in time of war, the boots and gloves were fine (unless ripped) and would not require replacement. The major commands soon became used to not purchasing protective suits; still, the levels began dropping due to consumption caused by training and gradual shelf life expirations. Some purchases were made to maintain an industrial capability, but this was not an area of high focus, resulting in the shortfalls seen in 1990.

Practicing CB defense during larger field exercises showed some problems; if a large body of soldiers, say 250 troops, were in protective suits that were contaminated, they needed to swap out of their contaminated suits within twenty-four hours and receive new suits. Chemical decontamination companies were primarily designed to support equipment decontamination; personnel took care of themselves by receiving new suits and moving out of the contaminated areas. Brigade and division supply officers worked with chemical officers to develop ways to enhance resupply of critical chemical defense equipment quickly and efficiently. One approach was called "Individual Chemical Equipment" or ICE packs. These were boxes, often converted Meals-Ready to Eat (MRE) boxes, that contained one protective suit, one pair of gloves and boots, new mask filters, one M256A1 kit, one M8 paper and one M9 paper roll, and one M258A1 decontamination kit. Each company supply shop would personalize an ICE pack for each individual, to ensure sizing requirements were correct, label the boxes with the soldier's name, and ship them to brigade supply centers. In the event of actual wartime, the ICE packs would be rushed forward. This would support troops at least through the first chemical attack.[5]

This practice was entirely dependent upon the division commander and his desire to implement some type of solution to a tough logistics issue. Other divisions were not as willing to invest the time to maintain even this degree of readiness. The light infantry divisions, in particular, were always trying to reduce their logistics footprint (the size of the logistics trains necessary to support the division). Their goal was to deploy anywhere in the world within eighteen hours of notice. Heavy armored or mechanized infantry divisions might take that long just to get their vehicles onto the railcars to move to their deployment sites. In addition, the 1980s light infantry divisions were all expecting to be deployed into areas of low-intensity conflict, e.g., Nicaragua, El Salvador, places where the enemy had only light armored vehicles, limited air cover, and no CB munitions. This philosophy drove the training to largely exclude CB defense training other than the mandatory six hours per year in MOPP gear and familiarization firing on the weapons range in masks. To reduce the logistics burden, many brigades decided that the military raingear available would be the first line of protection against chemical warfare. Those that remember the old olive-drab raingear recognize that it is liquid-resistant, not repellent, and of no protection against chemical vapors. Light infantry soldiers grudgingly kept the masks on their web belts only when it was pointed out that Central and South American military and police use tear gas much more frequently than their U.S. counterparts.

The end result of ten years of protective mask and suit design was seen in August 1990. Wearing a protective mask in the field was mandatory, and MOPP training was always somewhere in the annual training requirements, but that didn't mean that units knew how to operate during a battle in protective gear. After-action reports from the National Training Center proved that. Because the Air Force, Navy, and Marine Corps had relatively low inventories of suits and masks (as compared to the Army), their industry partners could not support the sudden wartime requirements on top of low wartime reserves in August 1990. This sudden demand by the other services caused a significant drain on worldwide inventories of protective suits and masks, and started cries for the Army to support all DoD wartime requirements. If anything, the 1990 Gulf War emphasized the need for a joint service protective ensemble program—not just as a sensible cost-saving effort, but as an important component of military readiness and sustainment practices when considering jointly managed military consumables.

Military protective suits and masks have been designed specifically for CB agents and tested against CB agents, all within safe limits for their line of work (operating on a high-risk battlefield).  Every soldier who has been through the Chemical Defense Training Facility at Fort McClellan leaves with the strong recognition that protective suits and masks work, providing a safe atmosphere in an otherwise deadly environment.  As pointed out earlier, however, there still remains a question of whether there might be an overdesign issue, or is a ten-gram-per-square-meter challenge still required after the Cold War.  Until the Army's combat leaders instruct the Chemical Corps to revisit this issue or there are sudden leaps in protective technologies, the heavy and hot protective suits and bulky protective masks will continue to be a fixture in the Army's future.

    This program area will always receive the most attention in CB defense, if only because the American public wants to see their sons and daughters return safely from combat, and they demand high standards for protection.  Military leaders and politicians echo this demand, which again puts focus on whether the suits and masks are adequately designed for future CB warfare conditions.  This chapter should highlight the point that the research and development is mature enough to meet high expectations of zero risk, but that carries a price—not just of higher unit prices for an item that is bought in the quantity of millions, but the price of lessened operational effectiveness on the battlefield.  Hampering the soldier's ability to operate on the battlefield because of bulky suits and masks is just as likely to cause casualties, if not more so, when our soldiers engage the enemy.  Combat leaders need to measure the risk of CB warfare agents against the risk of lessened operational effectiveness realistically and calmly, and determine what their forces need in terms of capability to fight the battle with a minimum loss of life and operational effectiveness.  While occasionally these military leaders do conduct these risk analyses, they often fail to make hard decisions about collective protection requirements—our next program area.

# CHAPTER 14

# Collective Protection and Decontamination—Part 2

These two program areas are grouped in this chapter not based on their functions, but rather because they share the same shadow cast by detection and individual protection programs. The basic research and development program for both areas did not accomplish much in the late 1980s, in part due to lowered funding and interest and in part due to a lack of breakthrough technologies. As mentioned earlier, collective protection systems (CPS) amount to air-conditioning for vehicles, vans, and shelters; decontamination can be seen as just plumbing and brushes. Without capable replacements for activated carbon (in the case of large CPS filters) and DS-2 (in the case of decontamination in general), there was not much new going on in the late 1980s other than basic research looking for new approaches and fielding new equipment designed in the early 1980s.

## COLLECTIVE PROTECTION, 1985–90

In July 1985 the Army type-classified the M20 Simplified Collective Protection Equipment (SCPE), with production scheduled in 1988. Initial test and evaluation issues related to the contractor delaying the immediate production. The M20 SCPE had initially been issued for command posts and forward medical units, but only in small numbers before the contract was canceled for technical problems related to the rubber fabric's chemical agent resistance (an important factor). Army units finally began receiving new M20 SCPEs in May 1990 (two years behind schedule). The system was well received; it did inflate and protect interiors of buildings very well, but it was next to useless in the field. It was not compatible with GP tents and their sharp poles, but then again, it was not designed to be used outside hard-walled buildings. This was an ideal system for Europe, but not for the Middle East.

In September 1985 a medical board decided that they did need a system to treat casualties in a contaminated environment, and the M51 shelter was as good as they were going to get during this decade. The M51 was recognized as an interim solution.  The target fielding number was set at 1,200 systems, of which 837 were already fielded.  No one else within the Army had really identified a mobile CPS requirement other than these two systems.  The medical community requested that the shelters fit within the 64-foot modular tents (Tent Extendable, Modular, Personnel [TEMPER]), used for modular set-up of mobile army surgical hospital (MASH) units.  CRDEC developed a shelter liner, protective entrance, and powered filtration system for these 64-foot-long tents, called the XM28 TEMPER SCPE.  This included a similar liner as the M20 SCPE, which would layer the inside of the large tents.  It featured a special airlock that could fit a stretcher on a table, allowing soldiers to decontaminate contaminated casualties before passing the patient within the tents for treatment.  This program had not begun formal production by 1990.  The Navy had looked into the XM28 program efforts for their shore installations, the only other service interested.

The Air Force continued their concern with fixed-site protection and, by 1985, developed a Survivable Collective Protection System (SCPS) based on a French design.  The SCPS-1 design weighed over 600 tons, supported 84 personnel in two-shift days, and was entirely self-sufficient with its own generator, water supply, and sewage system.  This gold-plated beauty cost only $493,000 each, with Air Force plans to buy about 1,700 systems through 1987.  Congress killed this system based upon poor justification for the requirement.  The Air Force turned its resources toward a more mobile CPS, called the Transportable Collective Protection System (TCPS).  This took an approach more similar to the Army's M28 program, with modular protective shelters that were environmentally controlled (air-conditioned).  The Marine Corps had embarked on a design similar to those of the Air Force and Army, with their Mobile Collective Protection System (MCPS); again, a modularly designed shelter system with environmental controls.  The Marines claimed they could not merge their program with the Air Force due to the advanced level of commitment they had made to the MCPS, and they could not merge with the Army's M20 program because of the Army's lack of a requirement for an environmental control unit (a.k.a. an air conditioner).  Neither system was ready by 1990.  While it appeared that the Air Force's TCPS, the Marine Corps's MCPS, and the Army's M28 SCPE all looked remarkably similar, no one could convince the three services to collaborate on one joint program.

The Navy had invested in using the Army's large filter technology for their ships, creating a shipboard collective protection system, protecting the more vital areas of the ships such as the bridge.  The Marine forces within the transportation ships were expected to wear their protective gear if they were attacked, as it was too much area to effectively protect with CPS.  Because of the cost of refitting ships, this was a slow process, only affecting a small quantity of ships by 1990.  The Navy's two hospital ships lacked a CPS, thus requiring contaminated casualties to make an intermediate stop (for decontamination) prior to boarding.  Needless to say, this effort did not include the Merchant Marine fleet.  The Navy's solution to collective protection was to button up and stay at sea, rather than in port. By presenting less of a target, the Navy fleet was hoping it would not require the extensive protective measures that hadn't been installed.

ODCSOPS had authorized the accelerated development of collective protection systems for all combat vehicles, bypassing the need for separate requirement documents for each vehicle. In response, CRDC had developed a modular CPE approach consisting of four different-sized filter units, three different free standing protective entrances, and a motor controller to allow for a mix and match depending on the size of the vehicle. Units that housed their command and control units in vans were the main customers of this (fire direction centers, communications vans). The M60 tank, M1 tank, M2/M3 Infantry/Cavalry Fighting Vehicles, and M109A2/A3 155-mm howitzers did not have either a ventilated facepiece or an overpressure system. The cost of redesigning or modifying these older vehicles to accommodate NBC defense equipment was seen as cost prohibitive. The entire family of M113 vehicles, to include the M901A1 Improved TOW Vehicle, M106A1 Mortar Carrier, M557 Command Post, and M1059 mechanized smoke generator vehicle, had no collective protection. This was more due to the age of the chassis (developed in 1960) and the decision made then not to include collective protection in the original M113 chassis. The M60A1/A3 and M551 tanks incorporated a ventilated facepiece for their crews wearing M25 masks, as did the M2A1/M3A1 IFV/CFVs. Due to space and operational requirements, the infantry squads within the M2A1s and M3A1s would have to rely on their individual masks, and not an overpressure system or ventilated facepiece system as the three-man crew had.[1]

The summer of 1986 saw the first M1A1 Abrams tank fielded with a hybrid collective protection system. This added (1) an overpressure system, which would force air out of the tank through positive pressure, keeping chemical agent vapors from infiltrating the tank's interior. Combined with (2) a ventilated facepiece system and (3) a microclimate cooling system for the crew, this would allow the armor crews to operate normally in a contaminated environment, without the intense degradation normally associated with a full protective posture. The M270 MLRS vehicle incorporated the hybrid system as well. These vehicles are the only two in the DoD inventory with a hybrid collective protection system.[2] The M93 Fox NBCRS has an overpressure and macro-cooling system, and its crew relies on the M17 or M40 masks for a back up (also if they have to dismount the vehicle while reconning contaminated areas). The next generation of armored vehicles (tanks, IFVs, howitzers, command and control vehicles) all promised to include the hybrid system in their development.

## DECONTAMINATION PROGRAMS, 1985–90

The M17 Lightweight Decon System continued to face redesign issues over the reliability of its engine, its water pressure, and the overall decontaminating effectiveness of the system up to its final type-classification in FY87, with a designated procurement date set in 1989. Units in Europe finally began receiving the M17 LDS (officially) in early 1990.  Its relatively light weight and portability (300 pounds) and lighter maintenance requirements would make it a good fieldable system, but it was one that still relied on large quantities of water in near by collapsible rubber fabric water tanks.  Because it did not use DS-2 but rather hot water, it was stressed that this only reduced potential chemical contamination.  It did not eliminate the need for protective suits and masks after the cleaning, but it did reduce the threat and reduce the spread of contamination across the battlefield.

The XM18 skid-mounted DAP fared no better than its predecessor (the XM14) in replacing the M12A1 Decon Apparatus.  It was approximately 1,100 pounds overweight for the 5-ton payload limit, when carrying 450 gallons of water in its holding tank.  In September 1985, based on a special review of the system, HQ AMC directed that the XM18 be terminated by 1987, leaving the Army with the old M12A1 warhorse as its primary decontamination system.   In 1989 the Chemical School gave up on the German C8 emulsion decontamination program, citing the higher effectiveness of DS-2 as the primary reason.  The added concern that C8 emulsion would not completely replace DS-2 (DS-2 was still required for the M11/M13 DAPs) was another factor.

The nonaqueous decontamination programs had not advanced much from the beginning of the decade.  The XM19 NAEDS ran into problems over its use of an ozone-depleting chemical (Freon-113) and was sent back into research and development until a substitute for Freon was discovered, much to the disgust of Air Force proponents.  They thought that the decision to hold up the decon system because of the Freon issue was not a proper consideration of the loss of real capability (not having a nonaqueous decontaminant for avionics and electronics) that would present itself in wartime.  The Army, however, had stringent require-ments to consider the environmental impact of any program in development.

Research and development programs continued to search for the magic "pixie dust": the substance that would work against all chemical and biological warfare agents, be environmentally safe, noncorrosive, safe for soldiers to use, require no water, and be as effective as or more effective than DS-2.  These efforts included the sorbent decontaminant, the enzymatic decontaminant, and the catalytic coating decontaminant.  Sorbent decontaminants would absorb CB agent contamination into a powdery resin base, to be swept off the equipment.  That eliminated the water requirement, but the CB agent was still present in the dust.  Enzymatic decon explored bioremediation efforts, where organic enzymes would literally consume the contamination, ideally much more than the enzyme weighed (for instance, one pound of enzymatic decon would absorb five pounds of agent).  Catalytic decon concepts suggested that one could spray on a liquid that would harden and peel off, taking the CB agent contamination with it.  While these ideas were noteworthy for their originality if not their practicality, identifying candidates that performed like "pixie dust" was ultimately not fruitful prior to 1990.  DS-2 and STB remained the Army standard decontaminants, although the Air Force and Navy were not fond of the corrosive substances and fell back on Fuller's earth and seawater, respectively.

The M258A1 individual decon kit was a decided advance over its predecessor, but there were some drawbacks. The small size of the towelettes limited the ability of soldiers to decontaminate anything much larger than a square foot per pair of decon packets. What soldiers wanted was an easier decontamination capability for their mask, weapon, helmet, and load-bearing equipment. CRDEC began investigating a larger towel-sized version of the M258A1, called the XM280 Decontamination Kit, Individual Equipment (DKIE). The basis of issue for the DKIE would run twelve packets in one box, designed for one squad's use. The second problem was the toxicity of the M258A1 packettes themselves. They included a caustic solvent that, if wiped on the forehead (as doctrine initially called for, if liquid chemical agents existed there), could drip into the eyes and burn (not causing any permanent damage). There was no easy solution here but to warn troops not to decontaminate above the eyes with the M258A1, but to use clear water instead. To avoid problems during training, the M58A1 trainer was developed, using rubbing alcohol for its solvent instead of the caustic solution. This became a great favorite for troops to remove camouflage paint and to erase plastic-covered mapboards marked with felt markers (as well as practicing emergency decontamination).

The medical community had a vested interest in decontamination of chemically contaminated casualties. The Chemical School had cast their Personnel/Casualty Decontamination System as a joint service medical NBC defense program among the four services and between the medical and chemical defense communities. Research conducted by the Medical Research and Development Command had led to the development of a new skin decontamination kit, the XM291. This kit featured a small pad with a mixture of ion exchange and charcoal-based resins, which literally pulled liquid chemical agents away from the skin. The M291 decon kit would be well received by the military, as military personnel discovered that the M1 CAM alarmed to solvents present in the current M258A1 and M290 skin decontaminant kits. Figures 14.1 and 14.2 summarize the equipment developed prior to 1990, with associated cost and density in the force.

## EXERCISING COLLECTIVE PROTECTION AND DECONTAMINATION IN THE FIELD

Collective protection was a difficult requirement to which to train, since there were little visible or measurable benefit to using the system correctly. While it was relatively easy to test soldiers on their ability to use detectors in the field, and one could use tear gas to test their speed in donning their masks and protective suits, armored vehicles could just race through a cloud of tear gas or liquid simulants without taking any real notice. If the vehicle CPS was turned on, who knew? There was no penalty and the NTC observers couldn't see whether they were cheating or doing what was required. All the crews understood that wearing the masks with the ventilated facepiece limited their ability to quickly engage and defeat the enemy. This limitation slowed down their reactions during exercises as

**Table 14.1**
**Representative Collective Protection Systems**

| Nomenclature | Intended Use | Basis of Issue | Unit Cost* | DoD Inventory* |
|---|---|---|---|---|
| M20A1 SCPE | Interior room CP shelter | 2 per battalion | $14,300 | 890 |
| M51 Shelter | Transportable CP shelter | special | $56,000 | 350 |
| KMU-450 Shelter Mod | Fixed shelter modification kit | special | $90,000 | 25 |
| 200-CFM filter | Used in various shelters | 2 per system | $735 | 3,000 |
| M12A2 Gas Filter | Used in M2A2 Air Purifier (part of Modular CPE for M2 Bradley) | 2 per system | $75 | 9,000** |
| M13 Particulate Filter | Used in M2A2 Air Purifier (part of Modular CPE for MRLS, M109 howitzer) | 2 per system | $28 | 9,000** |
| M18A1 Gas Filter | Used in M13A1 GPFU (part of MCPE for armored vehicles) | 2 per system | $160 | 42,000** |
| M19 Particulate Filter | Used in M13A2 GPFU | 2 per system | $70 | 36,000** |
| M48A1 Filter | Filter for M1A1 Abrams tank CPS | 2 per tank | $570 | 9,000 |

\* - FY98 costs and inventory figures, to give the reader a measure of the costs and DoD requirements
\*\* - Note: These numbers reflect requirements, not on hand storage, as CPS filters are notoriously understocked.

**Table 14.2**
**Representative Decontamination Systems**

| Nomenclature | Intended Use | Basis of Issue | Unit Cost* | DoD Inventory* |
|---|---|---|---|---|
| M11 DAP | Interior room CP shelter | 1 per vehicle | $38 | 76,500 |
| DS-2, 1 1/3 quart can | To fill M11 DAP | as needed | $9.50 | 214,000 |
| M258A1 decon kit | For immediate decon of skin | 1 per soldier | $4.65 | 2,500,000 |
| M13 DAP | Fixed shelter modification kit | 1 per vehicle | $313 | 65,500 |
| DS-2, M13 can | To fill M13 DAP | as needed | $72 | 110,000 |
| M17 LDS | Used in hasty decon opns for vehicles and equipment | 2 per battalion | $14,000 | 4,200 |
| M12A2 PDDA | Used in deliberate decon opns for personnel, vehicles and equipment | 12 per chem co | $12,600 | 520 |
| STB, 50-pound drum | Used in M12A2 PDDA and deliberate decon opns, to include terrain decon | as needed | $56.50 | 21,600 |
| DS-2, 5-gallon can | Used in deliberate decon opns | as needed | $83 | 321,000 |

* - FY98 costs and inventory figures, to give the reader a measure of the costs and DoD requirements

well as potential combat situations, which meant they didn't use the system unless they had to. In addition, keeping the CPS turned on meant one had to keep the tank's engine running or the battery supporting the CPS would die, which meant precious gallons of diesel slipping away each minute.

The M51 shelter was not often erected in the field, due to its large weight and time-consuming construction. By the time it was up, it might stay in place a day, and then soldiers would have to tear it down and move to a new location. While there was no question about the comfort of the air-conditioned system, it constantly required maintenance and the filters were costly. Similarly, while the M20 SCPE was a snap to erect, it wasn't much good in the field without a nearby building within which to erect the system. The system was useless for the mechanized infantry and light infantry forces, as their forces rarely operated in urban environments. It was good for logistics units and other large base operations, which didn't make it to the field as often as their combat brethren. Fixed-site shelters were not being maintained at airfields and critical installations, given the desire to maintain a high-speed, low-drag constantly moving combat force. The bottom line was that the concept of collective protection shelters was being lost.

The low level of training created a constant drop in stores of large filters. Since troops didn't use the collective protection systems while training in the field, they stopped ordering filters. The lack of peacetime demand slowly eroded war reserve stocks, as the filters expired and were not replaced. Most people were cognizant of the need to maintain a certain level of war reserves and the fact that they were dipping far under the safe limits. The problem was that it was not acceptable for logistics staffers to push field commanders on what they ought to be purchasing with their operations and maintenance (O&M) funds. Each commander, irrespective of service, saw as his/her prerogative the need to purchase materials for training and to maintain their warfighting systems in shape for wartime missions. If they had a heavy training schedule, the priority went to purchasing fuel and bullets and spare parts for the vehicles. This meant that CB defense consumables, such as large expensive filters that were not often used in training, were not purchased.

The thought process these commanders had was that if they had to go to war, they could just throw money at the problem and Defense Logistics Agency would have to meet their needs. This was not the case. The continued historical pattern of low peacetime procurements resulted in more and more firms leaving this sector for more profitable commercial areas, such as filters for heating and ventilation systems in private-sector buildings. The filters that were in the war reserves had a five-year shelf life, and they were expiring every year without being replaced. This created a very real shortage and lack of industrial capability by 1990.

Decontamination equipment and its procedures were much easier to practice in the field. For one, the M11 and M13 DAPs could be filled with water, allowing soldiers to get practical hands-on experience with the sprayers and what they could cover. Basic decon training using the M58A1 trainers was equally easy, with the training kits using rubbing alcohol instead of the real decontaminants. Since soldiers were often wearing camouflage in the field, it was very easy to see where one had missed when using the wipes. The combination of realistic training kits and the incentive of taking off protective gear after deconning oneself and individual equipment made these lessons both practical and easy to impress upon the troops.

Hasty decontamination procedures also required little effort to convince troops to practice. For hasty personnel decontamination, soldiers had to strip their protective suits while retaining their masks and don clean protective suits immediately. This was called a MOPP exchange, which allowed the troops to maintain their protection while near combat (rather than moving to the rear to clean up). The M17 LDS was a very easy tool to use to clean vehicles after muddy field exercises, which was practical in addition to practicing good decontamination principals. Hasty decontamination procedures took time, but soldiers could see the practical nature of the processes. While squads and companies practiced MOPP exchanges, this was not practiced often as battalions or brigades, meaning the leaders did not appreciate the time and logistics of moving hundreds of clean protective suits and thousands of gallons of water to support these operations.

Deliberate decontamination practice was a little more rare, due to the need to commit time and resources to planning out the exercise. Usually, each company-sized unit (120-plus troops) created a four- to six-man decontamination team, whose responsibilities included knowing how to organize a personnel decontamination line. This meant borrowing buckets and brushes from supply and creating a hot zone/warm zone corridor that, in stages, allowed soldiers to decontaminate their mask, individual gear, and boots with STB, warm water, and bleach solution, step into the "warm zone," strip their protective clothing and gloves, step across the no-contamination line, and unmask in a clean environment.

Equipment decontamination called for dedication of the chemical defense company's M12A2 decontamination assets, to include water haulers. It took time to coordinate between the chemical company and the combat unit to identify which vehicles would require decontamination, prior to their move to an established decon site. The chemical company had to select a decon site that would permit a large number of vehicles to enter and exit while controlling contaminated water runoff and maintaining the logistical flow of hundreds of gallons of water and decontaminants. Last, the combat unit was expected to contribute its own personnel for site security in addition to its drivers operating the vehicles.

The demand on logistics, personnel, time, and specialized chemical decon equipment meant it was very rare that a combat unit would actually practice deliberate decon during field exercises. It was more common to practice it on the way back to the barracks, as part of the "reconstitution" phase of field operations. As a result, not many battalions or brigades actually practiced the principles of deliberate decontamination until they had to at the National Training Center. The downside of this is that combat leaders and their staff had no real appreciation for the sheer scope of logistics involved in supporting deliberate decontamination exercises. The dilemma was that any vehicles or personnel that were contaminated meant a loss of combat power, which would only increase inefficiencies until the force was decontaminated and moved into clean areas. The sooner they were decontaminated, the sooner they got back into the fight without physical and physiological degradations caused by wearing MOPP gear.

The entire philosophy of decontamination operations was fight dirty until the military force had time to consider full decontamination during restoration and recovery operations. When the protective suit resistance to liquid agents was extended from six to twenty-four hours, that caused an immense relief that deliberate decon operations could be more carefully planned than when rushed into that six-hour period. What the combat arms and staff was missing from the entire context was the eternal question that the technical community was dodging all this time: How clean was clean enough? Since no field detector was sensitive enough to detect down to OSHA standards, it stood to reason that soldiers would be at some risk, albeit not life threatening, from equipment or terrain that had been previously contaminated. Being practical people, combat arms leaders noted that as long as their troops could remain fully operational during combat conditions, that was clean enough. Wartime standards meant some risk. Peacetime standards, for government civilians and military personnel working on CB warfare issues between wars, did not allow for any such risks.

For the chemical defense community, there was a technical answer (of course). When deciding how to deal with the possibility of leaking chemical weapons or contaminated equipment in the labs, there was a standard called X, XXX (3X), and XXXXX (5X). An agent symbol with a single X indicates that the item has been partially decontaminated of the indicated agent. This might be merely a field decontamination process, meaning that personnel conducting maintenance or repair might still have to wear protective suits. The standard 3X meant that the equipment was 99.99 percent clean, calling for surface decontamination and containing the item within an airtight bag with air monitoring tests showing that the agent concentration is below threshold weighted averages. The ultimate safe level, 5X, required that the equipment be completely decontaminated of the indicated agent and may be released to the general public in accordance with federal, state, and local regulations. The item is considered completely decontaminated only when the item has been subjected to procedures that are known to have completely degraded the chemical agent molecules. One method of achieving this is to expose the item to 538 degrees Centigrade (1,000 degrees Fahrenheit) for fifteen minutes (basically incinerate the material).[3] There were not many other options that could meet this level of proof, but this was the level required for peacetime acceptance of "cleanliness."

Obviously these standards could not be applied to all equipment and personnel, due to the destructive nature of the tests, especially during combat. There was just not enough time or specialized personnel to meet these standards and still effectively fight the battle. Still, not much thought was given to combat or post-war decontamination requirements in the 1980s. It goes without saying that other requirements such as large area decontamination (ports and airfields) and human remains decontamination were not even considered logistically or technically feasible without a huge dedication of personnel and funds. The priority was always aimed at enabling the soldiers to continue the battle through a CB agent-contaminated environment, and if sublethal levels of agent did not incapacitate the troops, the presence of low-level agents was an acceptable risk. After the conflict was over, there would be time to clean up the contaminated battlefield and ensure safe measures were taken prior to sending personnel and equipment back home. At least everyone thought so at the time. Political fallout after the Gulf War, questioning the possibility of CB agent exposure to military service personnel, would blur and confuse the line between peacetime and wartime standards.

# CHAPTER 15

# Smoke, Radiacs, and Medical CB Defense

In addition to CB defense, the Chemical Corps also has responsibilities for smoke and obscurants programs and radiacs. The Chemical School was also to coordinate with the Medical Corps for medical chemical defense material requirements: treatments, antidotes, and vaccines for CB agents and their effects. The Air Force and Navy had never considered radiation detection programs, smoke and obscurants programs, or medical CB defense programs as part of their CB defense programs, as did the Army, prior to 1990. Radiacs in particular remain a distinct research area due to the larger and more diverse requirements that arise in operating nuclear reactors and storing nuclear weapons. Likewise, smoke and obscurants were seen as a general survivability problem, not a specific CB defense concern; therefore, any interservice coordination was done on a case-by-case basis and not as a rule. The Marine Corps, in part due to their traditional ground force missions, took advantage of the Army's efforts in smoke and radiacs but remained subordinate to the Navy's primary service role in medical CB defense. This chapter reviews the evolution of these cousins of the Army NBC defense/smoke program. If nothing else, the reader should understand that these programs had to compete with the better-established CB defense programs. While they were overshadowed by CB defense, there were important advances in the 1980s smoke, radiac, and CB medical programs that would play significant roles in the Gulf War.

## RADIAC PROGRAMS

Development of radiacs began immediately after the rumbles of Nagasaki settled. Prior to 1945, the military had access to civilian laboratory instruments; these had been used to detect alpha, beta, gamma, and X-ray emissions but were obviously not rugged enough to withstand field conditions. In 1945 the military saw the dawn of the atomic battlefield and recognized the need for simple and rugged instruments that would give the soldier information about the presence of radioactive fallout. Military leaders were not concerned about alpha particles that were stopped by the skin, or beta particles that clothing would block from harming soldiers. The only danger these particles posed was if they were ingested or inhaled, where their radioactivity could affect internal organs. It was the much deadlier gamma radiation that would penetrate solid objects and damage cells, potentially causing death, that had to be monitored.

Military leaders needed to monitor how much radiation their troops were exposed to, where the contaminated areas were and how hot they were, and what personnel and equipment were contaminated with radiological fallout, if they were so unlucky as to be traveling through contaminated areas. The general guidelines were that an individual could be exposed to up to 75 centigray (cGy, also called rads) with little effect other than headaches and nausea. Between 75 to 150 cGy, about 5–30 percent of the exposed personnel would suffer mild nausea and vomiting within a day, but no deaths, and the force would still be combat effective. The highest soldiers were supposed to be exposed to without exceeding emergency risks was 150 cGy. Being exposed to over 150 cGy would mean accepting moderate fatigue in half the force within two days, and 10 percent deaths due to radiation-related illnesses. Over 450 cGy meant immediate nausea and vomiting and moderate fatigue for the entire force and possibilities of death in 50 percent of exposed soldiers; over 800 cGy meant certain death in three weeks. It all depended on how close one was to ground zero or how long one traveled through or remained in an area contaminated with radiological fallout.

The Atomic Energy Commission and the Department of Defense initiated several programs to modernize and ruggedize laboratory instruments into field monitors. The Army Chemical Corps took the lead, with its interest in radiological contamination as the new member of the Atomic-Biological-Chemical (ABC) threat. While Edgewood had no real experience in radiac design, the Army Signal Corps did (given the nature of nuclear-induced radiation as part of the electromagnetic spectrum) and would be the executing laboratory creating the instruments under the Chemical Corps's direction. Initially, the design of these radiacs differed little from what was found in the Los Alamos laboratories; metal boxes about eight inches long, five inches wide, and six inches tall, about eight pounds weight, with bright chromium-plated probes that were not exactly suitable for stealthy troops trying to avoid detection. Scientists of the 1950s were more intent on giving troops an immediate capability than answering all military requirements. As one source book on radiacs dryly commented, "To date, the greatest emphasis has been placed on obtaining proper instrument response with the idea that once this has been achieved, some of the other characteristics will receive attention."[1]

There were three basic requirements for radiacs. First, there were individual dosimeters, designed to identify the total cumulative dose absorbed by the dosimeter's owner. Some of these were designed to be read by their owners, others required readers to identify the dose. Second, dose rate meters tracked the total dose rate, or radiation levels in an area in rads per minute or hour. These devices were important to identify when the peak radiation level had been reached and began falling. They were also used in the course of surveying contaminated areas, provided constant readings that could be recorded and plotted to identify the scope of contamination. They were also valuable during movements as warning devices that the area being entered was too hot for safe travel. Third, sensitive total dose detection meters identified point radiological contamination on personnel, equipment, and terrain. These devices existed in a number of configurations, some specific for only one kind of radiation, others for specific ranges.

Film badges were used as early individual dosimetry devices, but they were not reliable or exact indicators. They were inexpensive and offered a permanent record of exposure, so they remained in the labs, medical units, nuclear reactor working areas, and nuclear weapons storage areas, but they were not acceptable for the field. Engineers quickly developed the pocket dosimeter, about the size of a ballpoint pen, with a very thin metallic-coated quartz fiber within the device. When exposed to gamma radiation, the metal became charged by the ionization field created and moved across a scale which could be read if the pen was held up to the light. The dosimeter could be recalibrated with a charger. These devices ranged from 50 to 650 cGy in measurement. One of the first military dosimeters was the IM-9 and IM-9A model, which measured up to 200 cGy. Pocket dosimeters improved in accuracy and measurement through the 1960s, ending with the IM-147/PD and IM-93/UD dosimeters (0–60 cGy and 0–650 cGy, respectively).

In the 1980s, PM NBC Defense oversaw CECOM's radiac program and initiated an effort to improve the dosimeter to the IM-185. While retaining the distinctive ballpoint pen dimensions and clip, the dosimeter would replace the older 1960s veterans. This program failed in the mid-1980s in part due to problems created when the government chose a firm in a lowest-bid competition. The Army also investigated designing a wristwatch shaped individual dosimeter, the DT-236. This device would have read gamma and neutron radiation from 1 to 1,000 cGy. It could not be read by the individual; it required a radiac computer indicator (CP-696/UD), which weighed about fifteen pounds. The concept was that every soldier would turn in their wristwatch to the company medic, who would read and record their exposures. While this system was fielded in the late 1980s, the reader's weight and the fact that individual soldiers couldn't immediately read their exposure prevented its full acceptance in the field.

The radiacmeters used for monitoring dose rate increases and survey missions were largely built on the principles of ionization chambers. This design used a series of electrodes within a sealed container, creating a given volume of air under standard conditions of temperature and pressure. The radiation would produce ions between the electrodes, which created a current. The current fed the meter that would provide a reading of the proportional radiation creating the current. If the radiacmeter had a very thin mylar window, it could collect alpha and beta radiation in addition to gamma. Because these were not practical in the field, they generally detected gamma only. Radiacmeters were built for aerial surveys as well as ground surveys, beginning with the first field model AN/PDR-T-1.[2] Aerial surveys were safer than ground surveys, as personnel in helicopters were physically further away from the radiological contamination. They could take the radiation readings and then convert them to ground level readings using mathematical formulas. The modern Army equivalent (circa 1970s–1980s) was the IM-174B/PD, an aluminum-cased radiacmeter that displayed gamma radiation readings on its front panel meter from 0 to 500 cGy per hour.

The best-known radiacs include those detectors known as Geiger-Mueller counters, or simply Geiger counters. These devices feature a silver-colored probe attached to a portable container that has a panel indicator and power source. The probe has an internal sealed tube filled with halogen gas mixtures. When radiation particles enter the gas, ionized particles produce a pulse of electrical current. With higher voltages, the gas amplification permits very sensitive readings to occur. The pulses are of such magnitude that they can be heard in earphones like a loud static, rising in intensity with the level of radiation.

By designing different probes, the military has developed a number of sensitive detectors specifically for alpha detection, beta-gamma detection, X-ray detection, and so on. A number of commercial detectors already in use were the basis for the military's first AN/PDR-T-2, which was quickly surpassed by the AN/PDR-8 series with its fish-pole type extension for probing at a distance, the AN/PDR-15, and the AN/PDR-27. These all detected beta and gamma radiation, the last in scalable ranges of 0–0.5 cGy, 0–5 cGy, 0–50 cGy, and 0–500 cGy (to permit exact readings). The AN/PDR-27 evolved through the alphabet, with the last version as the AN/PDR-27J, still in use today (over forty-five years from its initiation). The AN/PDR-56F is used to monitor alpha radiation contamination on terrain, personnel, and equipment, using the same principle. It can also swap its probe for the DT-590 X-ray probe, used to detect radiation from plutonium-239 and americium.

One of PM NBC Defense's main goals for radiacs was to replace the Cold War veteran IM-174 and AN/PDR-27 series radiacs with one system that would meet both requirements of monitoring and detecting. The device that was chosen in the mid-1980s was the AN/VDR-2. This commercial adaptation was microprocessor-based and could measure gamma radiation from 0 to 10,000 cGy/hour and beta from 0.01 to 4 cGy/hour. When fitted with Geiger-Mueller probes, the radiac functioned as a detector, and its memory permitted simultaneous functioning as a dosimeter as well. A conversion kit existed to use probes designed to detect alpha, beta, gamma or X-ray radiation, creating the AN/PDR-77 detector. It featured a digital readout and self-test diagnostics and could be used on both ground and aerial surveys. The Air Force and Navy more slowly initiated their modernization efforts, opting to look at the ADM-300-series multifunction radiac (and similar separate radiacs on the market) as their candidate.

An aerial radiac system, the AN/ADR-6 (Airborne Dose Radiac), was in development in the early 1980s. This was a program designed to install radiac devices into scout helicopters for automated aerial surveys of radiologically contaminated areas and general aerial detection. Rather than manually jotting down radiac measurements along a route, the radiac could either send its readings to a ground station or record them internally. The debate arose over which helicopter to put the radiac on. The Aviation School had agreed to put the device onto its OH-54D helicopters, but the Chemical School, fearing that the OH-54s were on their way out (replaced by the Comanche), held out for the newer helicopter to include aerial radiation surveys in its job description. Because of the intense effort to lighten the Comanche (and perhaps the end of the Cold War in 1989), this program eventually faded away.

Radiac training was a high priority prior to Vietnam, but it died off quickly with the new Army. Although the interest in tactical nuclear weapons remained into the 1980s, few were expecting that kind of battlefield. It became a chore to keep the dosimeters calibrated and radiac teams trained for survey missions, chores that were abandoned in lieu of small unit tactical operations. There were training devices that used electronic signals transmitted to radiacs fitted with special receivers to imitate radiological fallout readings, but they were not often employed. As the 1980s closed and the Berlin Wall fell, training and preparing for nuclear battlefields fell out of favor.

## SMOKE AND OBSCURANTS PROGRAMS

The successful employment of thermite and smoke mortar shells in World War I caused the Chemical Warfare Service to continue research and development of smoke pots and generators. The main concern in the 1920s through the 1940s was the protection of strategic waterways, such as the Panama Canal and Great Lake locks in Michigan, against the strategic bomber threat envisioned by so many military theorists. Shortly after Pearl Harbor, the CWS deployed stationary M1 oil generators to protect the Canal, locks, and other important industrial sites. These generators were similar to smudge pots, generating oil-burning clouds within 20 to 30 minutes of being lit. Because of the weight and size of the M1 smoke generators, they remained at fixed points surrounding the Canal. As the U.S. military increased its overseas involvement, the CWS saw the obvious advantage to employing these systems in ports and harbors supporting theater military operations.

The M2 smoke generator, developed just prior to June 1944, allowed a more mobile employment of smoke generators around ports in Europe. Their lack of reliability still relegated them largely to fixed points, but the lighter weight allowed commanders to develop flexible options based on moving generators around the port perimeter, allowing for shifting weather conditions. Because the M2 generators used fog oil instead of pure oil, the volume of smoke and its staying power on the battlefield increased as the cost of smoke operations dropped.

Initially smoke generator companies were used to cover the Mediterranean Theater of Operations rear areas, such as the ports of Bizerte, Naples, and the Salerno beaches, from enemy bombers and artillery. At Anzio, the 24th Decontamination Company and 179th Smoke Generator Company provided round-the-clock obscuration after U.S. forces landed. Enemy artillery effectiveness was greatly reduced once the smokescreen rose. After the invasion of Normandy, as the Germans retreated and blew up bridges, smoke generator units screened the efforts of engineers building bridges over the many rivers in Europe. It became a Third Army standard operating procedure to use smoke generator units in front-line operations during river crossings and bridge building, which greatly increased the Allied effectiveness in contested crossings.

The Korean Conflict saw the same employment of smoke generators in rear areas, although it was rare that the new M3 smoke generators placed around Seoul had to obscure the city from enemy air operations. Development of the M3 smoke generator meant a much more reliable and efficient capability to support smoke missions. Chemical smoke generator companies remained in theater for the duration of the war to screen Seoul, Pusan, and Inchon against potential North Korean air attacks. Had the enemy been able to penetrate the Air Force's screen, these smoke units would have obscured the supply installations and harbors.

In addition to rear support functions, smoke units supported missions on the front lines at selected fixed points. In July 1951 the 68th Smoke Generator Company obscured the Kumhwa area with smoke to allow evacuation teams to recover lost vehicles while under enemy artillery fire because of smoke. Near the end of the Korean War during operations around Pork Chop Hill, American forces were forced to carry out construction, resupply, and evacuation operations under the direct observation of North Korean troops. The 338th Smoke Generator Company provided a smokescreen for four months (November 1952 to February 1953), causing enemy fire to be largely ineffective. When the commander of the 7th Division terminated the mission (due to manpower shortages) enemy fire resulted in increased casualties. The commander promptly brought the smoke generators back, where they remained until July 1953.

After the Korean Conflict, the four services' interest in smoke obscurants declined in proportion with their ability to dominate ground, air, and sea operations through superior firepower. The Vietnam conflict did not call for the doctrine of obscuring ports and rear area supply centers from enemy air and artillery forces. Some units used smoke generators mounted on helicopters (the M52 smoke generator) to screen the insertion of airmobile troops, but there was no call for smoke missions with large area coverage. The use of both smoke generators and smoke projectiles decreased, although the use of smoke grenades increased dramatically. However, these uses were more for signaling than for obscuration. It was not until after the U.S. military studied the lessons of the Arab-Israeli War of 1973 that they discovered the continual and more urgent need for tactical obscuration. The Syrian army had used smoke to obscure the vision of Israeli artillery observers on the Golan Heights. The use of smokescreens also greatly reduced the tank fatalities due to antitank guided missiles. The increasing lethality of antitank munitions began to emphasize the mantra "if you can see a target, you can kill it." This drove the search for smoke systems that supported mobile front-line forces.

Smoke and obscurants had been one of the earliest revived program efforts at Edgewood, beginning with the special formation of a Product Manager for Smoke and Obscurant Systems (PM-Smoke) in 1977.  The 1973 Arab-Israeli October War illustrated the new lethality of antitank munitions and the role smoke could play in reducing that lethality.  The Chemical Systems Laboratory showed how M60-series tanks could use the existing engine fuel pump to spray diesel fuel into the engine exhaust.  Upon activating the system, diesel fuel would vaporize in the high engine heat and condense with the ambient air behind the vehicle to form a dense white smoke screen.  The Vehicle Engine Exhaust Smoke System, or VEESS, added only 18 pounds to the tank and cost less than $400 per tank (FY79 dollars).  Since most antitank munitions were optically guided, armor units could greatly decrease the number of vehicles exposed on the move by altering their formations and allowing a few tanks to screen the force for any period of time.

VEESS was not a cure-all for protecting armored vehicles.  The engine had to be running at a high rate per minute if the vehicle was stationary; and this tactic still exposed a few tanks at the front of the formations.  The next material complement was a rapid smoke grenade launcher system.  By wiring four to six smoke grenades to both sides of the turret, the crew could trigger a volley of smoke grenades immediately before the tank.  This smokescreen would activate within one to three seconds, and last one to three minutes (weather permitting).  If a tank commander saw an antitank missile fired at his vehicle, he could launch the smoke grenades and immediately change direction.  Since antitank missiles took several seconds to impact, this simple maneuver could cause the anti-tank gunners to miss their target completely.

These types of countermeasure were exactly what combat arms branches wanted from the Chemical Corps.  It was a visible, measurably effective support system that increased their survivability on the battlefield.  Smoke and obscurant equipment became a hot source of demand as Edgewood's labs began improving their older smoke grenades, smoke pots, and artillery smoke projectiles of the latter decades.  The Chemical School began plans to develop new doctrine and organizations to improve their jeep trailer-mounted smoke generator companies.

The successful reemergence of smoke as a combat multiplier did not have a parallel for its counterparts, flame munitions and riot control agents.  Perhaps in part due to the bad press that napalm and CS gas received in Vietnam, and in part due to the lack of expressed interest from combat arms branches, flame munitions and riot control agents never progressed past the Vietnam-era M202A1 FLASH launcher, the M8 flame thrower, and common CS grenades.  Other than the use of fuel-air explosives in bombs, combat forces no longer had a defined doctrine for how flame munitions should be used in wartime.  M202A1 FLASH launchers continued to gather dust in infantry battalion arms rooms.  The Chemical School still taught the basics of *fougasse* emplacements, since these were field-expedient devices that could be manufactured from existing materials.  Outside of training exercises, the active Army saw little role for employing riot control agents. Edgewood had invested in some non-lethal weapon development in the 1970s for riot control missions, such as the softrag projectile (a bean-bag that was fired from a modified M16), but this area was dropped due to lack of interest and funding.

In January 1985 the Army began fielding the infrared defeating smoke grenade launcher, which was stockpiled in Europe by December 1986. That fall also saw the initial fielding of the M3A4 smoke generator, which greatly reduced the maintenance and reliability problems of earlier M3A3 smoke generator and led to the "robust concept of smoke employment" for which General Max Thurman had asked. It was mounted in pairs on a HMMWV, with a large eighty-gallon fog oil reservoir and a control subsystem, type-classified as the M157 wheeled smoke generator system and fielded to the dual-purpose smoke/decontamination chemical defense companies by 1988. The mechanized M113 version, designated the M1059 tracked smoke generator system, followed in the same year, using a 120-gallon fuel tank to provide large-area smoke screening.

One major advantage these new systems had over the jeep trailer-mounted smoke generators was the ability to provide smoke on the move, rather than being relegated to one planned position on the battlefield, and that it could move quickly and in synch with combat units. This gave the division commander options to use smoke in the front lines or in the rear areas for deception or cover. A smoke generator system featuring infra-red defeating obscurants advanced to become the XM56 prototype late in 1989. PM Smoke had the new mission of attempting to add a millimeter-wave-defeating obscurant module to the system, in order to defeat vision and sensors across the electromagnetic spectrum. Its type classification would not occur until 1994.

Smoke grenades, smoke artillery shells, smoke pots, and finally smoke generators initially caused great excitement in the Army. Concerned that the massive number of Soviet tanks would force a "shoot and scoot" requirement to retain their survivability, tankers in particular welcomed the systems that increased their survivability. The problem was that it was not often that the smoke generator systems could create the large-area smokescreens for tank platoons and companies to exercise tactics. Smoke generator units had not had much opportunity to develop their training skills. The one smoke platoon at the National Training Center was too small of a unit to effectively display the capabilities of large-area smokescreens in the manners of the World War II and Korean War examples. Instead, instructors used the smoke platoon to simulate artillery smoke projectiles, or to smoke selective strongpoints from enemy observation (this was also common for U.S. field training exercises at other posts).[3]

Occasionally a commander would bring a smoke company to Fort Irwin and lay down an effective smokescreen that looked tremendous, and his unit's training would really benefit from the practical experience. There were not enough commanders with the background and foresight to grasp this tool, a situation aggravated because of the limited number of smoke generator units in the Army to supply that training opportunity. Many smoke generator units were in the reserves, making it more difficult to schedule training time with smoke support. Army leadership recognized that the use of smoke in general was a combat multiplier, but since smoke was executed more for platoons and squads and rarely for companies and battalions, the larger unit leaders never learned the true operational principles.

Major General (retired) Gerry Watson recalled a time in the mid-1980s at Fort Hood, Texas, when a division commander excitedly called him to examine a smoke mission executed in support of a river crossing. When he arrived at the site, there were two smoke generators pouring out dense, white smoke that drifted across the water. The crossing site was obscured; but if he walked thirty yards up or down from the site, he could see the terrain above the riverbanks. The convoy moving down to the river crossing was entirely visible to an observant enemy, disappearing momentarily as they crossed, and then emerging from the smoke cover on the other bank. Rather than screening the movement, the smoke made a very good artillery marker. The division commander erroneously felt that it had been a tremendous exercise, because as he crossed the river, he had been obscured from sight. Again, this misapplication was not the rule—some commanders recognized the benefit of obscurants and developed the experience to employ smoke platoons in support of combat operations.

## MEDICAL PROGRAMS

The medical NBC defense community had conducted a significant amount of research for nerve agent antidotes since the discovery of nerve agents. Atropine antidotes of one kind or another had been developed since the 1950s, along with the advent of nerve agent munitions. The current Mark-1 nerve agent antidote kit (NAAK) program had been developed in the early 1980s and was well integrated into the Army as an essential survival item. The NAAK consists of an atropine autoinjector and a pralidoxime chloride (2-PAM) autoinjector. Each soldier carried three NAAKs in their protective mask carrier.[4] Amyl nitrate tablets had been used in the early 1960s as an antidote against blood agents. By cracking one ampule and inserting it under the mask, near the eyes, it helped expand blood vessels, thus minimizing the effects of hydrogen cyanide. Because this did not directly counter the effects of blood agents, its use was discontinued.[5]

The Air Force had initially decided to buy pyridostigmine bromide tablets off the shelf in June 1984, based on the British tests of its use as a pretreatment against nerve agents. The FDA had approved pyridostigmine bromide for use against the nerve disorder myasthenia gravis, which causes extreme weakness in affected individuals. The pyridostigmine bromide doses create additional acetyl-cholinesterase to overcome antibodies that are blocking neuromuscular junctions. It is also authorized for use to counter the effects of anesthesia, another neuro-muscular blocker. For myasthemia gravis, dosages could reach 120 milligrams every three hours; for anesthesia, it is a one-time fifteen-milligram dose. The Army and Navy had reservations about the formulation of the drug and decided to continue research and development, looking at 1987 as a more feasible time to consider adopting it. The three services continued efforts to identify blister agent antidotes, blood agent pretreatments and antidotes, and vaccines for all biological warfare agents. The Army Office of the Surgeon General (OTSG) saw the late 1980s and early 1990s as the timeframe for all these products.

In 1985 the Army Surgeon General's office began their trials of pyridostigmine bromide. By reformulating the dosage, the Army could adapt the drug to aid the effectiveness of the atropine nerve agent antidote. The change in converting from the civilian to the military requirement involved reducing the 60 or 180 milligram dose to a 30 milligram dose. This "new application" resulted in the FDA's labeling it as an Investigational New Drug (IND), until efficacy tests would prove its effectiveness. Its formal military designation was Nerve Agent Pyridostigmine Pretreatment (NAPP). A soldier's one-week supply is contained in a 21-tablet blister pack. During this period, the only producers were two foreign firms: a Dutch firm, Solvay-Duphar, and a British firm, Rouche Laboratories.

Diazepam, more commonly known as Valium, was developed as an autoinjector (similar to the British autoinjector kits). The OTSG proposed that this drug be used as an antidote for convulsions resulting from nerve agent poisoning, as a New Drug Application (NDA). This did not fall under the IND label by the FDA, since this drug had been used by the military for other purposes, but it did require efficacy testing for its new role. Instructions on its use included how and when to use the drug and stressed strict accountability to prevent inappropriate use. Its military nomenclature became Convulsant Antidote for Nerve Agent (CANA). The only FDA-approved source of production was, again, Solvay-Duphar. Solvay-Duphar had produced NAAKs as well, but a congressional requirement to retain U.S. companies as suppliers of critical medical antidotes resulted in the closing of Solvay-Duphar's U.S. production line. This would mean that prior to August 1990, there would be no producer identified for either the CANA or NAAKs.

Research into antidotes or pretreatments for blood and blister agents had not made significant progress in this decade. The GAO criticized the medical community for its work in the 1980s, developing biological treatments and vaccines for dangerous organisms not necessarily identified as biological warfare agents. Part of this criticism was unfounded, as the medical community had developed vaccines and treatments for many BW agents, anthrax in particular, in the 1970s. Because Congress forbade the military to expose human volunteers to CB agents, the medical community used animal tests to determine the efficacy of these treatments. It should also be noted that their own doctors working in BL-4 labs, in addition to field workers, ranchers, and veterinarians, all use these treatments without harmful effects while in the presence of these deadly diseases. The problem in the medical community was not R&D, however, it was in stockpiling the vaccines.

A continuous shortage of vaccines and antidotes for BW agents remained (anthrax and botulinum toxin, for instance), in part due to the costs to produce and store the millions of doses that would be required in the event of biological warfare. Vaccines and medical treatments had been developed for most natural infectious diseases and related illnesses where soldiers might be deployed, and everyone kept their shot records up for cholera, yellow fever, and other possible indigenous medical threats.  Although some in the military were beginning to note these deficiencies, the military leadership was not funding the project adequately, and industry was not rushing to maintain facilities for producing CBW medical treatments.  The combination of liability issues, high malpractice insurance rates, FDA testing and compliance, and low profitability of medical drugs that had no use outside the military field kept industry at arm's length.

Recently, many service personnel have questioned the anthrax vaccination policy, although they have no medical background and have never investigated the Army's medical research.  Still, they question the need to vaccinate our soldiers against the most optimally designed biological organism weaponized for warfare by using phrases like "untested," "legitimizing biological warfare," and "creating vulnerabilities to other BW agents."  They freely mix pseudomedicine theory, arms control diplomacy, military leadership, and CB defense in a matrix of why the United States should not vaccinate its soldiers.  While people have a right to their own opinions, it should be an informed opinion, one based on the realities of prior experiences with these vaccines and the requirement to protect soldiers if exposed to BW agents.  No one is suggesting vaccination is eliminating the chance of biological warfare by itself.  On the other hand, anthrax is the one BW agent everyone wants because of its lethality, persistence, and ease of weaponization.  If vaccination does lessen one aspect of the threat, that could translate into fewer American casualties in future battles.

Medical training was limited to understanding how to use the NAAKs on oneself and for one's buddy.  Plastic spring-loaded trainers emphasized the realism of pressing the autoinjector against the meaty part of one's thigh until one heard and felt the hard plastic "needle" hit into the flesh.  Occasionally, a training instructor would bring out a live kit and, using a piece of cardboard, press the autoinjector until the needle burst through.  Everyone saw that it worked and was convinced that this was needed to save oneself against the deadly, fast-acting nerve agents.  Everyone knew the mantra—three autoinjectors for yourself (one at a time), then the medics apply any additional atropine.  If your buddy went down because he was too slow getting his mask on, you use his autoinjectors on him and not yours.  That was the extent of medical chemical defense training: focus on surviving the nerve agent threat, recognize the blister agent symptoms, and get treatment.  Everything else (blood agents, choking agents, biological agents) was covered by using the protective suits and masks.

The resurgence of the Chemical Corps had only begun to have an impact on the Army's ability to survive and sustain combat operations in an NBC-contaminated environment.  The new chemical agent detectors and protective ensembles were quantum leaps ahead of their 1970s predecessors.  There were still challenges.  Individual NBC defense skills were being taught as stand-alone survival skills.

There was very little unit training, as noted by a GAO report,[6] in which soldiers would attempt to continue normal operations while wearing the protective clothing. As the CANE reports showed in quantifiable data, soldiers had difficulties accomplishing combat operations in bulky, hot, and isolating protective gear. The lack of training simulants meant that soldiers lacked the positive feedback to understand that properly using CB defense equipment would work during wartime.

This was not the case in all units. Major General Barry McCaffrey, as he was commanding the 24th Infantry Division, had always believed that if a unit trained in protective suits simulating NBC warfare, they were prone to be better fighters when they were not in protective suits. He had personally gone through the Chemical Defense Training Facility with Brigadier General Bob Orton (then Project Manager for Binary Munitions) in 1988. There were isolated cases throughout the Army of units who would survive and fight on despite NBC contaminated environments.

GAO reports through the 1980s and into the 1990s were (and remain) overly pessimistic and critical of the DoD NBC defense program. The program was a good deal improved from 1972, and admittedly not in its optimal condition. Chemical defense units were just beginning to find their place in the divisions' training programs and field operations. Those Chemical Corps officers more comfortable in laboratories than in chemical defense companies were relieved and replaced with younger, more aggressive chemical commanders. As the years progressed, division and corps operations officers learned how to best utilize these units. The important facts were that the CB defense equipment was arriving, along with chemical specialists to train and assist the men and women across the armed forces, filling a critical warfighting deficiency. The only thing the Chemical Corps could not control is how quickly the military leadership and their fighting forces would assimilate the necessary experience to retain a strong defensive capability. Unfortunately, many leaders still believed that a chemical weapons retaliatory capability and protective suits for their troops was all that was necessary. That would change.

# PART IV

# Current Events

One of these days it's going to happen, we're going to have to fight a chemical war. When that happens, we need to be as ready as we can possibly be and we need to be as well trained.

—General H. Norman Schwarzkopf, CINC CENTCOM, 1991

Materials and expertise to build chemical and biological weapons are ever more readily available. Nuclear materials and technologies are more accessible today than they have ever been before in history. The likelihood that state or non-state actors will attempt to use weapons of mass destruction against U.S. interests is growing. That seems to be, defined in broad terms, a really dangerous and immediate threat.

—Dr. John M. Deutsch, Director, CIA, May 1996

# CHAPTER 16

# Iraq's CB Warfare Program

To understand the threat CENTCOM faced in 1990, one must travel back in time to examine how Iraq grew to become the fourth-largest army in the world. Its ambitions to become the lead nation in the Middle East began in the early 1960s and grew in scope and power during the oil-rich decade of the 1970s. The war against Iran was perhaps a poor decision, based on Iraq's overinflated estimation of its military strength (the best equipment money could buy) and an underestimation of Iran's ability to counter the Iraqi offensives in 1980–82. However, the Iran-Iraq War did allow Iraq to test and develop its ability to use chemical agents against a modern (if ill-trained and ill-disciplined) army, the first case of documented chemical warfare since the Yemeni civil war in 1968.

The Iran-Iraq War provided a wake-up call for arm control groups; although the conflict initiated much debate about chemical warfare, no real sanctions from the global community came through. More to the point, it has been hotly debated whether the war showed that chemical munitions contributed to the success of any battles, whether chemical warfare merely preserved Iraq's army from falling to Iranian counteroffensives, or whether it was just another facet of an ugly war that had no real impact at all.

## LOOKING FOR WEAPONS OF MASS DESTRUCTION

Iraq's search for weapons of mass destruction began shortly after the success of the Nasser-influenced, army-led coup against King Faisal II on July 14, 1958. The Baath party officially took control of the Iraqi parliament from the Iraqi Communist party in 1963, with deputy secretary-general Saddam Hussein. The armed forces became the major force in Iraqi politics. In the early 1960s, Iraq began sending its officers to the Soviet Union for formal training, which included chemical defense training and offensive employment tactics. Diplomatic relations with the United States had been broken off since the U.S. government backed Israel in the 1967 Arab-Israeli war. Saddam Hussein had become the moving force behind the Baath party as early as 1969, and was already given to his ruthless political maneuvering, which included purges. By April 1972 Iraq and the Soviet Union had signed a "Friendship Treaty," which promised Soviet support for external and internal issues. The Soviet Union became Iraq's greatest supplier of military equipment. The Iraqi army soon took on Soviet military equipment and organization, to include a chemical defense company in every division. These chemical companies had the (then) state-of-the-art Soviet decontamination vehicles and reconnaissance vehicles, which in many ways were superior to the U.S. equipment at the time. Soviet support may have extended to supplying mustard gas munitions, with Egyptian military trainers teaching the Iraqis how to handle and store them.

After reports of Egyptian possession of chemical weapons and Israeli possession of chemical and nuclear weapons in the October 1973 war, the Iraqi government decided to create their own production facilities for CB agents and delivery systems. Increased oil revenues allowed the government to increase allocations to industry, provide funds for transportation and housing, and support other improvements of living standards. They began by approaching the Pfaudler company in 1975, and asking that U.S. company about purchasing a small pesticide production facility. The production goals of this facility included handling 600 tons of Amiton, 300 tons of Demiton, 150 tons of Paraoxon, and 150 tons of Parathon. All these pesticide agents are extremely toxic and had been abandoned by most customers as outdated and dangerous agricultural insecticides. These chemicals are all organophosphates, the basic building blocks for nerve agents. Pfaudler soon recognized what they were being asked to perform and begged off the contract. The Iraqi government next turned to Imperial Chemical Industries (ICI) of Great Britain. The British government had given all their domestic chemical companies a list of potential chemical agent precursors, and ICI immediately recognized Iraq's goals. They also refused to cooperate.[1]

Iraqi government officials were not deterred, and they continued investigating West German, Swiss, Dutch, Belgian, and Italian firms. Their main commercial cover lay behind the Ministry of Industry and Military Industries (MIMI), who fronted the requests for chemical precursors and industrial equipment through a number of academic and industrial organizations. Gradually, they gathered their components and built a special pesticide plant with the support of a West German laboratory equipment supplier, Pilot Plant, a unit of Karl Kolb. They also contracted technical support from a West German firm called Fritz Werner. A Belgian consortium called "Sybetra" built their chemical complex at al-Qaim in the early 1980s. The plant would include a phosphate purification complex and a separately contracted uranium extraction facility by the time it was completed.

Water Engineering Trading, GmbH, another German firm, sold Iraq about $11 million of equipment and tons of chemicals. Other equipment was provided by a German firm called Quast. Some thirteen German firms would later come under investigation by the West German government for these export arrangements. Iraqi scientists also began investigating the production and weaponization of anthrax and botulinum toxin in the mid-1970s and began searching for a company to build a nuclear power plant. With Iraq's increasing wealth, few Western companies were eager to turn Iraqi customers away. By 1980, Iraq was importing $700 million of American goods a year. However, Saddam continued to rebuff U.S. diplomacy, especially as the 1978 Camp David Egypt-Israel accords took place. Iraq's stand against the Camp David Accords also had the effect of making Saddam Hussein a major leader in Arab affairs.

As a result of the increased economic ties with the West, by 1980–81 Iraq had initiated its major chemical agent production plants southwest of Samarra, a town about seventy miles northwest of Baghdad. This would become the Muthanna State Enterprise for Pesticide Production. Some mustard gas was probably in production, with plans for nerve agent production before the war with Iran started. The majority of their stockpile remained mustard gas and CS shells from previous Soviet purchases, as their early plants did not have the ability to support large-scale gas warfare operations.[2] The Osiraq nuclear facility was nearly completed. Iraq erected fifteen CB agent obstacle courses to train soldiers on how to operate in a contaminated environment. With its state-of-the-art Soviet decontamination equipment, training, and stockpile, the Iraqi army became another example of the global proliferation of chemical warfare.[3]

As will be seen, this did not necessarily mean Iraq was prepared to conduct offensive chemical warfare. British chemical warfare expert Julian Perry Robinson points out that a stockpile alone does not mean it is militarily useful or significant. The armed forces must have logistical channels to link the stockpile to the delivery systems, trained military operators to use the chemical munitions, defensive equipment for combat troops, a strong research and development capability to support all this, and the direction of a command and control structure to coordinate the use of the munitions in the overall context of the operations.[4] Iraq's early experiences and learning curve in using chemical agent munitions would emphasize this point. As for biological weapons, the Iraqis were not about to seriously throw themselves into that arena at least until they learned more about chemical weapons production and storage operations.

## THE IRAN-IRAQ WAR

In 1980 Saddam Hussein decided to go to war against Iran. He had just taken over the presidency a year, replacing President Ahmed Hassan Bakr as president of the republic, as secretary general of the Baath party, as chairman of the Revolutionary Command Council, and as the commander-in-chief. Iran and Iraq had sparred over the rights to the Shatt al Arab, the deepwater shipping channel that ran between the two countries for decades. After the Ayatollah Khomeini took power in Iran, he called for the overthrow of the Iraqi Baath party and actively supported the Kurdish and Shi'ite rebel groups in Iraq. Iran was going into its second year of intense civil war and internal disorder in 1980. It had alienated the

United States through its hostage crisis the year previous and was therefore unlikely to be able to logistically support its mostly U.S.-equipped forces. This meant that Iran was weak, and the Iranian Sunnis might also rebel against the fundamentalist Islamic regime in Teheran, if given a reason. The Gulf States feared Khomeini's clerics calling for their revolution to expand into their countries, and would welcome the war. Saddam predicted that the war would take only three to four weeks.

Iraq's first offensive attack in September 1980 began with a massive air attack, and a two-corps ground offensive soon pushed into Iran. The Iranian air bases survived the attack, and the slow pace of the Iraqi advance allowed Iran to muster its forces and begin to assemble a defensive position the next month. By late November the Iraqi offensive was halted on all fronts, but it held onto its limited gains of one captured city. The major powers all became politically involved, as nations began to take sides in the conflict. The United States set up an underground major command and control center, at Saudi Arabia's request, that controlled an airborne warning and air control systems (AWACS) force of four E-3As, two KC-135 tankers, and three hundred support people. While the Soviet Union declared its neutrality, it allowed the East European countries to send arms shipments to Iraq. Syria, Libya, Yemen, Algeria, and (covertly) Israel supported Iran with arms and supplies. The other Gulf States and Jordan, France, and North Korea supported Iraq with further arms shipments and oil purchases to help pay for the war. France had a historical relationship of supplying arms to Iraq since 1975, especially in the area of aircraft and missiles, which would continue throughout the war. This had very quickly developed into a regional conflict being played out, in a figurative sense, on an international stage.[5]

During the spring of 1981, Iran began counterattacking, but achieved no real success until the fall. While the major powers observed, the Gulf States formed a Gulf Cooperation Council in February 1981, in part to show their displeasure against Iran's rhetoric of exporting revolution to the rest of the Arab world. Both Turkey and Saudi Arabia supported the building of Iraqi pipelines through their countries to keep the Iraqi oil flowing to market. Saudi and Kuwaiti political support and funds poured into Iraq's war effort. On August 12 Iran charged Iraq with using poison gas against attacking Iranian troops. At this stage, Iraq may have been experimenting with CS or mustard gas weapons. There was little indication of any extensive use of chemical weapons in 1981. Iranian counterattacks kept Iraqi forces on the defensive throughout the year, with some loss of territory on the part of the Iraqi army in September.[6]

On June 7, 1981, eight Israeli F-16s sneaked across their border into Iraq feigning the radar signature of a commercial airplane. They hit and destroyed Iraq's Osiraq reactor at Tuwaitha, stopping Iraq's first major (and at the time, it's only) nuclear power plant. Israel's justification was self-defense, that the preemptive strike would halt the production of nuclear bombs intended for Israel. Iraq had initiated their nuclear program as far back as 1976. Saddam Hussein, as deputy president in 1976, had traveled to Paris to negotiate the sale of a French reactor. The reactor design was unusually large and had special features to irradiate uranium, which produced plutonium. In 1980 Iraq purchased sizable quantities of natural uranium from Brazil, Portugal, Niger, and Italy. As the plant was being finished in 1981, Iraq was negotiating to buy a heavy-water power reactor from Italy. Some experts theorize that Iraq was following the pattern of Sweden's 1960s nuclear program of developing a legitimate open nuclear program and was developing the ability to handle plutonium while clandestinely stockpiling it for weapons. After the attack, both the United States and France publicly expressed their outrage at Israel's actions, but secretly, they were satisfied that the nuclear program had been stopped. Despite promises of French assistance to rebuild the reactor, the Osiraq reactor was not rebuilt.[7] It remains open to speculation whether Iraq would have used a tactical nuclear device against Iran, once that capability had been realized.

Iran continued its offensive against Iraq in 1982. In March, Iranian forces launched a wide offensive against the entire southern front. This pushed the Iraqi army back thirty miles and captured thousands of prisoners. Syria officially announced its support for Iran and cut off Iraq's pipeline through its country, costing Baghdad about $30 million a day. Syria would remain on Iran's side throughout the war. The U.S. government moved decisively toward relations with Iraq in February, as it removed Baghdad from its State Department list of regimes supporting international terrorism. Iran's second offensive in May resulted in the recapture of Khorramshahr and tens of thousands of Iraqi POWs. On June 9–10, Saddam ordered a cease-fire and withdrawal, supposedly to allow both Iran and Iraq to support the PLO and Syria in Lebanon against the Israeli invasion that had begun on June 6. He requested a UN cease-fire, which Khomeini made clear would only take effect upon Saddam's ouster.[8]

These successes fueled Iranian desires to march into Iraq and take the oil fields around Basra that summer. The first major attempts occurred in mid-July, when Iraqi artillery began firing CS-filled artillery shells into the infantry to break up the unprotected troops. This tactic, combined with massive air attacks and mechanized infantry counterattacks, stopped the Iranian advances. The CS caused additional panic and disorganization among the Iranians, who thought they were being attacked by chemical agents. The flow of foreign arms sales continued to favor Iraq by three to one, especially as France's deliveries, constituting 40 percent of all Iraq's arms imports that year, arrived. This permitted Saddam to build up a heavy defensive position that Iran was unable to breach that fall. In addition, Iraq began a strategic air and missile campaign to attempt to force Iran back to the negotiating table. The first Scud-B rockets fell on Dezful on October 27, killing several civilians and wounding several dozen others. The Scuds were more accurate and destructive compared to the sixty-four FROG missiles fired in 1980–81, increasing the warhead payload from 455 kg to 900 kg, and increasing the range from 60 km to 290 km. The targets remained cities and rear-area military concentrations, in an attempt to bring political pressure on Tehran. In December, Iran began its human-wave attacks and night attacks against Iraqi lines. The success of using CS-filled artillery shells in the summer may have encouraged Saddam to use mustard gas against these human-wave attacks and night attacks. This was particularly effective against the unprotected and ill-trained infantry.

Iran launched a series of offensives in 1983, in February, April, July, and October. Iraqi counterattacks did little but stop the Iranian forces from achieving token gains into northern Iraq, an Iranian move that threatened the pipeline to Turkey. Iranian casualties had climbed to 180,000 killed since the war began, as compared to 65,000 Iraqis, partly due to Iran's use of human-wave minesweepers. In the last two offensives, Iraq used mustard gas delivered by Su-22 Fitter ground-attack aircraft bombs, Mi-8 helicopter sprayers, and artillery shells to stop the human-wave attacks from breaching their lines. Not all these chemical attacks were successful. The Iraqis learned that if one bombards an enemy on a mountain peak with mustard gas, the heavy density of the gas causes it to flow down into your own positions. Later mustard attacks in November showed that they had learned and applied that lesson. Iran credited the lack of success of their last offensive to the use of mustard gas, which they claimed caused several thousand of their 7,000–10,000 casualties.[9]

Iran filed its first major protest over the use of chemical agents to the UN. Evidently, Iraq had contacted a branch of Phillips Petroleum Company in Belgium the year before to obtain 500 metric tons of thiodiglycol, a precursor for mustard gas. It was ordered by the Iraqi State Ministry of Pesticide Production through a Dutch trading firm. Phillips was not alerted until the Dutch firm ordered a second shipment of 500 metric tons of thiodiglycol in early 1984, which Phillips refused to ship. The Iraqis used the initial order as feedstock for their plants to produce the munitions for limited gas warfare attacks, and they began producing the thiodiglycol domestically at the al-Fallujah complex.

Iran switched its strategy to attack central and south Iran in 1984. It started three limited thrusts against central Iraq, intended to draw Iraqi troops away from the south. Then a major infantry assault struck across the Hawizeh marshes near Basra in late February. The Iranians counted on an amphibious light infantry attack breaking through the lightly guarded wetlands before Iraqi armor and artillery could respond. Between the wetland terrain, Iran's daytime assault without artillery or air support, and Iraq's massive firepower, strong defensive positions, and mustard gas attacks, the offensive was stopped dead in some of the fiercest fighting of the war. In one operation, the Iraqis isolated the forward elements of the attacking force with mustard, cutting them off from resupply by land. When the Iraqis counterattacked days later, they encountered the same forward Iranian units, which had been without food or ammunition. In late March, Iran tried to launch a second supporting offensive against Iraqi positions near

Majnoon, which was also hurled back with conventional forces and chemical munitions. Estimates of Iranian casualties lay between 12,000 and 20,000 men. As a result of this offensive, Iran ceased any major offensives up to March 1985. They had to redefine their tactics that were costing so much manpower for so little gain.[10]  The rest of the year saw limited attacks, but mostly just the two forces shifting behind their defensive positions.

Iraq may have used its first nerve agents in the spring offensive of 1984. The State Ministry had received nerve agent precursors from American, Dutch, and West German chemical companies in 1983 and purchased large amounts of equipment that Iraq claimed was for producing organophosphate fertilizer. Some analysts believe it was tabun that was produced, since it is the one nerve agent that does not require a multistage production process. One production method for tabun is as simple as the mixing of four chemicals in a two-stage process. Iraq completed the construction of its production plants at Samarra by the end of 1984 and established two more chemical munitions production plants at Karbala and Fallujah. This allowed the Iraqi government to begin its major gas warfare offensive.[11]  In March, Iraq took the additional step of attacking the Iranian nuclear power reactor construction site at Bushehr, ensuring that Iran would not have access to potential nuclear material throughout the war.[12]

The U.S. response to Iraq's use of chemical weapons was mixed. The Commerce Department, perhaps alarmed by the reports of chemical weapons use, began updating and expanding its list of chemical controls. In February 1984 Customs intercepted seventy-four barrels of potassium fluoride destined for Iraq. Customs rarely screened outgoing deliveries and had to request additional authority from Congress to conduct overseas investigations. By September, Commerce had imposed export controls on eight chemicals used as chemical agent precursors.[13] Nevertheless, the State Department continued its diplomatic initiatives with Iraq. After threatening to halt chemical feedstock shipments to Iraq in March, the Reagan administration restored diplomatic ties with Iraq in November and offered crucial military information on Iranian movements and lavish credits to purchase food products and agricultural equipment. This allowed Saddam to purchase both "guns and butter" from West Germany, the United States, Britain, the Soviet Union, France, and other western countries. The Stockholm International Peace Research Institute estimated that in 1984 Iraq had spent nearly half its GNP—nearly $14 billion—on arms and defense.

Not all the U.S. exports to Iraq were sound decisions. Over the next five years, Commerce would approve 771 export licenses for dual-use goods, valued at $1.5 billion. The DoD objected to at least fourteen instances of those export shipments, which may have directly assisted Iraq in developing its NBC and missile capabilities. These included forges, special furnaces, and low-level computers. Commerce claimed it had no legal entitlement to deny most of the applications, and to hold up the licenses would have resulted in a loss of competitiveness for U.S. industry.[14]

## ACCELERATED USE OF CBW AGENTS

Iran began attacking in March of 1985, with a more controlled and limited focus than before. Its first major offensive was, once again, in the Hawizeh Marshes north of Basra. Iran's eight divisions were better prepared logistically, and they were equipped with German-made protective masks, protective capes, and Dutch atropine kits. While this protected them from nerve agents, the mustard gas was still effective due to its persistency, particularly when the Iranians were forced to stay in a gassed area for a prolonged period. The Iraqi response to this offensive was a full commitment of the Republican Guards and Air Force, and heavy use of mustard agent and some nerve agents. Iraq did not have an extensive stockpile of tabun built up yet, but the mustard gas was more than sufficient to degrade the Iranian forces. While Iraq found that they could not use mustard gas near the front lines without affecting their own forces, it was very effective against exposed Iranian forces in the rear areas. Iran's failure to gain any real success from this offensive halted any further major attacks for the year. They attempted a number of minor attacks, some of which made limited gains, but the lines kept relatively stable.[15] The only other actions in the war were an escalation in stopping and inspecting shipping traffic in the Gulf on Iran's part, and increased targeting of population centers and industrial centers, such as Khark Island, by Iraq.

In late 1985 Iran began preparing its final offensives by placing an increased emphasis on logistics capability as well as improving its operational training, which now included amphibious assaults. Iran bought more chemical defense equipment for its troops and began its own chemical munitions production with Syrian aid in 1986. Prior to 1986, Iran's chemical munitions were limited to what they could capture from the Iraqi forces. This led to some limited and ineffectual chemical attacks against Iraq in 1984–85. Iran had no internal industries capable of producing poisonous agents, and, like Iraq, turned to European firms and industries to develop a "pesticide" plant capability. This production eventually would include hydrogen cyanide, mustard gas, and phosgene, with research and development on developing nerve agents. Iran's new strategy was to attack Basra from the north, seize and retain the al-Faw Peninsula to block Iraq's access to the Gulf, disrupt Iraqi oil production in the south, disrupt their access to Kuwait, and support a Shi'ite uprising in southern Iraq.

The two-pronged offensive began in early January. While the offensive in the north was stopped, the Iranians were successful in taking al-Faw. Iraq had mistakenly assumed that the northern offensive was the main attack and hurried their counterattacks to throw the Iranians off the peninsula. Throughout February, despite the heavy use of mustard gas and some tabun, the two forces battled to a stalemate. Iraq was able to keep the first 200 kilometers of the peninsula. While Iraqi chemical attacks did hurt the poorly trained Iranian troops, the overall attack was not successful. One reason was the lack of integration with conventional infantry and air operations. The other was a lack of skill in chemical target analysis. Several Iraqi units were gassed along with Iranian targets.[16]

Iran began a second offensive in the north in mid-February, which soon stalled down because of Iraqi defensive positions and chemical munitions. The al-Faw positions remained stable due to easy access of Iraqi logistics to support their defensive operations, but neither side was able to spare the manpower to break the deadlock. In May, Saddam ordered the first major offense in a long while, attacking east from Baghdad into Iran to block a key invasion route. While the attack was initially successful, Iran built up a counteroffensive and attacked the invaders in June with chemical agents. The counterattack not only repelled the Iraqi forces, it gained additional ground in Iraq. Some speculate that American arms such as the TOW missiles may have added to the success. The rest of the year boiled down to limited offensives and counteroffensives, with heavier raids and attacks against oil rigs and tankers in the shipping lanes.[17]

The year 1986 had seen Iraqi scientists initiate a new phase of their CB warfare program. Scientists at the Muthanna State Enterprise near Samarra began researching the potential production and weaponization of anthrax spores and botulinum toxins. Perhaps emboldened from their experience in chemical warfare and seeing biological warfare as a way to break the stalemate, Iraqi scientists spent over a year on feasibility studies of biological warfare. This would soon expand to pilot plant tests, producing batches of anthrax spores and botulinum toxin, and continue into other feasible agents.

Iraq's chemical specialists came into their own in 1987. They had been perfecting their chemical target analysis skills for the past two years, and the production of nerve agents had finally built up a stockpile that would enable them to use chemical agents in effective amounts. In addition, using non-persistent nerve agents would mean Iraq could target front-line enemy forces without fear of affecting friendly forces. These improvements came along with other advances in the Iraqi army, such as T-72 tanks for the Republican Guard, an improved road infrastructure for moving military forces and supplies to the front, and improved and new air bases. Advanced training in combined arms operations, to include coordinating artillery and close air operations, would improve the army's overall effectiveness.

They had also identified the appropriate target windows for use of chemical agents. Given the particular weather and terrain between the two warring states, there were distinct and brief opportunities when the use of gas was at its most effective. In the desert during the summer, even mustard gas was non-persistent and not as effective as in the fall and winter. The marsh areas and the rainy season would effectively neutralize the chemical agents to a degree by hydrolysis of the chemical compounds. And as they found out the hard way, the only time to use chemical agents in the mountains is when you own the mountaintops and the enemy is in the valleys.[18] The final needed ingredient to improve the use of chemical munitions came in the form of a change of command philosophy. Saddam agreed to delegate authorization to his corps commanders to use chemical munitions at their call. This would enable them to better coordinate the chemical attacks with conventional munitions within the operational plans.

The Soviet Union had sold a number of long-range Scud missiles to Iraq and provided technical and operational support in their use. This would allow Iraq to continue tests of mounting chemical warheads on the Scuds. In addition, the biological warfare program had moved from feasibility studies to active animal tests and field tests near Salman Pak, southwest of Baghdad. Engineers built a large-scale wheat smut production plant near Mosul and began production scale-up studies for anthrax and botulinum toxin. By the end of the year, Saddam had decided to go into full-scale biological warfare production. Beginning in 1988, al-Hakem began its role as a BW research, development, production, and storage site.

Iran had not been entirely successful in its offensive chemical munitions program. Throughout 1987 Iran's wartime industries continued to work toward a self-sufficient production capability of phosgene, chlorine, hydrogen cyanide, and mustard gas and to produce enough to stockpile for an effective chemical retaliation capability. Defensively, the Iranian army continued to improve their stocking and training in protective masks, clothing, decontamination kits, and antidotes, allowing them to survive chemical attacks (although casualties still occurred). They lacked the agent detectors, command and control system, and collective protection equipment to sustain operations in a CB warfare environment, which handicapped their ability to retain the initiative in offensive operations.[19]

Most of 1987 was spent in a stalemate as both sides rebuilt their forces and defensive positions. Iran increased the number of its artillery units to reduce the gap between the two antagonists and bought a number of tanks, armored personnel carriers, artillery, Scuds, and Silkworm missiles from China and North Korea. Iraq continued its arms purchases from the western countries and the Soviet Union and completed extensive defensive fortifications around Basra. The UN had tried, without much success, to broker a cease-fire between the two parties, but neither side could agree to terms. Iraq used mustard and nerve agents at least four times during the year to disrupt Iranian troop buildups around Basra. Iran shifted some of its offensive aims to the north again, using anti-Iraqi Kurdish forces to supplement their efforts. While these forces irritated Iraqi forces more than really threatening them, this caused Saddam to initiate bombing and bombarding Kurdish villages suspected of supporting the rebels. These attacks included the first use of mustard and nerve agents against the civilian populace in June–July. With the exception of minor border conflicts throughout the year, no major offensives from either side occurred.[20]

The war resumed slowly in 1988, with Iranian attacks on the northern front, which gained some ground and strengthened Iran's ability to supply anti-Iraqi Kurdish fighters. Iraq responded with an increased air offensive, striking Khark Island and probing Iranian air defenses. The more noteworthy escalation was the resumption of missile attacks against cities, this time initiated by Iran's 300 Soviet-bought Scuds. This gave Saddam the excuse to resume their missile attacks, to include the introduction of the al-Husayn missile, a modified Scud-B with a smaller warhead (500 kg) and increased range (650 km). The number of launches in March and April revealed that Iraq had been stockpiling this new weapon for months prior to its introduction. While the accuracy was not improved over the Scud, the al-Husayn's increased range allowed Iraq to attack Tehran with missiles for the first time. This new development grabbed worldwide attention, as during the 52-day war of the cities, Iran fired sixty-one Scuds toward Iraqi cities along the border. Iraq countered with 203 total long-range missile attacks against Iranian cities, including Tehran. The growing fear of chemical agent missile warheads initiated a mass exodus of millions of Iranian civilians from Tehran.[21]

In March, Iran began to press the offensive in the north, with more success, since Iraq was holding their better divisions in the south against any offensives against Basra and the oil fields. To compensate for the lack of manpower and Iranian strengths, Iraq once again turned to the use of chemical munitions to slow and stop the offensive. From March through August, Iraqi use of mustard and nerve agents caused heavy casualties and significantly slowed the Iranian northern offensive. Iraq also continued gassing towns suspected of harboring the Kurdish rebels, who had been scoring some successes of their own. Iran used these instances to gain a major propaganda success by releasing films and details of the thousands of civilian casualties. One of the more famous incidents was the gassing of Halabjah on February 26, a city previously holding 70,000 civilians before Iraqi crackdowns on the city's rebellion drove half the populace out. While it is generally acknowledged that Iraq did use chemical munitions on the city, some military critics point out that it was in response to Iranian forces that had entered Halabjah, and only after Iranian artillery and aircraft had used phosgene and hydrogen cyanide on the city. In fact, many of the victims' mouths and extremities were blue, evidence in line with the use of a blood agent, which meant they were victims of Iranian attacks. However, worldwide opinion and the media focused on Iraq as the genocidal killers.[22]

Iraq shifted toward conducting major counteroffensives to drive Iranian forces out of Iraq in late spring. One major offensive was the attack against the Iranian forces on the al-Faw Peninsula. Iranian forces had been reduced in preparation for rotating new forces into the area, and their defensive positions had deteriorated. Iraq built up its force, which included the Republican Guard divisions, to attack on the first day of Ramadan (April 17). With a six-to-one ground force advantage, the Guards smashed forward in a predawn attack (3:00 A.M. local). The Iraqi forces used artillery-delivered non-persistent nerve and blood agents on the forward defensive positions for two hours before advancing. Helicopters and fixed-wing aircraft delivered mustard gas and nerve agents on the rear-area troops, command centers, and reinforcements. Combined with two amphibious assaults and massive close air support, the Iraqi force was able to decisively defeat the Iranians within thirty-five hours. In addition to being a major propaganda victory, Iraq captured virtually all major combat equipment, armor, artillery, and stocks on the peninsula, weakening the entire Iranian southern front.  This victory, combined with Iran's failed naval attacks against U.S. naval forces in the Gulf (protecting the U.S.-flagged tankers), allowed Iraq to announce a unilateral cease-fire on April 21, stopping the missile war on the cities.  Saudi Arabia and Kuwait announced that they would officially break off relations with Iran, and the United States announced increased protection for any civilian shipping in the Gulf.

In late May, Iraq built up its forces around Basra and attacked Iranian defensive positions.  Although initially resistant, the combination of chemical weapons, armor and artillery, and close air support broke the Iranian forces and routed them beyond their 1987 gains.  In the north, Iraq had made several small, but important, victories that began driving Iranian forces back as well.  To combat increasing defeatist talk in Tehran, Iran launched a large offensive in mid-June against Iraqi forces east of Basra.  The battle included the Iraqi use of chemical weapons to drive the offensive back after nineteen hours of fierce fighting.  Continued Iraqi offensives in the central front, supported by nerve gas attacks, resulted in more major Iranian losses of personnel and ground.  In late June, in their fourth major offensive, Iraq attacked to regain the Majnoon Islands and Hawizeh marshes, again heavily supported by Iraqi use of chemical munitions.  In July, Iraq threatened to begin another major offensive in the south if Iran did not evacuate Halabjah and Kurdistan.  Because of the massive losses in the south, Iran knew that they were virtually defenseless and agreed.  Iran formally asked the UN to implement the cease-fire on July 17, 1988.  After some further negotiations, punctuated by sporadic clashes in the north and Iraqi air raids, the fighting came to a formal end on August 8, 1988.

Iraqi units continued to fight in Kurdistan to drive out all pro-Iranian Kurdish fighters.  Up to fifteen villages had been attacked with chemical weapons.  The Physicians for Human Rights sent representatives to Turkey to interview some of the survivors in 1988.  They met with a group of Halabjah refugees that had been attacked on August 28, 1988.  Those who survived described a complex of symptoms: difficulty breathing, burning throat, eyes burning and watering, runny nose, dizziness, nausea, vomiting, and headaches.  Their skin itched and formed large blisters filled with a clear amber liquid.  About half the gas survivors exhibited what the doctors called "severe" chemical injuries.  Another team had brought back a soil sample, which, when analyzed, showed degradation products of sulfur mustard (mustard gas similar to that used in World War I).  The other symptoms matched those of nerve gas poisoning.  The attack had both nerve agents and mustard gas to maximize the amount of casualties.  One eight-year-old girl, orphaned from her father, mother, and twenty-year-old brother, described the attack.  She was several hundred meters from her home when (in her words)

I saw two airplanes overhead and they dropped some bomb, it made smoke, yellowish-white smoke.  It had a bad smell like DDT, the powder they kill insects with.  It had a bitter taste.

After I smelled the gas, my nose began to run and my eyes became blurry and I could not see and my eyes started watering too. And I still have some of the effects like my blurry vision and I have these things [skin blisters] over my chest. I saw my parents fall down with my brother after the attack, and they told me they were dead. I looked at their skin and it was black and they weren't moving. And I was scared and crying and I did not know what to do. I saw their skin turn dark and blood was coming out from their mouths and from their noses. I wanted to touch them, but they stopped me and I started crying again.[23]

After the cease-fire, Iraq continued to fund its offensive CB agent programs and continued to purchase arms from western nations and the Soviet Union. This included a purchase of some thirty-three tons of "growth or diagnostic media" in which organisms can be grown.[24] In February 1989 the Commerce Department, perhaps sensitized to the ongoing weapons programs in Iraq, blocked Iraq's attempted purchase of specialized vacuum pumps. These pumps could be used in a uranium-enrichment plant, although they did have other legitimate purposes. Iraq began attempts to purchase the raw materials required to build the sophisticated equipment necessary for uranium enrichment. In West Germany, some industries were under investigation in December for selling equipment to Iraq that may have been used in a nuclear program.[25]

Iraq built five major chemical weapons plants and five facilities for manufacturing and testing ballistic missiles in the 1980s. In addition to tabun, sarin, GF (cyclosarin), and mustard, Iraqi scientists began developing VX nerve agent (but with no known munitions production). The Iraqi army maintained a large stockpile of assorted chemical weapons. In 1989 the biological agent production facility at al-Hakem began large scale production of anthrax and botulinum toxin. Over the next year, the biological agent production plant produced and stored nearly 5,300 gallons of botulinum toxin and 158 gallons of anthrax.[26] Weapons testing and BW agent weaponization continued at the Muthanna test ranges. In 1990 scientists began investigating aflatoxin, C. perfringens, and ricin as biological weapons. Iraq's rebuilt nuclear facilities and new CBW R&D facilities received heavy, layered Soviet-purchased state-of-the-art air-defense protection to guard against any attempts to repeat an Osiraq-type attack.

Ballistic missile research had continued as well, producing the al-Abbas missile. This was essentially the Scud-B modified to one-third the warhead size (300 kg), thereby increasing the range of the missile to 900 km. Although unconfirmed by U.S. intelligence, Israeli sources claimed that Iraq had developed the technology to produce chemical and biological agent warheads for the missiles. Their guidance systems were not necessarily improved, but with a large-area coverage such as that CB agent munitions provided, pinpoint accuracy is not necessary. Years later, the UNSCOM teams would confirm that Iraq had conducted live agent tests of CB agent warheads on Scud missiles in April and May 1990.

## LESSONS LEARNED

The lessons from the use of chemical weapons during the Iran-Iraq war are mixed. Most military analysts feel that the production and use of chemical munitions did not have any real effect on the overall war. Certainly Iran did not benefit, operationally or tactically, with its limited offensive chemical agent capability. Iran suffered chemical casualties from a lack of defensive training and equipment, but not excessively in comparison to conventional weapons (as was the case in World War I). In a war that caused over a million military and civilian casualties, 45,000 chemical agent casualties does not prove significant in the grand scheme of things. However, Iraq's use of chemical munitions does make several important points. There is a strong case that the use of chemical munitions did have one notable impact on the outcome of the war—chemical weapons gave Iraq the time it needed to purchase weapons and ammunition to defend itself against a numerically superior foe. Iraq benefitted from using chemical weapons throughout the war, and it may have saved the nation from collapse.

First, as seen in their defensive use in the 1983–84 period, chemical agents used in conjunction with natural terrain obstacles (mountains in the north, the marshes in the south) can compensate for a lack of manpower behind defensive positions. The chemical agents did not have to kill all Iranian troops, but effectively demoralized and degraded their physical ability to maintain the initiative. This stopped Iran's armies from taking Basra and a considerable amount of Iraqi terrain. Iraq's army was unable to effectively use chemical munitions in the offense until 1987. This was because of several factors, the major ones being the lack of training and experience in chemical target analysis and chemical munitions delivery. Other factors included the lack of coordination between the conventional attack and the use of chemical agents and overreliance on chemical munitions to make up for the lack of coordinated combined arms attacks.

As 1987 started, the Iraqis had all the factors that Julian Robinson pointed out (earlier in this chapter) an effective offensive CB warfare program needs: an adequate stockpile, a good logistics infrastructure, well-trained artillery and aircraft units that could deliver the munitions on target, chemical protective equipment for the military, and a good command and control structure to coordinate its use. Once again, throughout 1987 and 1988, chemical munitions significantly increased the Iraqi army's counteroffensive drives, not through their killing powers, but through their ability to demoralize, disrupt, and degrade the Iranian defensive operations.

This is the lesson that the major powers of World War I never learned: that conventional forces, using a coordinated combined arms approach, adequately backed by a sound logistics system, and using proper operational tactics of attacking weaker points with superior forces, will be successful in a *much shorter timeframe* because of the employment of chemical agents. This effect is what U.S. military tacticians call a combat multiplier effect. Chemical agents did not and will never give the edge to an attacking force in and of themselves, if both attacker and defender are equally matched conventionally, have equal chemical defense equipment, and are trained and prepared for the attack. The physiological and psychological degradation effects do lower the targeted force's abilities to attack or defend to some degree as compared to its optimal performance. *This*, combined with superior strategy and forces, is what makes offensive use of chemical munitions a success: a 35-hour battle instead of a two-week campaign, as in the 1988 al-Faw offensive; and a three-month war instead of a year-long war, as in the 1935 Italian invasion of Ethiopia.

There is a second lesson to note, this time in the development and production of biological agents. Iraq had initially developed a chemical weapons expertise before venturing into the area of biological agent research and development. This is a common pattern seen in countries developing an unconventional weapons program; those that initiate chemical warfare programs will soon be developing biological warfare programs as well. Since chemical agents and delivery systems are safer to develop and test, a country can develop the necessary expertise on a trial-and-error basis before moving on to the more dangerous area of BW agent programs. Often, the same front companies can purchase the necessary equipment and feeder materials on the global market, given the similarity of chemical and biological scientific research, development, and production equipment. The production facilities for biological agents can be developed on a much smaller scale than the large chemical plants, making them harder to identify by intelligence sources. Identifying biological weapons proliferation in other countries will continue to be a major problem for intelligence agencies in the future.

On August 2, 1990, at 2:00 A.M. Kuwaiti time, the eight divisions of the Republican National Guard Corps rolled over the Kuwaiti border. Twelve hours later, Kuwait City had fallen. Three days later, Kuwait had become the newest Iraqi province. Now it would fall to the U.S. military to respond, for the first time in forty-five years, against an adversary who had a very real offensive CB weapons capability.

# CHAPTER 17

# Operation Desert Shield/Storm

With all the progress made between 1980 and 1990 came promises that the U.S. military was now the best-trained and best-equipped force in the world, even within the realm of CB warfare. In truth, Army units had not quite adapted to the new Chemical Corps's doctrine and training. The GAO, which had revisited the Army chemical centers several times since 1977 to assess the NBC defense readiness, gave the Army a below average grade once more.

The GAO performed a study just prior to the onset of Operation Desert Shield (May 1989 to July 1990, more by coincidence than design) to determine the extent of the Army's ability to conduct combat operations in a chemical environment. This report focused on chemical warfare rather than nuclear or biological warfare in the tradition of past reports, chemical warfare being the most likely threat. This study was released to the public in May 1991 and confirmed many fears that soldiers were inadequately equipped and inadequately trained to survive and sustain combat operations in a chemical environment. They detailed their findings according to doctrine, training, leadership, and materiel programs.[1]

The GAO found that the Army Chemical Corps had updated and published their manuals according to the new AirLand Battle Operations. Other Army branches, such as the Signal, Armor, and Infantry schools, continued to emphasize individual survival tasks but not the effects of NBC agents on their combat operations. Ten of the twenty-three field manuals examined either paraphrased the Chemical School manuals, provided general discussions of chemical operations, or inserted a paragraph or appendix with descriptions of the individual survival tasks. Specific tasks, such as entering and exiting an armored vehicle in a contaminated environment, were not covered in the Armor School's field manuals. Nearly two-thirds of the doctrine writers at the Signal, Armor, and Infantry Schools had not been aware of the CANE tests, exercises, or results, and therefore had not changed any of their training approaches.

Training for soldiers had not fully developed by 1990. Army training requires soldiers to spend four continuous hours in full chemical protective gear during basic training and field training exercises conducted at branch schools; that they perform their duties and fire their weapons to standard in protective clothing; and that their unit chemical training be realistic and fully integrated into mission training. At least a third of the soldiers interviewed had not completed this training and doubted that they could survive a chemical attack. Realistic chemical defense training was difficult to impossible to execute during unit training because of the lack of a good chemical agent simulant, such as riot control agents, other simulants such as the PEG-200 (polyethylene glycol), and other mechanical training devices. The Program Manager for Training has the task of developing an environmentally safe chemical simulant, but prior to 1990, this program had received no funding and very low priority. Reserve chemical units rarely trained with active duty combat units during the year; and, since the distribution of active chemical companies is one per division, active units did not often practice deliberate decontamination exercises.

Army unit leadership did not attempt to integrate NBC defense training into mission training; in fact, some commanders discouraged it because it reduced mission performance. Often, including NBC defense conditions into a unit's normal training exercise effectively stopped operations, to allow soldiers to focus on individual NBC survival tasks. Other leaders could not lead their troops effectively because of the lack of professional training and doctrinal omissions at their branch schools. As a result, many commanders led their troops through mock battles either overprotected when no chemical threat was present or unprotected when a threat was present.

The results could be seen at the Combat Training Centers, where the lack of chemical defense training through the training year caught up to the units in evaluations. Units failed to emplace chemical agent detectors, or did not prepare supplies and personnel for possible decontamination requests, or slacked off at night when chemical-biological attacks were most apt to occur. The result was unprepared leaders and units suffering 25 to 80 percent simulated agent casualties. Controllers described such massive simulated casualties as common, usually suffered by units that crammed on CB defense training, rather than those units that had frequent and regular integrated training. Despite these obvious problems, commanders were not held liable for these weaknesses. Instead, their mission-essential tasks that the units were tested on focused almost exclusively on conventional operations in clean environments. A commander could achieve a passing rating on combat mission capabilities even if the unit failed on all CB defense tasks.

Many units lacked their full complement of decontamination equipment and detectors. These shortages had a direct impact on their ability to train, let alone operate in wartime. Theater reserve stocks of protective clothing and individual decon kits were significantly below authorized levels. Half the modernization programs promised in the 1982 and 1986 GAO reports had missed their delivery dates and were years behind schedule. While the GAO acknowledged that the Army had several research and development efforts with significant promise, the promised equipment was not due for several years.

The unspoken issue in this report is that its findings matched a similar GAO report published in 1986, which reported similar weaknesses. Not much had changed in four years, but CB defense for individual protection and survival had improved to a degree. Still, the ultimate goal of being able to sustain unit operations in an CB-contaminated environment had not been met. But now, time had run out. Iraq was poised to invade Kuwait, and Iraq's military had chemical weapons at its disposal. If the U.S. military was to face down Saddam Hussein in the desert, they had much ground to make up in NBC defense readiness.

## DEPLOYMENT AND PREPARATIONS FOR WAR

I will not try to discuss the entire preparations made for the Gulf War here, having done so in more detail in other sources. A few points should be made. When the XVIII Airborne Corps deployed in August 1990, they were unprepared for CB warfare to the extent that had Saddam chosen to use CB weapons with an attack into Saudi Arabia, the elite airborne corps would have been severely hurt, if not decimated. This weakness, well known by the military leadership, initiated a strong reaction in three directions. First, the ODCSLOG initiated a massive effort to identify the quantities of CB defense supplies and equipment required for troops deploying to the Gulf, focusing on protective masks, protective suits, and medical supplies. In particular, soldiers of the 82d Airborne Division, the first to deploy to the Gulf, discovered that they had not maintained their masks well during peacetime and were critically short of replacements. It immediately became obvious that there were insufficient quantities of protective suits for a large force operating for an extended period, and Defense Logistics Agency released several contracts to initiate production to meet that shortage. Because these clothing firms required time to start up their lines, it would be several months before new suits arrived. This delay was minimized by stripping all warehouses in the United States of their suits, and eventually, most military stores in Korea and Europe. There were plenty of rubber gloves and boots for the soldiers, not that these were welcomed wholeheartedly in the desert heat.

Second, ODCSOPS identified active and reserve chemical defense companies to deploy in support of the XVIII Airborne Corps. Their current "light" force structure, one not designed for sustained CB warfare, meant that they required augmentation to face the threat posed to them. The first chemical defense units would not arrive until the end of September, meaning for two months the early troops were very thinly protected with only their own organic smoke/decontamination units. Last, the Edgewood and other service labs released several R&D items that were on the verge of being produced. This eventually included sixty-plus XM93 Fox NBC recon systems, a dozen XM21 RSCAALs, the ICAD, a number of commercial and military biological agent detector prototypes, the M291 decon kits, CANA, PB tablets, and other CB defense systems. While the biodetectors were not "real-time," they did permit a capability to determine if and when Iraq had initiated biological warfare, and to support charges that would stand up in international court. Other items, such as the M1 CAM, came in numbers from the Canadian military and United Kingdom contractor, as the U.S. production line could not ramp up quickly enough to support the demand.

Based on observations of the Iran-Iraq war, the political and military leadership was convinced that Iraq would use chemical weapons against the coalition force, at the least. Defense Intelligence Agency estimates were that Iraq had at least 3,000 to 4,000 tons of nerve and mustard agents, weaponized in 90mm helicopter rockets, 155mm artillery projectiles, 250/500 kg aerial bombs, and 122mm rockets for multiple rocket launchers. The biological warfare threat was less clear, but there were strong suspicions that anthrax and botulinum toxin had been weaponized and that Iraq was examining other BW agents as possible weapons. Whether Saddam would authorize biological warfare was unknown; Iraq's military capability to deploy BW munitions and exploit the advantages was not shown in the Iran-Iraq war, and no one was willing to guess.

It was not until October 1990 that enough chemical defense equipment was in theater, combined with chemical defense specialists both manning decon-tamination sites and training the soldiers, that Saddam's potential advantages started to wane. By January 1991, with a second corps in theater, the supplies were stretched further. To support all these forces, the U.S. military eventually had over forty chemical defense units in theater. This included three chemical battalion headquarters, seven heavy decontamination companies, three smoke generator companies, seven smoke/decon companies, several NBC staff cells, and four chemical recon platoons from U.S. forces in Europe. Six months of training and stockpiled supplies had transformed the vulnerable U.S. force into a capable, although untested, juggernaut that would not be stopped by CB weapons. The question on everyone's mind was how many casualties would they take from CB weapons, not whether they would take CB casualties.

One of the policy questions to face in the first few months was whether to threaten Iraq with retaliation in kind, which was the current U.S. policy in place. The U.S. administration had decided earlier to transfer U.S. chemical weapons in Europe to Johnston Atoll, as part of the U.S.-Russian bilateral chemical weapons agreement. Chemical Corps officers argued that the presence of chemical weapons in Saudi Arabia would give Saddam a pause, as his force remained much less capable of defending against such weapons than of using them. The aging unitary rounds might not even be usable, but there was also the idea of publicly shipping and storing half the binary artillery projectiles in Saudi Arabia as part of the retaliatory strategy. Even if it were all just a military bluff, the entire reason for the chemical weapons stockpile was for this one purpose; deterring the threat of chemical weapons use against U.S. forces. Because President George Bush was very committed to the goal of ridding the U.S. military inventory of chemical weapons, he chose to deny that request. It wouldn't do for the United States to be using these weapons in one breath and then after the war, to go back to negotiations on ridding the world of them. Even so, this decision meant that the soldiers had to rely on defensive equipment and training even more than before.[2]

The decision to add a second corps (VII Corps) to the conflict had an immediate impact on CB defense plans, both operationally and logistically. The decision to commit additional forces to develop an offensive option was not unexpected, but the decision had revealed a lack of expertise in planning logistics for a modern CB warfare scenario. As the military planners reviewed their options, they realized that if Saddam used CB weapons, they did not have enough chemical protective suits to support operations past April 1991. Division commanders, air commanders, and naval fleet commanders had all assumed that, once their shortfalls of chemical defense equipment were known and the threat emphasized, "someone" in DoD would get their supplies in short order. That wasn't happening. The CB defense sector of the military-industrial complex that had been dormant for years could not just spring into life. Cold production lines required time to reestablish; critical materials needed to be shipped; personnel on the line required training. The medical community could support one corps's demand for BW vaccines, but not two. The new equipment requested, such as the new XM93 Foxes, CAMs, and biodetectors, continued to roll into theater up to the day of the ground offensive. While individual training was completed and chemical defense units were in place by February 1991, supplies of CB detectors, detector batteries, extra protective masks and clothing, decontaminants, and large collective protection filters had just barely met the necessary requirements to support a short ground offensive.

As the air war began in mid-January, Iraq responded with Scud attacks. After an extremely nervous coalition force realized that the Scuds were not CB-armed, they got into the rhythm of how to respond to missile attacks. After tentatively identifying the Scud's targets, troops in that immediate area were warned to go to MOPP4. For downwind hazards, a more detailed map was required. The Defense Nuclear Agency had upgraded a software package called ANBACIS (Automated Nuclear, Biological and Chemical Information System) and supplied the corps and division headquarters with faxes, STUIII phones, and computer terminals to connect to a 24-hour operations cell in Washington, D.C. This system permitted real-time evaluation support across the theater for potential hazard areas created by the Scud attacks. The XM93 NBCRS vehicles rushed out to examine all impact areas and any troop areas that reported multiple chemical alarms going off. While there was an increase in chemical alarms, the overwhelming majority were due to low battery power, false alarms caused by the oil-smoked skies, or nervous troops overreacting to detector system tests.

Political pressure mounted very quickly that the Scud threat had to go. The CB production plants had been targeted very early in the air offensive, but that only meant that Saddam couldn't make any new munitions. That didn't account for all the stored munitions ready to move toward the front lines. While suspected storage areas near airfields and ammunition depots were targeted, postwar analysis showed that the overwhelming majority of munitions had escaped harm. Special forces groups and increased air missions tried to destroy the Scud launchers, but with the exception of a few, these escaped (although the number of launches dropped dramatically). Iraqi use of decoys and "shoot and scoot" tactics kept the launchers a threat all the way through the war.

Final preparations for the ground offensive included developing deliberate decontamination sites (at the point of entry into Iraq, preplanned sites throughout the movements, and in the rear area), delivering Fox vehicles to every division in theater, moving twelve special biodetection teams into position, and maneuvering smoke generator companies to the front of the lines. Each soldier had two protective suits, a fitted mask, decon kits and medical CB treatments. The U.S. force was now as prepared as it would ever be, logistically and operationally.

When the ground war started on February 24, 1991, it was preceded by a massive air and artillery strike against any weapon system that could employ CB munitions. The Iraqi air force had long since left, leaving the South African-produced 155-mm howizters and Iraqi rocket launchers as prime targets. Still, all forces crossing into Iraq did so in MOPP 1, half expecting the chemical alarms to all sound off at every Iraqi artillery barrage. Marines entering the teeth of the minefields in Kuwait were especially alert, as the mines slowed their progress and made them easy targets. When engineers reported a possible chemical mine explosion, the Marines instantly went to full MOPP 4 and called for their Fox vehicles to check out the lane. When no traces of chemical contamination were discovered, they sounded "all clear," downgraded their protection to MOPP 1 and moved out. This was exactly how the concept was intended to work; minimizing the time spent in protective gear to maximize operational lethality.

Once the first twenty-four hours had gone by, the coalition force relaxed somewhat. The Marines and VII Corps had breached the Iraqi defenses without any chemical artillery attacks. XVIII Airborne Corps had swung out and enveloped the Iraqi right wing without entering any chemical contamination. The anticipated CB agent attacks never occurred. There are a number of ideas why this did not happen. Saddam and his military leaders may have lost their nerve when the U.S. administration threatened a response that "would be absolutely over-whelming and . . . devastating."[3]  Others credit the intense air offensive that interdicted most traffic moving from Baghdad (and the suspected CB agent production sites) into Kuwait, while others credit the fast-moving ground units that never stopped to present a target. Some thought that Saddam realized CB agents would not affect an obviously well-prepared military force such as the United States now had, and was reserving them for any moves against Baghdad proper. Yet others noted that this could had all been Saddam's bluff, which had success-fully frozen U.S. forces in place for six months.

Postwar analysis noted that Iraq's military had enough CB munitions to seriously impede the coalition force's progress and to make the price of victory high, but not enough to stop the force. Once again, these analysts had missed the point. Iraq had never counted on its CB agent munitions to win battles; they just tilted the odds for the combat arms forces to take advantage of the other side's inability to cope with CB contamination. Saddam had never counted on beating the U.S. military at its full strength; he had counted on making the price so high that a U.S.-led attack into Kuwait and Iraq would become politically impossible to support. Had Saddam hit the ports and airfields with CB agents early in September–October 1990 and driven his divisions into Saudi Arabia, maybe he could have scared the U.S. administration into backing out. It was these strategic errors in judgment that had lost the war, not the lack of CB agent use.

The lack of CB warfare caused more questions than answers. Many combat arms leaders had the attitude that the active use of aircraft and artillery systems, combined with good maneuver, had negated the CB threat. A follow-on thought was if Iraq had not been convinced to use CB weapons against the U.S. forces, no one would. This line of reasoning completely ignored the fact that "active defense" options had failed to destroy, or even find, the enemy CB agents at storage sites. As the CB defense equipment and specialized chemical defense companies returned untested, the question of how well the U.S. military would have fared in a CB warfare environment remained unanswered. Yet there were many points that the chemical defense community captured for future reference.

## DOCTRINE, TRAINING, AND LEADERSHIP

For the most part, Army units understood the doctrine behind CB defense (GAO report notwithstanding). Everyone was keyed to signs and symptoms of nerve agent poisoning, and everyone walked around in Saudi Arabia with a protective mask at his/her hip. This included government civilians, contractors, and the media. Chemical alarms were deployed from August through February, to the point that the units were running out of the special batteries required. During the dawn and evening, soldiers donned their one protective suit used for training to acclimate their bodies to the heat and isolation. Once the decon companies arrived, everyone practiced decontamination drills, to include personnel and vehicles going through full deliberate decon sites. Chemical officers noted that for once, everyone, from private to colonel, was paying very close attention to CB defense training. One chemical soldier joked that the level of training people required was proportional to their rank; the higher rank one was, the more individual training he required. This reflected the way newer soldiers took to CB defense training as second nature, as opposed to the old-timers who joined the Army prior to 1980, who had not appreciated the CB warfare threat as much.

HQ DA ordered the units deployed to the Gulf to train every soldier in theater on individual CB defense skills, such as donning the protective mask, using M256A1 kits, using decon kits, and so on. In addition, many division commanders called for small-unit exercises conducted in MOPP gear, incorporating the chemical detection teams and decon teams within their ranks. The level of training was very high, but the understanding of what to do after donning the suits was low. Still, because the Chemical School had developed doctrine and training that emphasized individual and squad survival actions, the troops were confident they could survive a CB agent attack.

The down side was that when the M8A1 chemical detectors alarmed, everyone lept to their suits, especially after the early December Scud launch conducted by Iraq. This was not a bad thing, except that the soldiers were losing confidence in the M8A1 alarm after M256A1 kits showed there was no agent. The leadership did not understand or did not communicate the point that the M8A1 detector was only an initial warning of *possible* nerve agents at very low levels. Doctrine was that all M8A1 alarms be checked by M256A1 kits, which eliminated many of the false positive alarms. Those troops that remembered this point made it through.

Training shortfalls came with the new equipment that was rushed to the field. While the Fox vehicles have been touted as the most effective contamination detection system fielded during the conflict. While these vehicles certainly added to the dimension of CB defense in a quantum leap, their success was diminished by operator errors. In the rush to field these vehicles and crews to the Gulf, the crews were force-fed a three-week training program on an extremely sophisticated detection system.[4] The Fox vehicles required heavy contractor maintenance to keep them operational in the field, as their spare parts and maintenance requirements were not within the U.S. military logistics system yet. The end result was that operators made mistakes, notably the Marine crews leading their divisions into Kuwait. The MM-1 mass spectrometer identifies vapor agents with a broad discriminator at first; if the detector identifies a possible agent, the operator is supposed to stop and run a more sophisticated discriminating test. During the air offensive, the crews took their time to run the instruments. As they led the ground forces under heavy fire, the crews did not avail themselves of that luxury of more detailed checks, leading to errors in judgment. As with any new piece of equipment, it takes time to understand how to operate it under combat conditions, time that was not afforded to the NBCRS crews.

The biodetection systems were a similar example of training shortfalls and lack of doctrinal guidance. Prior to the Gulf War, no one had seriously addressed the doctrinal or training requirements to implement a biological point detection system throughout a theater of conflict. The emphasis had always been on sampling the BW agent and verifying the existence of these agents, not on real-time detection and warning. Many soldiers, to include those within the chemical defense community, assume that it should duplicate the current chemical agent point detection system. This is one reason why many so-called experts mistakenly deride the biodetection system's lack of a real-time detection capability as a deficiency. They fail to acknowledge the real technical challenges biodetection represents, to include the different threat employment used for BW agents, all of which makes the goal of real-time detection questionable. Biological defense requires a high level of coordination between the medical, intelligence, and CB defense specialists. Understanding what BW agents constitute a threat and where the BW threat extends leads to the proper use of medical vaccines and treatments that can make that threat irrelevant. Because BW agents require a longer time to infect and disable a human host, the need for a real-time detection capability is not there. It is more important to quickly verify what is being used (say within twenty-four hours), rather than immediately jumping into protective postures as is required with nerve agent attacks.

### Organizational Support

Because of the buildup of the Chemical Corps in the 1980s, there were dedicated professionals experienced with CB warfare present throughout the Army force structure, and equally important, dedicated chemical defense companies within the divisions. In the haste to make light infantry divisions more mobile, military planners had cut back requirements on the heavy decontamination companies to design smoke/decontamination companies. While the flexibility to support either operation was attractive, the 82d Airborne Division realized how inadequate these dual-purpose companies were without augmentation from reserve decontamination companies. August and September 1990 were lean months for the airborne soldiers, relying on a few limited decon systems per brigade prior to the entry of active and reserve chemical soldiers from the United States. This challenge was corrected after the war with the creation of a headquarters chemical battalion and corps chemical recon company at XVIII Airborne Corps, to better plan and support early operations in theaters with a CB agent threat.

Most important was that when the reserve and active chemical companies, detachments, and platoons arrived in theater, they were the right force for the job. These chemical soldiers came prepared to decon and recon, supporting the combat operations as they were trained. Had the Chemical Corps not been reestablished in 1976, there would have been no chemical defense companies to support the troops. Equally important were the chemical specialists acting as staff to the company, battalion, brigade, division, and corps headquarters. These troops were pressed into action, refreshing the CB defense training their comrades required to survive and sustain combat operations in a CB environment. Had they been thinner in number or nonexistent due to some poorly planned downsizing exercise, again, the low level of training could have been disastrous both for the morale of the force and for their chances for success against the Iraqi army.

### CHEMICAL DEFENSE EQUIPMENT PERFORMANCE

**Chemical detection** received a mixed review. On the low end, troops understood and used the M8 and M9 paper and understood when to use the M256A1 kit without having chemical specialists around. Automated point detection took a hard slam based on the number of false alarms reported throughout the conflict.  Both the M8A1 detectors and the CAMs false-alarmed to diesel fumes, the nitric acid used as Scud missile fuel oxidizer, and shipboard firefighting foams, to name a few causes.  Low battery power and poor training contributed to the confusion as well.  As explained earlier in this book, the labs had emphasized the technical requirements of low-level agent detection while trying to maintain a rugged, field-survivable instrument that was affordable (since there were tens of thousands used throughout the force).  The important thing was that the chemical detectors never ignored the real presence of chemical agents (no false negatives), as seen by the lack of any chemical agent casualties through the ground offensive.[5]

Some politicians questioned the lack of an automatic mustard agent vapor detector, without understanding that the mustard agent doesn't vaporize very well to permit automatic detection in time to warn troops.  Still, that politically-driven observation became a goal for the next-generation ACADA to meet.  Later detractors had a double argument—first they said that the false-alarming chemical detectors were examples of an ineffective chemical defense program.  Then they used the many reports of chemical alarms during the war as evidence that the chemical detectors had correctly identified low-level agent concentrations, meaning there was an environment where the soldiers had been exposed to low-level agents. The fact that there was no clinical evidence that low-level concentrations of nerve agents caused any ill health effects was irrelevant.  The field detectors worked fine when they were using fresh batteries and trained soldiers were operating them. Other point detectors such as the ICAD have not remained in the inventory after the war, perhaps an indication of how well they performed.  Obviously lightweight detectors are a goal but not at the cost of sensitivities or accuracy.

The Gulf War illness controversy has led some military and political leaders to mandate that the Army should not settle for anything less than both low-level agent (sublethal) detection and zero false alarms.  Words such as "making soldiers as safe from toxic agents as civilians are in the city streets" have actually been used in congressional testimony.  First, I would question whether civilians in the city streets are enjoying safe, clean air, considering some cities' pollution controls (or the lack thereof).  But more seriously, why should soldiers be completely protected from CB warfare agents when they are at risk from so many other weapon systems?  Is the new goal to make warfare a nice, safe, casualty-free walk in the park?  Because if that is the goal, people are seriously deluding themselves and setting up the military for a future failure.  There is a price for such high goals, and that is operational effectiveness of those that have to react to sublethal alarms.  This means more expensive detectors, thicker, hotter clothing, and more corrosive decontaminants.

The success of CW agent standoff detection during the conflict was not well explored.  The few M21 RSCAALs in theater frequently tracked dust storms or false-alarmed off the hot sun, resulting in their limited use during dawn and dusk only (which were ideal times for CB warfare agent release, so this limitation worked out). Because they were largely stationary and could not support mobile operations, their visibility to combat leaders was limited. They were deployed only because many military leaders cried out for any and all capabilities for CB defense to be fielded, in their fears of the unknown consequences of these attacks. The performance of these detectors did not support any groundswells of movement for standoff detection, and combat leaders today remain unconvinced that these systems are worth the investment, although the concept still appears valid.

Last and not least, reconnaissance was very well accepted as a vital requirement, if the M93 Fox itself was not. On the one hand, it could keep up with the Bradley IFVs and Abrams tanks far better than the chemical recon platoons using M113A2 APCs. On the other, the concept of how fast-moving NBC recon systems work with their assigned combat brigades in marking contaminated areas is still being worked on. There remains a bit of mystique about the system, like the fact that it is considered state-of-the-art means that its technical accuracy should be unquestioned. Its capability remains only as credible as its trained operators, however. Its maintenance requirements have amounted to a hefty contract logistics support bill, and the Marine Corps never liked its heaviness and nonstandard parts requirement (but that didn't stop them from requesting ten systems for the ground war). Bottom line, it was a step in the right direction, but the doctrinal concept of how it identifies CB agent contamination and what leaders do with the information remains to be worked out in training exercises.

What would make both the point detection false alarm issue go away and standoff detection capabilities work is what is called "digitizing the battlefield." If these detectors were all networked together to share information on battle screens, division and corps headquarters could quickly determine whether a chemical agent detector was false-alarming (because it was the only detector of a series to alarm) and whether standoff systems are adequately covering the battlespace. The concept of networking these detectors is still in development and not field-tested; it depends on advances in military battlespace communications and control systems, in addition to the military's purchase of enough point and standoff detectors and communication interface devices to make it work. The Army's current emphasis on "situational awareness" and the concept of fighting on a digitized battlefield has created an opportunity to make the idea work.

**Biological detection**, as mentioned, took a hard rap due to the failure to detect on a real-time basis and warn troops of sublethal concentrations. Technically speaking, the devices used were not capable of the mission, but they represented the best that could be fielded considering that the military had never emphasized the need for biological detection. The reaction seen during the Gulf War was a bit of an overreaction caused by the ignorance of those not familiar with the unique characteristics of BW agents. Because medical vaccines were not in stocks sufficient to protect the entire force from anthrax, people imagined the worst. By using air and land weapon systems to destroy possible CB delivery systems,

CENTCOM had a strong influence over stopping biological warfare from occurring. The combination of agent samplers and SMART tickets with forward military laboratories at KKMC and al-Jubail enabled the theater commander to understand whether BW agents had been used against his forces covertly or whether BW agents had entered his area of responsibility as a result of destruction of far-off enemy BW stocks.

This "detect to treat" philosophy means that after biodetectors identify the threat agents, it becomes a medical mass casualty issue to treat the affected soldiers (to include government civilians and other U.S. civilians affected in theater). While this may not be an ideal capability, to say that troops were not protected against BW agents is untrue. At the least, has at least awakened the military leadership to emphasize the need to quickly develop a more robust "detect to warn" capability. Today, the geographical commanders-in-chief are all demanding point biological agent detection capabilities at any price. Detection still will not occur in real-time, but the time to detection is being reduced from 45 minutes (1990) to 30 minutes (1998) and possibly to fifteen minutes (2000+?).

**Individual protection** received a mixed grade as well, due to the lack of any CB attacks to test its principles. There is no doubt that individual soldiers were well familiar with the M17A2 mask and protective suit by February, having trained, eaten, and slept with them always nearby. While soldiers may have preferred the M40 masks, the M17A2 protective mask was fully qualified to protect its wearers. The qualifying statement is that the masks had to be checked for correct fits by chemical specialists and maintained in good shape by the soldiers and their supply clerks.[6] While many soldiers had not paid attention to mask fit in peacetime, they paid very close attention now. Because the M17A2, M24, and M25 masks were all on their way out, the number of masks available as backups was very low (numbering less than 500 for VII Corps and its thousands of soldiers) and M13A2 filters became a scarce commodity as well.

What no one had considered was who was to give protective masks to the thousands of Filipino, Pakistani, and other foreign contract workers under CENTCOM's command, who were driving trucks, cooking at the bases, doing the laundry, and acting as sentries to free up coalition soldiers. Added to this requirement were the equally numerous contractors and government civilians supporting equipment maintenance, the press media (while the Army may not have wanted them to have masks, the press was insistent), and U.S. citizens in theater working for the Saudis. No one had counted them, and they all demanded masks. At one point prior to the ground war, the contracted truck drivers had refused to drive until they got their masks (and they did receive the masks).[7]

The lack of an active production line had severely limited the number of protective suits in theater as well, but every soldier had at least two suits when the ground offensive started. The suits, designed for a European Cold War scenario with heavy chemical attacks, were seen as too hot and heavy for soldiers in the desert. The butyl rubber boots and gloves were even worse, trapping heavy sweat and softening the skin, making soldiers vulnerable to mechanical injuries and trenchfoot. While durability and protection were important, it had come at the cost of high heat stress and lessened capabilities to perform heavy-duty missions. While the Marine Corps had opted for British Mark IV protective suits, they were later reviewed as not being durable enough in addition to protecting against half the challenge of the U.S. suits. Natick engineers tried to explain that the heat stress problem would have been caused by any additional clothing over the standard battledress uniform (to include a wet tee-shirt). Lightening the BDOs would not have reduced the heat stress adequately without losing chemical protection capabilities. Still, the dissatisfaction with the suits stayed fresh in people's minds and into the next generation of protective suit designs.

The suits and masks were untested, but the real lesson is twofold. First, had infantry soldiers trained more in protective suits and masks during peacetime, they would have known what to expect in wartime. While Fort Benning trainees are familiar with the slogans "train as you would fight" and "spill blood in training, not in combat," the slogans hadn't been applied to CB defense training. Second was the sheer logistics nature of stockpiling protective suits and mask filters for such contingencies. As all good combat leaders stress protecting their troops to maximize their combat lethality for the right moment, they should understand the technical limitations of protective ensembles and how often they need to be changed out. The follow-on thought is that if your higher headquarters does not plan the logistics of resupplying said ensembles, they have just sacrificed your ability to sustain combat power. Easy lesson, tough penalties.

**Collective protection** systems just weren't in place to really support the force, other than the integrated vehicle CPS, and even these systems were in danger of being irrelevant due to the shortages of large CP filters. The Army had taken special measures to replace its M1 tanks in III Corps with brand-new M1A2 tanks; while the primary purpose was to increase the odds against Iraqi armor, part of that swap program included overpressure and cooling systems. The Marine M60A3 tanks had only air-blown mask protection with no cooling and overpressure, and the difference in performance was evident. The M20 SCPE shelters, because of their design to fit within buildings, were useless in the desert and used only in city warehouses. The few XM28 SCPE shelters given to medical units made little impact. Again, logistics played a large measure of the success and failure of these systems. Large CPS filters, demanding much more activated carbon than protective mask filters, were in short supply and had a very low production line supporting their manufacture, despite the urgent requirements. The millions of dollars thrown at companies to surge-produce filters and suits would have been too little, too late, had Saddam initiated CB warfare.

The most vulnerable areas of CENTCOM remained at the theater ports, airfields, and massive supply dumps. Protective covers, designed to protect these supplies, had been redirected to become cupola shelters for tank commanders. Given the absence of protective covers and CPS shelters, these areas were ideal targets for persistent chemical agents (had Iraq better targeting systems or better intelligence sources). Still, the post-Gulf War combat arms community (and more important the combat service support community) have chosen to ignore the vulnerability, choosing to focus on unproven theater missile defenses and dreams of smart bombs finding all their targets of CB munitions. Only the medics chose to continue improvements for collective protection after the Gulf War. In part, it may take major investments in technology to overcome the space and power requirements of CPS before the military finds CPS to be a convenient way to avoid contamination.

**Decontamination programs** were well represented if not very convenient. Once the sun hit the M258A1 decon kits, the heat swelled up the alcohol-laden pads until they burst. Their replacements, the M291 decon kits, would have done better if they were available in numbers to support the mission. Still, individual decontamination was taken care of by the sheer volume of M258A1 kits. Equipment was a different story. Because of the corrosive nature of DS-2, effective equipment and vehicle decontamination counted on volumes of water to rinse off the decontaminants after scrubbing. The 82d Airborne Division had few water haulers with its dual-purpose decon units to maintain an effective capability, and even within its supply units, the division could not spare the few water haulers it had strictly for decon missions. To augment this thin capability early on, the XVIII Airborne Corps turned to local Saudi companies, purchasing commercial calcium hypochlorite and plastic water tanks and renting water haulers.

Units were just receiving the M17 SANATOR lightweight decon systems, but of course these systems would not completely clean contaminated equipment. That would have to be accomplished by the aging M12A1 Power-Driven Decon Apparatuses, which were in the heavy decontamination companies that would not arrive prior to October. Even as these systems arrived, maintenance units were hard pressed to maintain the old engines that were constantly breaking down in the heat. By resorting to cannibalization, the chemical companies kept most M12A1 decon apparatuses operational. By the time the air war started, there was a robust decontamination capability in theater. By teaming with Army combat engineers, the chemical companies prepared deliberate decontamination sites that would have supported decontamination of hundreds of vehicles, had they been caught by CW artillery projectiles. Eventually there were enough decontaminants and systems in theater to perform the mission, but it took months to get the specialists and their equipment into theater. The vulnerability to early-entry forces, especially in a force projection mode, continues today.

What was not covered was the increasingly large number of sensitive avionics and electronics on the battlefield. Without a nonaqueous decontamination process, this equipment would have been junked if contaminated, which would have severely impacted the U.S. military's high technology edge. Another unmet requirement was the large-area decontamination mission. Had the ports and airfields been hit with CB agents, what options would there be but to abandon the area? The amount of DS-2 and STB required to clean a heavily contaminated port was astronomical, not to mention the time and resources committed to conduct the operation (to include assessment of contamination, cleanup, and verification of safe levels). The final point is that the civilian labor required to run these ports and airfields would have to be convinced that the area was safe; they were not military personnel who could be ordered to return. In essence, the port/airfield would be lost for the duration, shutting off a vital logistics or operational point. This problem landed very squarely into the "too hard" column, which made military planners shudder every time they heard the Scud alerts sound.

The medical community and quartermasters realized they had a serious decontamination issue that had not been previously addressed: the decontamination of human remains. The American public demands its posthumous war heroes back, and politicians all the way to President Bush were insistent that all their soldiers come home. The question was, what if the corpse were contaminated with chemical or biological agents? By returning the bodies, the military might be unwittingly spreading CB agent contamination back to unsuspecting mourners in the United States. This gruesome question was addressed Stateside by several agencies, who finally developed an interim solution. By heavily bleaching the remains and testing the body later with sensitive laboratory instruments, these bodies might pass the muster to come home in closed caskets.

Finally, once the battle was over and equipment that had been field-decontaminated was ready to return home, how would the force ensure that the equipment met federal regulations for government civilian exposure to CB agents? These agent levels, essentially requiring 3X standards just to stay in the inventory, could not be verified with field agent detectors. Specialists with more sensitive laboratory equipment would have to screen each item prior to its return to the United States. In practice, the Army was willing to bypass this in the interests of time and money. The interim solution was that the equipment would never return; it would become either donations to the host nations, or stockpiled for the return of U.S. forces to that region. Lieutenant General John Yeosock, ARCENT commander, commented that his solution was to dig a deep hole and drive all the contaminated tanks and vehicles into the hole, covering the hole over. Actually, leaving the equipment out in the desert weather for a few weeks would have, in most likelihood, been enough to eliminate the threat. The point is that no one had really examined this issue.

**Medical chemical defense material** met the challenge, which was not unexpected. With the exception of the debate over the efficacy of pyridostigmine bromide (PB) tablets, the medical community had long anticipated the threat and its effects on the human body. Using the NAAK was second nature, drilled into every soldier's mind. The shortage of biological vaccines for anthrax and botulinum toxin was the greatest failure of military medicine for the medics, one that they have done much to address since 1991. There was no excuse for not having adequate vaccines for the force, which happened only because of the failure by military leaders to commit dollars to a project that they felt would never really be required. They were wrong. The argument about efficacy continues, with detractors claiming that Army soldiers were nothing but guinea pigs for the "untested" vaccines and pretreatments. This argument is insulting and uninformed. Had the U.S. Army deployed into the Gulf without the anthrax vaccine and without the PB tablets and been hit with CB agents, the howls over why the military had withheld the INDs and vaccines would have been deafening. This was truly a lose-lose situation, but considering the guaranteed deaths that might have resulted had Saddam used his CBW arsenal, there really was no choice.

The future for medical CB defense material remains shaky, as this argument continues to be played out. By FDA regulations, vaccines and pretreatments for CBW agents will never be fully tested as everyday prescription drugs are, simply because the U.S. military cannot test and will not test human volunteers exposed to CB warfare agents. I would ask these detractors and idiots that refuse to take the anthrax vaccine today, what is the solution, then? Remain unprotected against a 90 percent lethal threat that is so easy to counter? It would make as much sense as saying that wearing helmets and kevlar vests was optional in wartime.

## GULF WAR ILLNESSES

The issue of Gulf War Syndrome (GWS) deserves more than a few paragraphs; in the interest of brevity, I will cover the high points. About eighteen months after the end of the Gulf War, soldiers began complaining of suffering a variety of illnesses. Thinking these were service-related, they reasonably turned to the Veteran's Administration hospitals, where they were initially told the generic symptoms couldn't be traced to any one source.[8] When the cries of "DoD coverup" and "Agent Orange again" started, the Army leadership (recalling firsthand the problems of ignoring veterans' health claims in the 1970s) made the decision to treat all soldiers for possible Gulf War-related complaints, regardless of the time or nature of the illness. The question was, where did these illnesses come from? The nature of the illnesses was so nebulous, and the suffering soldiers had been all over the battlefield, that the source of these illnesses was not readily identifiable. Common theories ranged from petroleum exposure, stress reactions, depleted uranium, pesticide exposure, smoke from oil well fires, indigenous parasites and bacteria, military vaccines and nerve agent antidotes, chronic fatigue syndrome, and multiple chemical sensitivity. Oh, did I forget one? Many soldiers suspected they were exposed to low levels of CB agents, intentionally or accidentally released by the Iraqi military.

It was the perfect set-up; poorly trained troops had their fears of invisible CB agents heightened to unparalleled levels against a very capable foe; they had been using special equipment with which they were unfamiliar; they had to deal with false-alarming chemical agent detectors, hot oppressive clothing, and unfamiliar medicines. After being warned that it was a certainty that Iraq would use CB agents, when it didn't happen, some soldiers began to suspect that their leaders didn't really know what had truly had happened. When the Army engineers blew up the Khamisiyah depot on March 4, 199., it was later found that nerve-agent filled 122-mm rockets were in one of the thirty-eight bunkers that had been blown. Although none of the engineers nearby or other military soldiers within miles of the depot suffered any signs or symptoms of nerve agent exposure, this event convinced many that DoD was covering up their exposure to nerve agents.[9]

The CIA presented an assessment of the depot explosion on July 9, 1996, using a contractor-developed computer model to worst-case the scenario. Without considering the afternoon desert heat and impurities in the Iraqi nerve agent, and maximizing the possible downwind hazard, the model concluded that troops four kilometers away might have suffered runny noses and miosis symptoms. Anyone up to twenty-five kilometers downwind might be exposed to 0.000003 mg per cubic meter of nerve gas (or 0.013 mg-min/m$^3$), if they stayed in that area for seventy-two hours.

The Army leadership decided that, to be on the safe side, the hazard area should include anyone within a twenty-five kilometer circle. This gave way to the initial estimate of 5,000 troops possibly exposed to chemical agents. When the Pentagon announced it had extended the hazard radius to a fifty-kilometer circle (just to be safe), the exposure estimate rose to 20,000. Allowing for all troops that might have been downwind of the depot for any amount of time within three days of the explosion, the estimate grew again to 100,000. To sum up the situation, the military had admitted that their troops might have been exposed to chemical agents, based on a conservative estimate of a worst-case Army analysis of a worst-case CIA analysis. This was done during an election year to confront claims of nerve agent exposure, without any medical evidence of exposure, without any validated models, and without any Chemical Corps input. The press ate up the story, blasting the Department of Defense for previously stating that there had been no CB weapons use or exposure to CB agents, without considering how sound the evidence was. Sound familiar yet?[10]

In November 1995 Dr. Bernard Rotsker was appointed as the Special Assistant to the Deputy Secretary of Defense for Gulf War Illnesses. His office immediately began investigating every suspected case of CB agent exposure, no matter the degree of credibility. Narratives outlining the investigations are available to the public for scrutiny on the Internet, to include the majority of military records discussing CB defense during the Gulf War. Because detractors didn't like the idea of DoD conducting its own investigation, President Bill Clinton formed a Presidential Advisory Committee on Gulf War Veterans' Illnesses in the spring of 1996, largely made up of civilian doctors with little or no military experience. Both groups interviewed scores of veterans, military experts and civilian medical experts, and investigated a number of wartime-related incidents, with a particular focus on potential chemical or biological warfare exposure.

Since 1996 both academic and government medical research agencies have failed to turn up any evidence of CB agent exposure to military troops. Dr. Rotsker's group has thoroughly documented nearly all cases of suspected CB agent exposures and documented their reports and raw data for all to see on the Internet. Several expert panels have met, failing to turn up any evidence except for anecdotal stories from soldiers who wouldn't know chemical agents from saltwater. As for the other areas under suspicion, conclusively proving what is causing these Gulf War illnesses may be impossible, given the inability to account for where all these troops were on the battlefield, what they were exposed to both during the war and in the United States for two years after the war, and the lack of data on how combinations of these agents may have affected the human body. No one denies that the veterans are sick and require DoD's support; it would be nice to know exactly what was affecting them prior to treating their illnesses. In the meantime, they should receive immediate treatment, and, given the utter lack of hard evidence pointing at CB agents, that line should be dropped.

The Central Intelligence Agency has recently admitted that their chemical warfare agent exposure models were too pessimistic, and perhaps (by their models) only a few thousand soldiers were exposed to sublethal levels of nerve agent instead of the higher estimate of one hundred thousand. DoD has bent over backward to treat all Gulf War soldiers regardless of their illnesses and investigated nearly every suspicious incident, and yet people still think CB agents were a cause of GWS. Even when the Senate Veteran Affairs committee admitted in September 1998 that they saw no evidence of chemical-biological warfare agents as the source of GWS, many remain suspicious that the government is covering up the "truth."

What should be obvious is that ignorance and fear of CB agents is driving the GWS agenda more than any evidence of DoD coverups. Over 4,000 chemical specialists were in the Gulf, with thousands of battle-tested detection equipment, providing the expert testimony necessary to close the case against CB agent exposure. The question remains, are our military and political leaders listening and, more importantly, to whom are they listening? The conspiracy buffs or the CB warfare experts? The fallout of this issue does not stop with the Gulf War history; it affects how the future military force will face CB warfare and what tools they will have at their disposal.

# CHAPTER 18

# Restructuring the DoD CB Defense Program

Several material areas sorely required attention during the Gulf War. The most clearly evident requirement was the need for improved airlift and sealift capabilities. While C-17 cargo planes, heavy trucks, and merchant marine ships will never be as sexy or alluring as F-22 fighter aircraft, Abrams tanks, and Seawolf submarines, there certainly was a strong case made when the military had to rely on commercial aircraft and ships older than the generals and admirals in order to get to the theater of operations. Of course, CB defense equipment was another area of concern. Despite the Gulf War (or because of the lack of CB warfare during this conflict), CB defense equipment continues to struggle on as a relatively insignificant portion of the Pentagon's R&D funds (less than one-fifth of 1 percent).

CB defense equipment has always been criticized by both the military troops that use the equipment and the chemical specialists that train with it. Protective suits are too hot; protective masks are too restrictive; collective protection shelters are not adequate; decontamination apparatuses use too much water; CB agent detectors false-alarm too often; and medical antidotes cannot be trusted. All these complaints came too late for the troops in Operation Desert Storm. These concerns were primarily a result of the combat arms sitting by the sidelines, allowing the Chemical Corps to determine what the combat troops were going to use. The Chemical Corps did deliver detectors that detected chemical agents and protective ensembles that would have saved lives, and decontaminants did work very well.

The *BUT* part is that the combat arms units did not understand that getting CB defense equipment that works is only half the equation; there remain such matters as false alarms due to overly sensitive detectors, hot burdensome suits, and corrosive decontaminants that degrade combat effectiveness. If the combat arms incorporated CB warfare considerations into their wargaming, they might see the benefits and challenges of CB defense equipment, and they might get more involved. This active involvement will become more and more important as the military destroys its chemical munitions and relies solely on defensive equipment in the face of future CB warfare threats.

## ORGANIZATIONAL CHANGES

When Congress developed the National Defense Authorization Act for fiscal year 1994, it added a requirement to force certain changes in the DoD NBC defense program. This legislation was named Title XVII—Chemical and Biological Weapons Defense, under Public Law 103-160. Its main goal was to improve the joint coordination and oversight of the NBC defense program and ensure a coherent and effective approach to its management. This is to be accomplished through a single office in DoD, a stronger coordinating role by the Army, and a joint coordinated and integrated NBC defense budget for all four services. The House and Senate committees noted some improvements in the overall DoD program since the end of the Gulf War but remained concerned over the need for a sustained effort to strengthen the program. They also recommended DoD assistance in training U.S. and international Chemical Weapons Convention inspectors and monitoring teams. Last, they encouraged the Secretary of Defense to adopt a verification and inspection regime for the 1972 Biological Weapons Convention.[1]

As a result of Public Law 103-160, there is an increased emphasis on better management of the NBC defense program. The Army punched up the authority of its one-star commander of the laboratory (CRDEC) into a Chemical-Biological Defense Agency (CBDA), and finally the two-star commander of U.S. Army Chemical and Biological Defense Command (CBDCOM) in October 1993. In a recent Army initiative to consolidate and streamline its organizations, HQ AMC merged the U.S. Army Soldier Systems Command (SSCOM) into CBDCOM, creating the U.S. Army Soldier and Biological Chemical Command (SBCCOM) in 1998. SBCCOM formally took charge of the two commands' responsibilities and programs on October 1, 1999.

The commanding general of CBDCOM also "wears the hats" of Deputy Chief of Staff for Chemical-Biological Matters (DCSCBM), Army Materiel Command, and Department of the Army's Implementing Agent (DA IA) for Chemical Weapons Treaties and Arms Control Agreements. SBCCOM is charged to manage all NBC defense programs for the Army and to coordinate with the other services to manage better the DoD NBC defense program. SBCCOM manages the chemical stockpile sites, to include Rocky Mountain Arsenal and several programs at Dugway Proving Ground, and is gaining command over Pine Bluff Arsenal, Deseret Chemical Depot, and other locations. This is not to suggest that the Army has gone full circle, back to the single consolidated DoD NBC defense program it had prior to 1962. SBCCOM still has no direct control over medical NBC defense programs or the chemical demilitarization program. But it does have a great deal of authority to request funds, conduct studies, and develop new NBC defense equipment for all four services.

Public Law 103-160 also meant reorganization for the entire DoD NBC defense community, as shown in Figure 18.1. The four services formed a Joint Service Integration Group (JSIG) to coordinate joint doctrine and training issues and a Joint Service Material Group (JSMG) to coordinate joint material issues. Both are chaired by Army generals, and both include all services' general officers as equal partners. The JSIG resides at Fort McClellan, with the Chemical School's commandant as its chair. Its sister organization, the JSMG, is chaired by the commanding general of SBCCOM at Aberdeen Proving Ground. These groups officially started their functions in January 1995, both overseen by a DoD Joint NBC Defense Board. The Joint NBC Defense Board is a high-level, general-officer panel (including civilian acquisition members and officers from all services) designed to oversee the DoD NBC defense program and to sort out interservice conflicts. The new joint groups may be more effective than their predecessors, primarily since they make recommendations on the annual NBC defense budgets through a joint consolidated CB Defense Program Operations Memorandum (POM) strategy. As the Golden Rule states, those who have the gold make the rules. This is what made the difference from past joint CB defense groups[2]

Defense Secretary William Cohen recently added his own organizational change to the DoD NBC defense management structure. In the continued search to downsize government, DoD suggested to Congress that they combine the Defense Special Weapons Agency (the former Defense Nuclear Agency), the On-Site Inspection Agency, and Defense Technology Security Administration into the Defense Threat Reduction Agency (DTRA). In addition to consolidating similar DoD agencies that worked on arms control issues, the goal was to create an agency with a new focus; less on the older threat of nuclear proliferation and more on the general topic of reducing the overall threat of "weapons of mass destruction" in general. DTRA now acts as the banker and policy coordinator for DoD's CB defense program in addition to its arms control agenda.[3]

Last, with the end of the Cold War, the Department of Energy (DoE) labs have realized that they aren't in the business of testing and storing nuclear devices anymore. Faced with the perception of a lack of mission (and therefore the threat of lack of funding), Sandia, Lawrence Livermore, and Los Alamos National Labs have focused their attention on how they could participate in the CB defense program and its millions of R&D funds. The Defense Advanced Research Projects Agency (DARPA) has also lobbied heavily for defense dollars to investigate novel biological detection technologies. While the reinvigorated research is perhaps a good sign, there are two disquieting facts. These newcomers have no history in CB defense research and development; and they refuse to coordinate their programs with DoD's science and technology efforts, claiming the need for independent thought. While some might argue that fresh perspective is a good thing, there is the disquieting flavor of interagency rivalry resulting in a dilution of resources, rather than the promised teamwork. The added funds have caused many agencies to create new expertise to justify going after this program area.

Figure 18.1
Today's DoD CB Defense Structure

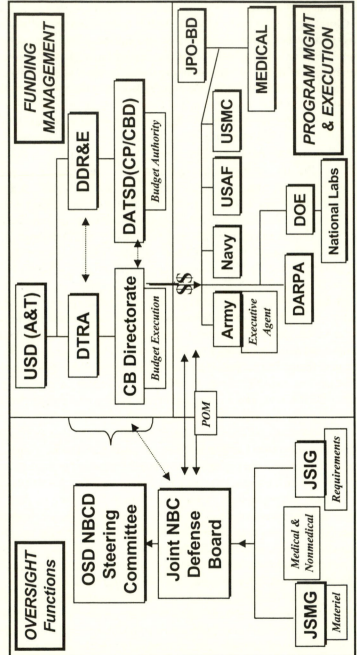

The other services still do not trust the Army to control the DoD NBC defense program entirely.  The four services still have difficulties agreeing on basic doctrine, or on roles and missions for the future.  The other services continue to fight tooth and nail to retain exclusive control over their own destinies in the NBC defense program areas.  Each service had its own offices, programs, and "rice bowls," specifically for NBC defense ever since DoD gave them leeway to initiate their own NBC defense programs in 1960, programs that became further entrenched when the Chemical Corps was downscaled in 1972.  The JSIG/JSMG have the budget authority and congressional language to make the tough decisions necessary to reform the DoD NBC defense program, but this does not guarantee any quick or near-term improvements.  Existing bureaucracies always fight change, the services still fight for "service-unique" requirements, and it will be some time before we see concrete results.  Surprisingly, the Army actually loses some power in this new relationship.  Although all CB defense programs are now funded through a "purple" DoD line where each service gets an equal vote in how things are done, it is still the Army committing the majority of its personnel and R&D facilities (upwards of 60–70 percent) to joint service CB program management.  Army units still  receive about half of all the fielded CB defense equipment, yet the Army seat gets only 25 percent of the vote.

The Army has made new tactical organization changes to develop its new fighting force for the next century.  Titled Army XXI, it features the traditional force structure of three brigades and supporting combat units, with a trimmed-down division support tail.  One of the goals was to reduce the size of the Army division from 18,000 to around 15,300 personnel.  While some combat slots were reduced, the majority of the cuts came from combat support and combat service support forces, which were moved to corps level or sent to the reserves.  Of note is that the division chemical companies were moved out of the organization.  The divisions are keeping their NBC recon platoons in the division cavalry regiments, while the decontamination companies and Biological Integrated Detection Suite (BIDS) companies are being moved to the corps as "recon/decon units."  The division chemical officer and staff remain in the division operations cell.

While this may trim down the force to a more deployable package, it also reduces the opportunities for soldiers to train with these units.  Out of sight is out of mind in Army training schedules.  The other problem is that, given the tendency to ship division combat arms units into theater prior to developing corps support assets, the early-entry forces are bound to have some time without any chemical specialist support.  The Army continues to examine better ways to quickly deploy packages of combat forces into theaters, and the division may not be the best way to move troops in the next century.  Many have pointed to Douglas Macgregor's combat group concept in *Breaking the Phalanx* as more feasible in future times of reduced troop strength and need for faster reaction times.[4]  Of note is that Macgregor acknowledges and plans for the inclusion of chemical defense units in his combat group structure.

## DOCTRINE CHANGES

Overall, the basic doctrine of the Army Chemical Corps remains the same: still oriented toward contamination avoidance, individual and collective protection, decontamination, and medical CB defense. One of the more notable changes is the decision to separate nuclear contamination avoidance from CB contamination avoidance (now in separate doctrinal field manuals).[5] In short, it is as close as the Army comes to stating that nuclear is not equal to biological or chemical weapons, almost moving them to break apart the NBC club—almost but not quite. Protection remained unchanged, while decontamination procedures changed from individual, hasty, and deliberate to immediate, operational, and thorough (the meanings are the same, the names were changed to project new thoughts). The 1993 Army field manual for decontamination also discusses decontamination of terrain, rotary-wing aircraft, and sensitive equipment.[6]

While the basic language remains the same, the new buzzword within the chemical defense community is "force protection." Force protection includes any and all efforts Army units would undertake to preserve the fighting force as it engages the enemy; naturally, NBC defense was included in this area. The down side of "force protection" is that it becomes the new amorphous descriptor for NBC defense doctrine and equipment. When closely examined, NBC reconnaissance and CB standoff detection benefits the Army concept of "dominant maneuver" by identifying clean and contaminated terrain in the battlespace. Leaders can engage the enemy with "precision engagement" only when they know what troops are able to operate without protective suits, which is a benefit derived of automatic point detectors. Of course, protective suits, masks, integrated collective protection systems, and medical CB defense items protect the force, allowing them to fight in contaminated environments. But decontamination, collective protection shelters, and manual CB agent monitors allow the logistics machine to work, enabling "focused logistics." Unfortunately, the Army leadership would rather play it safe and dumb the concept down to just "force protection"—a phrase that does nothing to explain how CB defense programs benefit the soldier.

The Chemical School has projected a Chemical Vision 2010—intended to leverage new concepts of Army Vision 2010 and Joint Vision 2010—which captures these ideas into four principles. These include: **sensing** the battlespace to provide a current NBC situation awareness (using recon systems and automatic early warning and standoff detectors); **shaping** the battlespace to provide commanders with a clear understanding of the current NBC threat (using an integrated NBC battle management software system linking the detection systems); **shielding** the force (medical pretreatments, CB monitors, protective ensembles, and collective protection systems); and **sustaining** the force (using decontamination systems and medical CB defense treatments). This vision captures the potential of the DoD CB defense program; the challenge is to educate the warfighters to understand and implement this concept throughout the military. Doctrine is one thing, seeing the concepts work in training exercises is another.

Biological detection is the big player on the block, with theater commanders-in-chief (CINCs) clamoring to get point biological detection systems into their theaters yesterday. The amount of funds being poured into this area is truly staggering, considering that the concept supporting how biodetection supports the warfighter is poorly explained. For instance, the concept of biological agent standoff detection is losing ground rapidly because the CINCs aren't convinced that the current technology and high cost give them a value-added capability. On the other hand, they have seen the Biodetection Advanced Technology Concept Demonstrations (ACTD) using BIDS and the commercially modified point biodetectors and they want it now, despite technical drawbacks and costly consumable antibody parts. Now some soldiers, airmen, marines, and sailors are fighting the biological vaccine program, largely fall out from the poorly explained Gulf War illnesses. Either the total biodefense program is not being well explained or the military leadership just is not understanding the concept.

It should not have come as a shock then, when in January 1996, the Joint Staff made recommendations to cut over a billion dollars from the five-year DoD CB defense budget. Of course it came as a blow to the chemical defense community, thinking that the Gulf War had proved the value of their mission. Counter-proliferation against weapons of mass destruction was the solution to future Saddams, encompassing active defense (attacking delivery systems and munitions dumps), theater missile defense, and passive defense (CB defense equipment).[7] Not surprisingly, the big fish of combat arms were crowding out CB defense equipment procurement plans in priority and funding. Searching for more support for special operations programs and bunker-buster air munitions, the Joint Staff recommended slashing purple CB defense program funds. Threatened with the incredible idea of losing DoD CB defense funding after the Gulf War, the chemical defense community at the Pentagon and Aberdeen Proving Ground outlined in a hasty series of memorandums what operational degradation in combat capabilities would result from the proposed cuts. Fortunately, Deputy Secretary of Defense John White agreed with the argument, and in fact raised the funding to compensate for identified weaknesses in decontamination and special operation's requirements.

## EQUIPMENT CHANGES

With the congressionally-mandated joint program, long overdue reforms in the R&D programs could take place. In the contamination avoidance program area, several duplicative programs merged into the Joint Chemical Agent Detector (JCAD) program. The troubled ACADA died one night, after $120 million invested in over fifteen years of work, and was replaced after a short competition by the British Graseby Ionics Detector (GID-3). The CB Mass Spectrometer also underwent a change from a government R&D program to an off-the-shelf Bruker model. Chemical stand-off systems such as the M21 RSCAAL and its progeny, the Joint Service Lightweight Standoff Chemical Agent Detector (JSLSCAD) continued their development. Biological detection programs flourished, first with the commercially equipped Biological Integrated Detection System (BIDS) and Navy Interim Biological Agent Detector (IBAD). Several joint programs with longer timelines grew out of the requirements community, including a Joint Biological Point Detector System (JBPDS) and standoff Joint Biological Remote Early Warning System (JBREWS). Because the technology was still very immature but the threat very highly emphasized, hundreds of millions of dollars of R&D funds were poured into the JPO-Biodefense programs. The recon concept solidified, with the Marines successfully arguing for the Light NBCRS program (returning the concept to the previously rejected LAV chassis).

Detection remains the king of funding, receiving over 45 percent of the budget. While real progress is being made in making these devices smaller and more accurate, there is a dangerous flip side. With DoD's and Congress's failure to come to terms with Gulf War illnesses, there is a politically mandated directive that all future detectors should detect sublethal levels of CB agents and never false-alarm. As discussed earlier, these goals are not always compatible with field-ruggedness requirements and funding challenges. However, lack of common sense has never stopped a military program from sucking down dollars and not yielding results. Some day, these technical and budgetary goals will be met, but the goal for an inexpensive CB agent detector that fits in a person's pocket while detecting traces of CB agents without false alarms is not achievable in the next five- or even fifteen-year timeframe. That means that the soldiers need a good contamination avoidance concept now.

Digitizing the battlefield may provide that concept. If all the point and standoff CB agent detectors were networked together to share information, commanders could see very quickly when one detector was false-alarming or when a pattern suggesting large area contamination warranted the move to protective measures. There are great strides being made in what the Army leadership calls "situational awareness" and digitizing the battlefield. So far, the chemical defense community has not been great players in this exercise, in part due to the difficulty in integrating CB agent effects into computer models. The few modelers in the CB defense community have focused more on agent cloud behavior and models that prove out R&D designs than on military command, communications, control, computers, and intelligence (C4I).

Individual protection saw a distinct coming together through the JSLIST program. With a Marine Corps project manager, the program examined over fifty textile candidates for protective clothing before choosing the Saratoga fabric (assembled by an American firm). The requirements driving the selection included meeting the ten-gram challenge (an Army demand), launderability (an Air Force demand), and reduced heat stress (the Marine Corps demand). The Navy joined the program late, recognizing that their current clothing stocks are rapidly dropping in scope with no replacements in sight. While the aging BDO inventory should be depleted by 2004, the JSLIST production will ensure that future soldiers get the state-of-the-art suits (although the JSLIST suits cost twice as much). The transition to a new suit will call for steady industry participation for several years.

There was less good luck with the boots and gloves. Faced with the challenge of creating gloves and boots that universally protected the soldier from heat, cold, petroleum products, and CB agents, Natick labs required more time to find the right candidates. Over the next ten years, we can expect to see a transition from the old butyl rubber standbys to lighter and more durable gloves and boots. The MULO boots should be out prior to the end of 2000, and the improved CP gloves (based on JSLIST technology) should be following.

The M40/M42-series masks quickly entered production, and after some initial production challenges, the entire military force structure is now prepared to retire the M17A2, M24, and M25A1 protective masks. Based on aviator input, the M43-series masks are already being replaced by more modern aviator protective masks. The fixed-wing community within the other three services still have service-unique masks, but have committed to developing a Joint Service Aviator Mask (JSAM) and Joint Protective Aircrew Ensemble (JPACE).

Collective protection programs have not really seen much improvement since the Gulf War. Since there have been no new armored vehicles or shelters, there has been no requirement for improving the filtration systems other than seeking replacements for the large charcoal filters and power-draining engines. The only source of requirements remains the medical community, which requested both a mobile shelter configuration and an improved field hospital shelter. The CB Protective Shelter is an air-inflated shelter that extends out the back of a medical HMMWV ambulance, creating a safe haven for medical stations in contaminated environments. The Air Force and Army medical community both used lessons learned from the M28 SCPE liner and designed the concept for protecting their larger field hospitals. These include the Air Force Chemically Hardened Air Transportable Hospital (CHATH) and Army CB Deployable Medical System (DEPMEDS). The Navy has invested in backfitting its ships with selective collective protection systems, and all new ships will include CB filter systems as well. Still, if the technology doesn't advance, these systems will soon fall into disrepair due to their bulk and the cost of supplying the military-unique large carbon filters.

Decontamination had a mixed reception after the Gulf War. At first, it appeared that there still was no resolution to the "how clean is clean?" question and, therefore, no substitute for DS-2 and STB. With the rise of the Domestic Preparedness Program (more next chapter) and the reexamination of the port/airfield contamination issue, there was an increased recognition that, like it or not, decontamination was a concern that had to be addressed if people were going to reoccupy formerly contaminated buildings and terrain and reuse equipment rather than replace it. There may be a replacement for DS-2 called sorbent decontamination, a dry absorbent powder similar to the M291/M295 decon kit technology. The question is, once it absorbs the CB agent, what does one do with the contaminated powder? Treat it as hazardous waste? Unless the sorbent powder destroys the CB agents, it is just exchanging one form of contamination for another. The current stores of DS-2 are rapidly deteriorating in Seneca Depot warehouses, and unless a substitute is identified soon, the military won't have any decontaminant to use. A decision is required very soon.

While more funds and technologies are being poured into this field, there are no near-term answers. The CB defense community is still hobbled with the politically motivated mandate that decontamination must be 100 percent effective, noncorrosive, environmentally safe, and not require water for rinsing (return of the pixie dust theory). Politicians, still looking at CB agents as a possible cause of Gulf War illnesses, are demanding that all future requirements drive for the absolute guarantees of cleanliness. Faced with this impossible demand, there is not any hope for a near-term solution other than sorbent decon, and little hope for far-term solutions unless the requirements are tempered with reason. Similar to CPS technologies, without a massive redirection of funds from detection to these program areas, there is unlikely to be any quick progress.

Medical CB defense programs have always been closely coordinated among the Army, Air Force and Navy. Most of the attention has been focused on the vaccine program, which has only just gotten the policy approval and requisite funding to build up anthrax vaccine stores. The media has latched onto the protests of a few service personnel who don't trust the vaccine as evidence that there may be something wrong here. Rather than examining the medical test evidence, these critics would make it appear that DoD is conducting illegal human experiments. Once this difficult policy issue is addressed by DoD and the FDA (and military leadership regains courage to counter political ignorance and election-year speeches), other safe and necessary vaccines should quickly follow. Chemical pretreatments and post-treatments should not change too much, as there have been no new CW agents weaponized. The medical R&D community is working on improving autoinjectors, decontaminable litters, and life-sign monitors to better treat CB warfare casualties.

In sum, the CB defense R&D program management has made drastic improvements since the 1980s. There is a larger investment of funds, more industry partners, and better cooperation among the services. The troublesome issue of CB defense logistics still looms. Since maintaining supplies for combat forces is still a service prerogative, there are no joint service funds to maintain the war reserves necessary to survive and sustain a long-term war, only operations and maintenance (O&M) funds that include training ammunition, fuel, spare parts, etc. For the seven years after Operation Desert Storm, the Army has ignored war reserve stores in favor of maintaining the equipment it has and conducting training exercises. This is in part due to the lack of growth of defense funds in the 1990s, and it is probably paralleled in the other services. As a result, while the U.S. military may have the best CB defense equipment in the world, it still doesn't have enough to fight two nearly simultaneous major theater wars. In short, we're not much better than we were at the crisis point of August 1990.

# CHAPTER 19

# Domestic Affairs

The fear of chemical and biological warfare agents, largely caused by overestimating their physical properties, poor training and ignorance of defensive equipment capabilities, has bled over into two domestic concerns. Decisions over how best to safely dispose of chemical weapons and bulk chemical warfare agents, and parallel concerns over the possibility that terrorists might use CB warfare agents against an unsuspecting public (such as the Aum Shinrikyo cult), have been a delicate policy issue for DoD, as regards their level of commitment and plans for action. Both chemical demilitarization and domestic preparedness for CB terrorism concern military-grade CB agents primarily designed for wartime use and possible public exposure to these agents during peacetime. The two areas have their distinct proponents and critics, which both claim they speak for "the Public" as a whole. While addressing "the Public's" concerns adroitly has never been a strong suit of the Chemical Corps (not for lack of trying), their technical expertise is demanded when well-meaning but ignorant laypeople start making decisions about CB agent matters. The nature of the threat and misinterpreted incidents such as Dugway Proving Ground (March 1968), Khamisiyah (March 1991), and the Tokyo subway incident (March 1995), have caused politicians, and the media in particular, to sensationalize these topics far in excess of what is deserved, resulting in an increased rather than decreased threat to "the Public."

Both these topics deserve much more discussion than can be allocated here, but there is an important point to observe. The American history of CB warfare, in particular the military and political views shaped by events since 1968, has a direct impact on how the issues of chemical demilitarization and domestic preparedness are addressed. It merits an examination to identify whether there is the chance to bring things to their proper scope, thereby enabling a calmer and more rational approach to real problems, enabling reasonable solutions. At the least, these topics deserve to be examined in terms of what is possible, instead of over exaggerating the threat into nightmare scenarios of gloom and doom, capitalized by politicians and those looking for their fifteen minutes of fame.

## CHEMICAL DEMILITARIZATION: HOW TO SUCCEED BY GIVING IN

In 1990 a little over 30,000 tons of chemical warfare agents sat in eight storage sites within the United States and one storage site at Johnston Atoll. Much of the stored chemical material had lost its original potency. Seven of these sites store bulk chemical warfare agents and munitions, with Newport and Edgewood holding only bulk agent in one-ton containers. Over 40 percent of the stockpile rested in Tooele Army Depot, with three sites holding less than 5 percent each and the remaining five holding between 5 and 12 percent each.[1]

As stated earlier, the deal President Reagan brokered with Congress in the mid-1980s was that for every newly manufactured binary chemical munition, one of the older unitary munitions had to go. This of course mean there had to be a tested and practical process of safely destroying the munitions as quickly as factories were manufacturing their replacements. This policy was discontinued by President George Bush when he announced the unilateral destruction of the U.S. military stockpile in 1990, but the Army was already on its way to building the Johnston Atoll Chemical Agent Disposal System (JACADS).

The Army's initial search for disposal processes experimented with chemical neutralization at Tooele and Rocky Mountain Arsenal. Between 1973 and 1975, Army engineers destroyed over 4,000 tons of sarin, but the process created up to six times that weight in additional waste products requiring treatment and disposal. In addition to being more costly and less efficient, the process still left the metal munition casings and containers, explosive fuses and bursters (termed "energetics"), and packing materials that required incineration.

In 1979 the Army had developed a Chemical Agent Munitions Disposal System (CAMDS) at Tooele, basically a small-scale test bed to evaluate disposal processes. Between 1981 and 1986, the Tooele engineers demonstrated incineration of GB and thermal decontamination of the munition bodies and ton containers, destroying thirty-eight tons of sarin at an efficiency of 99.9999995 percent.[2] CAMDS also demonstrated similar high efficiency in its incineration of eight tons of VX between June and August 1984. Over 6 million pounds of mustard agent and other chemicals had already been incinerated at Rocky Mountain Arsenal in the early 1970s. After an independent review of existing alternative methods of disposal, the National Research Council endorsed the Army incineration program in its 1984 report, while recommending a continued search for alternative approaches.

In 1985 Congress finally authorized the Army to begin building JACADS. In addition to disposing of the chemical stockpile stored at the island, the incineration facility would act as a prototype to evaluate how safe the process was and how future incineration sites would be constructed at the eight stockpile sites within the continental United States. Congress had passed Public Law 99-145 to direct the Army to dispose of 90 percent of its stockpile by the end of fiscal year 1994. The newly formed Army Program Manager for Chemical Demilitarization's (PM CD) reply was that it would take less than $2 billion to accomplish the job. They offered three options: eight incineration facilities (one at each site), two national sites (West Coast—Tooele, East Coast—Anniston), or one national incineration site at Tooele.

As these events unfurled, people living near the sites realized that the Army was really serious about destroying the stockpile (after the many years of studies and talk). Citizen groups began discussing their concerns that their respective site would be designated to destroy chemical weapons above and beyond the local stockpile. If the Army started moving chemical weapons around, their site might have to stay open longer. Then there were the nonstockpile chemical munitions, unearthed occasionally from old test ranges or forgotten storage areas. Surely the Army wasn't thinking about destroying those additional munitions at their site? Acting in true self-interest, "the Public" demanded that their politicians pass legislation forbidding the transportation of any chemical munitions or agent from other stockpiles into their sites.[3] This forced the government to build incineration sites at each location. The Army later stated that the option of eight incineration sites was probably less risky than transporting all the munitions and agents to one or two national locations. Less risky did not mean less expensive. The cost estimate rose to $3 billion and the completion date moved to 1997.

As the end of 1988 approached and JACADS was ready to come on line, Congress passed another law, Public Law 100-456, requiring an operational verification testing (OVT) period prior to the startup of any incineration site building in the continental United States (plans were being drawn up for Tooele). Between 1990 and 1993, the PM CD had to demonstrate safe destruction of each type of munition and agent in a series of four OVTs. JACADS destroyed more than 40,000 munitions containing GB, VX, and HD during this timeframe, at an efficiency of 99.9999 percent or better. Not only had the site successfully passed all tests, it had proven that the process was safe and had no adverse environmental impact.

In designing JACADS, the engineers had placed ninety-one chemical agent alarms within the facility and a dozen around the outside perimeter. Nearly seventy of these are the Automatic Continuous Air Monitoring System (ACAMS), gas chromatographs that are checked every twenty-four hours for faults. Located near every furnace and smokestack, they detect down to $0.00006$ mg/m$^3$ for nerve agents and $0.006$ mg/m$^3$ for mustard. They are in turn backed up by the Depot Area Monitoring System (DAMS), which collects air samples over a period of hours. These samples are analyzed for even lower levels of agent.

The last concern is that these incinerators might duplicate the problems of commercial and medical incinerators in their production of dioxins and furans and other products of incomplete combustion. EPA tests of the smokestacks revealed dioxin/furan concentrations of 0 to 0.16 nanograms per cubic meter, as compared to commercial incinerators that discharge 50–7,000 nanograms per cubic meter. The EPA noted that they had trouble taking air samples at times, as the air coming out of the stack was cleaner than the air surrounding the facility. According to detractors, any emission is still too high, since it adds to the overall exposure levels to the human population that some feel are too high. Yet these detractors continue to ignore commercial incinerators, diesel-belching trucks, and other combustive devices that account for the overwhelming majority of dioxins and furans.

With the completion of the JACADS OVTs, the Tooele Chemical Agent Disposal Facility (TOCDF) could initiate its test operations. Tooele has five improved incinerators and nearly one hundred automatic monitoring devices capable of detecting agent levels at one-fifth the Surgeon General's safe limits. The local citizen's group fought hard with several lawsuits and injunctions to attempt to stop its operations, as they were not convinced of its safety. All the group's attempts were thrown out of court, but it took an extra year to begin testing. Full operations began in 1996 and are expected to be completed by 2004. Completing JACADS and TOCDF operations would eliminate nearly 50 percent of the U.S. stockpile. Meanwhile, in 1993, PM CD adjusted the life cycle cost of their program to $8.5 billion and moved the end date to 1997.

At first, PM CD stood by its test results, stressing that independent scientific panels had verified incineration as the most effective and safe process of eliminating the weapons. As citizen groups at the eight stockpile sites grew more vocal and drew their local Congressional representatives into the fray, the Army felt the pressure building. Despite science on the side of incineration and test data positively showing no ill effects, Congress demanded the Army review alternative courses of action. The military posts at PM CD and its oversight agent, the Assistant to the Army for Installations, Logistics and Equipment, became very politically attuned to addressing these safety concerns.

The search for alternative technologies continued, with critics pressuring Congress to get the Army to adopt a "pixie dust" solution (i.e., anything but incineration that will eliminate the stockpile without harming people or the environment). The problem was, of all the alternatives to incineration, half of them were too similar to heat-induced solutions (such as molten metal or cryofracture and therefore as bad as incineration) and the rest did not fully destroy the agent and its metal shells as effectively. This led to the creation of two offices: the Alternative Technologies Assessment Program (ATAP) in 1994, and Program Manager for Assembled Chemical Weapons Alternatives (ACWA) in 1996. Since Edgewood and Newport held no munitions, just bulk agent, the ATAP office focused on determining the feasibility of neutralization and treatment technologies. They formed committees of government, industry, and the citizen groups within Maryland and Indiana to determine criteria, examine processes, and evaluate potential candidates. Based on their findings, they proposed neutralization followed by biodegration at Edgewood's chemical site, and neutralization followed by supercritical water oxidation for Newport. On January 17, 1997, ATAP received permissions to proceed with full-scale pilot testing at the two sites. The unmentioned part of this successful collaboration? Neutralization creates six to nine times as much hazardous waste as incineration, which has to be treated and disposed of separately, increasing the overall cost while raising questions about the long-term health effects.

PM ACWA is really the same process, revisiting the possibility that there can be an alternative technology for disposing of the chemical munitions. Again, a group of government, industry, and citizen group representatives have met to evaluate the available processes, but with the desire to have the stockpile eliminated by 2007, time is growing short to identify alternatives, test them for efficiency, build a plant, and run the disposal process. Anniston's and Umatilla's incinerators are already being built; Pine Bluff's incinerator contract has been approved. That leaves only Lexington Bluegrass (less than 2 percent of the stockpile) and Pueblo Chemical Depot (less than 9 percent) to benefit from this program. Until the ACWA assessment is complete (expected December 1999), all funding for incineration projects at Blue Grass and Pueblo have been put on hold by congressional mandate.

The issue of nonstockpile chemical munitions will continue to be a problem for years, if not decades. At least thirty-eight of the fifty states are suspected of having at least a few buried chemical munitions (back when environmental laws were more lax), none of which can be destroyed at the storage facilities by law. To accommodate this, the office of the Project Manager for Nonstockpile Munitions (established in 1992) has had to develop a mobile munitions assessment and destruction capability to blow up the munitions where they are found, with a containment system that traps the vapors and the explosive. If the munitions are stable, they can be transported to the nearest federal post and blown up there.[4] If they are not stable, they are blown up in place. It is of course more costly to destroy the munitions in this process, given the cost of the mobile system, the training and transportation of the personnel, and the safety measures required for the workers and the public. Estimates are that the nonstockpile program will be at least as expensive as the chemical stockpile disposal program, and it may run past 2030. Much of these costs could have been avoided had local politicians allowed for transportation and disposal at the currently run disposal sites.

When Congress accepted the U.S.-USSR Bilateral Destruction Agreement, the deadline moved once more to 2004. After the Senate ratified the Chemical Weapons Convention (CWC), again the end date moved to 2007. Every time the date has moved, it gives critics extra fuel to demand a reexamination of alternative technologies. These constant demands for more studies result in more program delays, which has accounted for the $12.5 billion program cost. Had the Army been allowed to build the plants as scheduled, the stockpile would have been gone by now at half that cost. As a final footnote, the Johnston Atoll Chemical Agent Disposal System (JACADS) had destroyed over 1,645 tons of chemical munitions by May 1999 with only three minor leaks and no injuries since starting operations. This represents over 80 percent of its stockpile, including all the GB munitions and all the M55 rockets. Tooele's incinerator has destroyed 2,703 tons by May 1999, including nearly all the GB-filled M55 rockets, without any injuries or threat to the public—not that this is any surprise to the plant designers. They know incineration can be a safe process, especially when safety is designed into the process. If it makes "the Public" sleep better moving from incineration to more costly, more wasteful, and untested processes, that's what our politicians (and the Army by default) are going to give them.

## DOMESTIC PREPAREDNESS: TRYING TO POP THE MYTHS

When the Aum Shinrikyo gassed the Tokyo subways on March 20, 1995, they ignited concern in Congress that terrorists had finally demonstrated the capability to use CB agents against large audiences.  Not much later, the tragedy of Oklahoma City rocked the nation (April 19, 1995), leading to the addition of very large amounts of explosives to the category of "weapons of mass destruction."  In June 1995 President Bill Clinton executed Presidential Decision Directive 39 (PDD 39), stating the administration's new policy on counterterrorism.  This directive gave the Federal Bureau of Investigation (FBI) and the Federal Emergency Management Agency (FEMA) new responsibilities to coordinate federal assets in response to CB terrorism.  The FBI would lead federal response during crisis management, ideally a period prior to and up to the intentional release of a CB agent (primarily a law enforcement role).  FEMA would head the consequence management phase, which was seen as the recovery and restoration after the incident.

Congress soon followed suit with its own directions.  On September 23, 1996, they passed Public Law 104-210, the National Defense Authorization Act for FY97, Title XIV Defense against Weapons of Mass Destruction.  Among the details of Title XIV, Congress directed DoD to initiate a Domestic Preparedness Program that included training "first responders" of 120 major cities, creation of a rapid response force, and the development of a secure hotline to provide information to the first responders.  The Public Law also directed FEMA to support the Domestic Preparedness Program by identifying all excess stores of equipment that might be directed toward this type of major incident.  DoD responded by tasking the Director of Military Support (DOMS) to act as the DoD member of the Federal Senior Interagency Coordination Group (SICG), a collection of representatives of all the federal agencies supporting the CB terrorism response.[5]

Other laws already existed to support the act of CB terrorism as a federal crime.  The Biological Weapons Anti-Terrorism  Act of 1989 made it a federal crime for individuals to develop, plan to use, or store BW agents as weapons.  When Larry Wayne Harris attempted to procure BW agents from the American Type Culture Center in 1995 for "defensive research" under the Biological Weapons Convention (BWC), Congress passed the Anti-Terrorism and Effective Death Penalty Act of 1996 to require all private and academic institutions to register potential BW agents with the Centers for Disease Control and Prevention.

The Marine Corps commandant, General Charles Krulak, decided that he had not seen a credible DoD response capability.  He directed the formation of the Chemical-Biological Incident Response Force (CBIRF) in April 1996, to be formed at Camp LeJeune, North Carolina.  To fully equip this force, he had to strip much of the Marine Corps of its trained CB specialists.  When the CBIRF was fully manned and equipped, however, it proceeded to steal the show from the Army Technical Escort Unit (TEU) as what many called the premier response force for CB terrorist incidents. While the TEU was more capable of providing expert advisers and disarming and transporting CB devices, they lacked the manpower that the CBIRF had at its call. The CBIRF leveraged this strength to market their capability to provide mass decontamination and casualty treatment at the scene of an incident. This was really not a duplication of functions, as the Army TEU supplied a crisis management supporting role, and the CBIRF supplied the consequence management. In the public relations blitz that accompanied the creation of the CBIRF, the Marines managed to emphasize their importance, overshadowing the TEU.

The first test of the federal response capabilities came during the 1996 Summer Olympics at Atlanta. While most talking heads focus on the no-notice terrorist event, federal agencies have the most impact when they support preplanned incidents, such as the Olympics, national political conventions, events with other national leaders attending (Group of Seven, the Pope's tour, etc.). Atlanta proved a test-bed of sorts as the federal agencies tried to sort out who was leading what efforts, where they would all stage their forces, how they would communicate amongst themselves, who was in charge at what times—it was a challenge that required everyone to rip up their original plans and collaborate toward a truly joint concept.

Since this was a crisis management situation, the FBI led the federal response, which included TEU, CBIRF, mobile Army and Navy laboratories from Maryland, EPA, CDC, and FEMA. They drew up plans for a CB Response Team and procedures to quickly assess any incidents that might occur months prior to the Olympic's opening in June. There were thousands of other Army and law enforcement officials involved in the security effort as well. When the pipe bomb blew up in Centennial Park on July 27, there was an immediate response by the Atlanta police and firefighters, in addition to the FBI task force. Most of the responders, to include the federal representatives, rushed into the park without considering any CB agent exposure risks. The CB Response Team did take soil samples and bomb fragments to their labs, which declared the bomb as clean of any traces of CB agents. This was the first true field test of how the federal-state-local coordination would work, and where the potential pitfalls existed in training, equipment, and procedures. The federal response teams continued to practice coordination that summer at the Democratic and Republican National Conventions in Chicago and San Diego, respectively.

FEMA and the FBI formalized PDD-39 by changing the Federal Response Plan on February 7, 1997.[6] Change 11 (Terrorism Annex) carefully illustrated the two lead agency roles prior to a CB terrorist incident, during and after the event, to include command responsibilities, coordination with the states, and how other executive agencies (such as DoD) would support the event. Of note is the point that during the crisis management role, the FBI is in charge of the crime scene with the city/state officials tasked to support (all the better to gather evidence for the future federal court case). During the consequence management phase, FEMA is at the direction of the city/state officials for what they require and where to send the supplies. While DoD has the most technical expertise of the group due to the nature of CB warfare agents (designed for military purposes), they remain in a support role only, called in by the FBI or FEMA as circumstances dictate.

The Secretary of Defense appointed the Army as the executive lead on Domestic Preparedness, again not a surprise due to the resources of the Army Chemical Corps. The Army designated HQ AMC as the lead Army agency (based on the perceived need for technical knowledge and supplies), who in turn looked to the Army Chemical and Biological Defense Command (CBDCOM). Major General George Friel appointed Jim Warrington as the Program Director for Domestic Preparedness (PD DP) in the fall of 1996. While DOMS acted as the policy lead and representative to the SICG, it was the PD DP office that had to execute the mission. The most challenging aspect of the program was the training of 120 cities' firefighters, police, emergency medical service technicians, emergency managers, and others within a three-year period.[7] Seems like a lot of time until one considers that there were no course plan, no training materials, and no instructors since preparedness against CB terrorism had never been taught.

The obvious solution was to turn to the Chemical School, home of the DoD instructors of CB defense. The problem was that Fort McClellan was facing a Base Realignment Committee (BRAC) closing date of 1999, and many at the Chemical School grasped this initiative as the way out. At a meeting held at Fort McClellan between the Chemical School, the PD DP office, and a representative group of emergency responders, the School proposed that they adapt a two-week NBC defense specialist training into the DP course. This two-week initiative would be topped off with a run through the CDTF to gain that same confidence that military personnel had. The problem was that there was no way the fire and police chiefs would agree to letting their best people travel to Fort McClellan for a two-week training course. It would be too costly in terms of travel and manpower require-ments, taking their best people away from the cities when they were needed on shifts. The Chemical School curriculum didn't parallel the traditional Firefighter Academy curriculum, and they really didn't see the need for the CDTF training. While several School officials insisted this was the only correct approach (as it had obviously worked for years in the military), it was not acceptable by the DoD leadership or by the city emergency managers. The PD DP office began to develop a training program at Aberdeen Proving Ground that was politically and fiscally acceptable to the cities.

To successfully train the responders, PD DP saw that they had to bring the instruction directly to the cities, at no extra cost to the host city (other than supplying the bodies). The training had to match National Firefighter Academy (NFA) standards, and it had to be short (four to eight hours per module). At a series of meetings, a group of SBCCOM employees and consultants hashed out the basic requirements. They had to avoid teaching what the city responders already knew (dealing with mass casualty incidents and hazardous material spills) and focus on training what was different because of the element of CB warfare agents. This was called the "NBC delta." The training courses, paralleling the NFA requirements, evolved into an introductory four-hour awareness course (for the cop on the beat), a four-hour operations course (for those requiring more guidance to make immediate decisions), a twelve-hour hazmat course (for hazmat specialists—identification and handling of agents), and a six-hour incident command course (for the chiefs and emergency managers). Two eight-hour medical courses, one for EMS and one for hospital providers, rounded out the program.[8]

Months prior to the trainers' arrival to the city, the city managers chose their students. Ideally, the students were to be trainers themselves, so that as the trainers were trained, they could repeat the process within their city. Therefore, the PD DP office didn't have to train the entire city's emergency responders, just a representative sample. The instructors paired up for each course, matching a seasoned emergency responder (usually a firefighter or police officer with over fifteen years experience) and a military CB defense expert to tag-team the course.[9] This maintained a sense of trust and credibility in the instructors, talking the right talk and supplying the necessary expertise on new topics. After the training, the instructors gave the city POC a set of training materials (books, slides, training equipment, etc.) so that the city could immediately go to work. These courses were repeated over four days so hundreds of trainers could rotate through the courses, or in the case of senior fire/police chiefs, take multiple courses. On the fifth day, the trainers held a city table-top exercise with the senior city managers (many of whom had attended the training) to examine how their city might respond to a CB incident. Each city trained also received a "loan" of $300,000 to purchase equipment above and beyond the training materials left behind.

Simultaneous with the training program, the PD DP office developed a CB hotline concept and a CB helpline. The hotline was intended for emergency use, a 24-hour open line through the National Response Center to the FBI and CBDCOM Emergency Operations Center. This hotline would be the trigger to notify the FBI and other DoD assets of a potential no-notice CB incident, as well as the source of immediate technical experts to guide emergency responders prior to the arrival of federal forces. The CB helpline would be the nonemergency technical assistance source for emergency responders as they developed plans, bought equipment, and trained for the possibility of CB incidents. The HelpLine started receiving calls in August 1997 (answering over 2,500 calls to date), with the Hotline going operational in January 1998.

In June 1997 the PD DP office had its first real test of its training program. The city of Denver, Colorado, had two major events planned for that summer: the Summit of Eight was meeting there, a very major international VIP event with heads of states attending, to include President Clinton. The Timothy McVeigh trial was also expected to start, and the city managers were very nervous that their city would be a target. Since the city had no time to institute a "train-the-trainer" course, the DP instructors trained the majority of the police and firefighter force directly. As the two events unfurled, the usual entourage of federal response teams were there, to include the FBI, Secret Service, TEU, CBIRF, and others. They applied the lessons learned at Atlanta and had a very smooth and uneventful stay at Denver.

Congress had arranged funding and priorities for first twenty-seven cities, specially chosen based on their large population, ongoing special events, and political importance.[10] The cities are listed in Table 19.1. In August 1997 the city of Philadelphia became the first city to receive the "train-the-trainer" course. Boston was next, followed by a stay in Detroit. Both the instructor pool and the cities were learning what they really needed to instruct, and over time the course smoothed out. Ironically, because of its success amongst the city responders, critics from the National Firefighter's Association (who had their own training school) and others both within and outside the federal government attempted to smear the DoD training program as a bloated, overly expensive benefit for retired military and government civilians-turned-contractors. While it was true that many contractors were attracted to the DP program (as they would be to any congressionally mandated, well-funded defense program), the training spoke for itself. What the emergency responders were learning was that with the right knowledge, equipment, and training, CB terrorist events became manageable. True, it might force a city to the brink of its resources and personnel, especially the smaller cities, but in all, a CB terrorist event became a special hazmat incident with the possibility of mass casualties. Denied the Hollywood glamor and media-induced ignorance, CB agents became less frightening. Table 19.1 identifies the first twenty-seven cities that received this training.

As more cities received training, more emergency managers became heavily involved in preparing their cities for CB terrorist events. They discovered that reacting to a chemical agent incident was much akin to responding to a dangerous hazmat incident; it required immediate actions from firefighters, police, and EMS. On the other hand, a biological agent incident was seen as more of a major medical incident, since it involved more public health agencies than police and firefighters (especially if it was a covert attack). Here is another example where specialists have observed that chemical warfare attacks must be handled differently from biological warfare attacks, although the same equipment might be seen in both incidents. A prominent New York City emergency responder noted that the DoD DP training was flawed because it attempted to address nuclear, biological, and chemical in one training program. Of course this was an exaggeration; the federal DP trainers knew very well there was a difference and explained the difference, but the program was always billed as a response against "weapons of mass destruction." The city emergency responders were just finding out that there are subtle (but important) differences between the classes of agents, and they had realized that CB terrorism was a manageable event.

This short introduction does not do the DP program justice. For the sake of time, I have not mentioned the extensive involvement of the Army medical community and the Public Health Service in developing their programs aimed at readying hospitals for this scenario, the roles of other Federal partners such as the

**Table 19.1**
**First Twenty-seven Cities Trained**

| City | Training Date | Number Trained |
|---|---|---|
| Philadelphia, PA | Aug. 25–28, 1997 | 220 (est.) |
| Boston, MA | Sep. 8–11, 1997 | 210 |
| Detroit, MI | Sep. 15–18, 1997 | 201 |
| Chicago, IL | Sep. 21–25, 1997 | 157 |
| New York City, NY | Sep. 28–Oct. 11, 1997 | 1,892 |
| Los Angeles, CA | Nov. 3–7, 1997 | 163 |
| Aberdeen Proving Ground, MD | Nov. 17–20, 1997 | 128 (federal employees) |
| San Antonio, TX | Dec. 1–4, 1997 | 275 |
| Washington, DC | Jan. 5–9, 1998 | 224 |
| Memphis, TN | Jan. 12–15, 1998 | 198 |
| Kansas City, MO | Jan. 20–23, 1998 | 293 |
| San Jose, CA | Jan. 26–30, 1998 | 208 |
| Honolulu, HI | Feb. 2–5, 1998 | 152 |
| Indianapolis, IN | Feb. 9–12, 1998 | 387 |
| Dallas, TX | Feb. 17–20, 1998 | 424 |
| Seattle, WA | Feb. 23–26, 1998 | 202 |
| Miami, FL | Mar. 9–12, 1998 | 292 |
| Baltimore, MD | Mar. 9–12, 1998 | 318 |
| Houston, TX | Mar. 16–19, 1998 | 263 |
| Atlanta, GA | Mar. 23–26, 1998 | 311 |
| San Francisco, CA | Mar. 30–April 2, 1998 | 356 |
| Portland, OR | Apr. 6–9, 1998 | 337 |
| Jacksonville, MS | Apr. 16–9, 1998 | 362 |
| Phoenix, AZ | Apr. 14–17, 1998 | 405 |
| San Diego, CA | Apr. 20–23, 1998 | 200 (est.) |
| Columbus, OH | May 4–7, 1998 | 360 |
| Anchorage, AK | May 11–14, 1998 | 198 |
| Denver, CO | Jun. 1–4, 1998 | 192 |

Environmental Protection Agency, Department of Energy, Department of Transportation, FEMA's ongoing technical assistance efforts, the National Guard and Army reserve component trainers, and the many academic institutions that are offering their support in this very complex program. While the DP program is often criticized because of the many federal, state and private organizations involved, it really takes a group effort to ensure all possible expertise is tapped. The question isn't just why so many agencies are involved, it's that there are so many cities asking for this guidance and only so many experts. No doubt a national preparedness "czar" could ensure there is minimal overlap and maximum return on the taxpayer's investment. But can one agency get its arms around such a wide-ranging issue, that encompasses law enforcement and emergency response?

By October 2000, the FBI will have taken over the entire program under their National Domestic Preparedness Office (NDPO). The transition is fraught with concerns that the FBI will try to "Lone Ranger" the job without DoD assistance, thinking that somehow they can succeed without the over seventy-five years of experience at Aberdeen Proving Ground. While there are a lot of experts outside the DoD that could assist the NDPO, the program will suffer if the FBI emphasizes the law enforcement role over the firefighter/hazmat/EMS (technical) roles. It is impossible for any one federal agency or group of agencies to train all the cities, given the urgency and sheer number of emergency responders out there. Private and public agencies are quickly filling in the gap, offering courses and equipment tailored to domestic preparedness. There is no doubt that as the DoD leaves this mission area, the DP program will continue to evolve and change beyond the scope of its humble beginnings.[11]

There remains much more to discuss about CB terrorism, the military's role in preparing federal, state and local agencies, the need for sustainment training for new responders, the need for specialized and tested equipment, and the continuing struggle to avoid unnecessarily exaggerating the threat while underestimating the capability to respond. The threat is not just the potential of mass casualties resulting from CB agents. There is the concern for treating long-term contamination after the immediate incident, dealing with panic-stricken citizens, emergency responders trying to save lives while avoiding becoming casualties themselves, the economic cost of recovering from a terrorist attack, and the loss of face to the authorities and resulting lack of faith from its citizens.[12] This is a very complex issue, one that becomes easier to manage if an educated public, or at the least, an educated political leadership exists. As the psychological and political aspect of CB incidents is so much larger than the actual danger from terrorist attacks, it is incumbent on the experts to identify the true nature and scope of the threat.

# CHAPTER 20

# Conclusions

Knowledge is power in gas defense. It saves casualties, increases the confidence of men in their own ability to protect themselves, and reduces fear.

—Brigadier General Alden Waitt, *Gas Warfare*, 1943

Chemical and biological warfare can be dangerous to your health. So can fighting with maces, bayonets, automatic rifles, tanks, cluster bombs, antipersonnel mines, cruise missiles, and five-inch naval guns. Weapons of war exist to give a military force the capability to exert its will against an adversary for a specific objective during a specific timeframe, ideally resulting in your side receiving the fewest casualties in the exchange. The United States invested in the design and development of CB weapons in an effort to gain an advantage over its adversaries, thus reducing the cost of personnel and equipment necessary to win. Even if one were to argue that these weapons were designed only as a retaliatory capability to respond and punish the offender in kind, the end result is that by discouraging the enemy against using CB weapons, the U.S. military gains an advantage in a conventional war (because its highly trained soldiers using state-of-the-art equipment aren't degraded). Chemical and biological agents are weaponized because they will incapacitate and/or kill the enemy, and they can be dropped with precision and with predictable consequences (at least as well as any smart munitions). That matches the requirements of any modern weapon system. CB weapons are not the "poor man's atomic bomb," they don't even come close with the long-term devastation caused by even a small tactical nuke. Bad press is more responsible for that label than any historical incident.

We have only to look at the historical examples. At Dugway Proving Ground, even if one overlooked the overwhelming lack of evidence, there was no threat to people and no human casualties. All that was seen was the whiff of dirty politics and the sound of howling reporters looking for blood. Even as the Army leadership settled out of court before the evidence was completely in, the popular opinion is that this was an admission of guilt. The faulty assumption that a small amount of liquid chemical agent could float thirty-plus miles from its impact point over mountains and slaughter thousands of sheep (but nothing else) has paralyzed common sense within the chemical demilitarization program, let alone how it retarded the military CB defense program.

When the Khamisiyah depots blew up, again there were no casualties due to chemical agents or any other weapon. All DoD offered were poor guesses of how far traces of nerve gas might travel in a perfect worst-case scenario, which they used to unduly alarm soldiers by telling them that they might have been exposed to low levels of agent because they were within 50 kilometers of Khamisiyah during one day. While some CENTCOM files may be missing, there are too many medical reports in addition to the corps and division logs that indicate the utter lack of CB medical casualties. Nevertheless, as the press trumpeted DoD's admission that 100,000 troops *may* have been exposed (ergo, by the media's logic they *were* exposed), Congress moved swiftly to review whether DoD had an adequate CB defense program. Great strides were made in improving how the four services coordinate their requirements, yet in response to unprovable allegations of Gulf War Syndrome, Congress feels the need to act.

The House of Representatives, in particular, is urging DoD to review and modify its policies and doctrine to "provide for adequate protection of personnel from any low-level exposure to a chemical warfare agent that would endanger the health of exposed personnel because of the deleterious effects of (a) a single exposure to the agent, (b) exposure to the agent concurrently with other dangerous exposures, . . . (c) repeated exposures to the agent, or some combination of one or more exposures to the agent and other dangerous exposures . . . over time."[1] Congress just forced every military person to wear overly heavy and hot protective suits, and each unit to man very expensive, overly sensitive, false-alarming detectors. They also have inadvertently ensured that the U.S. military will never be able to leave DS-2 as its standard decontaminant, instead of moving on to newer and safer decontaminants.

In Tokyo, where the world saw CB terrorism up close and personal, only twelve individuals died, and fewer than seven hundred actually required treatment for nerve agent exposure. Are twelve deaths the result of a weapon of mass destruction? More havoc has been wrought by a pair of handguns at one crime incident. Now with the heavy effort being poured into preparing our cities from a similar attack, people are beginning to grasp what a fantastically complicated effort it is, not unlike the civil defense program of the 1950s and 1960s. The target of 120 cities, the major metropolitan population centers that could marshal an adequate interim response to such an incident, is growing to 156 cities. There is a good deal of credit to be given that this program has educated thousands of emergency responders to the true scope of the threat, that it is a manageable incident. Still, this leaves a lot of small cities on their own, or at the least, subject to teaming with a major city for immediate training and assistance. How all the federal partners will play roles when a no-notice event hits is still unclear, especially how quickly DoD forces will respond and what real value they will have when they get on the scene. DoD's role at preplanned, large media events is a more certain success of minimizing casualties.

There are two big fallacies in the DP program. First, Congress and the media like to pressure the federal partners for assurances that because this training program is taking place, the Tokyo subway incident will never happen here. That is sheer foolishness; only an intrusive and hyperactive law enforcement effort would stop a terrorist act, be it conventional or unconventional explosives. All this DP program promises is to (1) reduce the number of emergency responder casualties as they respond to the alarms, and (2) minimize the number of post-incident casualties among the public, as in any hazmat/mass casualty incident. But you won't get any federal partner in the DP program to state that in public, on the record, because that's not the answer Congress or the press wants to hear.

The second fallacy is seeing a highly ranked government official solemnly raise a five-pound bag of sugar stating that, if it were anthrax it would wipe out Washington, D.C., or quoting a report that states 100 kilos of anthrax would cause three million casualties. The only result of this "education" is that every nut that has ever wanted to issue a bomb threat has just got a new tool to use. Between November 1998 and February 1999, police and firefighters in California, Texas, Georgia, Ohio, Illinois, and other states had to deal with literally hundreds of anthrax hoax letters and boxes. Many of these stories didn't hit the press, but they did alarm both the state/local officials and federal forces. Kids trying to close school early, a man who didn't want to show up in federal court, anti-abortion protesters acting against family planning clinics, people responding to the anti-abortionist organizations—anyone with a grievance now knows that you can get attention by writing "ANTHRAX" on a letter and pouring cinnamon into an envelope. The cost of responding to these hoaxes is mounting, since emergency responders have to deal with each case as a full hazmat operation until the lab tests come back. The major cities are learning and refining their operations, but responding to CB terrorism incidents is a new frontier for all.

Dr. Ken Alibek, the first deputy chief of the Russian biological warfare program from 1988 to 1992, states that even biological weapons should be called "mass casualty weapons, not weapons of mass destruction."[2] That's the first step in bringing this issue into focus. Even with this qualification, it must be stated that while one gram of anthrax or one drop of VX might kill a thousand people, if the agent is not perfectly dispersed, there is no way that one will see those numbers. When the Aum Shinrikyo hit the judges' apartment building in Matsumato in 1994, they had a heavy concentration of pure sarin pouring into a heavily populated area. It only killed seven unfortunate individuals, not seven thousand. Just as one bullet can kill one individual, very often one bullet will not kill one individual, especially if there are factors such as the target is running, it's nighttime, the shooter is inexperienced, etc. Similarly, while one drop of VX and one gram of anthrax will surely kill one individual, it will not if the person is inside a building during a hot summer day. We need to bring the correct perspective to this situation if we are to create the most reasonable and optimal defense for our soldiers and for our civilian populace.

Nowhere is this more evident than in the Army's chemical demilitarization program. Here is a program that has grown from a $2 billion, six-year project into a $15 billion, twenty-year project. And for once, DoD had the correct technology and experts in place, the particular incineration process having been tested and accepted by various scientific panels and environmental specialists. Because of a small group of people's paranoia and the political knee-jerk reaction to the special interest that screams the loudest, the government has adopted the most expensive and most drawn-out process it could ever desire. The Army leadership, of course, just wants the problem to go away with the least friction (just like they wanted for the DPG incident). HQ AMC hates having the albatross of chemical demilitarization draining their research, development, and acquisition funds. Any military piece of equipment must have a disposal strategy (cradle to grave, as they call it), but demilitarizing chemical munitions just takes too much political energy as well as program funds.

The easiest way for this problem to go away is to do whatever "the Public" demands, the leaders think, thus relinquishing all better sense to the mobs. So what if the government could move all the munitions safely to one or two disposal sites, thus saving billions of dollars? Not through my backyard! So what if alternative technologies cost more and create more waste? Anything but evil, evil incineration technologies! "The Public" doesn't believe the government's insistence that if the incineration process is controlled and monitored at every step, the vapors filtered, the whole area rigged with sensitive detectors, that it can be a safe process. And who can blame them, it's probably an X-File.

Chemical warfare agents can be defined, they can be analyzed and cleaned up. They are just chemical compounds, and like any chemicals (acids, water, fertilizer, pesticides), they can be studied and handled safely. Across the country, industry handles dangerous industrial chemicals not unlike chemical warfare agents every day. Sometimes there is an accident, sometimes people die, but these accidents are manageable. Emergency responders don't have any choice but to manage these incidents, and as a result of their experience, training, and equipment, they can develop the confidence to deal with a mass casualty incident combined with a hazmat spill. It's not something one wants to deal with every week, but the bottom line is that once they eliminate the fear that freezes their minds and bodies and rely on education and properly designed equipment, they manage.

Biological warfare agents require different considerations. While the same protective equipment can be used, they act differently from chemical agents, and there is a higher responsibility for medical personnel to analyze, track, and predict what outcomes will occur. Still, there are no doomsday bugs out there (yet). Every BW agent has its strengths and flaws; in fact, because of their slower rate of action, it becomes easier to lock down, isolate, and treat the contaminated populace once the problem has been discovered. With claims that "millions" of people will be infected and will die without treatment, one must come back to the notion that the BW agent will always be anthrax, that the 100 kilograms are perfectly dispersed over a populace that is all standing outside, just waiting to inhale the bugs. Assuming that any terrorist or sponsor state manufactures any BW agent, will they make just a few grams to fill up a small "bomb," or are we really expecting someone to fly over our cities in a crop-duster filled with hundreds of pounds of agent a la *Goldfinger*? What has become apparent is that responding to domestic terrorism is very different from responding to CB warfare during military operations. What is the same is that both military CB warfare and domestic terrorism involving CB agents can both be managed with strong leadership, the right expertise, and correctly designed equipment.

Our military and political leadership live in a world that states that one must prepare for the worst possible situation anyone could possibly dream up, rather than for the most credible situations that could occur. At the eight chemical stockpile sites, planners are forced to accept the idea that planes will plummet into their bunkers causing a chain reaction exploding all their munitions at once, with all the munitions releasing all their agent fills simultaneously. Then of course the perfect weather conditions for maximizing the spread of agent through the local city/county will take over, risking thousands of lives. Somehow, the sites have lasted over thirty years without these horrible accidents; in fact, they have gone without any accidents that caused the death of any human. Instead, all the site commanders have had to deal with is the occasional leaks inside the bunkers, which are found, moved and taken care of without any risk to the populace.

The same exaggeration happens in the military scenarios. We used to envision large clouds of nerve agent sweeping the front lines, devastating our troops standing before the enemy's onslaught. In wargames, either everyone is wiped out as a result of a surprise CB attack or everyone survives unscathed because all their protective masks and suits worked perfectly. There is no understanding of the costs or benefits of NBC defense equipment, because it just gets too complicated to model in the effects. Therefore the military leadership falls back to what it knows and understands. Ensure that protective suits and masks save the force, then retaliate with nukes.

Arms control agreements are important, but right now their only purpose is to demonstrate how pure the "good guys" are. Those nations that don't require CB weapons for an edge because they have state-of-the-art conventional munitions are glad to be the moral leaders of the world. ("Yes, we only kill our adversaries with the finest in advanced weaponry.") For those nations that cannot afford billion-dollar conflicts, they will exert all efforts to achieve their nation's goals with the lowest amount of casualties and lowest consumption of equipment. If CB agents can speed up that process and allow them to reach that end goal, they will continue to research and develop CB munitions. That logic is proven every year by the annual proliferation statistics demonstrated by DoD and the CIA, as the number of nations suspected of conducting CB warfare programs continues to inch up.

The Department of Defense has invested in CB warfare and CB defense for decades, with mixed results. There are specialists with a strong understanding of the CB threat, that have designed defensive equipment of all shapes and sizes that work in protecting personnel from that threat. Because the threat is often invisible and not immediately threatening, individuals require detectors to "see" the agents, protective masks, suits and shelters to survive the agents, medicines to recover from the agents, and decontaminants to eliminate the agents. This requires a true system of systems to both survive and fully sustain combat operations. To enable this system of systems throughout the military force, the military leadership needs to invest in developing doctrine, training its troops, designing equipment that can be integrated into combat operations without burdening the troops, maintaining logistics support to sustain operations, and (most important) maintaining a body of full-time specialists.

Unfortunately, the worst enemy that the Chemical Corps has ever had is not "the Public," soapboxing politicians or scandal-sniffing media persons, but the Department of the Army. Few Army leaders (the three- and four-stars) has wholly supported the CB defense program, but they did like binary chemical munitions and promoted them strongly before Congress. There is a saying that the work force only does well what the boss checks, and it is a fact that, despite the numerous GAO reports and criticisms through history, the Army leadership has rarely ever seriously brought down the heat on the Chemical Corps (with one or two exceptions) for failure to meet Army requirements. We narrowly missed being completely unprepared for CB warfare in 1990, when U.S. forces faced Saddam Hussein's CB arsenal, yet the conventional wisdom is that massive conventional retaliation, or threats of nuclear retaliation, is all that is required to stop the threat. Massive conventional airstrikes didn't stop Germany in World War II, it didn't stop the North Vietnamese from overrunning Saigon, it didn't stop the Chinese "volunteers" from pushing UN forces nearly off the Korean Peninsula, it didn't make Saddam leave Kuwait or destroy any Iraqi CBW munitions, and it didn't make the Serb military forces leave Kosovo.

Let me be clear here—strategic bombing will never be the solution to stopping the proliferation of CB weapons. No matter how many smart munitions, cruise missiles, or B-2 bombers the United States has to throw at the enemy, there is always the chance that the adversary of the future will use CB weapons to eliminate the high technology edge our ground troops have. They can produce these weapons in deep underground bunkers and in commercial laboratories built next to hospitals and schools. They use these weapons not because they are the "poor man's atomic bomb" but rather because U.S. forces remain vulnerable to their effects, and the U.S. public is so fearful and ignorant of these weapons.

In 1936 a logistics planner within the War Department noted: "It is apparent that there are critical deficiencies in our chemical preparedness. On the other hand, these requirements must be balanced against other vital needs in our military program." Army staffers had to plan funds for purchasing tanks and trucks, new rifles, a thirty-day ammunition supply for the active force, and equipping the Army Air Corps.[3] This same statement could apply to the U.S. military force today. Challenged with numerous programs and a need to maintain a highly trained and motivated force, DoD CB defense programs struggle to make their presence known. While the DP program has given the effort some new life, like all congressional fads, it will fade and then the Chemical Corps is back to fighting for the one-fifth of 1 percent of the defense budget.

The way the American public views CB warfare and how military leaders view the possibility of CB warfare largely influences how the military develops its defensive policies to prepare its forces. The trap that the military, and especially the DoD CB defense community, falls into, is the desire to utilize cutting edge technology to create a zero-risk environment, even if that capability is still years away in practical form. There is a saying, "better is too often the enemy of good enough." What this means is that when people ought to be satisfied with a good, inexpensive solution that meets 80 percent of the challenge, sometimes that is better than waiting for the 100 percent solution that is ten years away and costs three times as much. Because as soon as you get within view of the original "100 percent" goal, someone changes the standard and you're being told, if you wait a few more years, it will be 2 percent better. That's how 15-year defense programs (that should be 5-year defense programs) are created.

Final thoughts—there is a way out of this box, a way to resolve America's internal struggle with the morality of CB warfare. Accept the fact that the use of CB weapons is not inherently an immoral act, rather the use of CB weapons against civilian noncombatants is immoral (as would be the case with any conventional weapon). Accept the fact that CB agents are not doomsday devices; they are supertoxic agents that have definable characteristics and limitations, and therefore they can be handled and disposed of just like tanker spills that the EPA deals with every day. Emphasize to people that the terms "NBC" and "CB" and "WMD" do not mean nuclear, biological and chemical warfare aspects are equal or treated the same. Accept the fact that military personnel, with the proper training and defensive equipment, can and will be prepared to fight in CB-contaminated environments to the point where they can complete their mission because these agents are irrelevant. Accept the fact that, in order to prepare our troops for this eventuality, America needs a Chemical Corps with strong leadership, to develop the doctrine, design the equipment, organize the specialists, train the soldiers, and advance these discussions. Look at our current state of readiness and decide if this is good enough for future conflicts. Most likely, Congress and DoD want our forces to be fully prepared for fighting in a CB warfare environment, to suffer a minimum of casualties without overburdening the troops with gear that interferes with their operational effectiveness. Now what are our military and political leaders prepared to do to accomplish this state of readiness?

# Notes

## CHAPTER 1: SWORDS OR SHIELDS: THE DEBATE OVER WMDS

1. More precisely, the military makes a distinction between toxic chemical agents (which create casualties) and herbicides and riot control agents (which temporarily incapacitate and do not create casualties if properly used). Some arms control advocates claim that riot control agents (RCAs), developed in the 1960s, and incendiary munitions (such as napalm) should be considered as chemical warfare agents. Technically, CS and other riot control agents are chemical compounds and are often referred to as chemical agents in 1960s Army technical manuals. It must be noted that RCAs such as CS tear gas do not permanently maim or kill their targets as a result of exposure to the powder or gases alone (when used in typical employment scenarios). While pumping a room with burning CS gas may cause casualties, that is caused by the absence of oxygen rather than the actions of the tear gas. In a similar fashion, the jellied substance napalm is not harmful until it is burning, as opposed to the actions of mustard gas on contact with flesh. For these reasons, the United States has always differentiated between the applicability of incendiaries, RCAs, and chemical warfare agents under the laws of combat while often developing the agents and their munitions in the same laboratories.

2. Edward M. Spiers, *Chemical and Biological Weapons: A Study of Proliferation* (New York: St. Martin's Press, 1994), p. 5.

3. Carbamates are also categorized as nerve agents, but they are solid and not organophosphates as opposed to tabun, sarin, soman, and VX. Carbamates were not weaponized, as they are not as intrusive as liquids and aerosols.

4. See Public Law 105-736, House language section 1045, Chemical Warfare Defense.

## CHAPTER 2: THE CHEMICAL CORPS ENTERS THE COLD WAR

1. Frederick Brown, *Chemical Warfare; A Study in Restraints* (Princeton, NJ: Princeton University Press, 1968), pp. 191–95.

2. Senate Committee on Labor and Public Welfare, *Chemical and Biological Weapons: Some Possible Approaches for Lessening the Threat and Danger* (Washington, DC: GPO, 1969), p. 47.

3. The Chemical Corps Association, *The Chemical Warfare Service in World War II* (New York: Reinhold Publishing, 1948), pp. 20–21, 36.

4. The Chemical Corps Association, *Chemical Warfare Service*, pp. 97, 206–19. Camp Sibert (named after the first CWS chief) lay about thirty miles northwest of what is now Fort McClellan, Alabama.

5. Norman M. Covert, *Cutting Edge: A History of Fort Detrick, Maryland, 1943-1993* (Fort Detrick, MD: HQ Garrison), pp. 17–18.

6. Robert Harris and Jeremy Paxman, *A Higher Form of Killing* (New York: Hill and Wang, 1982), p. 103. Harris and Paxman outline the British–American partnership, which is described as being more secretive than the Manhattan Project and second only to the Manhattan Project for funding. The British had had a BW program since the mid-1930s, and so they supplied the research and America supplied the resources. They also claim a heavy American interest in anticrop biological agents. According to Army records, the first pilot plant designed for botulinum toxin was completed in October 1942, and the second in March 1944, which manufactured both anthrax and anthrax simulants (*bacillus globigii*). While Camp Detrick probably investigated anticrop agents, there is no evidence that they weaponized them.

7. Operation Paperclip primarily sought German rocket and nuclear scientists such as Dr. Werner von Braun, the head scientist of the German V-weapon program. However, upon discovery of the German nerve agents, chemists and biologists involved in Germany's CB agent weapons program were also included in the sweep.

8. Jeanne McDermott, *The Killing Winds: The Menace of Biological Warfare* (New York: Arbor House, 1987), p. 145.

9. Contrary to the popular notion that the U.S. Army had a biological warfare capability in 1944, the effort had never been completed. Factories had started manufacturing four-pound N-bomb shells in 1943 (the "N" designation being the code name for anthrax). However, the planned filling of the anthrax bombs was running behind. The Vigo plant in Indiana had successfully produced *bacillus globuli* (BG spores) in shakedown trials but had not initiated anthrax production by June 1944. The War Department shelved plans for using anthrax bombs for the war's duration.

10. Colonel Donald H. Hale, "Atomic Energy Indoctrination Training in the U.S. Army–Europe," *Armed Forces Chemical Journal* 4, 1 (July 1950).

11. Jeffery K. Smart, *U.S. Army Chemical and Biological Defense Command: Historical Highlights* (Aberdeen Proving Ground, MD: U.S. Army CBDCOM, 1994), p. 11.

12. Arthur E. Brown, "The Strategy of Limited War," *Military Strategy* 3 (Aug. 1973), p. 36.

13. William R. Brankowitz, *Chemical Munitions Movement History Compilation* (Aberdeen Proving Ground, MD: Office of the Program Manager for Chemical Munitions [Demil and Binary] [Provisional], 12 June 1987). The records show unspecified quantities of unspecified chemical agents moving from Concord, California, by sea to unspecified locations throughout 1951 and 1952. Colonel (ret.) Carl Burke, Senior Chemical Officer for U.S. Pacific forces in 1959, recalls these to be toxic agents moved in theater to provide a retaliatory capability as needed. In October 1953 the Army shipped nine tons of mustard agent to Japan from that port. There was similar movement of chemical munitions to Fort McClellan, Edgewood Arsenal, Yuma Test Station, Dugway Proving Ground, and Pine Bluff Arsenal, but records do not indicate what the munitions were.

14. Sterling Seagrave, *Yellow Rain: A Journey through the Terror of Chemical Warfare* (New York: M. Evans, 1981), pp. 92–93. The plant was mothballed in 1957 after producing 10-15,000 tons of dichlor. Rocky Mountain Arsenal shut down its production line of sarin munitions in 1957 as well, after finishing its run of the sarin-filled projectiles and

bombs.  The arsenal is still cleaning up chemical waste products from government and private industry activities under environmental remediation projects.

15.  Soviet military leaders and arms control analysts later claimed that the Soviets made the statement emphasizing their concern that the United States would employ CB weapons, creating the future battlefield image they described. The Soviets claimed they would not be the first ones to use CB weapons, and their stockpile was for retaliatory purposes only.

16.  Stockholm Peace Research Insistute (SIPRI), *CB Weapons and Programs* (Stockholm, Sweden: SIPRI, 1972), p. 195.

17.  Mark S. Watson, "Nerve Gases Gain Favor As Weapons," *Baltimore Sun*, Apr. 3, 1960, p. 1; William Johnson, three-piece exclusive (titles as in text), *Baltimore News-Post*, Jan. 4-6, 1960; and Peter Andrews, "In a War, Russ Might Put Gas Before A-Bombs," *Baltimore News-Post*, Nov. 1, 1961.

18.  William A. Buckingham,, Operation Ranch Hand: The Air Force and Herbicides in Southeast Asia, 1961-1971 (Washington, DC: GPO, 1982), p. 52.  Olenchuck went on to become the senior Chemical Officer (Major General Peter Olenchuck) in 1974.

19.  Seagrave, *Yellow Rain*, pp. 101–2.

20.  Hoyt Gimlin, *Chemical-Biological Weaponry* (Washington, DC: Congressional Quarterly, Inc, 1969), p. 468.

21. UPI and AP, "War Foes Plan to Burn Dog in Protest at U. of Cincinnati," *New York Times,* Nov. 8, 1968.

22.  Charles Mohr, "A Daring Captain Saves a Company," *New York Times*, p. A1, Jan. 10, 1966.

23.  Seagrave, *Yellow Rain*, pp. 124–25.  Military experts suspect Soviet pilots dropped the munitions in part due to the  pilots' ability to drop the munitions upwind of the target, resulting in maximum effectiveness.  Some sources suggest that Israeli alarm over Egyptian use of nerve agents in Yemen added to the decision for an Israeli preemptive attack.  The U.S. military sent thousands of protective masks to the Israeli army for the Arab-Israeli conflicts.

24.  Smart, *Historical Highlights*, p. 23; and Brankowitz, *Chemical Weapons Movement*, p. 11.

## CHAPTER 3:  THE CHEMICAL CORPS BEGINS ITS FALL

1.  Harris and Paxman, *A Higher Form of Killing*, pp. 216–17.  The costs included $60 a head for 4,377 sheep killed outright and 1,877 disabled—a price about double the market value. Gimlin, *Chemical-Biological Weaponry*, p. 457.

2.  C. Grant Ash, *History of the Skull Valley Sheep Deaths in 1968* (Deseret, Utah, 1994).  This personal account is based both on Dr. Ash's experience while at Deseret and newspaper reports of the period in question.  He wrote up his accounts for Major General (ret.) John Appel and the Chemical School in an effort to recollect what they had seen.  The Army's report is titled "Report of Investigation Concerning Sheep Deaths in Skull Valley, Utah," prepared by Brigadier General William W. Stone for the Commanding General of Army Material Command, April 1968.

3.  Deseret Test Center was established in 1962 at Fort Douglas, near Salt Lake City, Utah.  It was authorized for a staff of 227 military and civilian personnel and jointly staffed and supported by the Army, Air Force, Navy, and Marine Corps.  DTC was to coordinate the requirements for, plan, conduct, and evaluate testing of CB weapons and defense systems.  While it was led by an Army general officer, it was funded and its tests approved

by the Joint Chiefs of Staff, with review and approval by OSD (DDR&E) and the President's Scientific Advisory Committee. This was hardly a loosely run testing organization, as later press reports and pundits would imply.

4. HQ TECOM was the overseer for DPG as a test and evaluation center since 1962, when the realignment of the Chemical Corps under the Continental Army Command occurred and all arsenals, laboratories, and proving grounds were transferred to the new Army Material Command.

5. The original fact sheet did not specify the agent or the airplane, as these were considered classified at the time of the incident. Identifying the actual agent and delivery system would have allowed the Soviets to learn more about U.S. capabilities in offensive chemical warfare. This was disguised by stating that it was "a persistent agent" dispersed from "a high speed type aircraft."

6. Dr. Bernard McNamara was chief, Toxicology Department in the Medical Research Laboratory at the time. The newest building at Aberdeen Proving Ground, Edgewood Area (the Life Sciences Building), was named after him. He was joined by Mr. Ed Owens, Major John Ferrell, and Captain John Everts.

7. "Report of Investigation Concerning Sheep Deaths in Skull Valley, Utah," prepared by Brigadier General William W. Stone for the Commanding General of Army Material Command, Apr. 1968.

## CHAPTER 4: BAD NEWS GETS WORSE

1. Richard D. McCarthy, *The Ultimate Folly*, pp. 83, 94. This resolution was H.J. Res. 691, issued on April 30, 1969, and was cosponsored by Congressman Edward Koch (D–NY). Congress mandated Public Law 91-441 signed by President Richard Nixon on October 7, 1970, which required an extensive study of the effects of herbicides in South Vietnam. This law mandated that the Secretary of Defense contract this study through the National Academy of Sciences. The NAS investigators released their final report on February 15, 1974. The report failed to find any clear evidence of direct damage to human health from herbicides. They also could find no evidence linking the human birth defects to the spraying, despite making a considerable effort. However, outside scientists were still critical, and charged bias, noting that the president of the NAS, Frederick Seitz, was also the chairperson of the Defense Science Board. The chief investigator, Geoffrey Norman, was a former biochemist and division chief at Fort Detrick (1946–52).

2. McCarthy, *Ultimate Folly*, pp. 102–9; and Brankowitz, *Chemical Weapons Movement History Compilation*, p. 11. There was one last sea dump, CHASE X, of Anniston Army Depot stocks of M55 rockets in concrete-filled vaults on August 10–12, 1970 (two years after CHASE XI and XII). The Army had filled the vaults up with concrete earlier but delayed the dumping due to circumstances beyond their control. The Army received permissions to dump this last load, due to fears that the rockets were leaking and there were no incineration plans in place.

3. Seagrave, *Yellow Rain*, pp. 268–69.

4. Office of the Chief Chemical Officer, "Estimate of the Chief CBR Situation" (Washington, DC: Dept. of the Army, 1958) p. 1. This policy came about due to the "limited" warfare situation resulting from the Korean War. Many chemical officers (and other combat soldiers) felt that needless casualties could have been avoided had President Harry Truman permitted the use of CB weapons against Chinese and North Korean forces. General Douglas MacArthur himself endorsed the idea of using radiological contamination in the demilitarized zone to ensure that enemy forces could not readily cross and attack the

U.S. and South Korean forces. Truman had thought that by keeping the conflict "limited," i.e., without the use of CB weapons or nukes and not expanding against other countries, he would keep the Soviet Union and China from escalating the war across the world.

5. Kathleen Teltsch, "Thant Urges Halt on Germ Weapons," *Washington Post*, July 3, 1969, p. A1.

6. On October 12, the Army released testimony from Brigadier General William Stone before the House subcommittee, in which he revealed the Army's efforts to develop binary weapons.

7. Mr. Bill Dee, interview with author, June 1994.

8. Seagrave, *Yellow Rain*, p. 269; and personal interview with Mr. Bill Dee. The eight sites include Anniston Chemical Activity, AL; Blue Grass Chemical Activity, KY; Deseret Chemical Depot; Edgewood Chemical Activity, MD; Newport Chemical Depot, IN; Pine Bluff Chemical Activity, AR; Pueblo Chemical Depot, CO; and Umatilla Chemical Depot, OR.

9. Ibid., pp. 258–70.

10. *New York Times*, "Laird Defends Chemical Weaponry as a Deterrent," July 29, 1969, p. 4.

11. McCarthy, *The Ultimate Folly*, pp. 141–42.

12. Public Law 91-121 was amended on October 7, 1970, to include prohibitions against the disposal of CBW agents. This amendment was added under Public Law 91-441. It also added a requirement to investigate the ecological and physiological dangers inherent in the use of herbicides, and more specifically, the defoliation program carried out in South Vietnam. The PHS duty is executed by the HHS's Centers for Disease Control and Prevention (CDC), National Center for Environmental Health, Special Programs Group.

13. Wilbert Taylor, Frank Massaro, and 2d Lieutenant Gwen Marshall, "A Summary of Chemical Munition Testing and Disposal Operations at Dugway Proving Ground" (Dugway Proving Ground, UT: Joint Operations Directorate, HQ DA, 1988), pp. 1–2. During World War II, Dugway Proving Ground had tested only three systems: various incendiary munitions, the 4.2-inch chemical mortar, and aerial spray tanks. In the eighteen years after its reopening, it had tested everything from aerial spray tanks and artillery systems to mortars and land mines, and both guided and unguided missiles. Deseret Test Center had been consolidated into Dugway Proving Ground in June 1968, expanding its acreage to nearly 850,000 acres.

14. *New York Times*, "Nixon Renounces Germ Weapons, Orders Destruction of Stocks; Restricts Use of Chemical Arms," Nov. 26, 1969, p. 1.

15. G. B. Carter, *Porton Down: 75 Years of Chemical and Biological Research* (London: HMSO, 1992), pp. 74–75.

16. H. R. Haldeman, *The Haldeman Diaries: Inside the Nixon White House* (New York: Putnam, Sons, 1994). Two lines mention CB warfare; on page 110, Nov. 21, 1969, Nixon tells Haldeman "Leave [Senators] Griffen and Scott . . . out of the briefing meeting Tuesday about CBW," and later, Nov. 25, "Johnson couldn't have gotten NPT, CBW, Okinawa and the draft because . . . [he] didn't have the confidence of the people."

17. Pine Bluff Arsenal held antipersonnel agents such as anthrax spores, botulinum toxin, shellfish poison, and a variety of other agents. They were incinerated at a cost of $10.2 million, which took place between May 10, 1971, and May 1, 1972. Beale AFB neutralized and incinerated their anticrop agents between Aug. 2, 1971, and May 10, 1972, at a cost of $500,000. Rocky Mountain Arsenal held about twenty-five times the quantity of Beale, and was similarly destroyed between Aug. 2, 1971, and Feb. 15, 1973 (costing $2.4

million).  Fort Detrick's limited quantities of biological warfare agents were destroyed between Jan. 17, 1972 and Mar. 16, 1973, at a cost of $990,000.  HQ DA, *U.S. Army Activity in the U.S. Biological Warfare Programs,* 2, Feb. 24, 1977.

18.  Two died of anthrax in the 1950s, and one died of Venezuelan equine encephalitis (VEE) in 1964.  Since 1969 only five people have become sick from laboratory-bred diseases, and none have died.

19.  Gimlin, *Chemical-Biological Weaponry,* p. 459; Elaine Landau, *Chemical and Biological Warfare* (New York: Lodestar Books, 1991), p. 84.

20.  Alibek, Ken and Stephen Handelman, *Biohazard* (New York: Random House, 1999), pp. 225–40.

21.  Seagrave, *Yellow Rain,* pp. 271–72.

22.  The shipments were executed on Jan. 13 on the USNS *Robinson*; Aug. 3 on USNS *Sealift*; Aug. 18 on the USNS *Private McGraw*; Aug. 29 on the USNS *Miller*; Sep. 4 on the USNS *Sealift*; and Sep. 19 on the USNS *Private McGraw*.  Brankowitz, *Chemical Weapons Movement,* p. 12.

23.  The first article spelled out the broad terms of the agreement:

Each State Party to this Convention undertakes never in any circumstances to develop, produce, stockpile or otherwise acquire or retain:

1.  Microbial or other biological agents, or toxins whatever their origin or method of production, of types and in quantities that have no justification for prophylactic, protective or other peaceful purposes;

2.  Weapons, equipment or means of delivery designed to use such agents or toxins for hostile purposes or in armed conflict.

The BWC was signed on April 10, 1972.  W. Michael Reisman and Chris Antoniou, *The Laws of War* (New York: Vintage Books, 1994), pp. 58–59.

24.  Lawrence J. Korb, *The Fall and Rise of the Pentagon: American Defense Policies in the 1970s* (Westport, CT: Greenwood Press, 1979), pp. 36–42.  New programs under consideration included the Army M1 tank (replacing the M60A2), the Navy F-14 and Air Force F-15 (replacing their F-4s), the Navy Trident missile submarines (replacing the Polaris subs), and the Navy Spruance-class destroyer DD-963 (replacing the DD-800).  These new programs represented a unit increase in price of 150% to 700% over their predecessors.

25.  Office of the Chief of Staff of the Army, memorandum for the Secretary of the Army, subject: Chemical Corps Consolidation, dated Jan. 4, 1973.

26.  Edgewood Arsenal (the installation grounds) became Edgewood Area of Aberdeen Proving Ground.  Edgewood Arsenal (the organization) still continued as the chemical commodity center for Munitions Command.

27.  Smart, *U.S. Army Chemical and Biological Defense Command,* p. 13.  The Army discontinued most Technical Service headquarters establishments (including the Chemical Corps) in 1962.  All arsenals, laboratories, and proving grounds were assigned to HQ AMC.  AMC, in turn, assigned all Chemical Corps arsenals to MUCOM, replacing the Chief Chemical Officer's logistics responsibilities.  The Combat Development Command and Continental Army Command took over doctrine and training missions, respectively.

28.  General Creighton Abrams, memorandum for DCSPER: "Plan for Consolidation of Army Chemical Corps," Oct. 16, 1972.  This deliberate oversight was especially galling to Major General Appel, since he was sitting as the Director, Chemical and Nuclear Operations Directorate, Office of the Assistant Chief of Staff for Force Development in the Pentagon.  This was the prime Chemical Corps advisory position to the Chief of Staff, yet Abrams deliberately kept him out of the loop prior to the memo's release.

29. Chemical Study Group, memorandum for CSA, "Consolidation of Chemical Corps Functions," Dec. 15, 1972.

30. Eric Pace, "Army Reshuffles Commands in U.S.," *New York Times*, Jan. 12, 1973, p. A1.

31. Major General (ret.) Watson, interview with author, May 25, 1995; and Brigadier General (ret.) Pete Hidalgo, phone interview with author, Dec. 2, 1995.

32. Notes from the Abrams Collection, Army War College library, Carlisle, PA. These notes include the advantages of consolidation as establishing a chemical weapons specialist field similar to the nuclear specialists found in the Artillery Branch, Engineer and Ordnance Corps, and freeing up facilities at Fort McClellan to the Women's Army Corps (WAC) School and Center. The report also optimistically called for closing Fort Dix; truly visionaries before their time, if not a bit naive (considering what the government has had to do up to the Base Realignment and Closing committees).

33. "The Posture of the Army," statement by General Creighton W. Abrams before the Committee on Armed Services, House of Representatives, Second Session, 93d Congress, February 14, 1974. Ironically, at that same briefing, he admitted to Congress that the U.S. Army had been surprised by the sophistication and quantity of Soviet CBR equipment of the Arab forces (equipment captured from the Arab-Israeli October 1973 war), and was determined to improve the Army's defenses. While congressmen were being told in one brief that the Chemical Corps' disestablishment caused no vulnerabilities, they were told in another brief that the Army had no one to evaluate the Soviet chemical defense equipment captured in the Arab-Israeli War. Lieutenant Colonel Rudolph S. Malooley, "Gas Is Not a Dirty Word in Soviet Army," *Army*, September 1974, pp. 21–23.

34. While Major General Appel was one of the strongest proponents of the Chemical Corps even after his retirement in June 1974, he (intentionally or unintentionally) fell into this category. With the exception of one year in Korea as the chief chemical officer for the Eighth U.S. Army, his assignments from January 1949 through January 1973 were either instructor positions, staff positions in DC, or commanding officer of arsenals and test centers. He was a relentless advocate of a strong CBW program, but perhaps he did not know how to translate that into combat arms terms (or the combat arms leaders did not perceive him as credible when talking about the Army's future combat requirements).

## CHAPTER 5: REGAINING CB DEFENSE CAPABILITIES

1. Brig. Gen. Robert Scales, *Certain Victory: The US Army in the Gulf War* (Washington, DC: Brassey's, 1994), pp. 10–14; John L. Romjue, *From Active Defense to AirLand Battle: The Development of Army Doctrine 1973–1982* (Fort Monroe, VA: HQ TRADOC, 1984), pp. 2–3.

2. Discussion with Col. (ret) Gary Eifried, former Director of Combat Developments, U.S. Army Chemical School.

3. Anthony H. Cordesman and Abraham R. Wagner, *The Lessons of Modern War: The Arab-Israeli Conflicts, 1973-1989* (Boulder, CO: Westview Press, 1990), p. 268.

4. General Creighton Abrams had died of cancer while in office on September 4, 1974.

5. Anthony Ripley, "Clements Won't Rule Out A-Bomb Use," *New York Times*, Jan. 12, 1973 p. A15.

6. Charles H. Bay, "The Other Gas Crisis—Chemical Weapons," *Parameters—Journal of the US Army War College*, Sep. 1979, pp. 70–72.

7. "Report of the Chemical Warfare Review Commission" (Washington, DC: GPO, June 1985), pp. 98–99.

8. GAO, *Chemical Warfare: DoD's Reporting of Its Chemical and Biological Research* (Washington, DC: GAO, Aug. 1991), p. 8. This report, titled the *Annual Report on Chemical Warfare—Chemical/Biological Defense Research Program Obligations*, was compiled by Edgewood Arsenal. Congress terminated this reporting requirement in 1986 as part of a cost saving measure and to reduce the administrative burden on DoD. In 1989 Congress reinstated the report (now being developed by the Joint Staff), citing the need for better oversight. More likely this was due to the resumption of binary 155-mm shell production, and Congress decided it should stay aware of the stockpile growth.

9. Ibid., pp. 73–74.

10. In 1990–91, these individuals were Brigadier General Bob Orton, commandant of the Chemical School; Brigadier General Walt Busbee, commander, U.S. Army Chemical Materiel Destruction Agency; and Colonel Rick Read, Chief Chemical Officer, Nuclear and Chemical Branch, ODCSOPS.

11. The Military Police Center and School relocated to Fort McClellan from Fort Gordon, Georgia, in July 1975. The Signal Corps Center and School had moved from Fort Monmouth, New Jersey, to Fort Gordon, pushing the MPs out of Fort Gordon.

12. The Missile Munitions Center and School agreed to move the live agent training to Fort McClellan upon the completion of that post's toxic agent training facility.

13. Interviews with Major General (ret.) Watson and Colonel (ret.) Bob Thornton.

14. Dept of Defense Directive 5148.2, effective 1978.

15. GAO, *Chemical Warfare: Progress and Problems in Defensive Capability*, (Washington, DC: GAO/PEMD-86-11, 1986), pp. 87–89.

16. Dept. of Defense Directive 5160.5, effective in 1977.

17. GAO, *Chemical Warfare: Progress and Problems in Defensive Capability*, p. 55. The Public Law was passed in 1978. The first (and only) armored vehicle with both overpressure and ventilated facepieces is the M1A1 tank, due to the fact that all other vehicles had already been developed. This is discussed in more detail in the materiel program chapters.

18. Bay, "The Other Gas Crisis," p. 74.

19. "Administration Wants to Build Plant for Binary Gas Weapons," *Washington Post*, October 20, 1978.

## CHAPTER 6: CHANGES IN DOCTRINE AND TRAINING

1. President Boris Yeltsin admitted that the accident had occurred at a biological weapons plant and acknowledged the existence of the Soviet biological warfare program at Camp David in February 1992. He conceded that "a number of centers and a number of programs dealing with this issue have been closed," and that "from 1992 [forward], there will be no [military] budget allocations coming to that program." Edward M. Spiers, *Chemical and Biological Weapons: A Study of Proliferation* (New York: St. Martin's Press, 1994), p. 37.

2. Office of the Program Manager for Binary Munitions, *Binary Chemical Munitions Fact Sheet*, Aberdeen Proving Ground, MD, September 1989, p. 1.

3. Sen. Howell Hefflin, "The Russian Chemical Warfare Menace: The Ability to Retaliate in Kind," delivered at the Senate, Washington, DC, June 30, 1985.

4. Senate Armed Services Committee, *Chemical Warfare* (Washington, DC: GPO, 1980), pp. 3–4.

5. Ibid., p. 21. Soon afterward, the 8-in. binary projectile was shelved due to the plans to replace all 8-in. artillery batteries with the MLRS batteries in the latter 1980s.

6. HQ DA, *The Airland Battle and Corps 86*, TRADOC PAM 525-20, dated July 30, 1982.

7. Final copies released include FM 3-3, *Contamination Avoidance*, dated May 1987; FM 3-4, *Protection*, dated Oct. 1985; FM 3-5, *Decontamination*, dated Jun. 1985; FM 3-6, *Field Behavior of NBC Agents*, dated Nov. 1986; FM 3-50, *Deliberate Smoke Operations*, dated Oct. 1984; FM 3-100, *NBC Operations*, dated Sep. 1985; FM 3-101, *Chemical Staff and Units*, dated Apr. 1987.

8. Smart, *U.S. Army Chemical and Biological Defense Command*, p. 13. The new CRDC was a subordinate of the equally brand-new Armament, Chemicals and Munitions Command (AMCCOM), headquartered at Rock Island Arsenal, Illinois. The AMCCOM Deputy Commanding General for Chemical Materiel also became the commanding general for CRDC. AMCCOM also took custody of Pine Bluff Arsenal and Rocky Mountain Arsenal, which did not come under the DCG, CM, but reported directly to HQ, AMCCOM. All procurement and manufacturing orders for chemical materiel went from Edgewood to Rock Island.

9. U.S. Department of State, *Chemical Warfare in Southeast Asia and Afghanistan*, Special Report #98, p. 6.

10. Seagrave, *Yellow Rain*, p. 35.

11. Ibid., pp. 14–16.

12. Anthony H. Cordesman and Abraham R. Wagner, *The Lessons of Modern War: The Afghan and Falklands Conflicts* (Boulder, CO: Westview Press, 1990), p. 218.

13. Philip M. Boffey, "'Yellow Rain': New Support for Honeybee Theory," *New York Times*, Aug. 12, 1985, p. A13; Laurence Pringle, *Chemical and Biological Warfare: The Cruelest Weapons* (Hillside, NJ: Enslow Publishing, 1993), pp. 48–51.

14. This DoD directive has been re-released as DODD 5134.8, Assistant to the Secretary of Defense for Atomic Energy (ATSD[AE]), dated June 8, 1994.

15. Spiers, *Chemical Warfare*, p. 169.

16. L. B. Taylor and C. L. Taylor, *Chemical and Biological Warfare* (New York: Franklin Watts, 1985), pp. 89–91.

17. Major General (ret) Watson, interview with author.

18. Steven Browman, *U.S. Chemical Warfare Preparedness Program* (Washington, DC: Congressional Research Service, 1982), pp. 13–14.

19. U.S. Arms Control and Disarmament Agency, *Chemical and Biological Weapons Reader*, June 1994, pp. 117–18.

20. Peter Dunn, *A Journey to Iraq—A Personal Account* (Melbourne, Aus.: DoD, Defense Science & Technology Organization, Materials Research Labs, 1984), p. 24.

21. Congressional Research Service, *Binary Weapons: Implications of the US Chemical Stockpile Modernization Program for Chemical Weapons Proliferation* (Washington, DC: GPO, 1984), p. I.

22. Office of the Chief of Public Affairs, HQ, TRADOC, "The Chemical Strategy," *Army Chemical Review*, January 1988, pp. 23–24.

23. Major General Alan A. Nord, "Views from the Top," *Army Chemical Journal*, Fall 1985, pp. 11–12. Because the Army was having difficulties adopting the Norwegian lightweight decon system called the Sanator, most units, although authorized to receive the decon system, did not receive their Sanators until 1990. This made it very difficult to practice the new philosophy.

## CHAPTER 7: RECONNAISSANCE, DETECTION, AND IDENTIFICATION

1. While the DoD did not immediately form this task force group, this report was the basis for forming the Joint Service Review Group in 1984. The JSRG would have a role in developing a prioritized list of R&D defense programs for acceleration and would review and report on the four services' NBC RDA efforts.

2. Chemical Warfare School, "Study Guide—Chemical Warfare: Questions, Answers and Practical Exercises" (Edgewood, MD: Chemical Warfare Center, 1943), p. 43.

3. The M18A1 kit replaced the M9A2 chemical detection kit. There was also an M19 CBR sampling and analyzing kit, intended for use by specially trained personnel in a technical intelligence team, military intelligence team or chemical service organization. In addition to identifying over forty types of chemical warfare agents, it allowed for the preliminary processing of unidentified samples. It required that at least one member of the team be a trained chemist that could evaluate and translate the findings.

4. One of the aims of the M256 kit was also to lessen the logistics involved. The M256 kit had a five-year shelf life, replacing the M18A1 and M15A1 chemical detection kits that had three-year shelf lives. Thus the Chemical Corps reduced the logistics footprint and made it easier to identify chemical agent vapors.

5. The M8's reaction was called "Spontaneous Electrolysis Alarm" or SEA. Some people wonder why mustard agent is not often considered for automatic chemical agent detectors. While mustard agent remained a very potential threat, it was not considered a lethal agent like the nerve and blood agents. Also, mustard gas did not readily vaporize to readily permit vapor agent detection. Mustard agent would have to land very close to the detectors for the alarms to sound, which defeated the purpose of an "early" warning at low agent levels. The Army chose to stick to a manual paper detection method (M8 paper) for that particular agent identification.

6. The modifications included mounting kits and power supplies for the M8 detector. These became the M11 detector system (for 1/4 ton trucks), the M12 detector system (for the 3/4 ton truck), the M13 detector system (for the 2½ ton truck), the M14 detector system (for the M113 personnel carrier), the M15 detector system (for the full tracked vehicles), the M16 detector system (for the 1/4 ton truck using the M10 power supply), the M17 detector system (3/4 ton truck with M10 power supply), and the M18 detector system (for the 2½ ton truck with M10 power supply). This allows the reader to bridge the gap to the next developmental detector system, the M22 ACADA.

7. The Automatic Chemical Agent Alarm Set, A/E 23D-1, also known as the Ionization Detector Set, was sponsored by the Air Force as an attempt to replace the M8 alarm with a system that would permit essentially unattended operation. It used a tritium source (beta emitter) to ionize air drawn into the detector cells. If an atmospheric contaminant caused a change in the current across the cells, the detector signaled an alarm. It only alarmed to nerve agents due to technical constraints.

8. The Air Force continued to power their IDS detector and the M43A1 from a generator, not being happy with the limited life of D-cell batteries in the BA-3517/U power pack of the detector (approximately 24 to 72 hours). Their version of the Army M43A1 was developed as the A/E 23D-3 detector. The Navy eventually bought some of the modified Air Force detectors for their Mark 21 Chemical Agent Protective Detection System (CAPDS), which tied two detectors (port and starboard) into their ship survivability systems. So while everyone was using the same basic nerve agent detector, three separate modifications existed.

9. The CAM used a nickel-63 beta emitter source as its ionization source. This required an NRC license to operate, which caused a real bureaucratic mess for the U.S. field units in storing and maintaining the CAMs.

10. Note on mustard gas—mustard gas was chosen as a nonlethal CW agent, as it disables troops rather than killing them. While it does not kill in low or moderate doses, it can be fatal if ingested or if personnel are exposed to very high levels.

## CHAPTER 8: INDIVIDUAL PROTECTION

1. The Air Force Systems Command and Air Force Logistics Command has combined into the Air Force Materiel Command. The Marine Corps Research, Development and Acquisition Command has now changed into the Marine Corps Systems Command.

2. In 1984 the Joint Logistics Commanders were composed of the commander of Army Materiel Command; the commander of Air Force Systems Command; the commander of Air Force Logistics Command; the Deputy Chief of Naval Operations (Logistics); and the commanding general of Marine Corps Research, Development and Acquisition Command. The commander of the Defense Logistics Agency and the J-4 (Joint Staff) sat in as observers. The JP-CBD began as a low-level panel in the late 1970s, when Brigadier General Bobby Robinson (AMC's chief chemical officer) brought it into the front as the tool for joint service NBC defense program development.

3. This technique should not be confused with equipment used with scuba (self-contained underwater breathing apparatus) diving. These tanks use negative pressure system to release compressed air into the diver's mask.

4. Jeffrey Smart, *Preparing for Chemical Warfare: The History of the Infantry Protective Mask* (Aberdeen Proving Ground, MD: HQ CBDCOM, undated [circa 1992]), p. 9. Excellent and in-depth discussion of the evolution of protective masks.

5. The Army chemical defense community had always shown an interest in developing collective protection systems for tanks and aircraft at least since the 1950s (collective protection was prototyped in late World War II for the Sherman tank).

6. The XM30 mask was a joint program between the Army and Air Force in October 1978. When the Army ordered the project to be terminated by 1984, the Air Force objected and continued the program with the Navy under the new program name of MCU-2/P with a fielding date of 1984. The Air Force planned a buy of 11,000 MCU-2/P masks, and the Navy, 4,000 masks, with deliveries scheduled to begin in 1984. The Navy remained with the Mark V protective mask for shipboard and shore support use until the MCU-2/P masks became available.

7. Edgewood scientists claimed the British suits didn't offer enough protection against mustard agents. What they didn't state was that they were purchasing CPOs based on a technical data package that was at least a decade old (definitely not state of the art). The need for a breathable suit was made very clear in the 1975 Unit Chemical Defense Study, which demonstrated the need for CPOs designed to accommodate heat stress during combat. This data was developed using the Goldman Heat Stress Model (Dr. Goldman was a Natick scientist).

8. All clothing programs, to include chemical defense clothing, were consolidated under a new program manager, PM CIE, who championed the Natick lab's R&D programs. This office was located at Falls Church, VA, near to the Pentagon. Their programs included anything that the soldier wore to the battlefield; rucksacks, load-bearing equipment, canteens, helmets, boots, gloves, etc. They petitioned for taking over the protective mask programs, but those remained at Edgewood after bitter fighting. This rivalry caused many

bad feelings between the two labs, which only hurt Natick more when they were told to merge with Edgewood in 1998.

9. The Navy, not satisfied with the heavy overgarments and convinced that their ships did not face a high chemical weapon threat, adopted the British Mark III protective suits in 1983. These suits provided roughly half the protection (2 to 3 grams per square meter) but reduced the heat stress tremendously with a woven fiber technology, and they were flame-retardant. They also took up much less space when stored. The Navy later modified the Mark III for U.S. production, calling it the Chemical Protective Overgarment (CPOG).

10. While the 7-mil gloves were more tactile and allowed greater dexterity, they ripped easily on rough edges. Combat soldiers used the 25-mil gloves, while radio operators might use the 7-mil gloves.

### CHAPTER 9: COLLECTIVE PROTECTION

1. The exception are some chemical detectors used on vehicles and ships. The Navy integrates their detectors into their ship systems, and chemical detectors can be mounted on tanks and HMMWVs. However, this is usually an afterthought, rather than planned into the vehicle design as collective protection often is.

2. This attitude resurfaced briefly in 1990, when the Air Force Chief of Staff declared that collective protection was not an area in which the Air Force would invest. His concept was that if the air cover failed and the air base was contaminated, the entire base population would move lock, stock, and barrel to another air base. He canceled all CP programs, and it wasn't until after he left (after Operation Desert Storm) that the Air Force staffers were able to bring them back. This area is still considered a serious deficiency for AF planners.

### CHAPTER 10: DECONTAMINATION

1. This is one of the reasons why it became so important to have chemical agent detectors that the individual soldier could use. If they identified the agent positively, the leaders could determine whether decontamination was necessary. If the chemical agent was not a persistent agent, they could move out and wait for the agent to dissipate. Otherwise the clock was running.

2. This process was investigated and developed at Fort Detrick. As stated, the technology had laboratory appeal but could not be transferred easily to the field.

3. The term "ABC" stands for "Atomic-Biological-Chemical," a term predating CBR by a few years (1945-62).

4. Interview with Major General Jan Van Prooyen, August 1996.

5. CARC paint initially came in the three woodland colors of olive green, brown, and black. As more and more exercises were held in the Middle East, the Army developed the sand color just in time for Operation Desert Storm.

### CHAPTER 11: POLITICS OF CHEMICAL ARMS AND CHEMICAL DEFENSE

1. Union Carbide had a methyl isocyanate (MIC) production plant in Bhopal, India. On December 3, 1984, about 40 tons of MIC leaked from the plant and killed some 2,500 people and injured 177,000 others. The accident caused some U.S. Congressional and environmental leaders to examine whether such an incident might occur in the United States. In response to one newspaper's claim that the binary weapon components were as lethal as MIC, CRDC and USANCA prepared a public report showing that the binary weapon components were one to two orders of magnitude less hazardous than MIC.

2. Public Law 98-525, Department of Defense Authorization Act for 1985, directed the president to establish a "Chemical Warfare Review Commission" to review the overall adequacy of the chemical warfare posture of the U.S. military with particular emphasis on whether the U.S. government should produce binary chemical weapons.

3. Walter J. Stoessel, Jr., et al., *Report of the Chemical Warfare Review Commission* (Washington, DC: GPO, 1985), p. 79. This Commission's charter included a review of

- the relationship of the U.S. chemical stockpile modernization program with the ultimate goal of achieving a ban on chemical weapons
- the adequacy of the existing stockpile of unitary chemical weapons in providing a credible deterrent to use by the Soviet Union of chemical weapons against the US and allies
- whether the binary chemical modernization program proposed by the DoD is adequate to support U.S. national security policy by posing a credible deterrent to chemical warfare
- the ability of defensive measures alone to meet the Soviet chemical warfare threat and the adequacy of funding for current and projected defensive measure programs

4. Ibid., pp. 73–75.

5. HQ DA, *Collected Works of the 30th Chief of Staff, USA: John A. Wickham, Jr., General, USA, Chief of Staff of the Army, June 1983–June 1987* (Washington, DC: HQ DA, 1987), p. 86.

6. Captain Richard M. Bartosik, "Chemical SPR," *Army Chemical Journal*, Fall 85, pp. 51–52.

7. GAO, *Chemical Warfare: Progress and Problems in Defensive Capability* (Washington, DC: GAO/PEMD-86-11, July 1986), pp. 98–100.

8. U.S. Arms Control and Disarmament Agency, *Chemical and Biological Arms Reader*, pp. 137–39. The INF treaty contains on-site inspection provisions (except for challenge inspections) similar to that initially proposed for chemical warfare verification. It provides for stationing U.S. and Soviet inspectors at destruction and production sites and twenty-short notice inspections during the first three years of the treaty. These practices became the starting point for working out CWC inspection protocols.

9. HQ DA dissolved the PEO-CN position in March 1989, due to the lack of major programs in the NBC defense area and the need to reduce the total number of Army PEOs. The OPMBN transferred to the control of the commander, CRDEC.

10. PM for Binary Munitions, *Binary Chemical Munitions Fact Sheet*, Sep. 1989, pp. 15–18.

11. Spiers, *Chemical and Biological Weapons*, p. 87.

12. Ibid., pp. 65–67. Libya had been one of the "horizontal proliferation" cases identified in 1982. It had obtained chemical munitions from East Germany in 1980 and acquired training in offensive and defensive NBC programs in the Soviet Union and Poland. Libya had begun building what intelligence sources identified as a chemical factory at Rabta, some 80 kilometers southwest of Tripoli, around 1983. What set it apart from other chemical factories in Libya was first its remote location in the desert; second, the projected size that seemed to exceed the expected fertilizer and pesticide requirements of the country. The last indicator, perhaps the damning one, was the security provisions surrounding one particular building. These included a twelve-meter earthen wall surrounding the complex,

an elaborate surface-to-air missile system, a highly sophisticated and oversized ventilation system, special pumps and noncorrosive piping, airtight windows and doors, and escape routes. All this could have been construed as circumstantial evidence, considering the paranoia of a country that had been bombed by U.S. planes in 1986. Other evidence, however, to include accidental chemical leaks and animal kills in the area, seemed to confirm the assessment.

In the summer of 1987, Chad's government reported that Libyan troops had attacked across the border, and that the attack had included the use of chemical weapons (mustard and nerve agents). The U.S. government responded by shipping 2,000 M17A2 protective masks to the Chad government. Reports later suggested that the Libyan use of chemical munitions was very inaccurate and short-lived; in any event, it did not appear that the Libyans were about to repeat their experimental use after their troops were summarily routed by the Chad army. The continued operation of the suspected chemical warfare plant would eventually raise suspicions that West German chemical industries were supplying the plant with chemical stock and equipment. This controversy caused an unwelcome stir in relations between the Reagan administration and the Kohl government in 1989. The Rabta incident became a case study in the difficulties in controlling chemical weapons proliferation across a global economy. For military scholars, they would note that the mere use of chemical agents did not guarantee victory for the Libyans. As was the case in so many conflicts, without a sound tactical plan and supporting combat arms, chemical weapons offered no real advantage to soldiers in defensive equipment (and therefore were not as "terrifying" to the Chad forces).

13. Ibid., pp. 69–73.

14. Ibid., p. 88.

15. USACDA, *Chemical and Biological Arms Reader*, pp. 118–19.

16. Under Secretary of Defense, memorandum for Secretaries of the military departments; Chairman, JCS; etc. subject: United States Chemical Programs, dated July 12, 1990.

17. GAO, *Chemical Warfare: DoD's Successful Effort to Remove U.S. Chemical Weapons from Germany* (Washington, DC: GAO/NSIAD-91-105, 1991), pp. 6–9.

18. Debra Fowler, "Removing Chemical Weapons from Europe," *Army Logistician*, Mar./Apr. 1991, pp. 36–39.

19. Public Law 100-456 required demonstration of the safety and effectiveness of the facility prior to the beginning of full operations. These tests were conducted in a four-phased program called Operational Verification Testing. From 1990 to 1993, the Army demonstrated that the Johnston Atoll Chemical Agent Disposal System (JACADS) could operate safely with any munition and agent type while protecting the workers and the environment. Since then, over one million pounds of nerve and mustard agent have been destroyed. This includes all stockpiled M55 rockets, one-ton containers of mustard and nerve agent, and one class of mustard-filled projectiles on the island. Several government-related organizations and agencies exercised oversight of the operations, to include the National Research Council of the National Academy of Sciences (technical aspects); Department of Health and Human Services (public health); Environmental Protection Agency and the Council on Environmental Quality (environmental aspects); DoD Explosives Safety Board (safety aspects); Defense Nuclear Agency (base operations and maintenance); congressional committee surveys, investigation teams, and the General Accounting Office (congressional oversight).

## CHAPTER 12: RECONNAISSANCE, DETECTION, AND IDENTIFICATION —PART 2

1. To confuse the reader further, there are also civilian program directors in the acquisition community, and Program Manager for Chemical Demilitarization (which is not considered an acquisition agency in the normal sense of the term).

2. The position of Product Manager for Smoke and Obscurants was later reduced to Project Manager, perhaps because of the fewer number of systems and reduced management requirements. Saga of the PEO-CN story was told to me by Brigadier General (ret.) Hidalgo and Billy Richardson, circa 1996.

3. As of January 1999, the Marines have abandoned the ICAD (none are with the combat units), the Air Force has given up on the ALAD (although some are still in depot), and the Navy has just started fielding its twenty IPDSs.

4. The forty-eight systems included six vehicles each for four divisions and two armored cavalry regiments, four maintenance floats, and eight vehicles for the USACMLS. The Product Manager for NBC Defense Systems, Col. Jan Van Prooyen, recommended that the XM87 program be halted in 1987 because of continuing problems. The task force recommended that FY88 money be used to purchase German Fuchs.

5. There had been two XM87 prototypes built by TRW by that time. Both were stripped of their equipment to provide the government-furnished equipment for the shoot-off between the LAV and the Fuchs. As a side note, General Motors had to team with TRW, a Canadian-based company (ironic since it was protesting the shutout of "American" companies).

## CHAPTER 13: INDIVIDUAL PROTECTION—PART 2

1. The British AR-5 was referred to as "the wheezing gasbag" by its operators in the Royal Air Force, perhaps an indication that they were not fond of the mask. One has to wonder why the Navy invested so much time and effort into the program, unless it was just because the AR-5 wasn't an U.S. Air Force program.

2. There continues to be a great amount of debate over the pros and cons of one-piece protective suits versus two-piece protective suits. On the one hand, a one-piece offers fewer gaps to allow aerosols and dry spores access to the individual. However, quickly donning a one-piece suit and taking care of one's bodily functions in a one-piece suit while in a contaminated environment was very unwieldy. The requirement to quickly process people through a decontamination line favored the two-piece protective suit as well. It was another example of weighing acceptable risk versus desired operational capabilities.

3. The powered exoskeleton is not an exaggeration; that was an actual requirement at one point (and may still be out there). Ironically, there are advertisements in 1950s defense magazines for a similar integrated soldier system concept for the atomic battlefield. The more things change, the more they stay the same.

4. Tech Escort troops did use the interim STEPO (STEPO-I) during the Gulf War to handle Iraqi chemical munitions. With the onset of the DoD Domestic Preparedness Program, the Air Force and Navy are reexamining the STEPO to see whether they can use it for their CB incident response forces.

5. This was a popular concept with heavy divisions that had the vehicles necessary to carry the boxes from division/brigade support areas forward to their combat units. In the light infantry divisions, supply officers tried to carry this concept forward but were

hampered by the lack of vehicles to support the number of ICE packs required. As a result, this logistics exercise was rarely practiced outside the heavy divisions.

## CHAPTER 14:    COLLECTIVE PROTECTION AND DECONTAMINATION —PART 2

1. This is not an all-inclusive list. These vehicles also use the ventilated face piece system: M9 Armored Combat Earthmover (ACE), M88A1 Recovery Vehicle, M109A4/A5, M578 Light Recovery Vehicle, M728 Combat Engineer Vehicle (CEV), M730A1/A2 Chapparal Missile Carrier, M981 FIST Vehicle Combat Carrier, M992 Ammunition Support Vehicle, and M993 MLRS Carrier. GAO, *Chemical-Biological Defense: Collective Protection Systems* (Washington, DC:GAO/NSIAD-91-273, 1991).

2. Live fire exercises using the hybrid system versus wearing protective gear has conclusively proven the worth of the system. Wearing protective gear often robbed the crew of an accurate and timely first shot, which in their line of work could make the difference between life and death.

3. To meet 3X standards, agent levels could not exceed $0.0001$ mg/m$^3$ for GA/GB, $0.00003$ mg/m$^3$ for GD, $0.00001$ mg/m$^3$ for VX, and $0.003$ mg/m$^3$ for H or L. One procedure was exposing the item to 350 degrees Fahrenheit for four hours, thus decomposing the agent. Complete guidelines for decontaminating equipment for peacetime use are covered in Department of the Army Pamphlet 385-61, *Toxic Chemical Agent Safety Standards*, dated March 31, 1997.

## CHAPTER 15: SMOKE, RADIACS, AND MEDICAL CB DEFENSE

1. Lt. Cdr D. C. Campbell, *Radiological Defense, Vol. IV: RADIAC, An Introduction to Radiological Instruments for Military Use*, (Armed Forces Special Weapons Project: Washington, DC, 1950), p. 43. This attitude from the technical community was not uncommon and can be seen with the CB defense community as well. The priority seemed to be to design an instrument that worked in the laboratory, then see if it could be adapted to the field, instead of designing in the military requirements first.

2. AN stood for Army-Navy (radiac program sponsors). PDR stood for Point Dose Radiac.

3. The Chemical School had asked the Army to create a chemical smoke generator company to be stationed at Fort Irwin, CA. The Army leadership denied the request, instead forcing the smoke generator company at Fort Lewis, WA, to split off a platoon to be stationed at NTC. As stated, this did not allow a fair portrayal of the true capabilities of smoke operations.

4. The atropine injector held 2 mg of atropine and 220 mg of obidoxime chloride. The 2-pam injector held 600 mg in two ml of pralidoxime chloride. Only medics were supposed to inject additional atropine into a soldier who had received three injections of atropine. The kits had a five-year shelf life in controlled storage.

5. Also, hydrogen cyanide was not seen as a very high threat, since it took a great number of munitions to deliver in volume, it evaporated quickly, and if an individual was to be unlucky enough to inhale a less-than-immediately-lethal concentration, the body could metabolize the effects away.

6. GAO, *Chemical Warfare: Progress and Problems in Defensive Capability* (Washington, DC: GAO/PEMD-86-11, 1986).

## CHAPTER 16: IRAQ'S CB WARFARE PROGRAM

1. Anthony H. Cordesman and Abraham R. Wagner, *The Lessons of Modern War, Vol II: The Iran-Iraq War* (Boulder, CO: Westview Press, 1990), pp. 507–10. Hereafter, *Iran-Iraq War.*

2. Ibid.

3. Spiers, *Chemical and Biological Weapons*, p. 45.

4. J. P. Perry Robinson, "Chemical Warfare Capabilities of the Warsaw and North Atlantic Treaty Organizations: An Overview from Open Sources," *Chemical Weapons: Destruction and Conversion* (New York: SIPRI, 1980), p. 14. One could probably say the same thing about the American chemical warfare capabilities during the 1970s and 1980s.

5. Cordesman and Wagner, *Iran-Iraq War*, pp. 103–5.

6. Ibid., p. 127.

7. Ibid., pp. 518–19.

8. Ibid., p. 141.

9. Ibid., p. 176. See also Stephen C. Pelletiere and Douglas Jackson, *Lessons Learned: The Iran-Iraq War* (Carlisle Barracks, PA: Strategic Studies Institute, 1991), pp. 97–98.

10. Cordesman and Wagner, *Iran-Iraq War*, pp. 178–83; Pelletiere and Jackson, *Lessons Learned*, p. 99.

11. Cordesman and Wagner, *Iran-Iraq War*, pp. 511–2. Iraq may have begun a biological agent pilot plant at this time, according to a report of Iraqi germ warfare program in the *Washington Post.* The report suggested that Muthanna hosted a biological R&D program for less than a year in 1985. R. Jeffery Smith, "Iraq Had Program for Germ Warfare," *Washington Post*, July 6, 1995, pp. A-1, A-17.

12. Leonard S. Spector with Jaqueline R. Smith, *Nuclear Ambitions* (Boulder, CO: Westview Press, 1990), p. 190.

13. Spiers, *Chemical and Biological Weapons*, pp. 56–7.

14. Judith Miller and Laurie Mylroie, *Saddam Hussein and the Crisis in the Gulf* (New York: Times Books, 1990), pp. 168–72, and Spiers, *Chemical and Biological Weapons*, p. 58.

15. Cordesman and Wagner, *Iran-Iraq War*, pp. 200–4.

16. Ibid., pp. 217–24.

17. Ibid., pp. 225–40. The first 100 TOW missiles delivered to Iran through Israel arrived on August 30, 1985, and the remaining 400 on September 14, 1985. This resulted in the release of one American hostage held in Iran (Rev. Benjamin Weir).

18. Pelletiere and Johnson, *Lessons Learned*, pp. 99–100.

19. Ibid., pp. 354–58.

20. Ibid., pp. 359–62.

21. Ibid., pp. 362–67.

22. Pelletiere and Johnson, *Lessons Learned*, pp. 370–71; *Chemical Warfare Chronology Bulletin #11* (Cambridge, MA: Harvard University, Mar. 1991), p. 5. This propaganda later backfired on Iran, as the reports of intensified chemical agent use had a significant negative effect on recruiting efforts and number of volunteers.

23. Robert Mullen Cook-Deegan, M.D., "Iraq's Chemical War against the Kurds," in Gary McCuen, ed., *Poison in the Wind*, pp. 41–43.

24. "Biological Weapons Program in Iraq Larger Than Believed," *Baltimore Sun*, Feb. 28, 1995.

25. Miller and Mylroie, *Saddam Hussein*, p. 168.

26. Smith, "Iraq Had Program for Germ Warfare." Later admissions from Baghdad suggest that the biological agent pilot plant at Muthanna had produced up to 20,000 liters of botulinum toxin and anthrax since 1985. Iraqi officials claim all this was destroyed in October 1990, and the program was abandoned. "Saddam Hopes BW Confession Is Enough to Convince USA," *Jane's Defense Weekly*, September 2, 1995, p. 27.

## CHAPTER 17: OPERATION DESERT SHIELD/STORM

1. GAO, *Chemical Warfare: Soldiers Inadequately Equipped and Trained to Conduct Chemical Operations* (Washington, DC: GAO/NSIAD-91-197, May 1991). On Jan. 15, 1991, the GAO released a classified version of this report to Congress, to avoid raising public fears immediately prior to the ground offensive. The public version was released on May 29, 1991. GAO officials visited thirty-six active combat units in the continental United States, seventeen active combat support units in Europe, and four of the nineteen reserve component chemical decontamination companies. They also visited thirty-four local field training exercises of Army units and four training exercises at the National Training Center and Joint Readiness Training Center. This report probably had as a direct result four congressional committees calling for hearings into the DoD NBC defense program immediately after the Gulf War.

2. The U.S. Army had at least 3,000 tons of usable unitary rounds of its over 30,000 tons in storage in 1990. While this could not effectively be claimed as adequate to support a sustained chemical warfare scenario, it still provided a credible threat of retaliation in kind. While the option was rejected by the Bush administration, the point remains that the U.S. leadership had no idea whether nuclear or massive conventional retaliation were feasible options. They had never seriously faced this scenario.

3. Secretary of Defense Richard Cheney, December 23, 1990. On Jan. 9, 1991, President George Bush also delivered a message through Secretary of State Jim Baker to Prime Minister Tariq Aziz at Geneva warning Iraq against using weapons of mass destruction. British and French politicians also warned Saddam against using CB weapons and discussed their planned retaliations in these events (most denied holding the nuclear retaliation card in reserve). U.S. News and World Report, *Triumph Without Victory: The Unreported History of the Persian Gulf War* (New York: Times Books, 1992), pp. 203–06.

4. Chemical reconnaissance platoons, normally staffed with M113A2 APCs, attended an abbreviated three-week training course either at the German Army's NBC School at Sonthofen, or at Fort McClellan, Alabama, the assignment depending on whether they were stationed in Europe or the continental United States. As these crews were attending training, the German government, in partnership with Thyssen-Henschel and General Dynamics Land Systems, refitted sixty-two Fox vehicles with American accessories such as U.S. radios, radiacs, M8A1 chemical alarms, U.S. machine-gun mounts, and an air-conditioning system to protect the delicate MM-1 mass spectrometer.

5. The one chemical casualty of the war, PFC David Fisher, came into contact with mustard gas while clearing an empty ammunition bunker in northern Kuwait. By brushing against a wall, he contacted the liquid, which was absorbed into his uniform and kevlar vest. Medical doctors confirmed the blisters that rose eight hours later as caused by mustard gas. He suffered four blisters measuring about one inch in diameter on one arm, was treated, and subsequently returned to duty.

6. Since the Gulf War, a Marine study on protective mask fit stating the failure of 26-40 percent of M17-series masks in mask-donning tests has been misinterpreted by those seeking evidence that CB agent exposure might have caused Gulf War illness. The truth is

that untrained individuals trying to fit themselves caused the high failure rate. When trained specialists fitted the individual and tested the mask with banana oil or CS-chambers, the failure rate became negligible. During the Gulf War, a special team of Pine Bluff Arsenal mask specialists arrived to assist the two corps in repairing masks. In addition, a team from Edgewood assisted in fitting soldiers with hard-to-fit heads (too small and too large) with M40-series masks, aided with a protective mask fit validation system.

7. This is still an unanswered requirement, as no combat unit wants to assume the costs of purchasing equipment for personnel outside their unit and there is no DoD regulation to do so. Yet these personnel are a necessary part of mission success, and someone will have to take it out of hide when the moment presents itself.

8. The symptoms described on the Persian Gulf Registry include abdominal pains, facial pain, chest pain, blood clots, flushing, night sweats, blurry vision, shaking, vomiting, fatigue, swollen lymph nodes, weight loss/gain, intestinal disorders, sore gums, cough, memory loss, dizziness, inability to concentrate, labored breathing, depression, neurological disorders and leg cramps. Some even claim Lou Gehrig's disease as a result of GWS, which is unusual as it takes several years for this disease to manifest itself, not one or two years after "exposure" to the Gulf War environment.

9. The loss of the CENTCOM logs was another incendiary event on the DoD coverup story. In reality, because the Chemical Corps had not seen any CB warfare, the soldiers reviewing the files probably did not attach any importance to the logs. As a result, while tens of thousands of documents were being routinely destroyed in Saudi Arabia or shipped back to the United States, there were only two complete sets that returned. One set was compromised by a computer virus and the other lost, leaving an incomplete set on record today. There are a number of other records that "conspiracy buffs" should review, however, such as the many Army division and corps records that are intact and that do not reveal any "missing" CB warfare attacks.

10. If this passage doesn't sound familiar, reread chapter 3.

## CHAPTER 18: RESTRUCTURING THE DOD CB DEFENSE PROGRAM

1. The law included five sections, which included

- Section 1701: *Conduct of the Chemical and Biological Defense Program.* Improve the joint coordination and oversight of the NBC defense program and ensure a coherent and effective approach to its management. This is to be accomplished through a single office in DoD, a stronger coordinating role by the Army, and a joint coordinated and integrated NBC defense budget for all four services.
- Section 1702: *Consolidation of Chemical and Biological Defense Training Activities.* The Air Force's Disaster Preparedness School would move from Lowery AFB, Colorado, to Anniston, Alabama. This allows the Air Force to use the Chemical Defense Training Facility and increases the likelihood of compatible training of NBC defense specialists.
- Section 1703: *Annual Report of Chemical and Biological Warfare Defense* demands an annual report reporting the overall status of the DoD NBC defense program; it includes readiness issues, such as logistics status of stocks, training and readiness of the armed forces and war game/battle simulations; the status of the DoD NBC defense RDA program, to include future requirements, joint

program initiatives, management and coordination improvements, and problem areas; and the military's preparations for the Chemical Weapons Convention.

- Section 1704: *Sense of Congress Concerning Federal Emergency Planning for Response to Terrorist Threats.* It recommends an increased effort by the Federal Emergency Management Agency to develop a capability to detect, warn, and respond to the potential terrorist use of chemical or biological agents, or natural disasters and emergencies involving industrial chemicals or natural or accidental outbreaks of disease.

- Section 1705: *Agreements to Provide Support to Vaccination Programs of Department of Health and Human Services.* This gives the Secretary of Defense and Secretary of Health and Human Services permission to use excess peacetime biological weapons defense capabilities to support domestic vaccination programs. This ability would allow DoD to retain a surge capability to produce vaccines and antidotes for unusual diseases as the armed forces became involved in a future contingency.

2. The Joint Program Office for Biological Defense (JPO-Bio) was formed in 1993 and does not formally report to the JSMG/JSIG, although it has nonvoting members on the panels. After an interim plan dated March 1992 failed to reach joint consensus, the Joint Requirements Oversight Council developed a joint Mission Needs Statement for a new biological defense program. A joint body called the Joint Services Committee for Biological Defense, led by ODCSOPS, outlined a DoD Operational Concept for Biological Defense, which grouped needed improvements into detection (point and standoff), protection, decontamination, and immunization. About a year later, the Office of the Secretary of Defense created the Joint Program Office for Biological Defense, or JPO-Bio, which would answer directly to OSD rather than to or through the Army. Colonel Gene Fuzy, having led the Army's efforts to develop a biodefense capability, was selected to lead this office, supported by the four services' CB defense organizations.

3. This was part of the Defense Reform Initiative Report, released on November 10, 1997. The report noted that it was adopting best business practices to change the organization, streamlining and eliminating unneeded infrastructure. It also devolved chemical demilitarization to Army rather than OSD, disestablished the Office of the Assistant To the Secretary of Defense (Nuclear, Chemical, and Biological), and eliminated Assistant Secretary of Defense (International Security Policy). Congressional law still requires a central OSD position, which has been designated under the Under Secretary of Defense (DDRE) as Deputy Director for Counterproliferation and CB Defense.

4. Douglas A. Macgregor, *Breaking the Phalanx: A New Design for Landpower in the 21st Century* ( Westport, CT: Praeger Publishers, 1997).

5. FM 3-3 was retitled *CB Contamination Avoidance*; FM 3-3-1 is *Nuclear Contamination Avoidance.*

6. The new FM 3-5 discusses field measures that can be taken given the restrictions of current decontaminants (too corrosive, requiring water, etc.). Without any new technologies fielded, there were no real improvements in how these specialized decontamination operations were conducted during to the Gulf War.

7. In 1997 the CINC priorities for counterproliferation listed battlefield NBC detection and warning as priority no. 4, individual protection ranked no. 8, collective protection was at no. 11, decontamination no. 15, and medical NBC treatments last at no. 16. Numbers 1–3 were counterproliferation intelligence cycle, precision munitions, and SOF response,

respectively. Despite the Gulf War lessons, the leadership still thought that if they smashed the weapons they wouldn't have to deal with CB warfare.

## CHAPTER 19: DOMESTIC AFFAIRS

1. Amy Smithson, *The U.S. Chemical Weapons Destruction Program: Views, Analysis, and Recommendations* (Washington, DC: The Henry L. Stimson Center), Sep. 1994, p. 3. Ironically, the three sites with 5 percent or less (Newport Chemical Depot, Blue Grass Chemical Activity, Edgewood Chemical Activity), get the majority of press due to their very vocal citizen groups and the larger population centers close to the sites. TOCDF gets its share of attention since it is the largest depot. Umatilla Chemical Depot is a favorite of the press for some reason, perhaps because of its proximity to Portland (ninety miles away) or the story's appeal to the West Coast environmentalists.

2. Program Director for Chemical Demilitarization, *DoD Interim Status Assessment for the Chemical Demilitarization Program* (Aberdeen Proving Ground, MD: PM CD, Apr. 1996), p. B-2.

3. Public Law 99-145, passed in 1986, forbade the disposal of non-stockpile chemical warfare material at any of the chemical disposal sites. This forced the Army to develop a controlled destruction capability to demilitarize the munitions at the site of their unearthing.

4. In a rare moment of clarity, Congress passed Public Law 103-337, which prohibited chemical stockpile transport across state lines but permitted "regulated movement" of nonstockpile material to cross state lines.

5. The SICG included all the agencies traditionally involved in domestic counterterrorism, to include the FBI, FEMA, Environmental Protection Agency, Department of Energy, Department of Transportation, Public Health Services, and of course DoD. This body met frequently to coordinate the executive branch activities required to execute the Domestic Preparedness Program.

6. The Federal Response Plan was created in 1992 after Congress expressed its displeasure with FEMA's execution of federal aid after Hurricane Hugo hit Florida in 1989. The FRP spells out every executive agency's responsibilities and plans to support declared disasters, from search and rescue to communications to transportation assets. This plan, at the least, ensures that federal executive agencies and state officials understand who is charged with providing certain capabilities to the states during declared disasters.

7. The term first responders was shortly replaced by the more correct term emergency responders. It was seen that first responders obviously included firefighters, police, and EMTs, but what about the emergency managers at the operations centers, the bomb squad, the hospital providers, utility crews, and so on? Emergency responders encompassed a much more complete collection of the trainees.

8. There is also an "Employee Awareness" video for laypeople in high-risk areas such as federal buildings, utilities and communication centers, etc. This video runs for less than half an hour and is accompanied by a short discussion on how to recognize incidents that may be caused by CB warfare agents.

9. The instructors came from a diverse collection of individuals, to include police from New York City and Boston, fire chiefs from Washington, DC, and Philadelphia, DOE instructors from Texas (teaching the radiological threat), National Guard and active Army soldiers, government civilians, and consultants from Booz-Allen & Hamilton, SAIC, RPI, and EAI, Inc. Most of the consultants were prior Chemical Corps soldiers, whose inclusion came under fire by the NFA. The NFA claimed on a PBS interview that this was a revolving door payoff between the government and retired military, which was unwarranted sniping

by an agency that thought they should have gotten the federal dollars for training programs. All instructors had to be certified prior to going on the road. The instructors that didn't measure up were identified by post-training assessments by the city students and either shaped up or were removed from the program.

10. Originally it was the top twenty cities for the first phase of the 120-city program. Seven cities were added to account for "geographical balance and special events" (GAO report T-NSAID-99-16). For instance, Atlanta was not initially on the list of initial cities to be trained in 1997. Then retired-senator Sam Nunn (D-GA), as the sponsor of the legislation, made it very clear that that was not acceptable. Atlanta was subsequently moved onto the list, as were Honolulu, Hawaii, and Anchorage, Alaska.

11. The military remains concerned that their bases, ports and airfields within and without the United States could be vulnerable to CB terrorist incidents, which could disrupt their "power projection" capability. The Army Chemical Corps is trying to translate this new interest in CB terrorism into what is termed the "Homeland Defense" mission. While the formal definition and scope of homeland defense is still unclear, the Center for Homeland Defense will stand up at Fort Leonard-Wood in an effort to assess and prepare DoD bases, airfields and ports for the potential of CB terrorist attacks. Similarly, the newly-named Joint Forces Command (formerly Atlantic Command) will take over the mission of centrally planning the DoD response and managing DoD assets for CB terrorist incidents through the Joint Task Force for Civil Support (JTF-CS).

12. Richard A. Falkenrath, Robert D. Newman, and Bradley A. Thayer, *America's Achilles Heel: Nuclear, Biological and Chemical Terrorism and Covert Attack* (Cambridge, MA: MIT Press, 1998), pp. 5-7. This is an excellent book discussing the policy implications of CB terrorism incidents.

## CHAPTER 20: CONCLUSIONS

1. H.R. 3316 for Public Law 105-736, Section 1045, Chemical Warfare Defense. The language also calls for prevention of, protection against, and the detection of exposures (intentional or unintentional) of CW agents not sufficient to endanger the health immediately but greater than the general population maximum safe limit.

2. Alibek, *Biohazard*, p.22.

3. Frederick Brown, *Chemical Warfare: A Study in Restraints* (Princeton, NJ: Princeton University Press, 1968), p.156.

# Selected Bibliography

## BOOKS

Brown, Frederick. *Chemical Warfare; A Study in Restraints.* Princeton, NJ: Princeton University Press, 1968.

Carter, G. B. *Porton Down: 75 Years of Chemical and Biological Research.* London: HMSO, 1992.

Cordesman, Anthony H., and Abraham R. Wagner. *The Lessons of Modern War, Vol. 1: The Arab-Israeli Conflicts, 1973-1989.* Boulder, CO: Westview Press, 1990.

———. *The Lessons of Modern War, Vol. 2: The Iran-Iraq War.* Boulder, CO:Westview Press, 1990.

Harris, Robert, and Jeremy Paxman. *A Higher Form of Killing.* New York: Hill and Wang, 1982.

McCarthy, Richard D. *The Ultimate Folly: War by Pestilence, Asphyxiation, and Defoliation.* New York: Alfred A. Knopf, 1969.

McDermott, Jeanne. *The Killing Winds: The Menace of Biological Warfare.* New York: Arbor House, 1987.

Pringle, Laurence. *Chemical and Biological Warfare: The Cruelest Weapons.* Hillside, NJ: Enslow Publishing, 1993.

Rothschild, J. H. *Tomorrow's Weapons.* New York: McGraw-Hill, 1964.

Seagrave, Sterling. *Yellow Rain: A Journey through the Terror of Chemical Warfare.* New York: M. Evans, 1981.

Spiers, Edward M. *Chemical and Biological Weapons: A Study of Proliferation.* New York: St. Martin's Press, 1994.

Taylor, L. B. and C. L. Taylor. *Chemical and Biological Warfare.* New York: Franklin Watts, 1985.

## GOVERNMENT REPORTS

Ash, C. Grant. *History of the Skull Valley Sheep Deaths in 1968.* Deseret, Utah (self-published), 1994.

Brankowitz, William R. *Chemical Munitions Movement History Compilation*. Aberdeen Proving Ground, MD: Office of the Program Manager for Chemical Munitions (Demil and Binary) (Provisional), June 12, 1987.

Browman, Steven. *U.S. Chemical Warfare Preparedness Program*. Washington, DC: Congressional Research Service, 1982.

Campbell, Lt. Cdr D. C. *Radiological Defense, Vol. 4: RADIAC, An Introduction to Radiological Instruments for Military Use*. Washington, DC: Armed Forces Special Weapons Project, 1950.

Chemical Corps Association, *The Chemical Warfare Service in World War II*. New York: Reinhold Publishing, 1948.

Congressional Research Service. *Binary Weapons: Implications of the US Chemical Stockpile Modernization Program for Chemical Weapons Proliferation*. Washington, DC: Government Printing Office, 1984.

Covert, Norman M. *Cutting Edge: A History of Fort Detrick, Maryland, 1943-1993*. Fort Detrick, MD: HQ Garrison, Sep. 1994.

Dunn, Peter. *A Journey to Iraq—A Personal Account*. Melbourne, Australia: DoD, Defense Science & Technology Organization, Materials Research Labs, 1984.

Government Accounting Office. *Chemical Warfare: DoD's Reporting of Its Chemical and Biological Research*. Washington, DC: GAO, Aug. 1991.

———. *Chemical Warfare: DoD's Successful Effort to Remove U.S. Chemical Weapons from Germany*. Washington, DC: GAO/NSIAD-91-105, 1991.

———. *Chemical Warfare: Progress and Problems in Defensive Capability*. Washington, DC: GAO/PEMD-86-11, 1986.

———. *Chemical Warfare: Soldiers Inadequately Equipped and Trained to Conduct Chemical Operations*. Washington, DC: GAO/NSIAD-91-197, May 1991.

———. *Status of Department of Defense Programs to Improve Defensive Chemical Warfare Capabilities*. Washington, DC: GAO, 1985.

Office of the Chief Chemical Officer. "Estimate of the Chief CBR Situation." Washington, DC: Dept. of the Army, 1958.

Office of the Chief of Public Affairs, HQ, TRADOC. "The Chemical Strategy." *Army Chemical Review*, Jan. 1988.

Senate Committee on Labor and Public Welfare. *Chemical and Biological Weapons: Some Possible Approaches for Lessening the Threat and Danger*. Washington, DC: GPO, 1969.

Smart, Jeffery K. *U.S. Army Chemical and Biological Defense Command: Historical Highlights*. Aberdeen Proving Ground, MD: U.S. Army CBDCOM, 1994.

Taylor, Wilbert, Frank Massaro, and Gwen Marshall. "A Summary of Chemical Munition Testing and Disposal Operations at Dugway Proving Ground." Dugway Proving Ground, UT: Joint Operations Directorate, HQ DA, 1988.

## JOURNAL ARTICLES

Bay, Charles H. "The Other Gas Crisis—Chemical Weapons." *Parameters—Journal of the U.S. Army War College*, Sep. 1979.

Gimlin, Hoyt. *Chemical-Biological Weaponry*. Washington, DC: Congressional Quarterly, Inc., 1969.

Malooley, Lieutenant Colonel Rudolph S. "Gas Is Not a Dirty Word in Soviet Army." *Army*, Sep. 1974, pp. 21–23.

## NEWSPAPER ARTICLES

"Biological Weapons Program in Iraq Larger Than Believed" *Baltimore Sun*, Feb. 28, 1995.

Boffey, Philip M. "'Yellow Rain': New Support for Honeybee Theory" *New York Times*, Aug. 12, 1985.

"Laird Defense Chemical Weaponry as a Deterrent" *New York Times*, July 29, 1969.

"Nixon Renounces Germ Weapons, Orders Destruction of Stocks; Restricts Use of Chemical Arms" *New York Times,* Nov. 26, 1969.

Ripley, Anthony. "Clements Won't Rule Out A-Bomb Use" *New York Times*, Jan. 12, 1973.

Smith, R. Jeffery. "Iraq Had Program for Germ Warfare" *Washington Post*, July 6, 1995.

Teltsch, Kathleen. "Thant Urges Halt on Germ Weapons" *Washington Post*, July 3, 1969.

UPI and AP, "War Foes Plan to Burn Dog in Protest at U. of Cincinnati" *New York Times,* Nov. 8, 1968.

Watson, Mark S. "Nerve Gases Gain Favor as Weapons" *Baltimore Sun*, Apr. 3, 1960.

# Index

**About the Author**

ALBERT J. MAURONI is a management consultant working on Department of Defense chemical-biological defense programs. He has fourteen years experience as an Army chemical officer. His previous works include *Chemical-Biological Defense: U.S. Military Policies and Decisions in the Gulf War* (Praeger, 1998). He lives in Abingdon, Maryland with his wife Roseann and their three dogs.

ISBN 0-275-96756-5

EAN

9 780275 967567

90000>

HARDCOVER BAR CODE